MASTERING **CHILD PORTRAIT** PHOTOGRAPHY

A DEFINITIVE GUIDE FOR PHOTOGRAPHERS

RICHARD BRADBURY

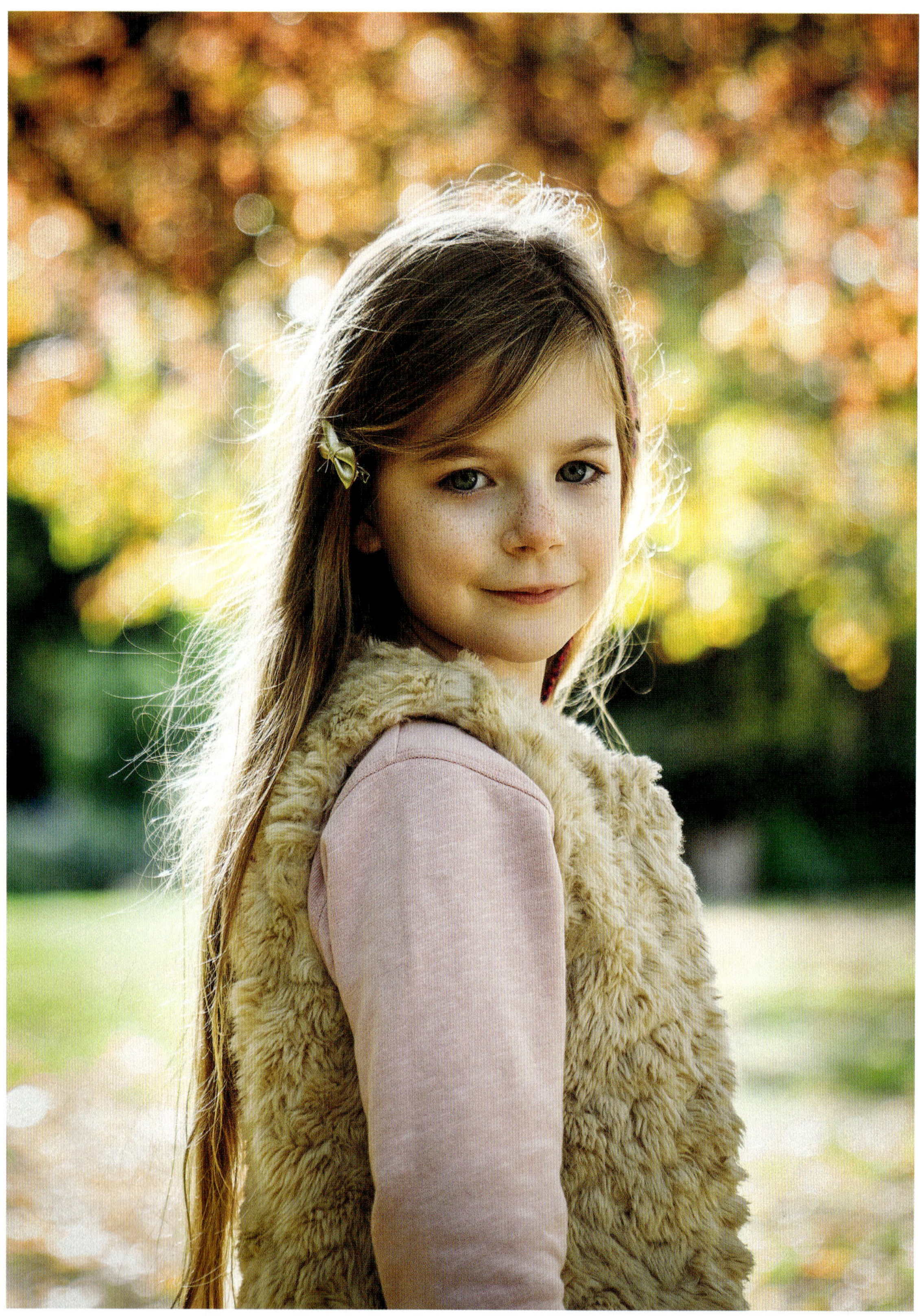

MASTERING **CHILD PORTRAIT** PHOTOGRAPHY

A DEFINITIVE GUIDE FOR PHOTOGRAPHERS

RICHARD BRADBURY

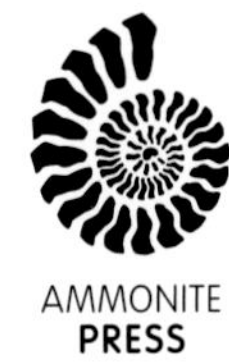

AMMONITE
PRESS

First published 2019 by
Ammonite Press
an imprint of Guild of Master Craftsman Publications Ltd.
Castle Place, 166 High Street, Lewes, East Sussex, BN7 1XU, United Kingdom

ISBN 978-1-78145-359-9

British Library Cataloging in Publication Data: A catalog record of this
book is available from the British Library.

Publisher: Jason Hook
Design & Illustration: Robin Shields
Editor: Chris Gatcum

Typeface: Helvetica Neue
Color reproduction by GMC Reprographics
Printed in China

Contents

Introduction

There is quite literally nothing in our lives that will ever compare to the way we love our children. They are more precious than gold, diamonds, and pearls; they are a reflection of everything that has passed, and represent all that is good about a bright and shining future.

Capturing the beauty of a child—their character, their happiness, their very essence—has been the obsession of artists throughout history. Painters paint and sculptors sculpt, but photography is the most accessible art form in the world, making it the perfect medium for recording every aspect of our children's lives. In doing so we can create a unique pictorial archive that brings joy to friends and relatives for many lifetimes to come.

Portraiture as an art form has a few fundamental requirements. Yes, you must capture a true likeness of your subject, but great portraiture offers more than that. You must also learn to capture their character and personality. So how do we ensure that the photographs we take are the very best representation of our most precious assets?

Photographing children is not easy, and they are certainly not like other models: they move around, they look the wrong way, they dribble, sneeze, and cry, and as any parent will tell you they never do what you want them to do—at least not when you want them to do it!

It is this unpredictability that makes child portraiture the fascinating challenge it is. It is easy to understand why we love our children so much, but capturing that in a single image requires a unique combination of creativity, technique, persuasion, and child psychology.

In this book we will explore each of these issues in detail. For the keen enthusiast this is a guide to capturing beautiful images of your children that will last a lifetime; for the professional it is the gateway to a wonderful lifestyle business that will bring pleasure to clients for generations to come.

I will start by advising you on the equipment you will need to ensure that you never miss that critical "once in a lifetime" shot. I'll explain some of the technical aspects that are unique to photographing children, including lighting, composition, and camera craft. You will also discover how to get the best from your child model—both on location and in the studio—and finally, I will explain the basics of good postproduction and reveal how retouching can enhance your finished images.

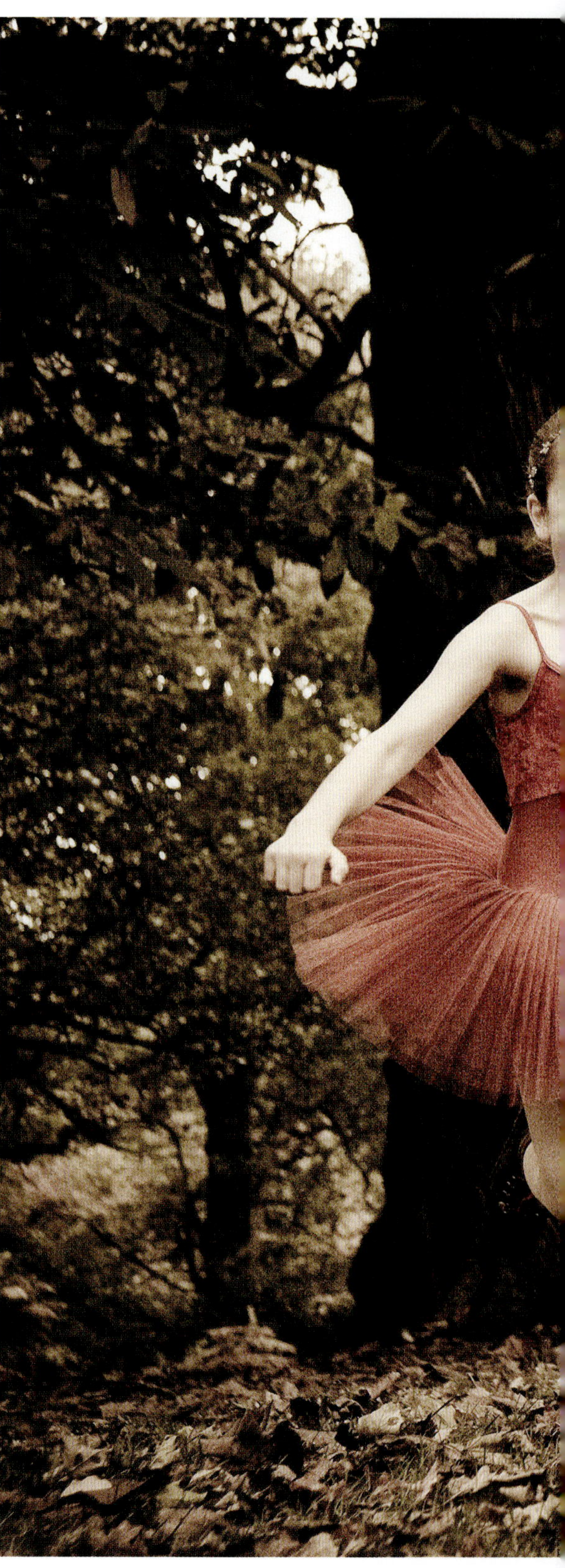

Right: Beautiful child portraits do not need to be stiff and posed. Try to bring out the essence of childhood with every shot you take.
Focal length: 55mm
Aperture: f/5
Shutter speed: 1/800 sec.
ISO: 6400

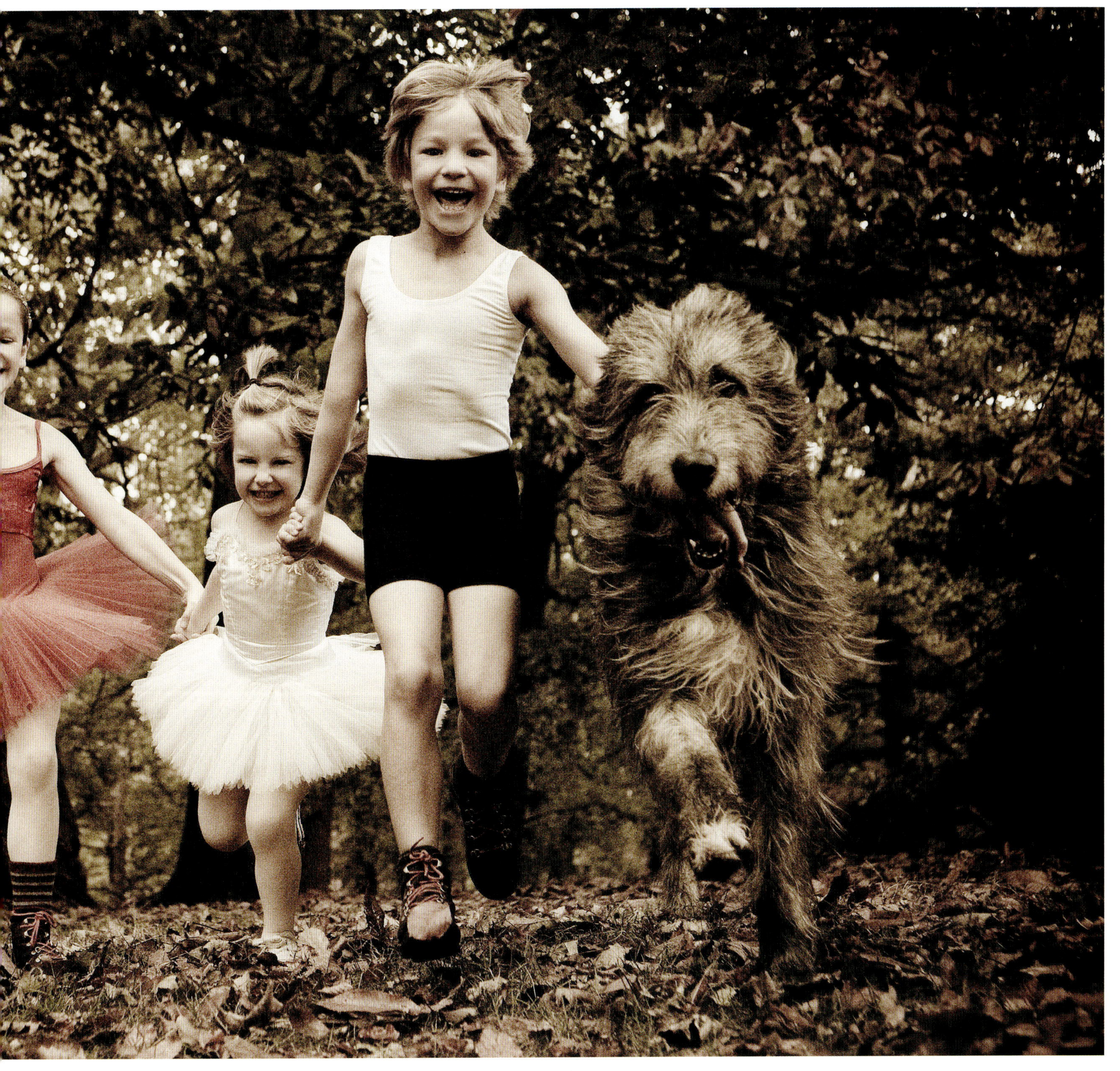

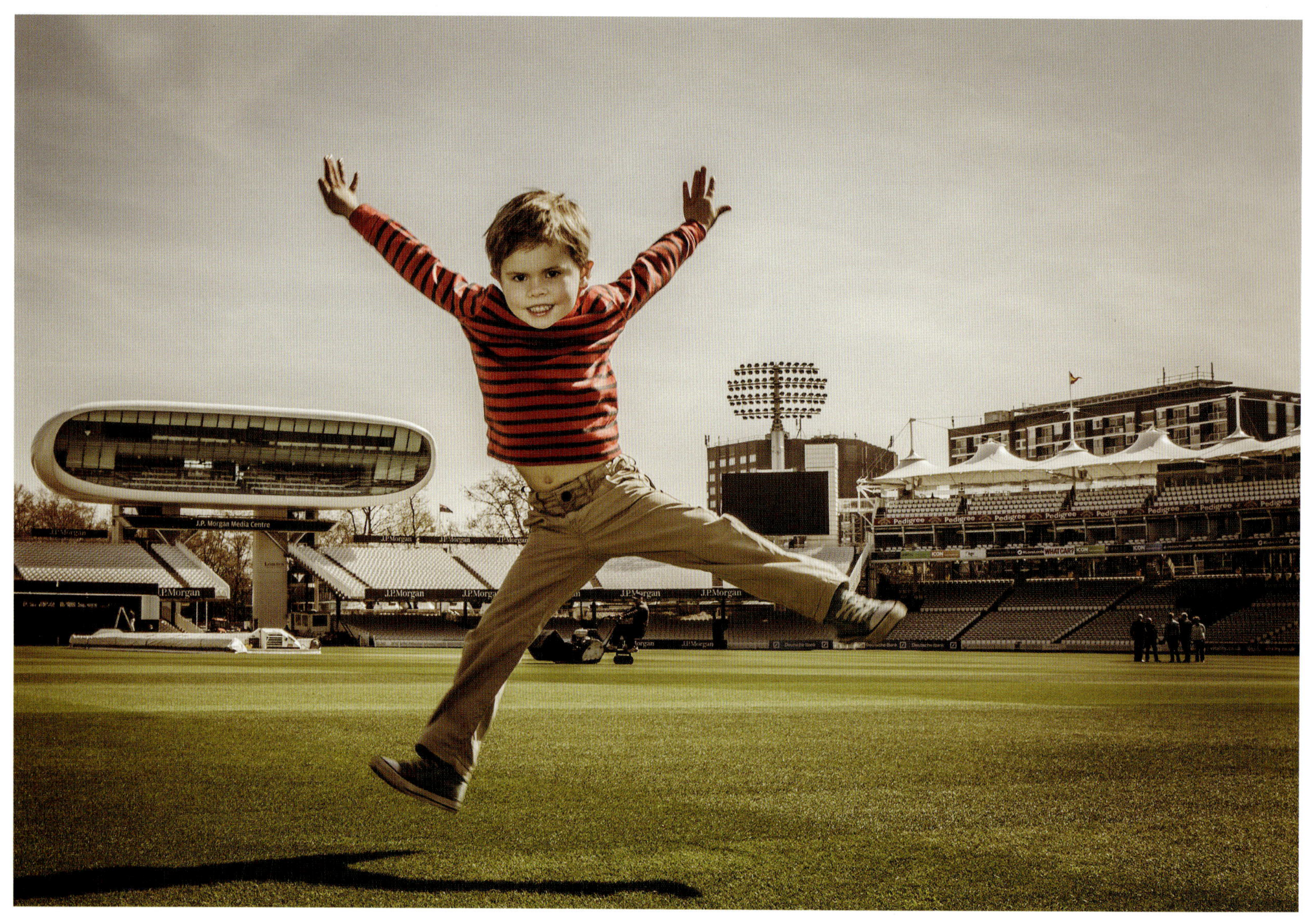

Above: Choosing the right location for your child's portrait can transform your photography. Children are happiest when they are doing the things they love to do.

Focal length: 42mm

Aperture: f/16

Shutter speed: 1/200 sec.

ISO: 500

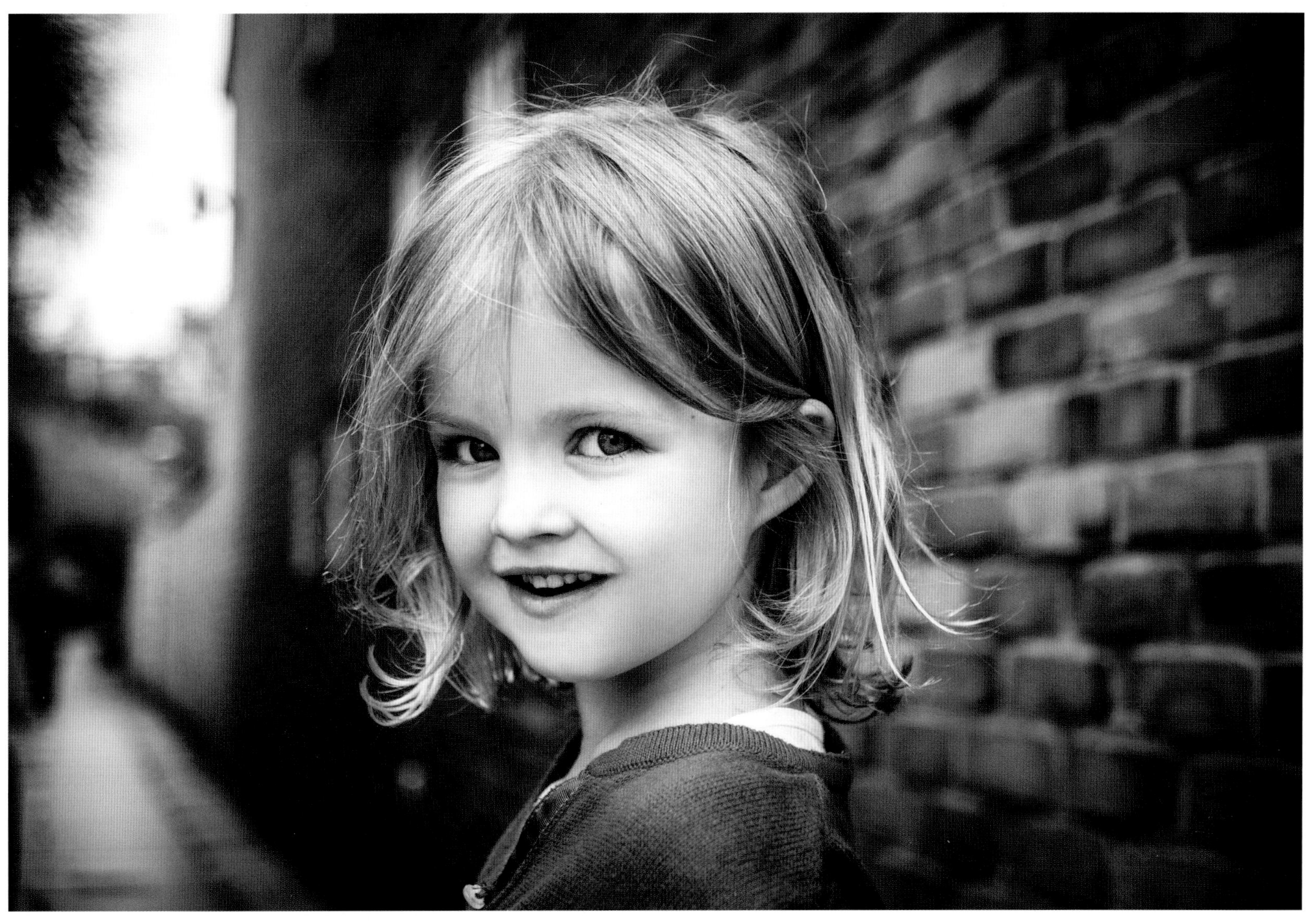

Above: Sometimes the perfect child portrait can be the simplest shot in the world. Great lighting, the correct angle of view, and a stunning expression are all key factors.
Focal length: 60mm
Aperture: f/4
Shutter speed: 1/1000 sec.
ISO: 2000

Chapter 1
Equipment

More than any other art form, photography is defined by the equipment used to create an image. The fundamental requirements for any photographer are a camera and the means to either create light or bend it to your will. The choice of which camera and lighting is best for the job will always be a subjective one, and I would not dictate a "one choice for all" equipment list. It is also worth noting that the equipment you use is not the most important element to a great photograph: it is the photographer that takes the photograph, not the equipment. Equipment is simply the means to help you create that photograph in the best way possible.

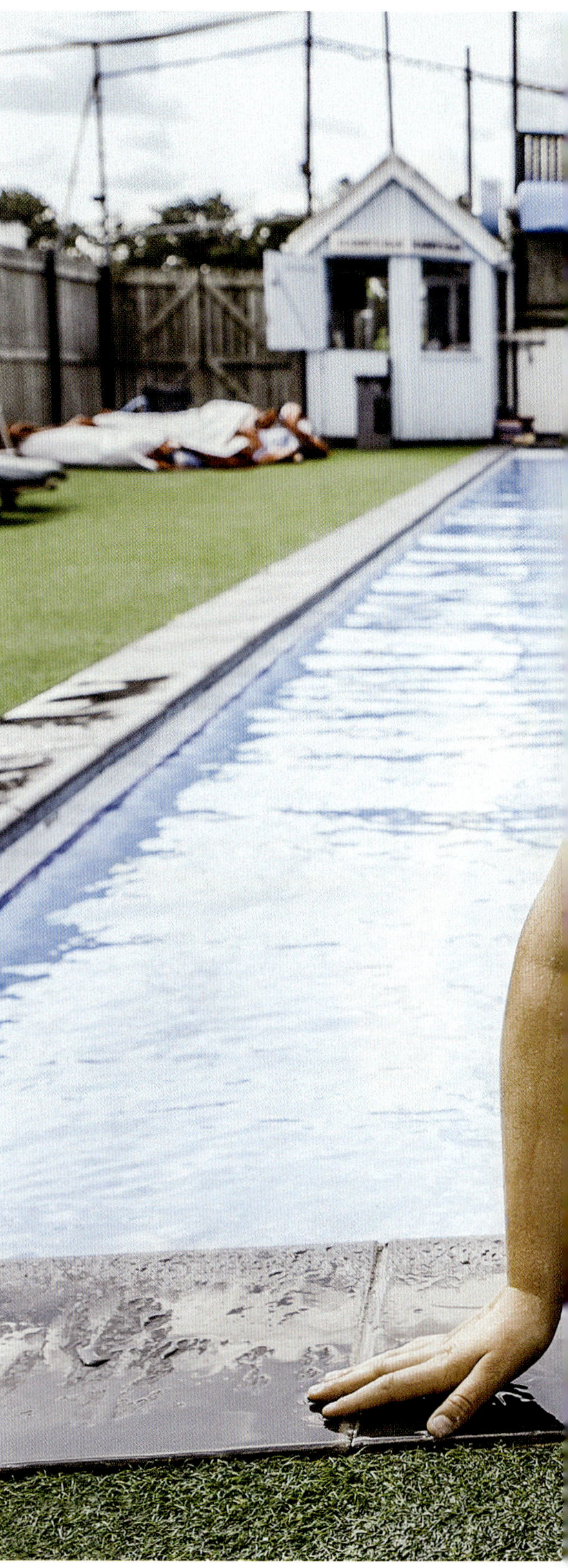

Right: Having the right kit enables you to be prepared for the perfect shot, whatever the environment.

Focal length: 25mm

Aperture: f/5

Shutter speed: 1/1000 sec.

ISO: 640

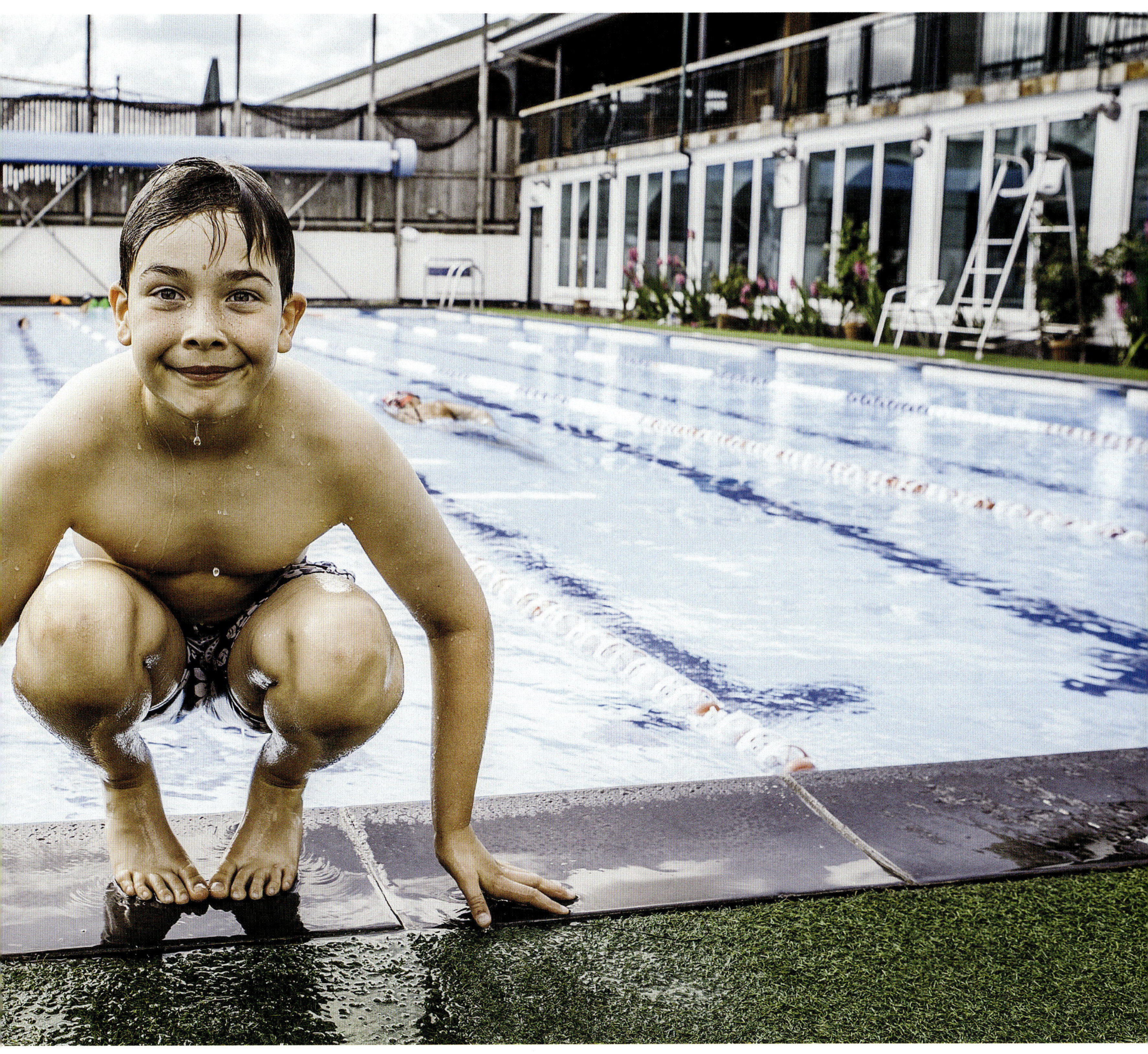

Cameras

Almost every one of us carries a cellphone with a camera and a built-in flash, and modern phones are more than capable of producing high-quality images. However, if you want to take the art of child portraiture seriously you will need a "proper" camera and the ability to change and adapt the light that is to be captured.

There are two main defining features of cameras available to the serious photographer: the size of the image that can be captured (which is largely a matter of the sensor size) and the features offered by the camera itself (including its range of lenses and accessories). The choice is huge so let's start with the different types of camera available.

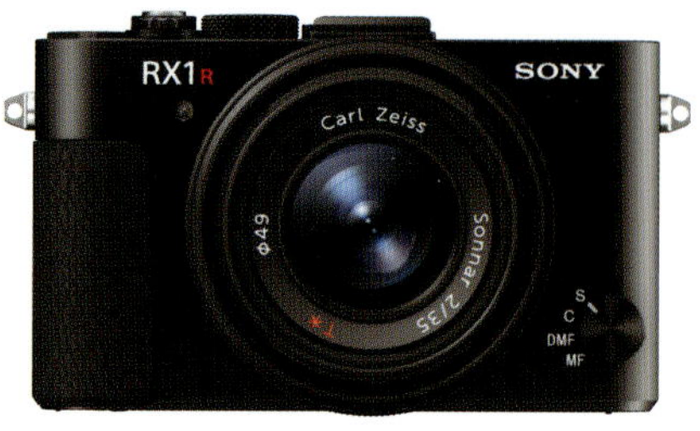

Above: The Canon G9 X MkII is a high-end, high-resolution compact camera with a useful zoom range.

Above: Sony's RX1R MkII is unique among compact cameras, as it has a full-frame sensor.

Compact Cameras

This type of camera comes with a fixed lens, which may be a single focal length or a zoom, and is—generally speaking—fitted with small-sized sensors. Beware of any mention of a "digital zoom" as this simply takes a smaller section of the sensor and electronically blows it up, severely affecting the final image quality in the process. If you want to use this type of camera for serious child portraits, look for a sensor size of at least 18 megapixels to ensure you have enough quality to crop and print your images at a reasonable size.

Some compact cameras have an optical viewfinder, others an EVF (electronic viewfinder), but most use the screen on the back of the camera to frame and view shots. Be aware that cameras with optical viewfinders do not show you exactly what the lens is seeing as you are looking through a separate viewing window, rather than viewing "through the lens." If you are shooting close-up images, this can lead to the final image being incorrectly framed (due to "parallax" error), but for more distant shots it is not noticeable.

Tips

- The right kit for you will be a collection of equipment that is both affordable and practical. It should enable you to deal with every reasonable situation that you find yourself in and will inevitably be a work in progress. As your experience grows you will want better and more varied equipment to deal with your increasing skill levels and to help express your developing creativity.

- Start with a basic kit and then gradually find out where your work is going. You may find you have a leaning toward studio photography, for example, in which case you can look at more advanced studio lighting, but if you find you enjoy photographing action portraits you will need to think about buying more expensive, faster lenses. Each of us has different priorities depending on the type of portraits we prefer to shoot.

Tips

- Cameras are changing constantly as technology offers better solutions to every conceivable issue, so read reviews and get friendly with your local camera store. Try different camera options until you find the system that suits you the best.

- A handgrip can often improve a camera's handling and also hold an extra battery for longer shooting sessions, so check whether your preferred camera has one available.

Interchangeable Lens Cameras

Sooner or later most photographers end up choosing to work with an interchangeable lens camera, as it offers a much wider range of creative options. DSLR (Digital Single Lens Reflex) and mirrorless cameras are by far the most popular choices for the serious photographer, although they have some fairly fundamental differences, which largely come down to the way in which you view the scene.

DSLRs are based on SLR (Single Lens Reflex) film cameras and the technology has been around a long time. A DSLR uses a mirror and a pentaprism contained within the body of the camera to project the scene you are looking at to the viewfinder. The mirror flips up the moment you take a photograph to expose the sensor located directly behind it.

Many photographers prefer this direct viewfinder system, finding it simpler and a more "real" way to preview images. DSLRs are also generally faster to operate and have little or no lag between shots, so for the fast shooter they are a good choice.

Mirrorless cameras are generally lighter and more compact than DSLRs, but the main difference is that they show the image using an electronic viewfinder (EVF) or the rear screen; there is no mirror and no mechanical action required to expose the sensor other than the shutter opening. Because of this, a mirrorless camera can also offer a preview of the photograph, showing you the exposure level, white balance, and other image qualities on the EVF or LCD screen. This gives you an accurate representation of the image in the viewfinder *before* you take a shot, avoiding the need to check the exposure between frames. When you are photographing children who need to be captured "in the moment" and often require your full attention, this can be a huge benefit and help speed up your shoot.

Although the viewing systems differ, a key thing to remember is that both DSLR and mirrorless cameras provide a view through the lens, so both will enable you to see what the sensor will record. They also offer a vast array of lens and accessory options to suit almost every shooting situation. Although DSLRs are more popular overall (partly because they offer a greater range of lenses and accessories), the latest mirrorless cameras are stunning, and many people see them as the "future" of photography.

In both cases, a key aspect of camera choice is how it handles. Try models from different manufacturers to see which you prefer, as your camera needs to feel good in your hand, and we all have different preferences. You then need to spend time getting to know exactly how your camera works. This is the skill of becoming a truly professional photographer: you are an artist and the camera is your brush.

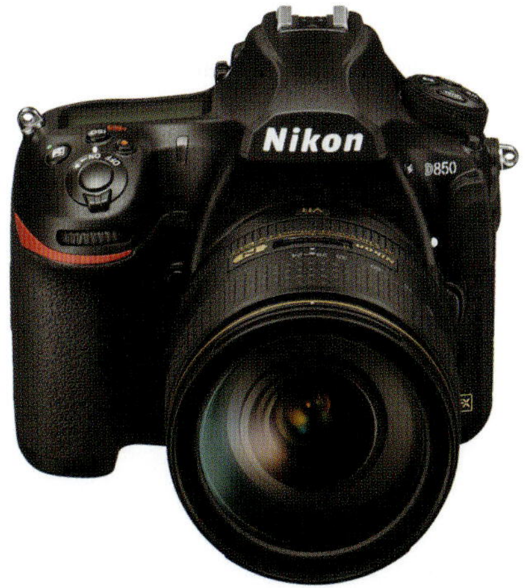

Above: DSLRs are the preferred choice for a lot of portrait photographers and there are numerous models available at a variety of price points, from entry level cameras through to high-end models like the Nikon D850.

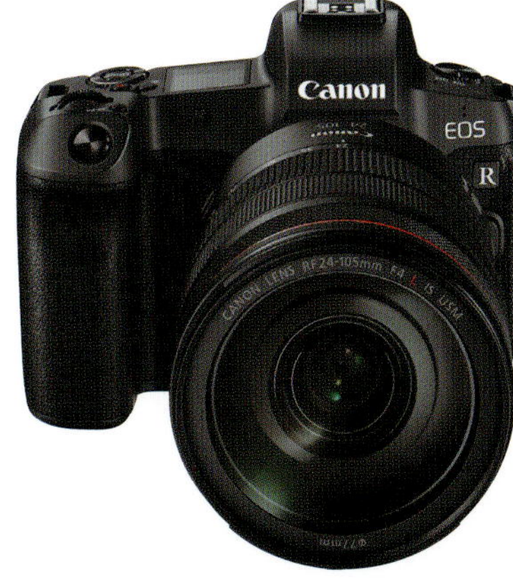

Above: There has been an large number of full-frame mirrorless cameras being released in recent years, which offer an alternative to a DSLR. The EOS R is Canon's first foray into this exciting new market.

DSLR CAMERAS	
FOR	**AGAINST**
• Direct view through the viewfinder • More established technology • Greater range of lenses and accessories • Faster to operate	• Heavier • Can't see exposure preview in viewfinder • Viewfinder hard to use in low light

MIRRORLESS CAMERAS	
FOR	**AGAINST**
• Lighter weight • In-viewfinder exposure preview • Illuminated viewfinder image works in low-light conditions • Rapidly developing technology	• Heavy reliance on electronic systems • Restrictive lens and accessory selection • Shorter battery life

Sensors

The image sensor is at the heart of every digital camera, and ensuring you have the "correct" sensor is vital if you want to produce high-quality images. This is the most restrictive factor of any camera: the sensor cannot be changed or adjusted, so think carefully about the size and performance that you want.

I am not going to go into a huge technical dissection of how sensors work and how they are made, but fundamentally there are two types of sensor: CCD (Charge Coupled Device) and CMOS (Complementary Metal Oxide Semiconductor). Most sensors today are of the CMOS type, as they are cheaper to make, work better at high speed, and are capable of delivering superb image quality.

The size of a sensor is not only measured physically (see right), but also in terms of its resolution or number of megapixels (MP). While there are other factors to take into account, generally speaking, the larger the sensor and the greater the number of pixels, the better the image quality will be. At the time of writing the accepted professional standard is around 24MP, but 30MP, 36MP, 42MP, and even 50MP sensors are increasingly common.

However, bear in mind that a higher resolution sensor will deliver larger image files, and this can lead to problems handling and storing the large quantities of data generated. I regularly shoot around 400 frames for an average outdoor child portrait shoot and this can take up a lot of hard drive storage space: an uncropped 24MP image is perfectly adequate for the largest wall art prints, so don't get too obsessed with huge file sizes.

The speed at which the sensor reacts is also a factor, and larger sensors are generally slower. As a result, many high-end, sports-orientated cameras have a lower resolution to allow a fast frame rate, enabling them to shoot hundreds of

Raw images in quick succession. Again, don't feel that you need to have the highest resolution sensor available: you might find that a faster shooting speed is more important for the work you do.

A final consideration is dynamic range. This is a sensor's ability to record a range of brightness levels in a single exposure, with detail in the shadows and highlights. The highest performing sensors have a dynamic range of around 15 stops, which means detail can be recorded in shadow areas and highlights that are 15-stops apart in terms of their brightness. The greater the dynamic range, the more options there are when it comes to processing your images and the better able the camera will be at shooting in extreme situations, such as low light.

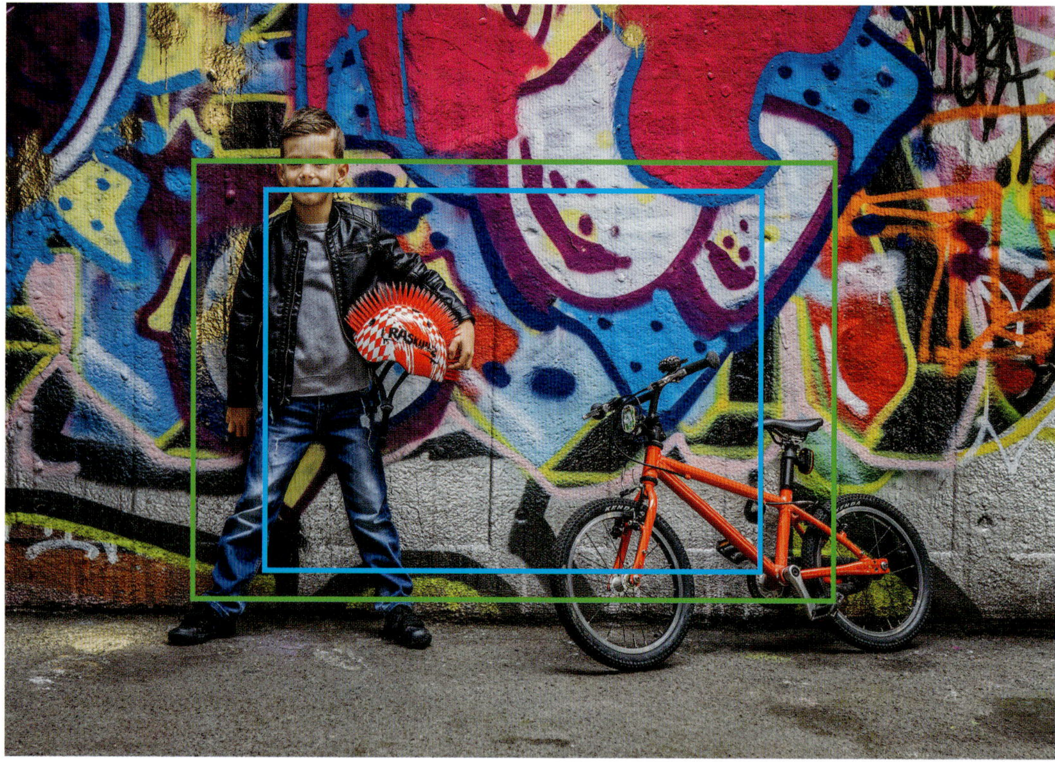

Above: This image was taken with a full-frame camera, which has a sensor measuring 36 x 24mm. The green box indicates how much smaller a cropped, APS-C sensor is (23.6 x 15.5mm), while the blue box represents the relative size of the sensor inside a Micro Four Thirds camera (17.3 x 13mm).

Focal length: 48mm

Aperture: f/5.6

Shutter speed: 1/160 sec.

ISO: 800

Lenses

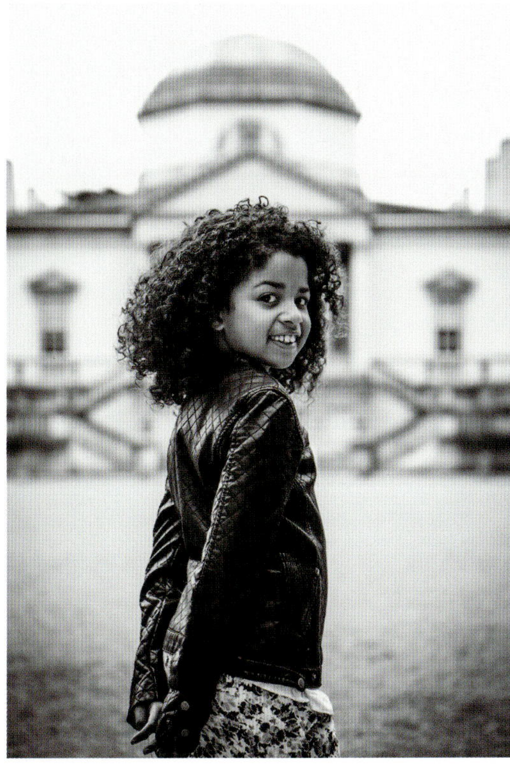

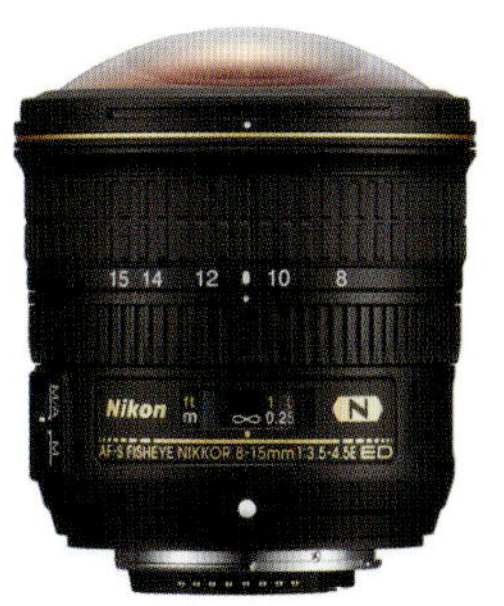

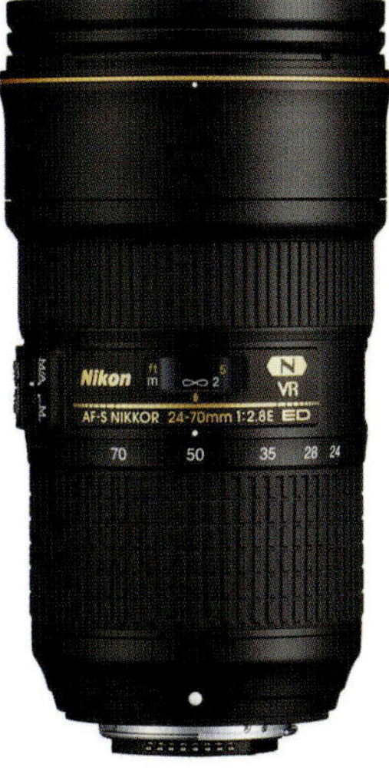

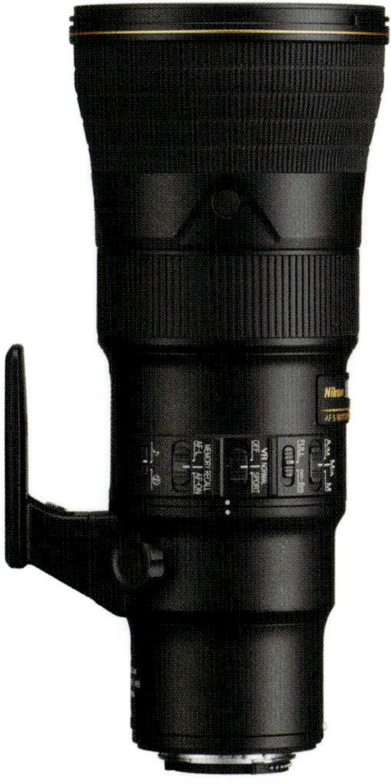

Above: Choosing the correct focal length can make or break an image. It is as important as lighting and composition when it comes to the final result.

Focal length: 70mm

Aperture: f/3.2

Shutter speed: 1/800 sec.

ISO: 500

Above: Like most manufacturers, Nikon's interchangeable lens cameras are backed by a huge number of lenses covering a wide range of focal lengths. Shown here is a tiny selection: 18–55mm f/3.5–5.6 "standard" zoom (top left), 8–15mm f/3.5–4.5 "fisheye" zoom (bottom left), 24–70mm f/2.8 zoom (center), 500mm f/5.6 telephoto (right).

No matter which camera system you decide to go for, or which sensor size you choose, it will be the lens that ultimately determines the quality of the final image. It is unwise to spend all your money on a camera body without allowing a reasonable budget for a decent set of lenses. In fact, most established professionals would tell you that the reverse is true: if you are on a tight budget, buy a decent—but basic—camera and spend more money on the lenses.

All manufacturers make their own lens systems and it is generally a good idea to stick with those lenses. However, there are several independent lens makers who produce lenses that fit different camera makes. These tend to be less expensive and are certainly worth considering if you want to try different lenses on a budget. There is a huge range of options, but the general rule is that the more expensive a lens is, the better it will perform within that particular category.

Again, speaking in general, fast lenses are usually preferable, with "fast" referring to a wide maximum aperture. A wider aperture lets in more light so you are able to use faster shutter speeds if required, but another benefit is that they can create a beautiful blurred background effect known as the "bokeh" effect. This is particularly sought after by portrait photographers, as its picks a subject sharply from the background. It is achieved by choosing a wide aperture to create a very shallow depth of field, typically with a high-quality telephoto lens.

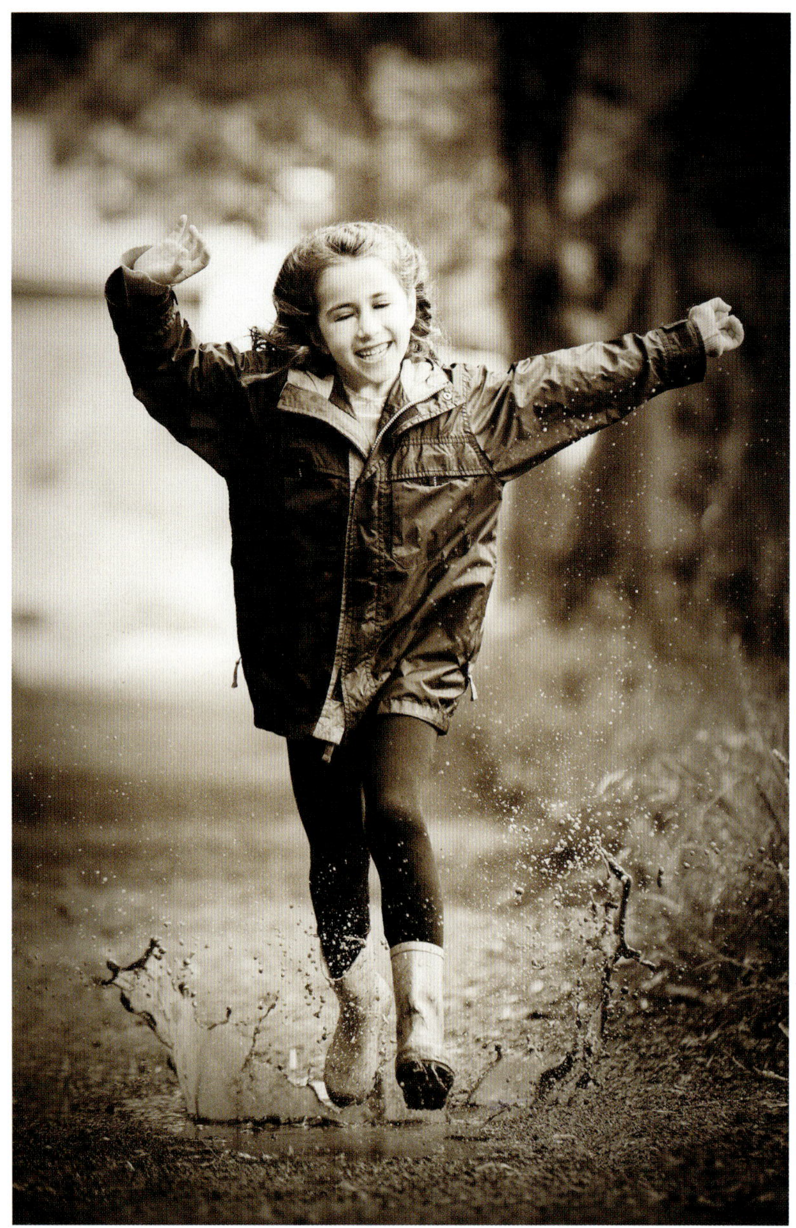

Above: Fast lenses enable you to freeze action and get some beautiful effects.

Focal length: 200mm

Aperture: f/3.5

Shutter speed: 1/2000 sec.

ISO: 4000

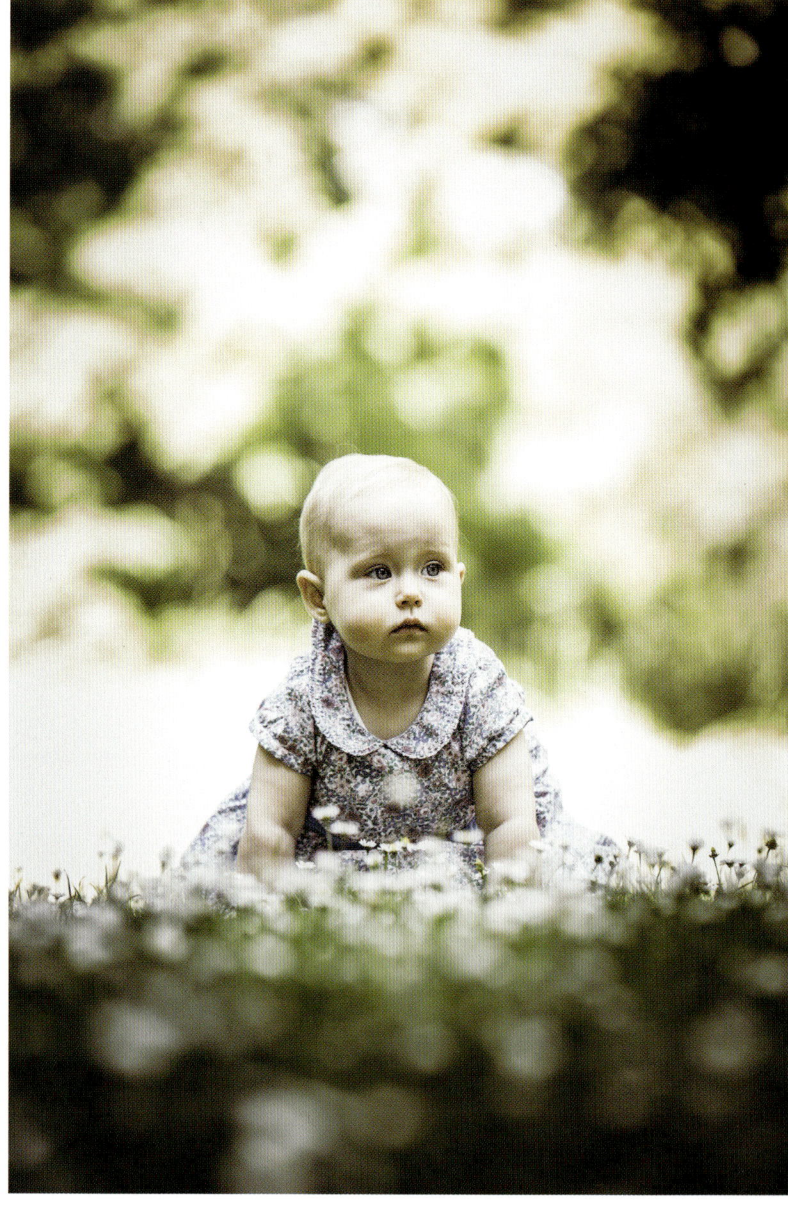

Above: The bokeh effect is particularly visible with longer lenses set at wide apertures.

Focal length: 200mm

Aperture: f/2.8

Shutter speed: 1/200 sec.

ISO: 640

Focal Length

Fixed focal length lenses (or "prime" lenses) generally have wider apertures than zoom lenses, with a maximum aperture of f/1.4 or f/1.8 being very desirable. However, wide apertures come at a price, and you will notice a huge price difference between a 70–200mm f/2.8 lens and a 70–200mm f/4 lens, for example. Anything less than f/4 is good, though, and f/2.8 is about as good as it gets for zoom lenses.

However, while they have distinct advantages, faster lenses tend to be larger and heavier, as they have to be constructed with more and/or larger lens elements. This can cause other problems, as heavy lenses can become unwieldy. Because of this, some larger lenses have built-in stabilization, which uses a tiny set of gyroscopes to stabilize the image as it passes through the lens, reducing camera shake and giving you sharper images. Some camera bodies—especially mirrorless ones—also have built-in stabilization, and this can assist any lens fitted to the camera.

The choice of which focal lengths are right for you is, once again, a subjective one, but it is fair to say that you need to cover a reasonable range. Most portrait photographers would agree that the best prime lens for most portraits is somewhere between 50mm and 100mm; 85mm is a popular choice. These lenses give what is regarded as a fairly neutral look to the finished image.

However, if you are working on location you need to have a range of focal lengths, so you can capture everything from close ups to distant shots. At the same time, you don't want to carry a huge amount of equipment, so for me, zoom lenses are a must when it comes to location shoots. My choice is simple: a 24–70mm f/2.8 and a 70–200mm f/2.8 with image stabilization. With these two lenses I can cover just about anything that comes my way, although I sometimes add a 16–35mm f/2.8 if I am working indoors or on location and the background is an important element of the image. Your decisions will ultimately be different to mine, but should always be based on quality versus practicality and, of course, price.

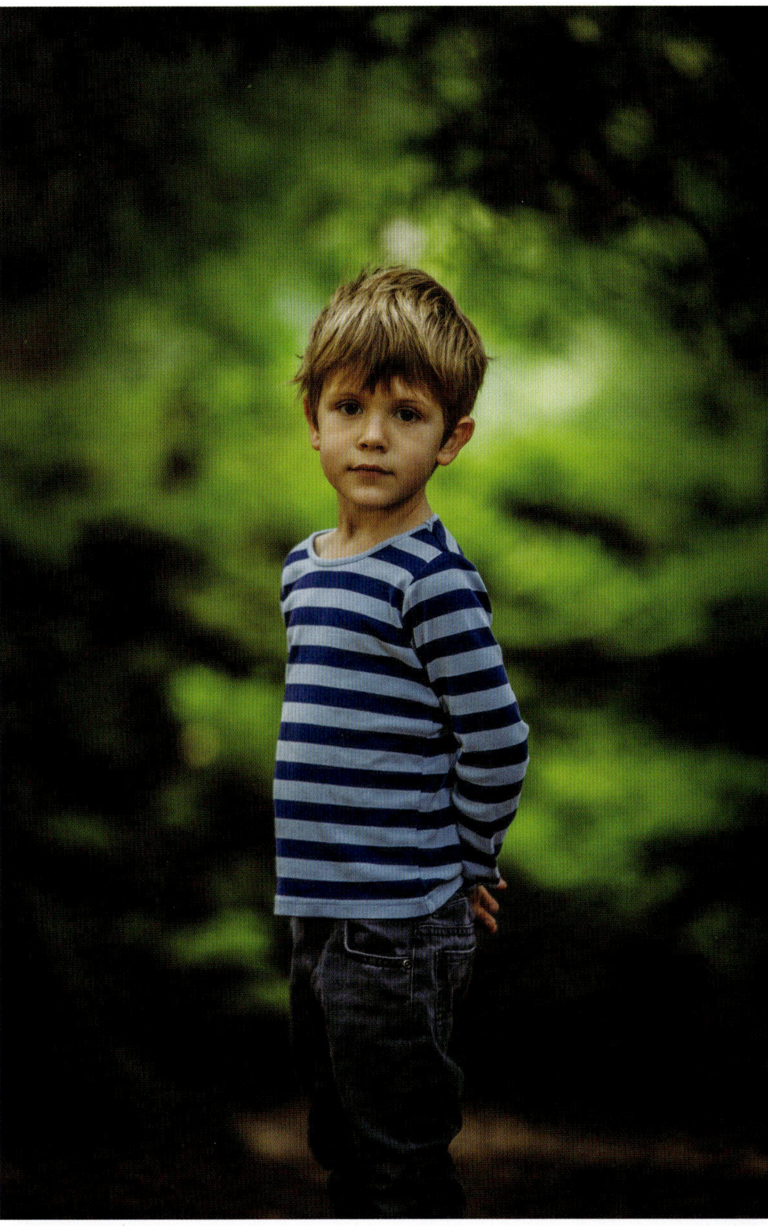

Left: Telephoto lenses give a very distinctive look to portraits, picking out the subject from their backdrop.

Focal length: 200mm

Aperture: f/2.8

Shutter speed: 1/160 sec.

ISO: 800

Tips

- While it may be tempting to go for a lens that offers a massive zoom range, such as 18–200mm, these are best avoided, as they will be slow to use and questionable in terms of their image quality.

- Buy the best lenses you can afford: there is no replacement for quality.

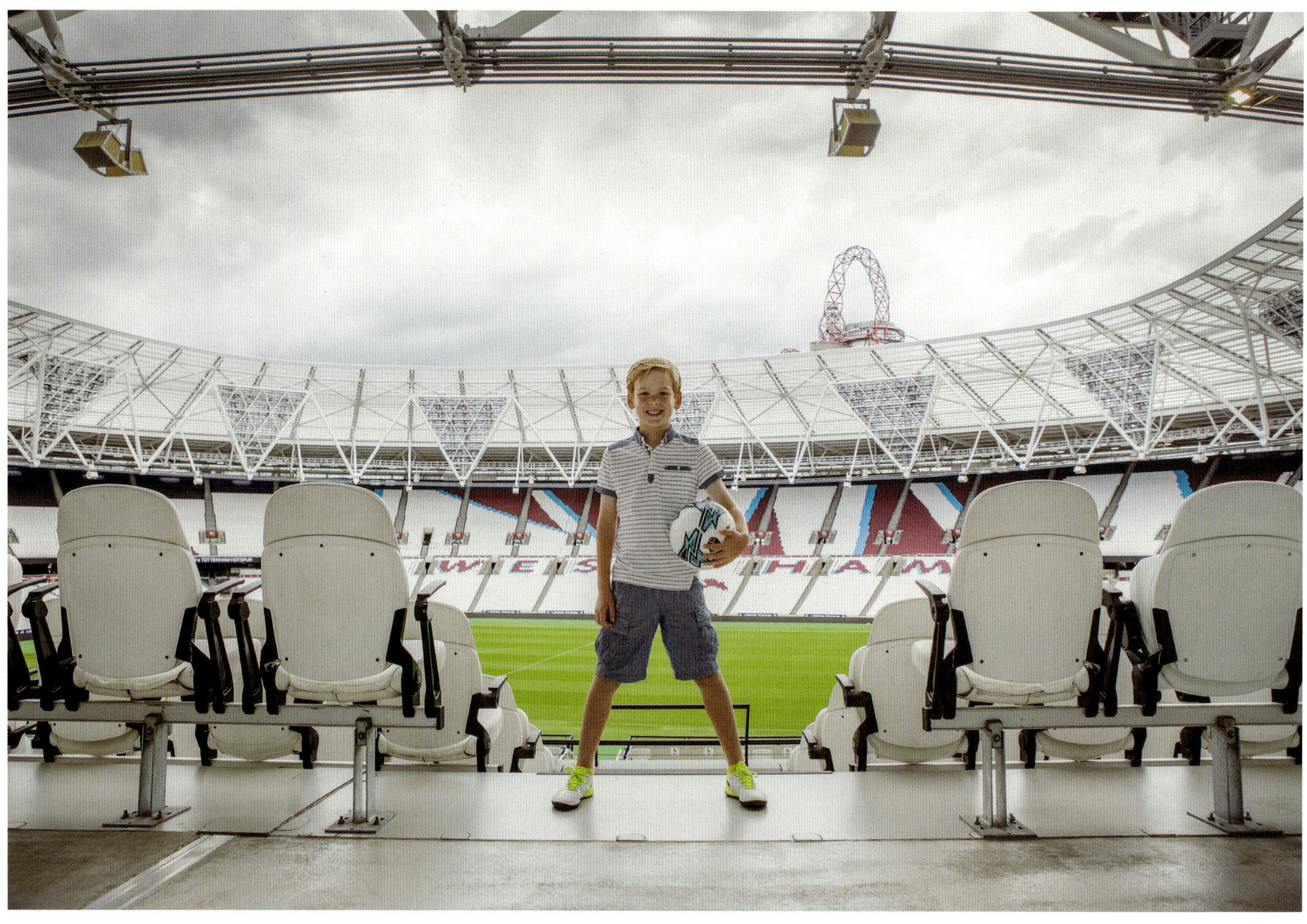

Above: Wideangle lenses let you show the grandeur
of a location and your subject within it.

Focal length: 24mm

Aperture: f/16

Shutter speed: 1/125 sec.

ISO: 400

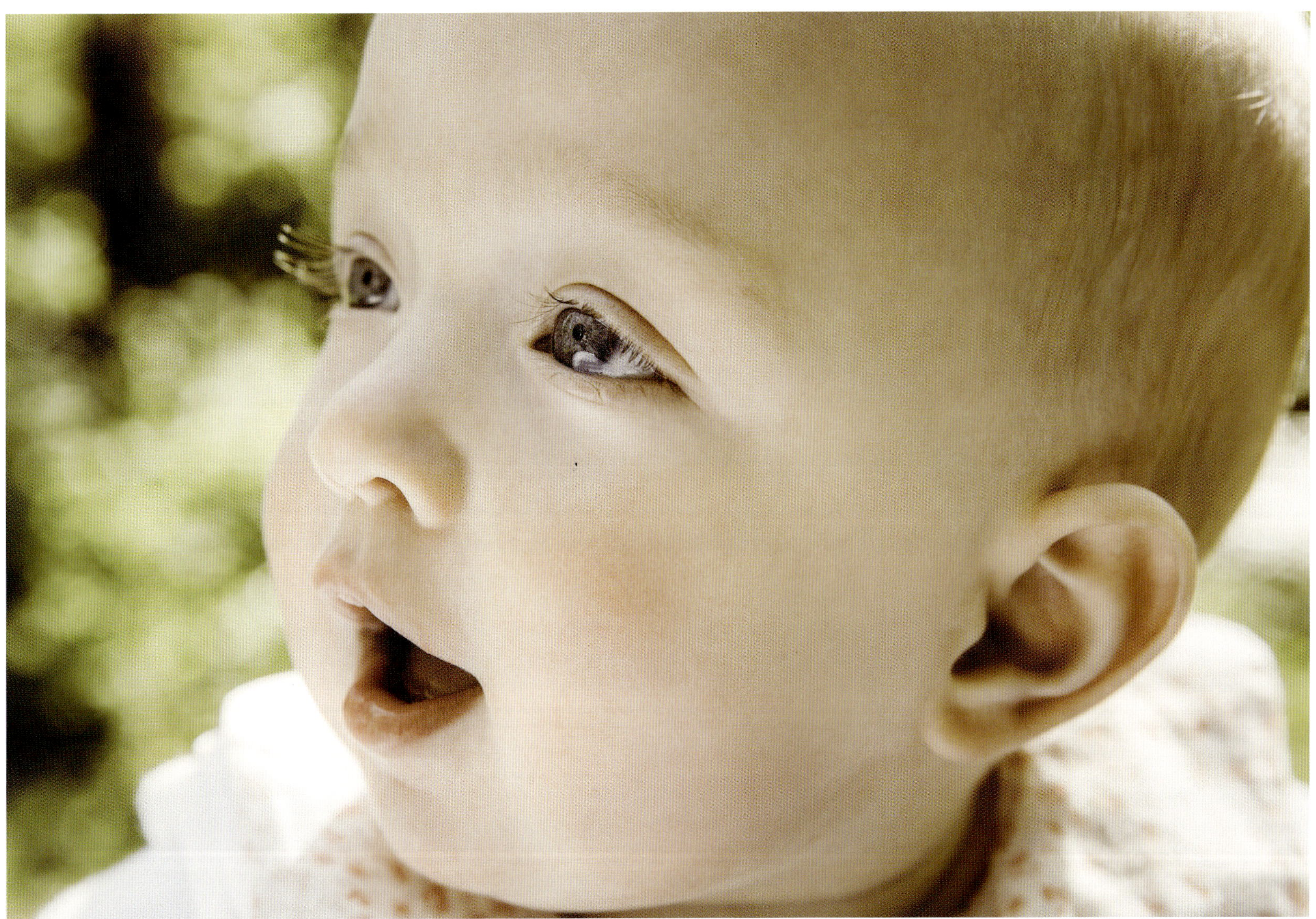

Above: Wideangle focal lengths used close to your subject
create a very "intimate" feel to an image, but care is needed
to avoid distorting facial features.
Focal length: 28mm
Aperture: f/4
Shutter speed: 1/250 sec.
ISO: 800

Lighting

On-camera lighting basically means a hotshoe-mounted speedlight flash or small, continuous light. Most manufacturers make their own dedicated flashes, but there are some very good independent manufacturers that are also worth a look. However, on-camera flash is rarely used for child portraiture, although it can be very effective for adding a little punch to a shot that needs it, introducing a highlight to the eyes, or to illuminate a room by bouncing the light off a nearby ceiling or wall. Some cameras have a small built-in flash, which can be a very useful feature (if only to add a slight sparkle to the eyes). I carry a small, lightweight LED unit in my kit bag, which is handy for adding a touch of light to dark areas where the shadows are just too difficult to work with.

For studio photographers, lighting is clearly one of the most important investments you will make, so it pays to get it right. Later in this book I will show you various different lighting setups, but you will need to decide whether you want to work with studio flash or continuous lighting. If it's the latter, LED lighting gets better and cheaper all the time and can provide a very good entry into studio lighting. The advantage of LED lights over older tungsten or HMI lights is that they weigh considerably less and do not get blisteringly hot.

Studio Strobes

LED lights will never compete with flash when it comes to power output, so studio flash or "strobes" are still the number one choice for most serious child portrait photographers. There are several different types of studio flash: some are mains powered, while others use batteries; some have the power pack built into the flash head, whereas others have separate power packs and flash heads. What they all have in common, though, is that they offer a very high light output and should have a reasonable number of light-shaping accessories that enable you to create different lighting effects. You can cover most lighting setups with no more than three lights, but two-head kits are commonly available in camera stores, so you might want to start there and buy more as your ability increases.

The power output of studio strobes is measured in watt seconds (often shortened to "watts" or "Ws"), and you will find lights available from around 200Ws up to more than 6,000Ws. Most flash heads come with two bulbs built into their design. The first is a "modeling light," which is a basic tungsten bulb that helps you to see what the finished result will be from that particular light. This acts as a continuous guide to help you to "model" the lighting, so you can see the effect it will have on the scene.

When you trigger the flash, the second bulb—the "flash tube"—will fire at a much brighter level, giving you the exposure you require. Modeling bulbs can be switched off to conserve power or set to flicker or dim to indicate that the light has fired correctly.

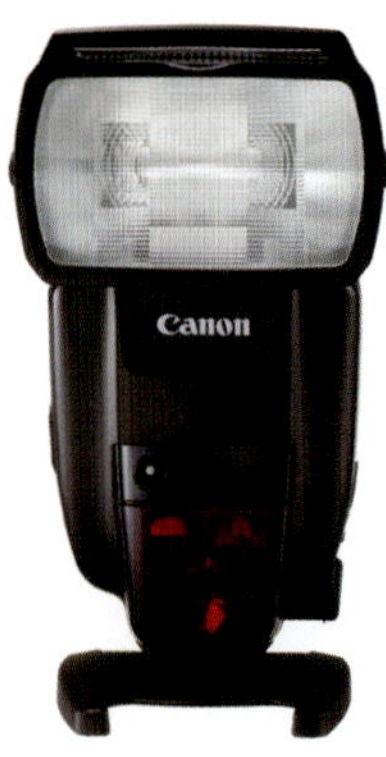

Above: Canon 600EX-II-RT Speedlite.

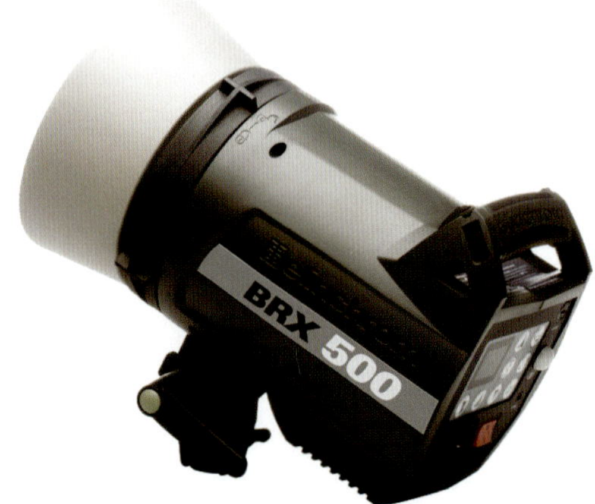

Above: Elinchrom makes a wide range of strobes, including monolights, such as this 500Ws BRX flash, packs and heads, and battery-powered location flashes with TTL exposure control.

Accessories

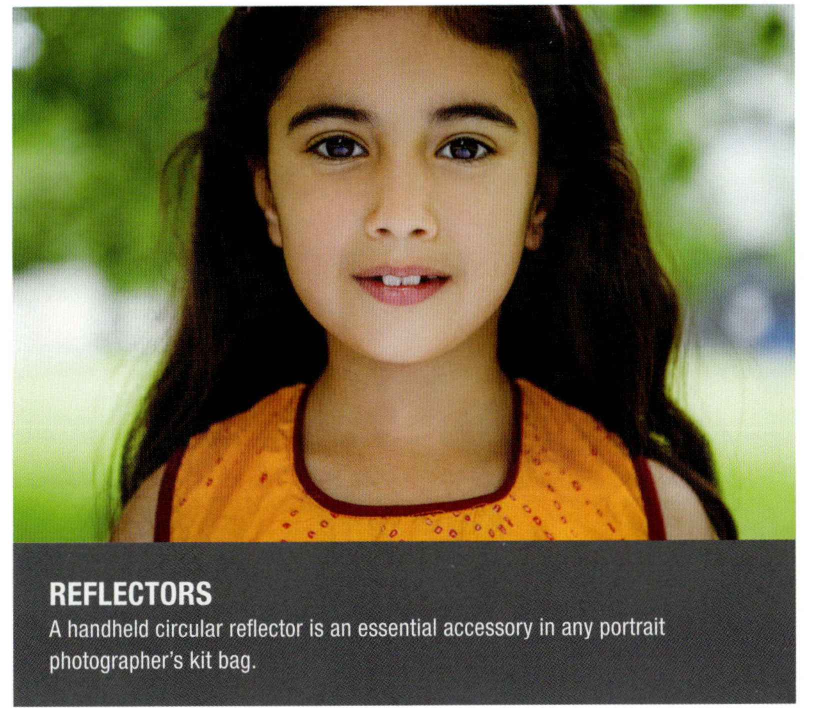

REFLECTORS
A handheld circular reflector is an essential accessory in any portrait photographer's kit bag.

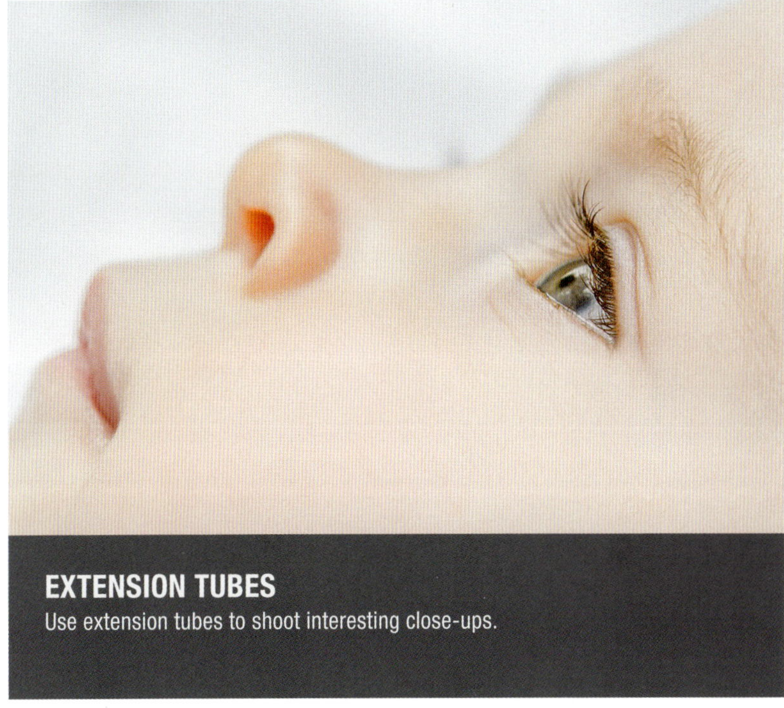

EXTENSION TUBES
Use extension tubes to shoot interesting close-ups.

Whether you are working in the home, in a studio, or on location, you will also need additional equipment. In many ways this additional kit will help to define your particular style of photography. I do most of my child portrait shoots on location and regard my collapsible bounce reflector as an absolutely essential element to my sessions. This type of reflector comes in various sizes, from small to enormous—I have many, but tend to carry a neat 30in. (75cm) circular reflector that folds down into my kit bag and gives me all the reflected light I could ever need. It is lightweight and comes with a white finish on one side and silver on the other. Made of water-resistant fabric these reflectors are very reasonably priced; I buy several each year and pass them on when they get too dirty or ripped.

In a studio you will need larger reflectors, so have a look in you local hardware store for polystyrene insulation boards. These are a cheap and easy way to create a mobile white wall to reflect light as required. Background materials are also a must for home or studio sessions. The cheapest are paper background rolls that come in all colors and a range of widths. You will need something to hold and support them, so once again have a chat with your local photo store and see what's available.

As well as the lenses mentioned previously, I also carry a set of extension tubes. They are lightweight and give me the ability to do beautiful close-up shots of eyelashes and lips that often result in gorgeous representative portraits that parents love to buy.

Although most child portrait sessions will probably have you moving around the child and being quite active, a tripod is a must for most photographers and studio photographers in particular will need a way to hold and stabilize their camera. Look at weight and extendibility before buying and don't forget that location photographers can use a monopod instead as a stable base to help prevent camera shake.

Finally, spare batteries and memory cards should not be forgotten: keep them in your camera bag at all times to avoid embarrassing mistakes! Every one of us at some point in time will forget to change our camera battery and take out the wrong memory card, so don't be caught out.

Memory cards are either SD (Secure Digital) or CF (Compact Flash) depending on your camera. Cards come in various different capacities and are rated at different speeds. Speed is really important, and you will pay more for the faster performing cards; size is subjective, as you want something that is large enough to take all the images from one shoot, but small enough so you don't risk losing too much if there is a technical problem. Modern cards are very stable, but they will one day let you down so don't be lulled into a false sense of security; some top-end cameras now have two card slots that can be set up to record simultaneously, so you never have a problem with a failing card.

Chapter 2
Camera Craft

Photographing children is challenging in many ways, and is often as much about managing the subject as it is about managing the photographic elements of the shoot. It is therefore more important than ever that the photographer has a clear and precise understanding of what he/she needs to be doing to ensure a result every time. There is rarely a second chance to capture that elusive moment: the smile, the laugh, the jump in the air may happen only once and there is no negotiating with a tired or stubborn child. Good camera craft is about learning everything there is to know about how your camera works and how you can master the techniques that will ensure you stay fluid and in control in any situation. The camera needs to be an extension of your eyes, your hands, and your creativity.

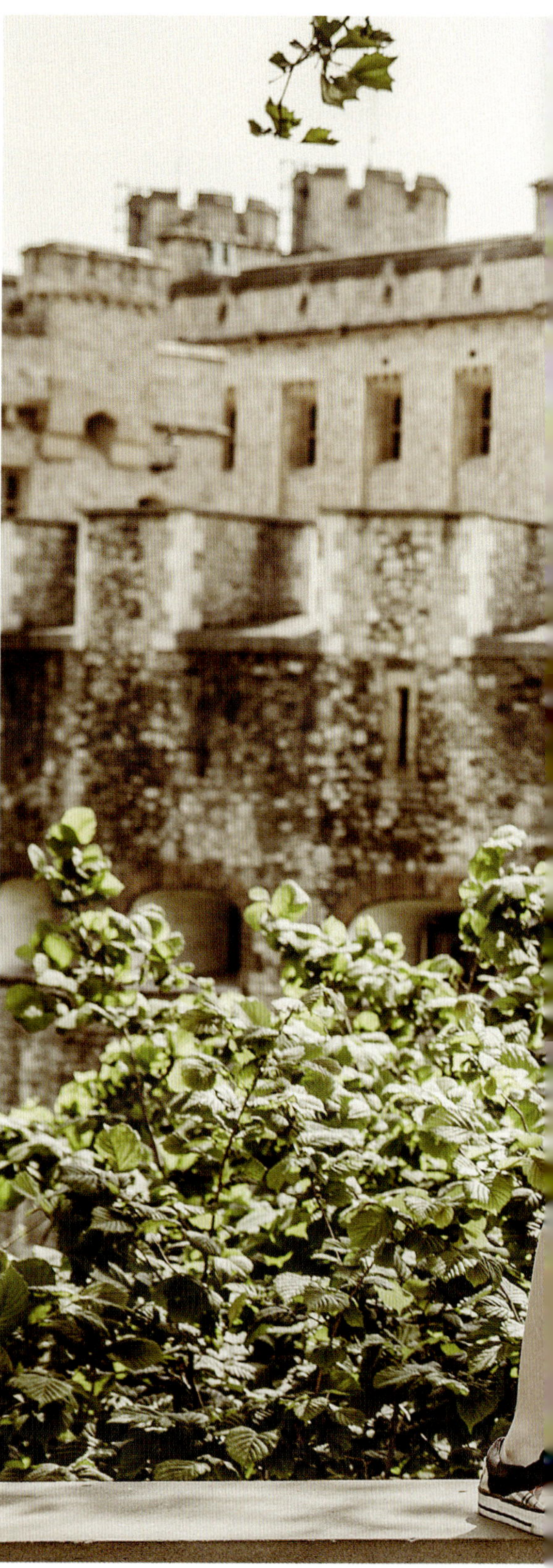

Right: With children you usually have just one chance to capture a moment.
Focal length: 50mm
Aperture: f/5
Shutter speed: 1/800 sec.
ISO: 400

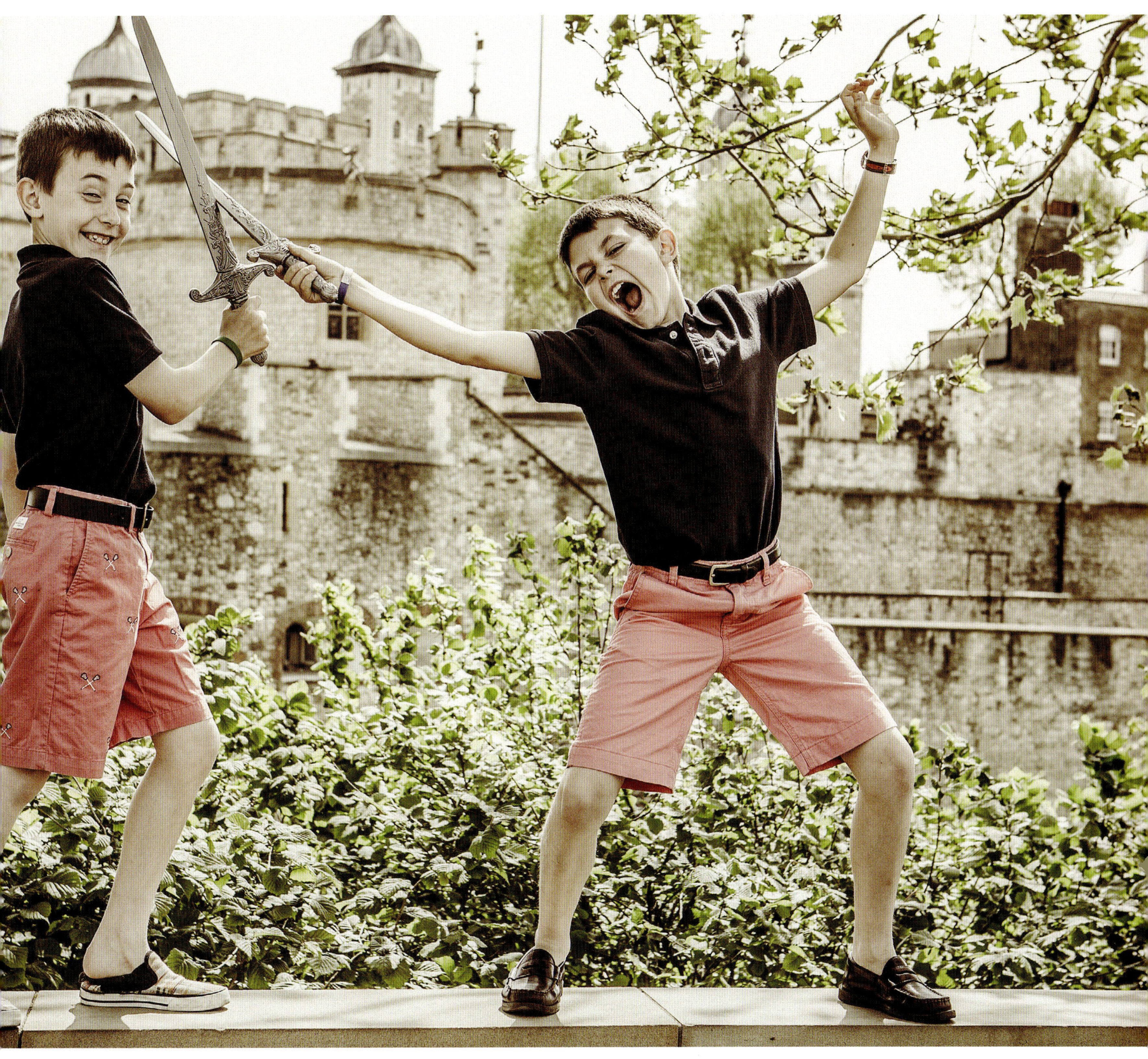

Handling Your Camera

Every camera is different, but you need to have the skill to operate the tools of your trade and be able to act, react, and respond to the changing situations that child portraiture will throw at you. There are few things more annoying or frustrating than watching a potentially great image float past the front of your lens because you are not ready or able to capture it.

When you first take delivery of a new camera it is normal to be slightly in awe. Modern cameras have a multitude of options and features, so it is important to quickly home in on the basics. Buttons may be in slightly different places and menus will be laid out differently, so start with the basics. How do you select an exposure mode, shutter speed, and aperture? How do you set up Raw and JPEG, and change the resolution? How do you adjust focus and what is the camera's LCD telling you that you need to be aware of? Even the simple act of half-pressing the shutter-release button and then fully pressing it can be different from one camera model to another.

In my early days in photography, shooting film, I had my first assignment for a new studio. The studio used Nikon equipment, whereas I was used to Canon. I was on location shooting for a beer company: production had stopped to accommodate me and I had established a complex lighting setup. I was ready to get the shot, when to my horror I could not make the shutter-release button work. No matter what I did, it simply would not let me press it.

Finding a phone (there were no cellphones back then) I rang the studio owner who quickly informed me that the Nikon I was using needed the winder lever to be pulled out before it would fire. This was designed to stop the shutter being released while it was in the camera bag, but was unique to this model and was a mystery to me. So get to know your camera before you go out on any child portrait assignment!

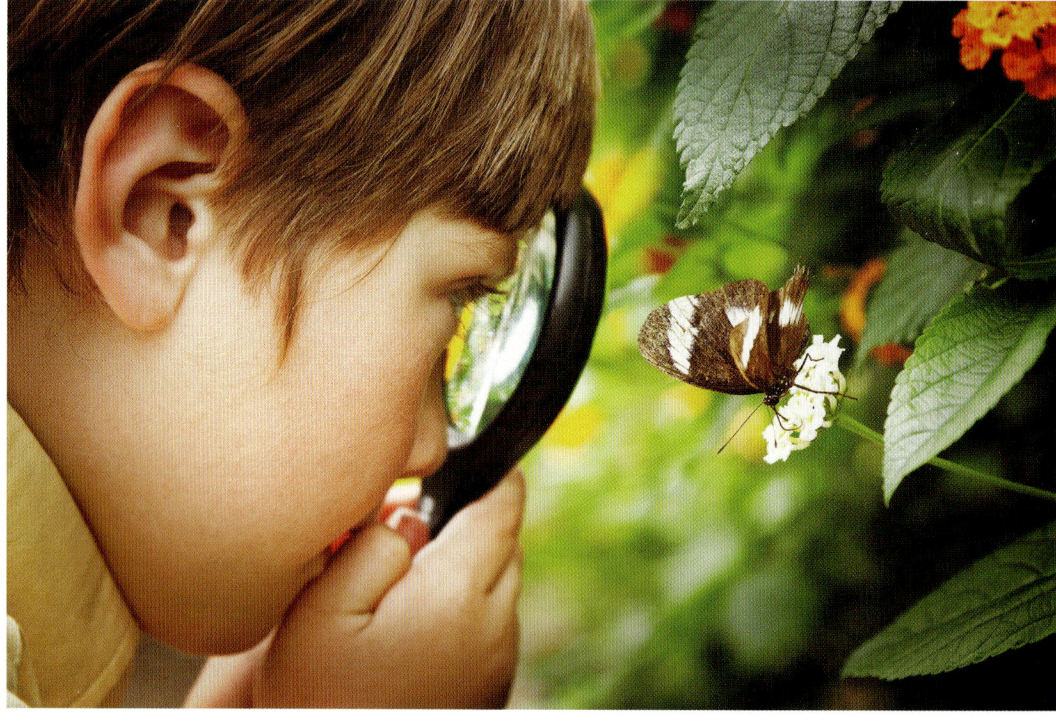

Above: With practice your camera should become a natural extension of your eyes. Good camera craft is at the heart of great photography.

Focal length: 105mm

Aperture: f/5.6

Shutter speed: 1/200 sec.

ISO: 400

The Basics

The balance of shutter speed and aperture is fundamental to shooting a correctly exposed image. Fundamentally there is a given amount of light available within a scene (whether you create that light or it exists naturally) and it is your choice as the photographer to adjust both the aperture and the shutter speed to suit your situation.

Shutter speed is the amount of time the sensor is revealed to light. It is usually measured in fractions of a second, but can be as long as you wish it to be. Many cameras have a shutter speed range 1/8000 sec. to 30 sec., plus a Bulb (B) mode that lets you hold the shutter open for as long as you hold down the shutter-release button. This is useful for exposures showing blurred movement or long exposures for still-life subjects, but is not relevant to child portraiture.

The aperture refers to the size of the variable opening in a lens that allows light to pass through into the camera. It is fairly obvious that the wider the opening, the more light enters the camera, so when it comes to balancing it with the shutter speed you can use a wide opening (or aperture) for a short amount of time (fast shutter speed), or you can use a small aperture with a long shutter speed and both will be correctly exposed.

But why is there a choice? It is simple: the shutter speed and aperture have other effects on the image, in addition to controlling the exposure.

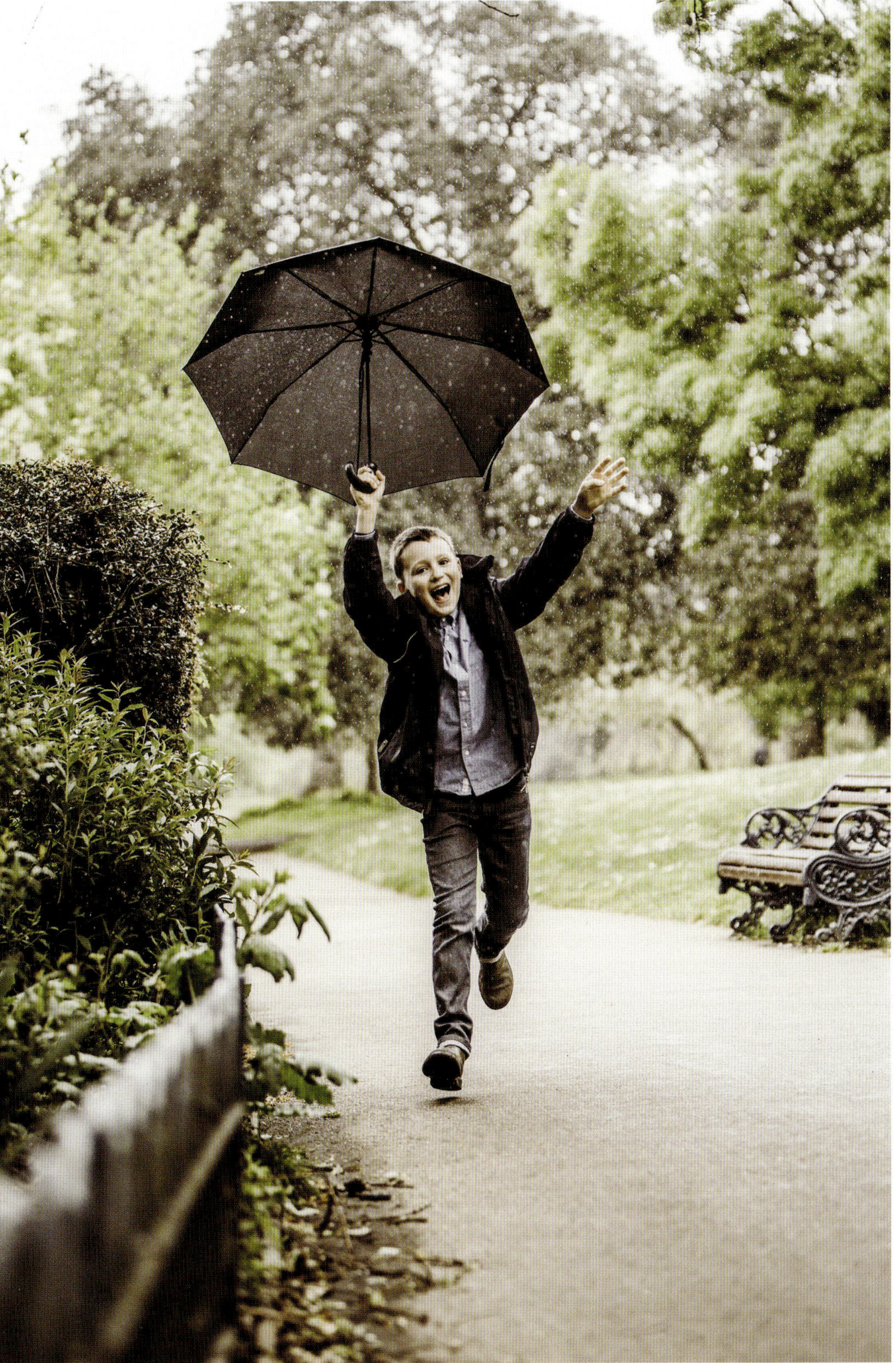

Right: A fast shutter speed will enable you to capture falling rain if the opportunity arises.

Focal length: 78mm

Aperture: f/2.8

Shutter speed: 1/1000 sec.

ISO: 800

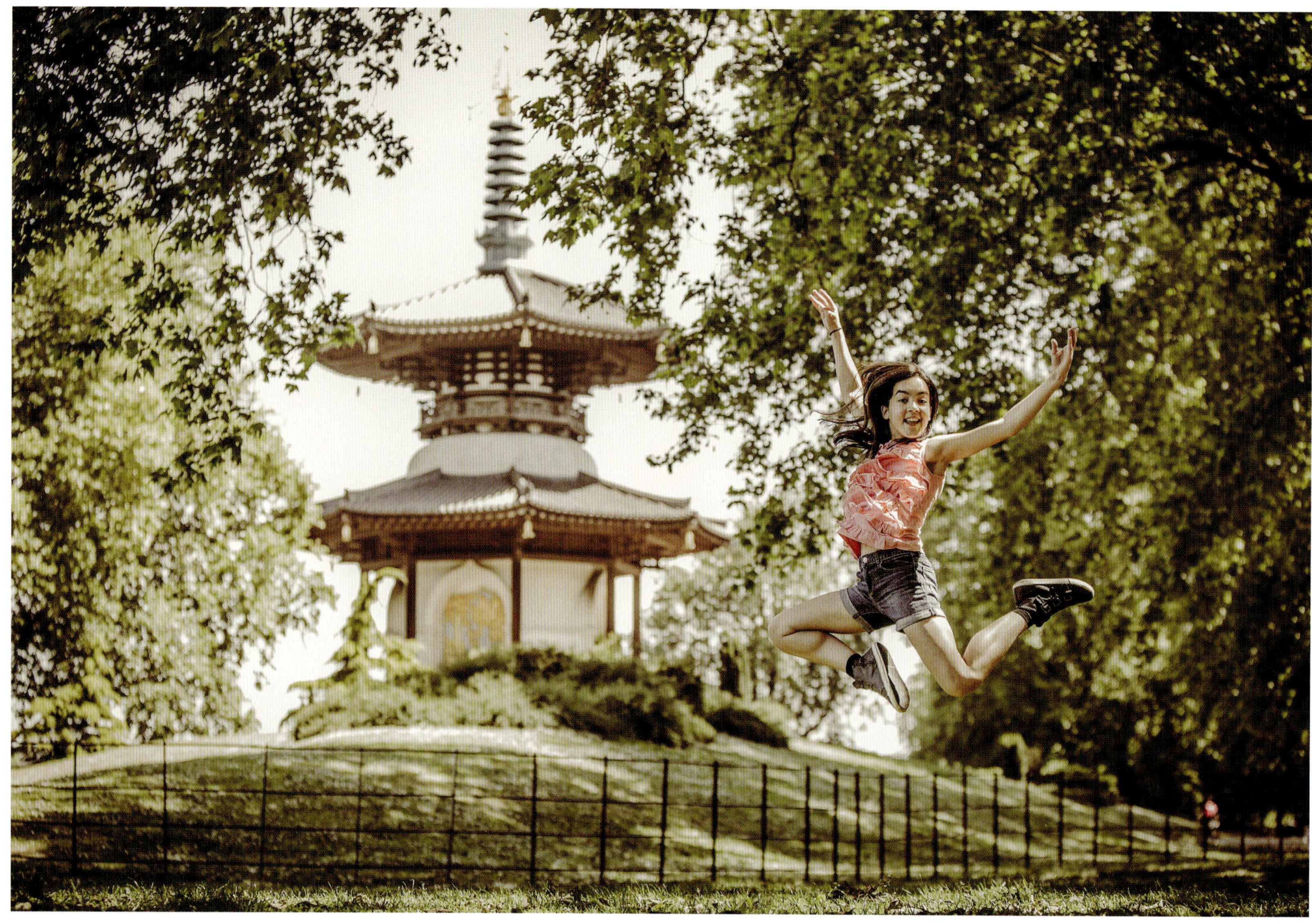

Shutter Speed

A short or fast shutter speed enables a photographer to "freeze" a fast-moving object (or child) sharply on the image. This can be fascinating, as it highlights the detail of a jump, falling rain, or a ball in mid-air having being kicked by a child.

A slow shutter speed has the opposite effect, showing blurred movement. It can be difficult to handle this effect (camera shake can be a problem), but shot correctly it can show hair flowing in the wind while the child's face is still, or you can pan the camera with a running child to blur the background and illustrate speed.

To avoid camera shake, a good rule of thumb is to ensure your shutter speed is always equal to or greater than the focal length of the lens. So a 50mm lens requires a shutter speed of 1/50 sec. or more, a 200mm lens needs a shutter speed of 1/200 sec. or faster, and so on. In-camera or in-lens image stabilization will help as well (as will your stance and the way you hold your camera), but if you stick to this rule you won't go far wrong.

Above: Freezing a dancer's leap in mid-air is only achievable with a fast shutter speed.

Focal length: 70mm

Aperture: f/3.2

Shutter speed: 1/1000 sec.

ISO: 800

Aperture

The effect of the aperture is slightly subtler than shutter speed, but it controls "depth of field." This is a zone of apparent sharpness that extends in front of and behind the point at which you focus. Controlling depth of field allows you to either blur the background and foreground in a shot to make your subject stand out, or try and keep as much of the scene as possible in focus.

The rule here is that the smaller the aperture, the greater the depth of field will be. Few DSLR and mirrorless camera lenses go below f/22, which is regarded as a very small aperture, offering a deep depth of field, although many professional large-format camera lenses offer a minimum aperture of f/32, f/45, or even f/64.

A wide aperture has the opposite effect and this can be very desirable to portrait photographers. The advantage of using a wide aperture setting is that it focuses all the viewer's attention on the subject. The best lenses are those that are said to give good "bokeh" (Japanese for "blur"), which creates beautiful out-of-focus areas that are very pleasing to the eye.

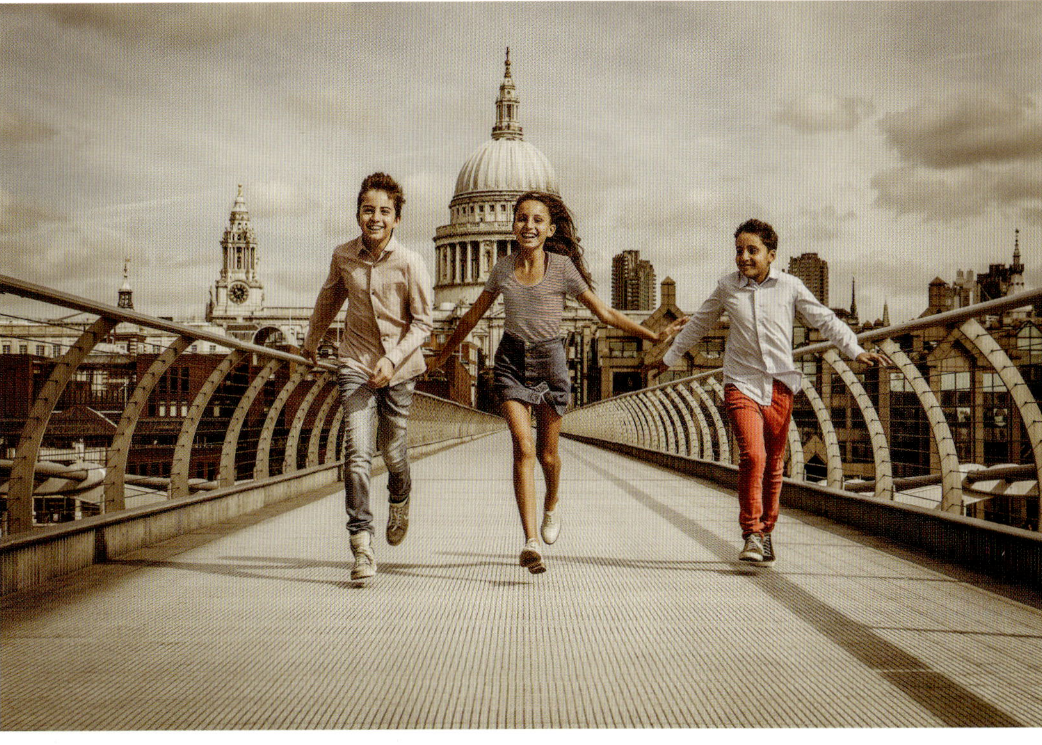

Right top: A small aperture will show detail from front to back, creating a huge depth of field throughout the image.

Focal length: 59mm

Aperture: f/16

Shutter speed: 1/1000 sec.

ISO: 1000

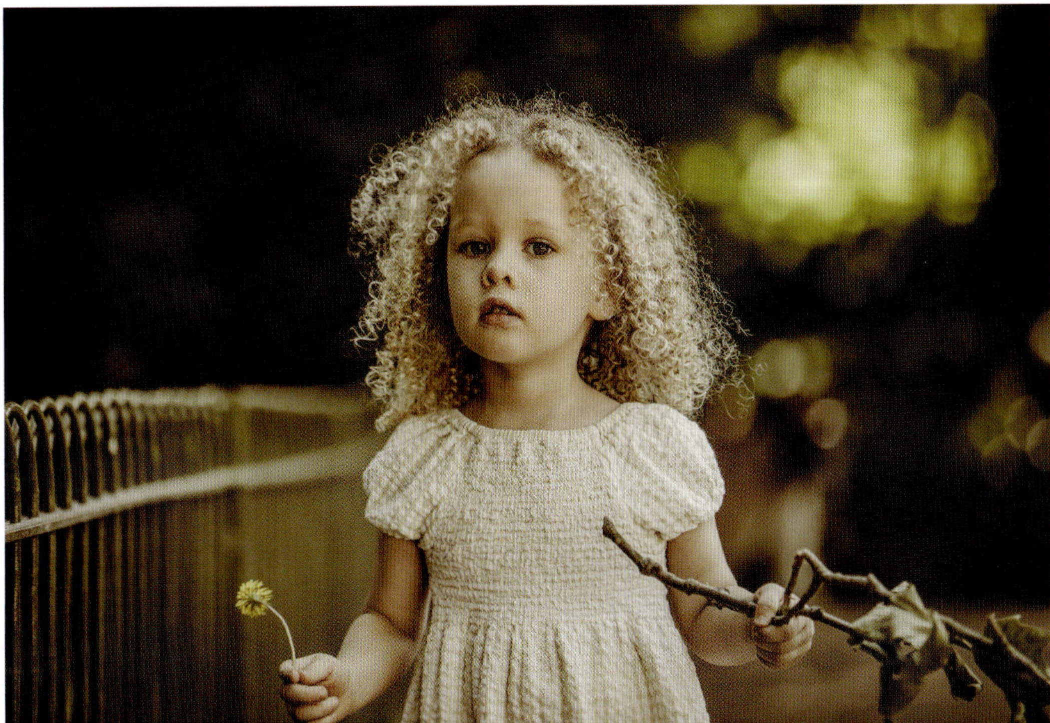

Right: A wide aperture will create a shallow depth of field, placing all the emphasis of the image on the subject.

Focal length: 148mm

Aperture: f/2.8

Shutter speed: 1/800 sec.

ISO: 500

ISO

At the beginning of every new photographic session it is important to check that the camera's ISO is set correctly. ISO (International Standards Organization) is the setting that denotes the relative sensitivity of the sensor to the available light. It is the means by which you set your camera according to the conditions, enabling you to shoot in low light, as well as brighter situations.

When you have low-light conditions you are generally forced to use slower shutter speeds to achieve the correct exposure. This leads to problems with blurring due to either subject movement or camera shake. If you reach the limits offered by your widest aperture setting, the only choice you have is to change the overall sensitivity of the camera itself. The problem with this is that you can only push it so far before the image quality starts to degrade, creating noisy images and discoloration. Although different cameras have different noise characteristics, a low ISO (ISO 50–100) will give you clean crisp images, while a high ISO (usually around ISO 1600+) will give increasing levels of noise and degradation,

The rule here is that it is better to get something in an extreme situation, rather than nothing at all, but you should always try to use the lowest ISO setting you can. It is also worth noting that manufacturers are constantly improving their camera's high ISO performance, and ISO 800—which used to be regarded as very high and almost unusable for professional work—is now a setting that is well-used by many photographers, myself included. In fact, some noise in an image can be regarded as stylishly desirable, giving the final image a "photo real" effect.

Metering Modes

How you and your camera determine the ideal combination of shutter speed, aperture, and ISO depends on the metering system you use to read the available light. You can set your camera to analyze the frame in several ways, from reading the light falling across the entire frame to placing emphasis on a smaller part of it.

The most extreme choice is spot metering, where the meter will take a light reading from a very small point. You would use this if you wanted to ensure that just one element of the overall image is correctly exposed. This is most relevant when there are areas within the frame that might make other metering options struggle, such as bright lights included within the photograph or if the subject is spot lit in a dark room.

However, the more general modes that cover more (or all) of the frame will be used more regularly. For example, you can set your metering to measure an average of the entire scene or maybe place emphasis on the center of the frame, while still considering the outer areas. It is up to you to choose the most appropriate setting for the location you are in. Like the ISO setting, this is something that is normally selected at the beginning of a shoot and is rarely adjusted unless the scene changes completely.

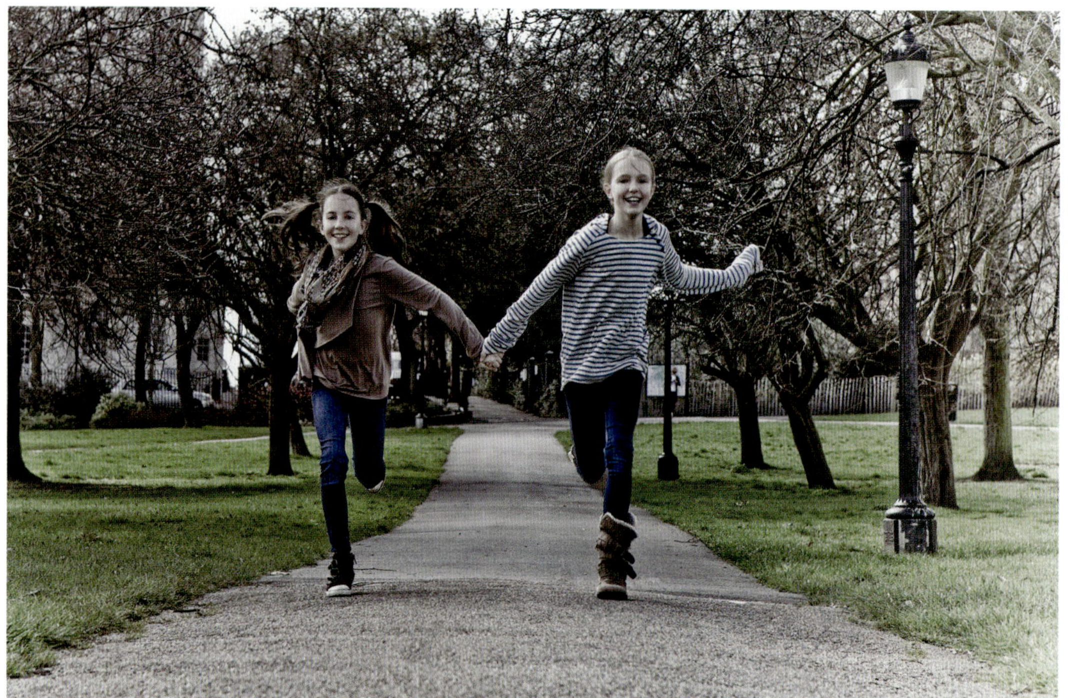

Above: High ISO settings are required in low-light situations where movement is important, although this will result in a noisier image.

Focal length: 70mm

Aperture: f/6.3

Shutter speed: 1/1000 sec.

ISO: 4000

Shooting Modes

Modern cameras are designed to help you shoot quickly and precisely in any situation. They do this by offering several different ways of combining aperture and shutter speed. It is important to have a full and clear understanding of what these modes are and when and why you should choose one over another in any given situation. Too many photographers select a mode for shooting when they buy their camera and then stick to that throughout the entire life of the camera. Pretty much every camera will have Manual, Aperture Priority, Shutter Priority, and Program, and these are the settings that most of us will use.

Manual (M)

In Manual mode the photographer is required to make all the decisions. It is up to you to choose the shutter speed and aperture as required and they will not change automatically, even if the lighting conditions change within the scene. In magazine articles and online video tutorials, much is made of how important it is to use Manual mode if you want to be regarded as a "true professional." It is true that there are occasions where Manual is the right way to set up your camera, but in my opinion there is far too much snobbery about using Manual exclusively.

The advantage of shooting in Manual is that once the shutter speed and aperture are set they will stay the same, no matter what. This can be useful when you have elements other than the subject changing in the frames; sunshine flickering through trees in the breeze is a good example, or someone running toward you who may sometimes reveal a sunny sky behind them as they run. In both of these cases manual exposure will not be swayed by any sudden changes in brightness.

Manual is also the best choice for shooting with flash in a studio, as the camera meter will not be able to measure external flash units.

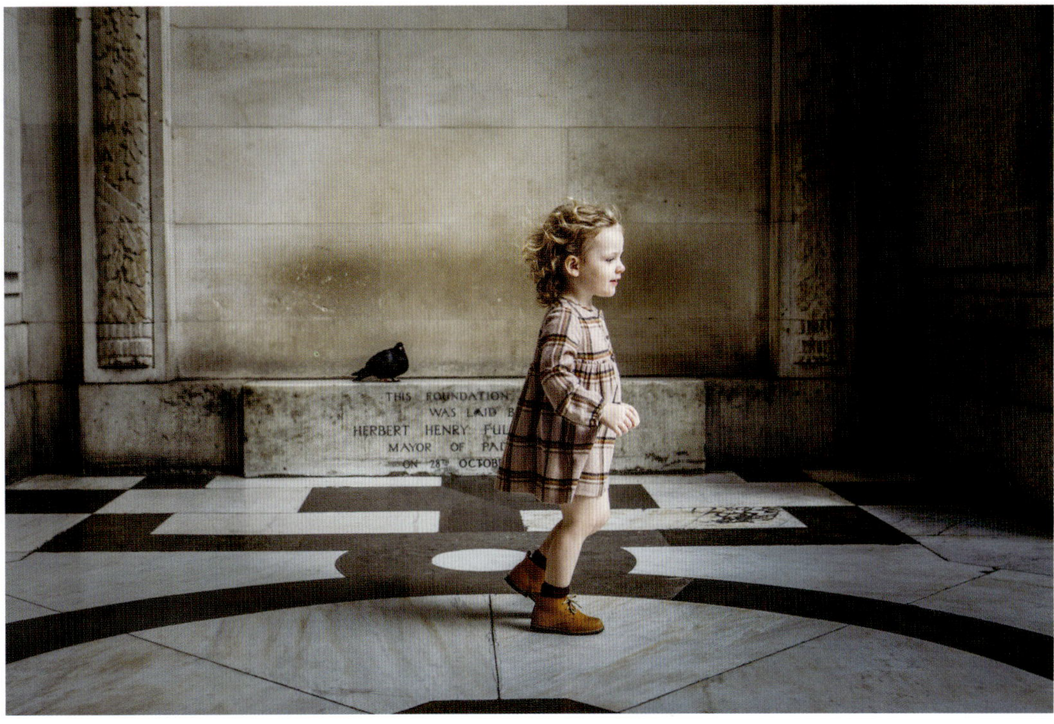

Above: Choose Manual mode when you need to be in control of every element of your photograph.

Focal length: 48mm

Aperture: f/5.6

Shutter speed: 1/200 sec.

ISO: 1000

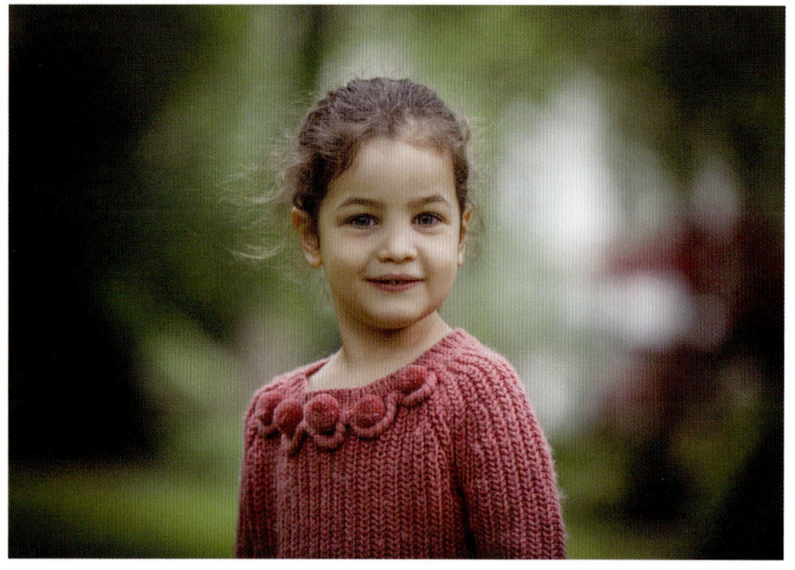

Above: Choose Aperture Priority when your primary
concern is to control the depth of field in the photograph.

Focal length: 170mm

Aperture: f/3.5

Shutter speed: 1/250 sec.

ISO: 500

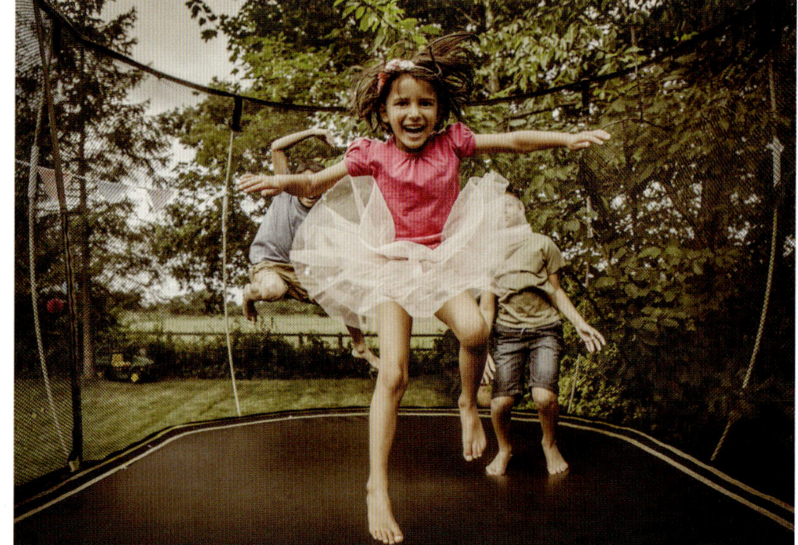

Above: Choose Shutter Priority when you want to control
the movement in your photograph. In this shot a fast shutter
speed freezes any motion.

Focal length: 24mm

Aperture: f/3.5

Shutter speed: 1/1250 sec.

ISO: 800

Aperture Priority (A/Av)

Aperture Priority lets you set the aperture and
the camera sets an appropriate shutter speed.
When photographing children, setting the aperture
can be very useful, as it lets you control depth of
field. However, you need to remain aware of your
shutter speed—especially if you are using a small
aperture—to ensure it is fast enough to freeze any
movement and avoid camera shake.

Shutter Priority (S/Tv)

Shutter Priority (also known as Time Value or Tv)
is my go-to mode for most location child portrait
sessions. This is because most of my shoots
involve children running about and being active,
and I need to ensure they are always sharp.
I don't want to stop their enjoyment, so setting
the shutter speed at 1/1000 sec. and letting the
camera choose the aperture is ideal for me. If the
child runs from a sunny part of the scene into a
shaded area, the camera will adjust accordingly,
so most images will remain correctly exposed.
I only change the setting if I am in close proximity
to the child and we are having a quiet moment
or engaging in a sensible manner.

Choosing a slow shutter speed can also be
effective, as it enables you to capture a soft, blurry
movement effect like spinning hair and fabric. By
choosing a reasonably slow shutter speed and
then panning at the same speed as a running child
you can get a beautiful blurred movement effect,
which is common in car adverts to show speed.
This is a difficult technique to master, as it involves
choosing a shutter speed that is slow enough to
blur the background, but fast enough to ensure
that detail in the moving subject is sharp. There's
no one shutter speed for every situation, so
practice is the only answer.

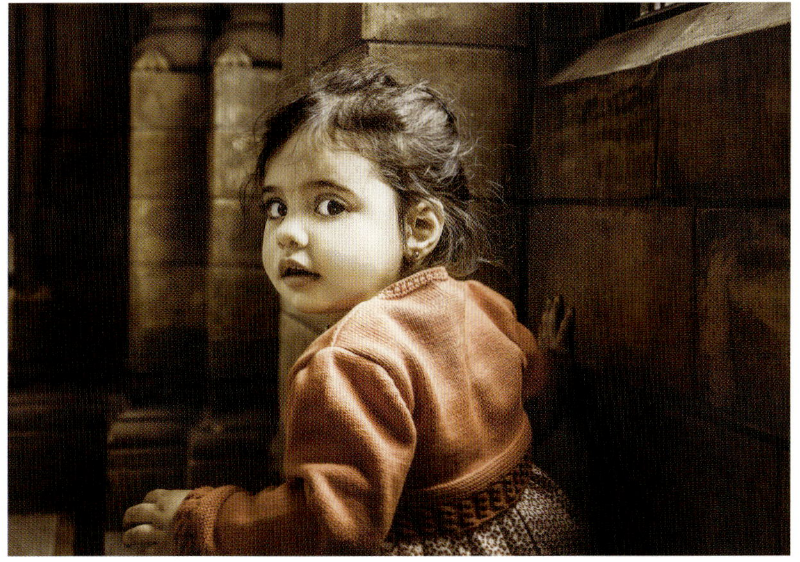

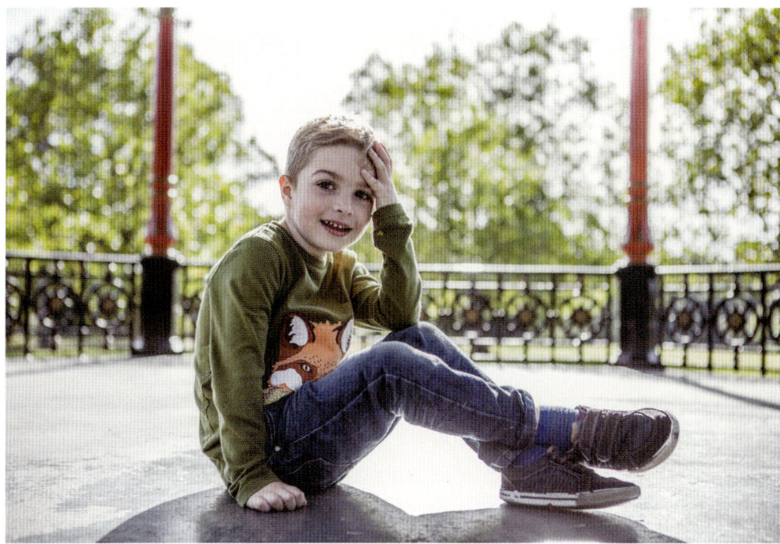

Above: Choose Program mode when you need to react quickly to a changing environment and make sure you get the photograph.

Focal length: 55mm

Aperture: f/7.1

Shutter speed: 1/160 sec.

ISO: 2500

Above: The bright sky in this scene would fool the camera into shooting an image that is too dark, so I set the exposure compensation dial at +2 stops to expose the boy correctly. This effectively changed the aperture from f/5.6 (the camera's recommendation) to f/2.8 (the correct aperture).

Focal length: 48mm

Aperture: f/2.8

Shutter speed: 1/800 sec.

ISO: 2500

Program (P)

Many professionals frown upon Program mode, but I use it often. If I see the children in a great position or locational setting and I need to be sure I will get the image, Program takes care of everything. It sets the shutter speed and aperture according to the situation, and with a lot of cameras it also takes the focal length of the lens into account, so it will try to avoid using slow shutter speeds with a long telephoto lens, while giving greater priority to small aperture settings with wideangle lenses.

It is true that Program can be a bit of a blunt tool, but is has got me many images that would probably not have been achieved otherwise. I usually leave my cameras set on Program when they're in my bag, as it means I can grab them if needed and don't need to think about whether the setting is correct or not.

Exposure Compensation

With the exception of Manual mode (where you have full control over the exposure), all of the previous modes can be adjusted using exposure compensation, which lets you fine tune your camera's automatic settings to compensate for any extreme lighting conditions. This is useful because when your camera's meter reads the light, it tries to calculate an exposure based on the best average setting between the brightest values and the darkest values in the scene.

This is great most of the time, but if there are exceptionally bright areas in a scene, such as the sky, this can throw the camera into setting a darker exposure than you need for the main subject. You need to compensate for the meter's lack of a creative brain, so would choose +1 stop of exposure compensation, or +2 stops or more if the sunlight behind your subject is very bright.

The same is true if a child is spot lit by a single ray of sunshine shooting through a dark wood: the camera will make the exposure too bright and wash out the detail in the child's face, so you would need to apply -1 stop or -2 stops of exposure compensation to get the desired exposure. Even the very best camera systems in the world cannot make creative decisions: you are the artist.

Focusing

Sharpness in your images is something that will become an absolute obsession. It sounds simple to make sure your images are sharp, but you will inevitably have sharpness issues at some point in your career. You will look at the wonderful once-in-a-lifetime shot on the back of your viewing screen and jump for joy when you get it, only to return home and see it is not critically sharp on the large screen of your computer. It's a crushing feeling, but something that all of us have experienced and sadly will experience again, especially when working with erratic subjects like children.

Today's cameras offer multiple focusing modes to help ensure the best chance of sharpness every time. They also offer multiple focusing points, which are the sensors that snap your lens into focus at a particular distance. The more expensive cameras generally have a greater number of focus points than cheaper models: the theory is that the more focus points you have, the greater chance you have of a sharp image.

However, it is *you* that determines where to focus, and having a thousand focus points won't help you if you choose the wrong one. So familiarize yourself with your camera's focusing options, as they are all a little different. From single points to cross points, four-point clusters and nine-point clusters, only you can choose the mode that best suits your style. There are even totally automatic focus settings that will jump around the frame finding the key areas for you as you frame and re-frame your image.

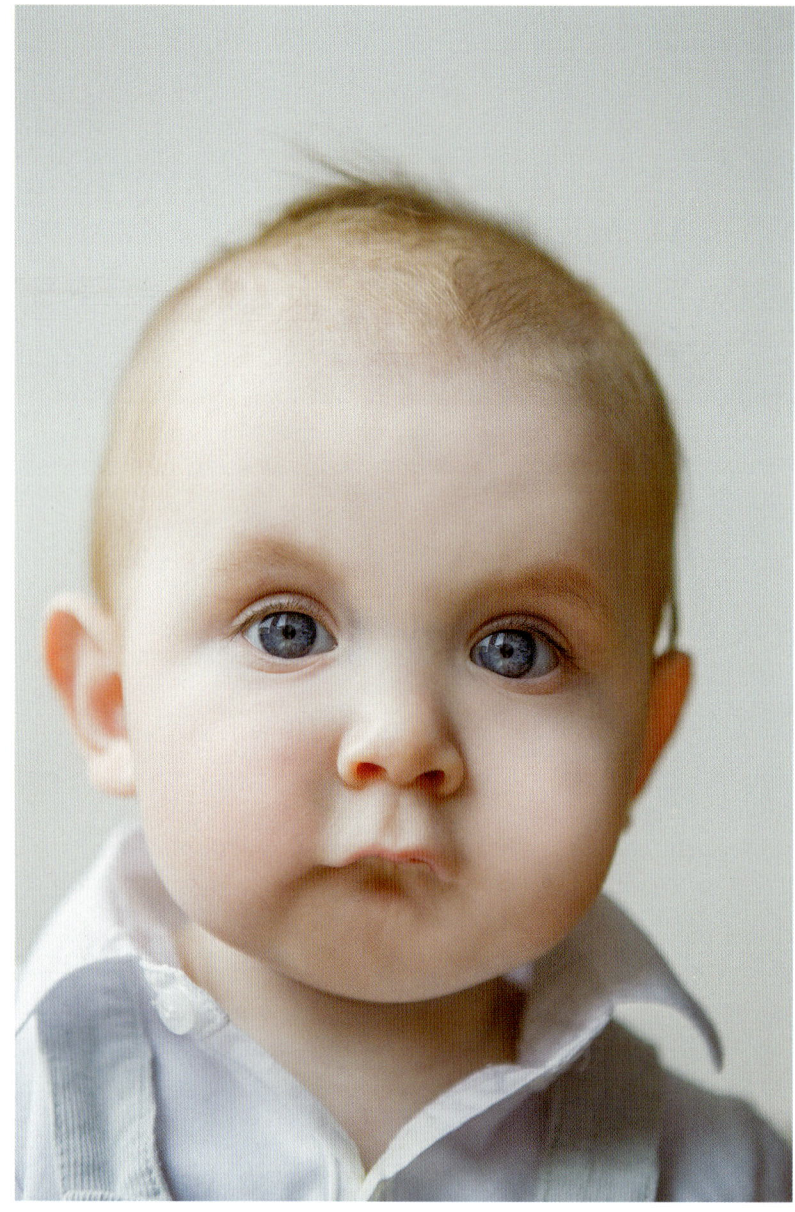

Left: The eyes are the windows to the soul: if the eyes are sharp, then all is well.

Focal length: 70mm

Aperture: f/3.2

Shutter speed: 1/500 sec.

ISO: 1600

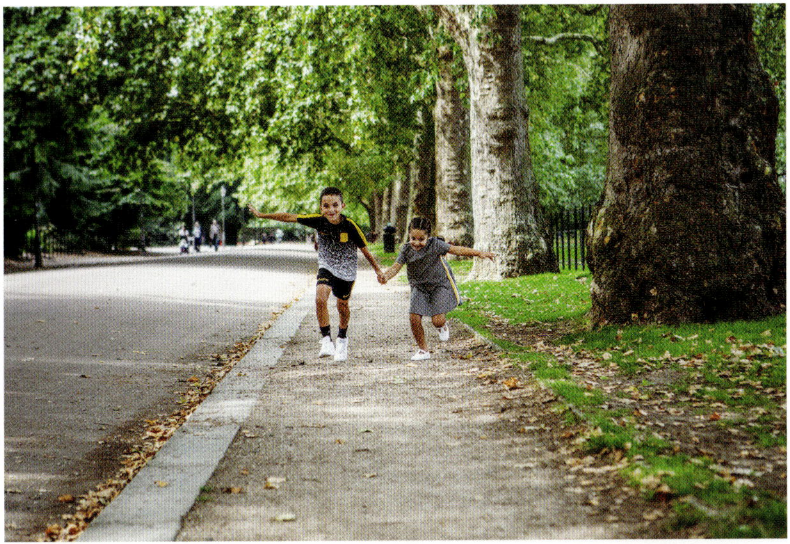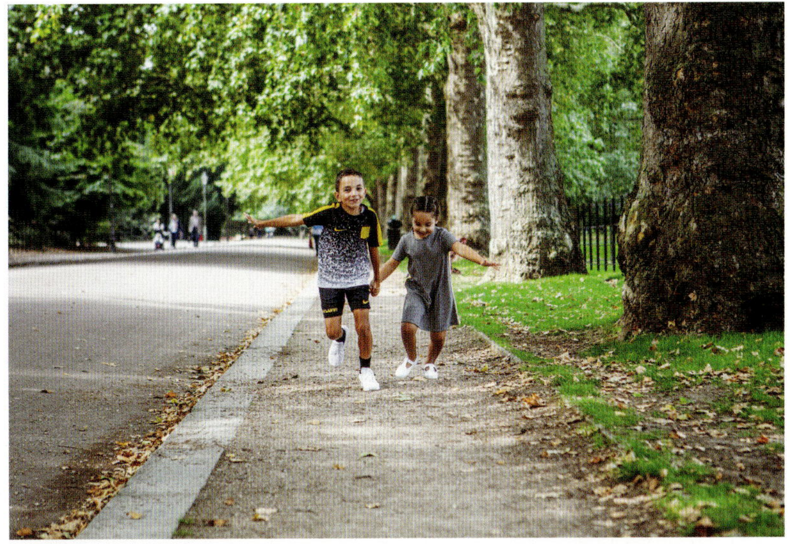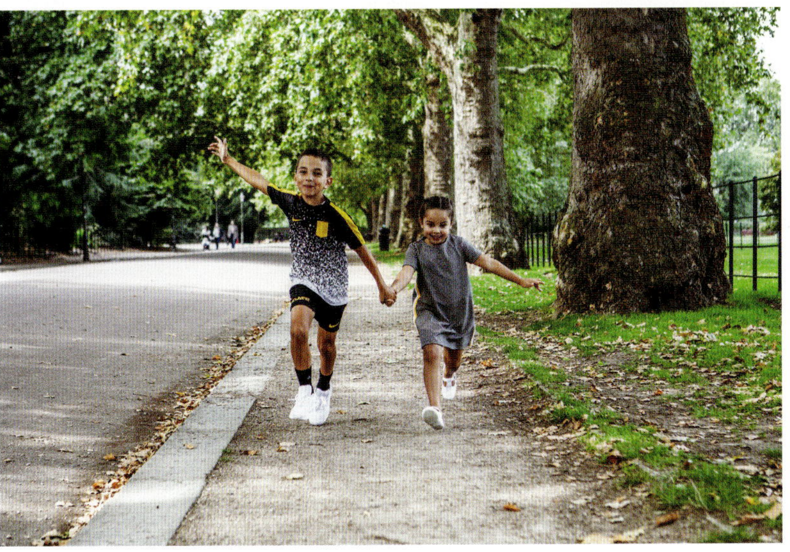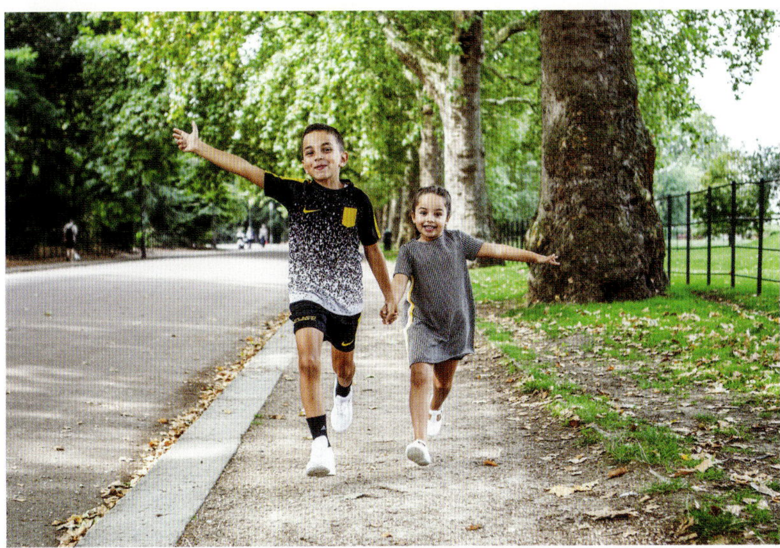

If there is one tip that applies to just about every child portrait you will ever shoot, that is: focus on the eyes. This is especially important when you are working with shallow depths of field, as it is the sharpness of the eyes that will define your picture. If all else fails in the image, but the eyes are sharp, the shot will often still be regarded as a success.

Some cameras now have a specific eye focusing setting or "eye AF," which can cleverly find the eye in a portrait scene and then keep the camera focused on that point, however and wherever it moves. Only a few years ago I would have been telling you to avoid such gimmicks, but the latest versions of this technology are incredibly effective.

Focus is generally set when you press the shutter-release button down half way, which enables you to focus using a single AF point (often the center of the view finder) and then recompose for a better composition before firing the shutter. Another common technique is to choose a focus point that's sitting over the critical area, although this can be slightly slower in practice. In any case, take the time to find the technique that you feel most comfortable with and make it a fluid part of your camera craft.

Above: Using continuous or predictive focus will let you track running children and shoot sharp images even if you are zooming as they move.

Focal length: 24–70mm lens (various focal lengths)

Aperture: f/2.8

Shutter speed: 1/1000 sec.

ISO: 640

White Balance

The human visual system is very sophisticated. It not only allows you to see in light and dark situations, but also computes subtle changes in the color of light so that—for the most part—we don't see any color shifts. If we go from incandescent indoor lighting to overcast daylight outdoors, the lighting appears to remain neutral to us, but the color of that light (known as the "color temperature") changes significantly.

If we take natural daylight as our yardstick for neutrality, then most household indoor lights are tungsten balanced, which means they are more orange than daylight. Color temperature is measured in degrees Kelvin (K), with daylight normally rated at anywhere from 5500–6500K depending on the time of day and weather conditions. By contrast, household bulbs are usually around 3300K, and you can see the difference quite clearly if you put a tungsten bulb in a wall fitting in a room where there is a large skylight: the reflection of the light on the wall will be yellow because your eyes have adjusted for the daylight conditions.

Cameras have a white balance feature that can either be set manually or set to auto. Auto white balance will make a good job of most situations, but it pays to keep an eye on how your images are looking, as some mixed light situations can give the wrong color temperature. The symbols on your white balance dial are self-explanatory, but try a test by shooting the same image outdoors with each of the settings so you can see the effect. It's not something that you will change that often, but it pays to know how white balance can affect your images if set incorrectly.

We will take a closer look at setting your white balance and the effect of color temperature in chapter five.

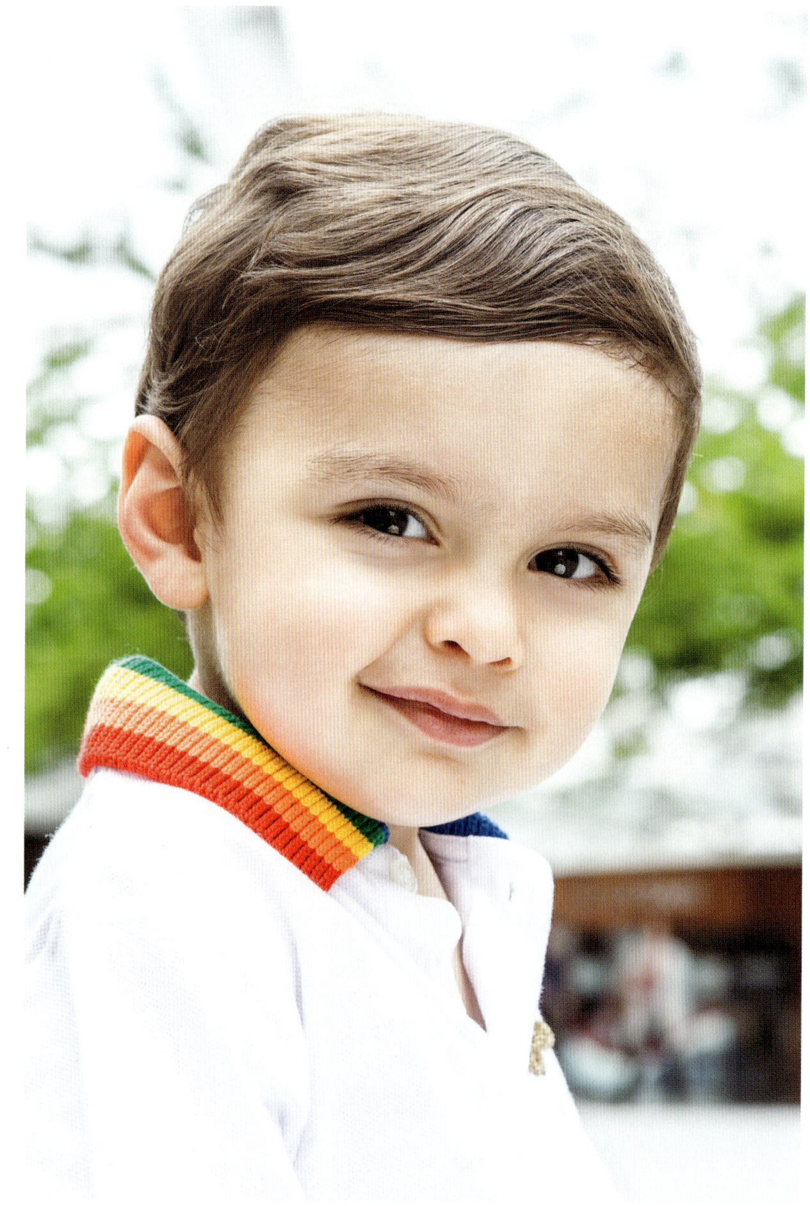

Left: Setting the correct white balance is essential if you want to ensure a perfect color rendition and clean and neutral whites in an image.

Focal length: 70mm

Aperture: f/7.1

Shutter speed: 1/400 sec.

ISO: 800

Choosing Focal Lengths

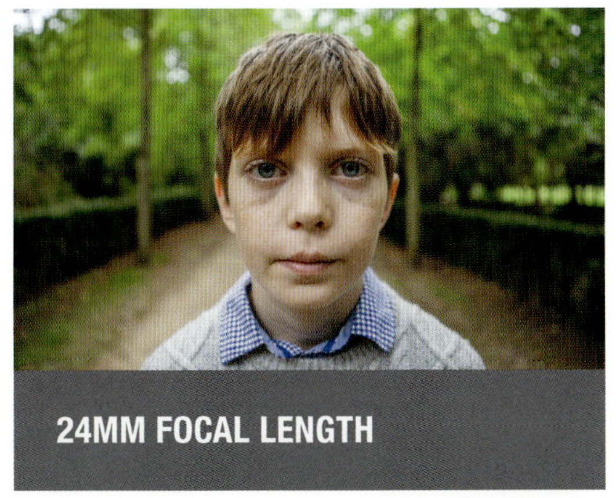

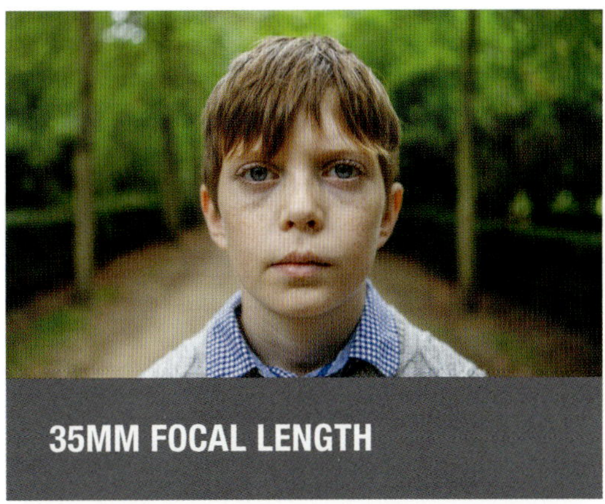

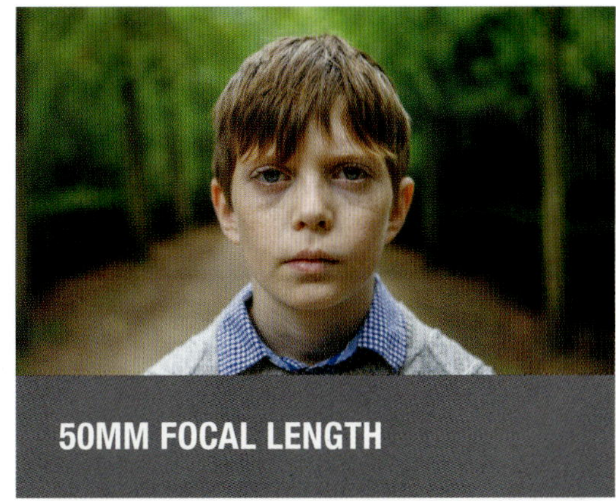

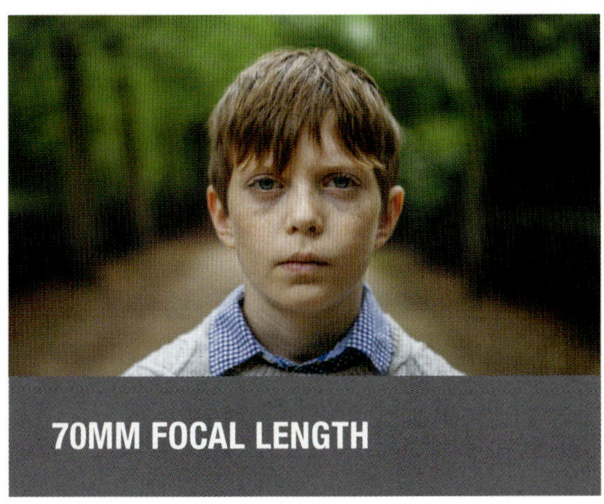

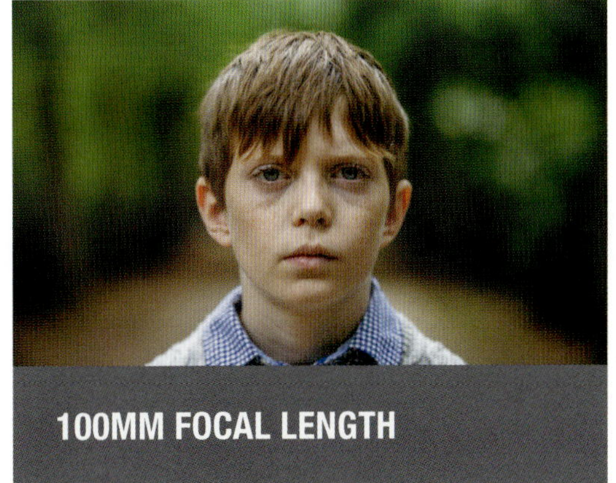

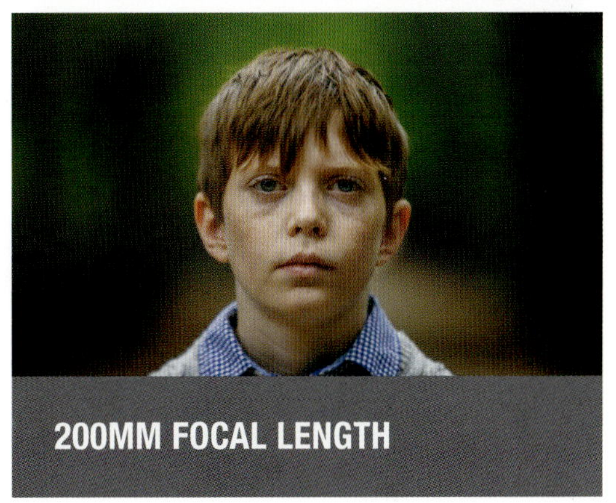

There is a huge choice of lenses for DSLR and mirrorless cameras, and the effect of choosing one over another is quite profound. It is fairly obvious that different focal lengths appear to bring the scene closer or farther away from the camera, from the narrow viewing angle of a telephoto to the extreme wideangle view of a fisheye lens, but that is not the only effect they have.

If you place your subject in the center of a scene and photograph them with different focal lengths—keeping the subject the same size in the frame—you will find your shots look quite different, as illustrated here. With a short focal length you will find yourself standing closer to your subject, while the magnifying properties of a long focal length will mean you have to stand quite far back.

However, even though your subject remains the same size in the frame, the background will appear quite different. With wideangle lenses there will be plenty of background and it will appear to be more sharply focused. With a telephoto the background appears to be enlarged, so less is contained within the scene; it also looks far less sharply focused, especially when you use a wide aperture and shallow depth of field.

These effects can be used to your advantage as an artist. Using wideangle lenses gives a very "inclusive" feel to the shots, which is a good choice when you want to tell a story and add context, such as "This is the day that Jack went to his favorite football ground." However, you need to beware of using a wideangle lens too close to your subject, as extreme wideangles can distort arms, legs, and faces, which can be rather unattractive!

A telephoto focal length does the opposite, and turns the background into nothing more than a beautiful pattern—a backdrop that frames your subject, leaving no doubt that the image is all about the child.

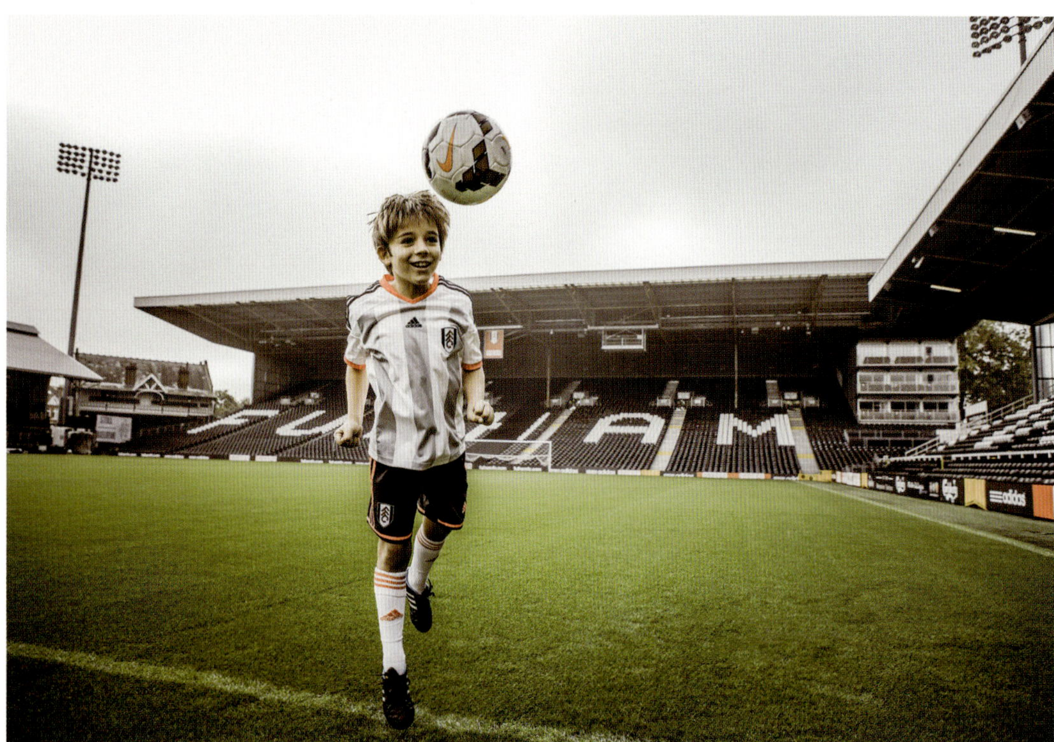

Left: Shooting with a 24mm wideangle focal length gives a wide view that tells a story about the location as well as the subject.

Focal length: 24mm

Aperture: f/5

Shutter speed: 1/1250 sec.

ISO: 1000

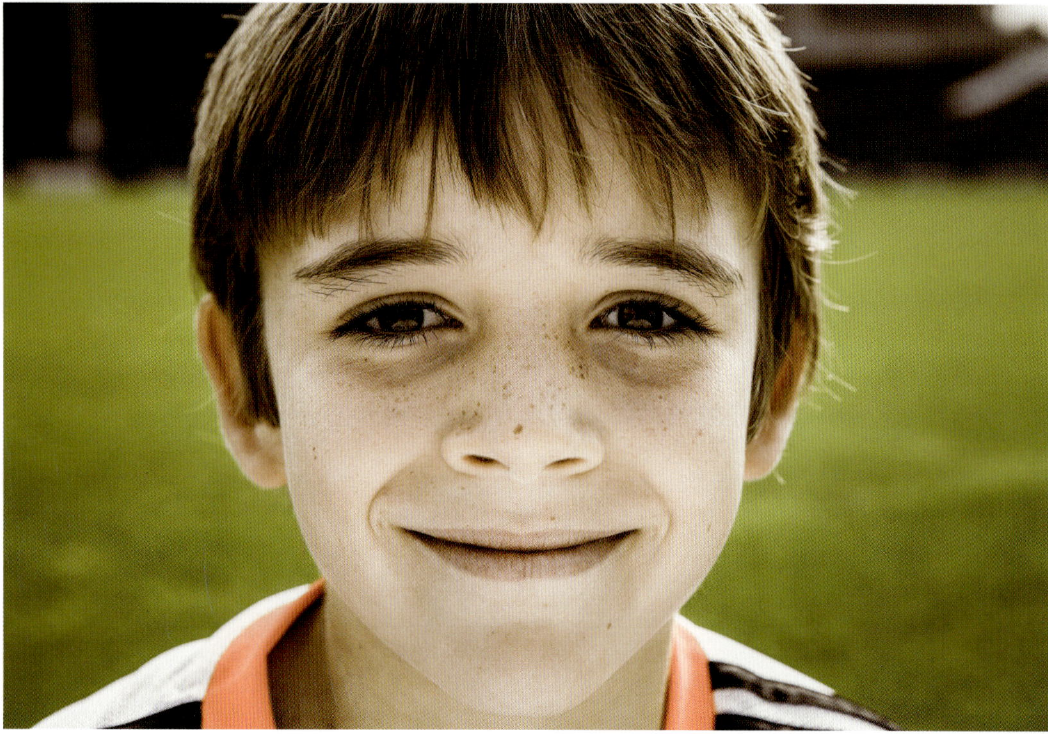

Left: A 70mm focal length flattens the background and magnifies the subject, placing far more attention on the subject.

Focal length: 70mm

Aperture: f/7.1

Shutter speed: 1/500 sec.

ISO: 640

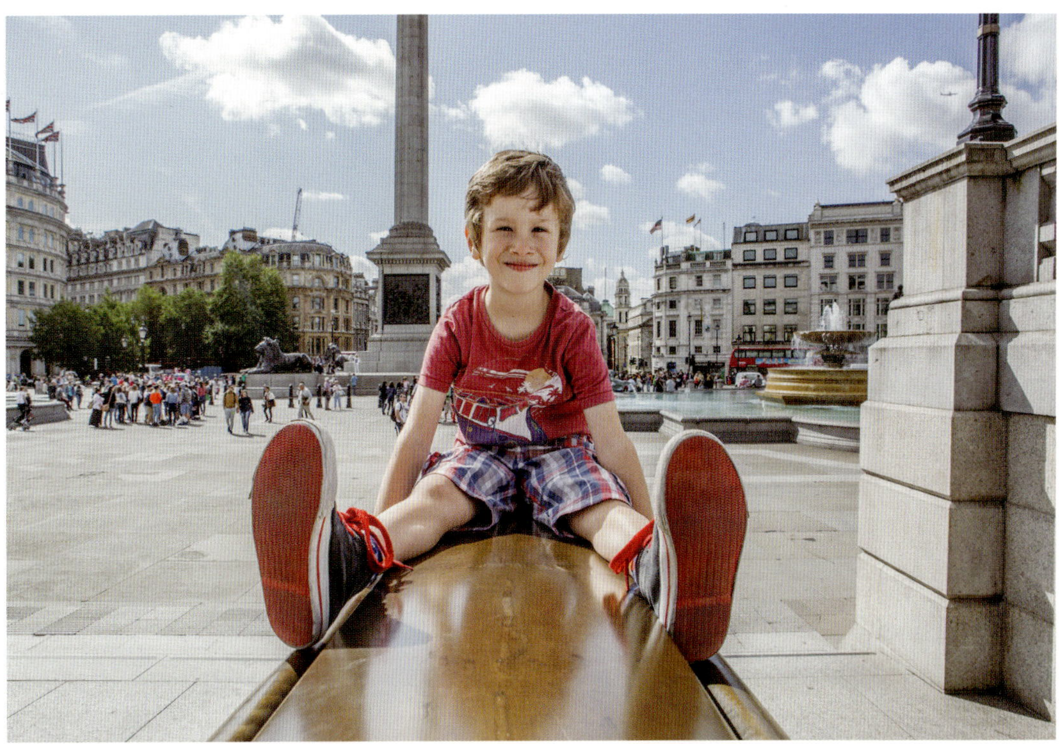

Right: The "bubble effect" you get from shooting too close with a wideangle lens can create large feet, hands, and even noses, but if you control it, it is perfectly fine.

Focal length: 24mm
Aperture: f/11
Shutter speed: 1/640 sec.
ISO: 800

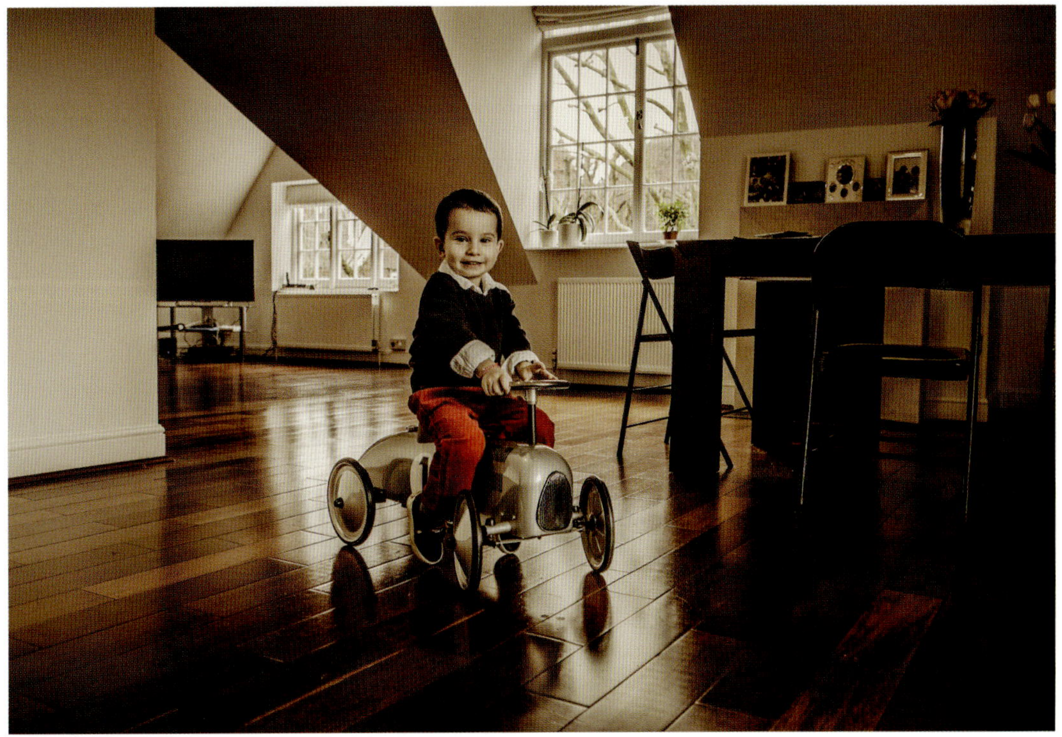

Right: Good camera craft is like learning to drive a car: once you have been doing it for a while your actions become instinctive.

Focal length: 34mm
Aperture: f/4.5
Shutter speed: 1/100 sec.
ISO: 800

Chapter 3
Composition

Producing a good photograph is the combination of many different elements, but at the heart of every great image is composition. Defining "good composition" is not easy, though, because it changes all the time with fashions and new views on what works and what doesn't. There are many traditionalists who will tell you that correct composition can only be acceptable if it falls into line with one of a very few solid rules. However, for me, the best definition of what constitutes "good composition" is that when you look at a shot with bad composition it will "hurt." What I mean by this is that it will make you feel a little uncomfortable, like when you walk into a room after an argument has taken place and you can feel that all is not right. Bad composition is the visual incarnation of a bad atmosphere.

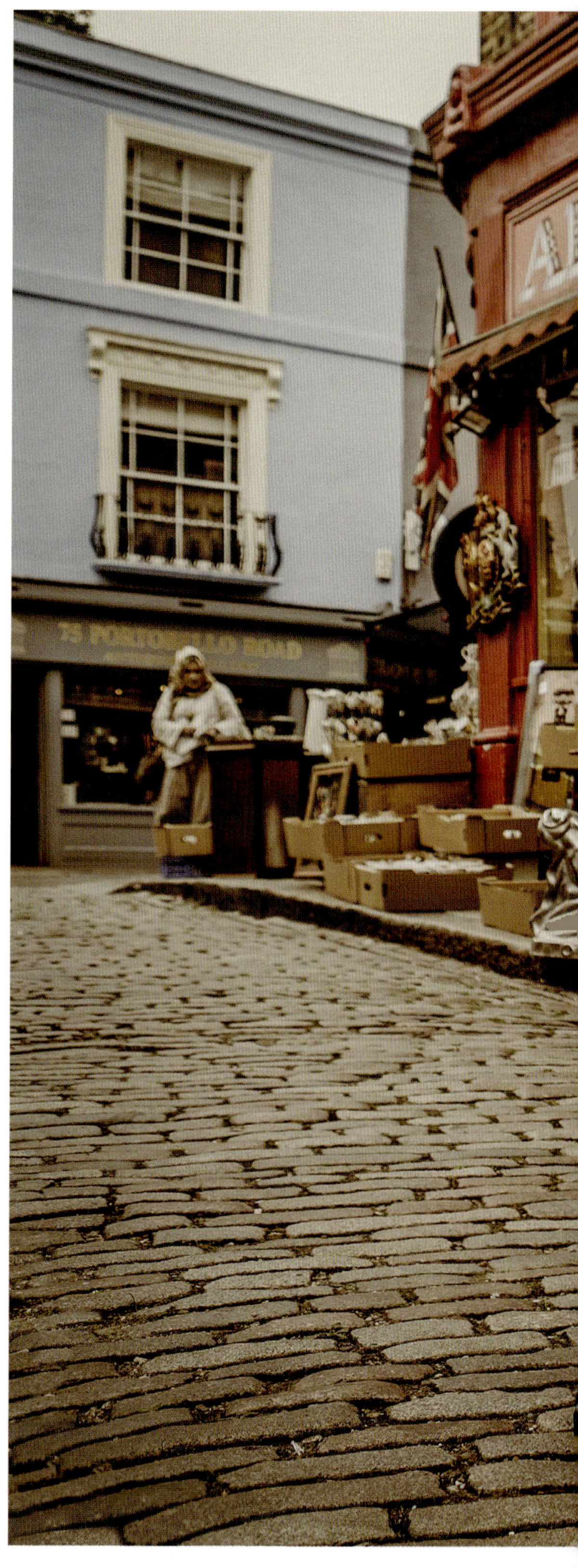

Right: A beautifully composed, well constructed image is a wonderful thing to behold. The art of good composition is at the heart of great photography.

Focal length: 27mm

Aperture: f/4

Shutter speed: 1/1000 sec.

ISO: 800

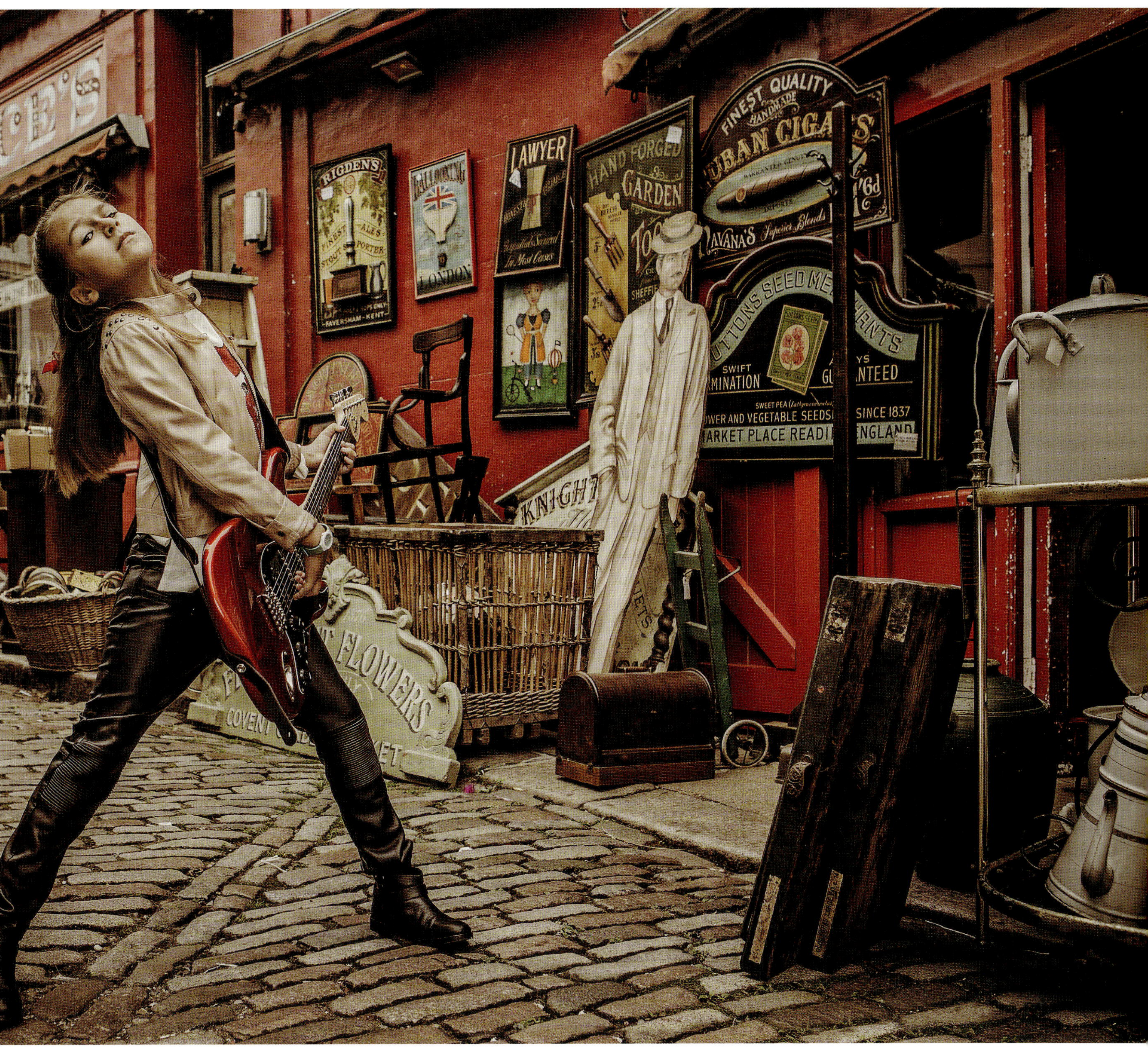
RIGDEN'S
FINEST ALES
STOUT & PORTER
FAVERSHAM · KENT
BALLOONING
LONDON
LAWYER
In Most Cases
HAND FORGED
GARDEN
TOO
SHEFFI
FINEST QUALITY
HANDMADE
UBAN CIGARS
HAVANA'S Superior Blends
6d
SUTTON'S SEED ME
ANTS
SWIFT
MINATION
GU
ANTEED
SWEET PEA
OWER AND VEGETABLE SEEDS SINCE 1837
MARKET PLACE READI
ENGLAND
KNIGHT
FLOWERS
COVENT
ET

Central Subjects

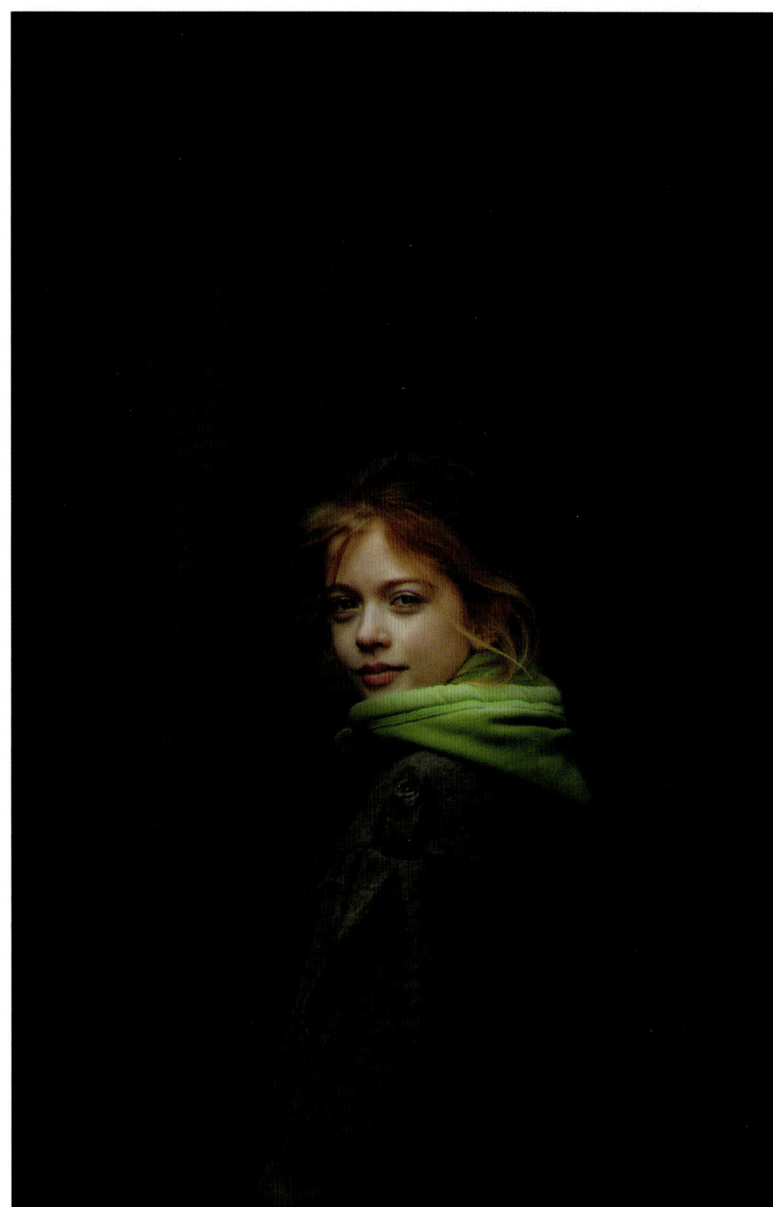

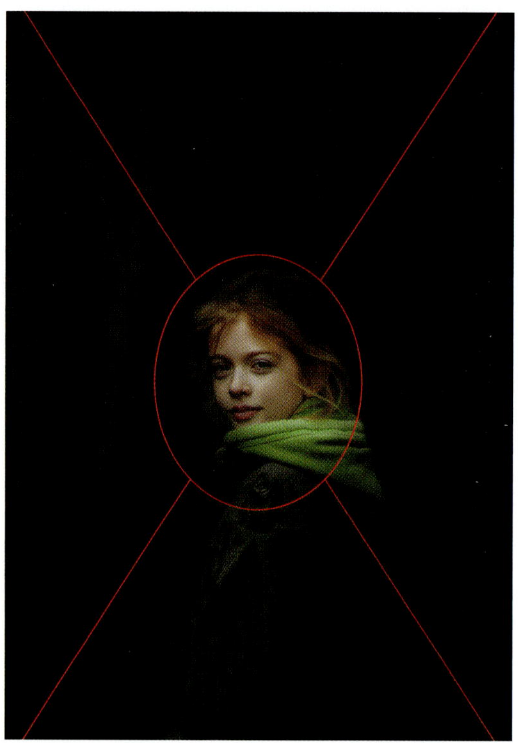

Left & above: A central subject is the most common compositional choice.

Central composition is so common that most people actually forget that it is a choice. It's a bit like breathing—we do it without thinking. Nevertheless, it is a choice that needs to be considered and used with care. If you place your subject at the center of your frame, you can't go wrong. It is obvious to the viewer that the person in the center is the main subject and you can use this to show authority within a group: a leader generally stands at the front in the center, while people on the sides are either subservient, supportive, or just modest.

With a group of children, older siblings are best placed at the center of the frame for an effect that parents will find pleasing; there is a natural hierarchy in groups of siblings and it is usually headed up by the eldest. Central compositions are powerful and straight to the point.

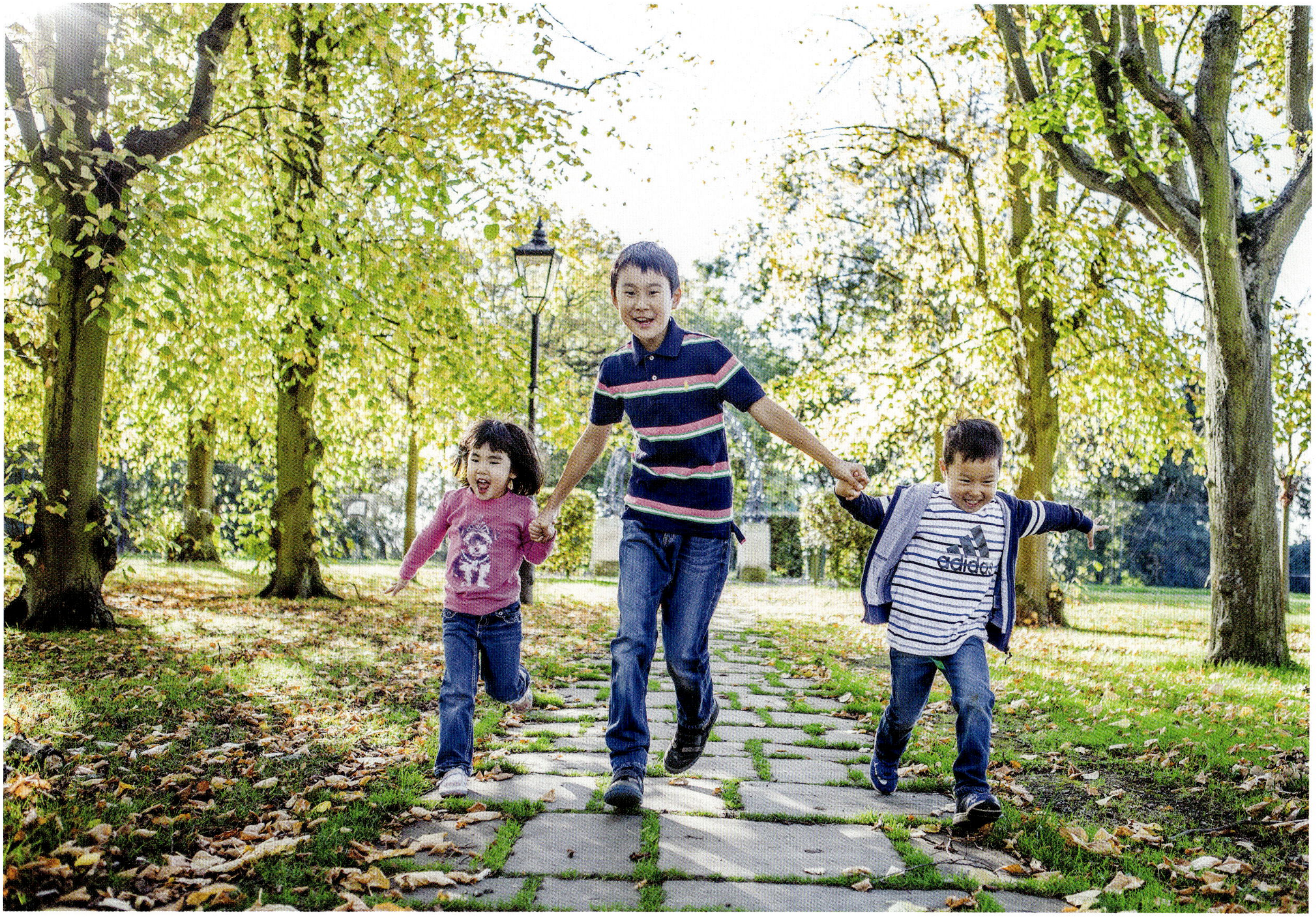

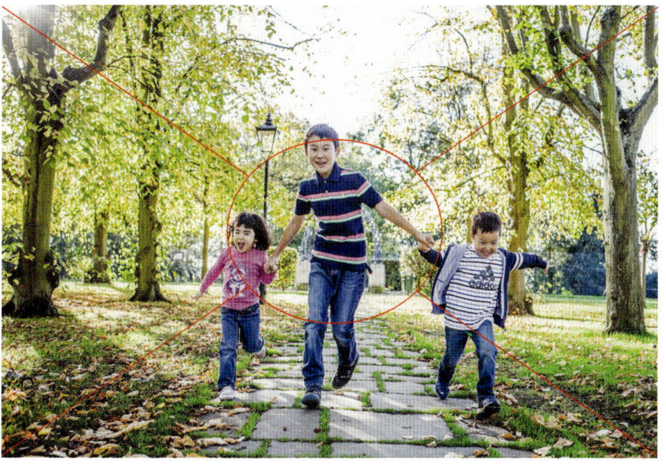

Above & left: You can use a central composition in a group shot to indicate who is the leader. With a group of siblings this is usually the eldest child.

Focal length: 34mm

Aperture: f/2.8

Shutter speed: 1/1000 sec.

ISO: 800

Rule Of Thirds

A grid overlay is a handy feature that you can find on pretty much every digital camera from compacts to DSLRs. It lets you change the display when you're looking through the viewfinder or framing your shots on the LCD screen, and will normally split the screen into nine blocks that are spaced evenly around the screen. This conforms to the rule of thirds and is my default option when I'm setting up a camera.

The rule of thirds is well documented and works by splitting the image into three, both vertically and horizontally. If you place the "hero" in the scene at any point where these lines meet it will have a pleasing effect. Using the rule of thirds will add variety and style to your images and is a great tool; it often adds to the image if you have the subject looking across the frame to the opposite intersection of thirds. The rule of thirds can also be combined with a central composition, as demonstrated here; mixing the two compositional rules creates drama and interest.

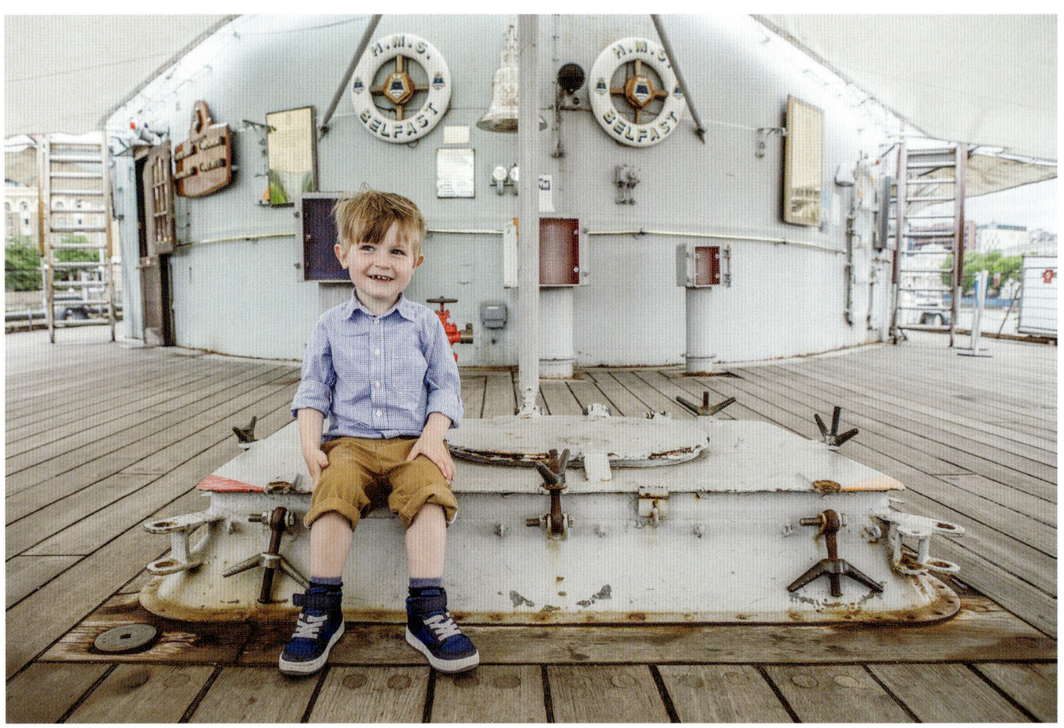

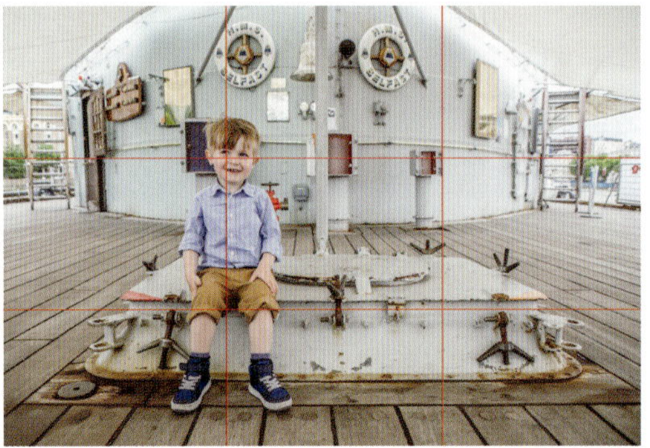

Above & left: Placing your subject or subjects at an intersection of the thirds lines naturally allows more of the background to show, which helps add context.

Focal length: 24mm

Aperture: f/4.5

Shutter speed: 1/640 sec.

ISO: 800

Leading Lines

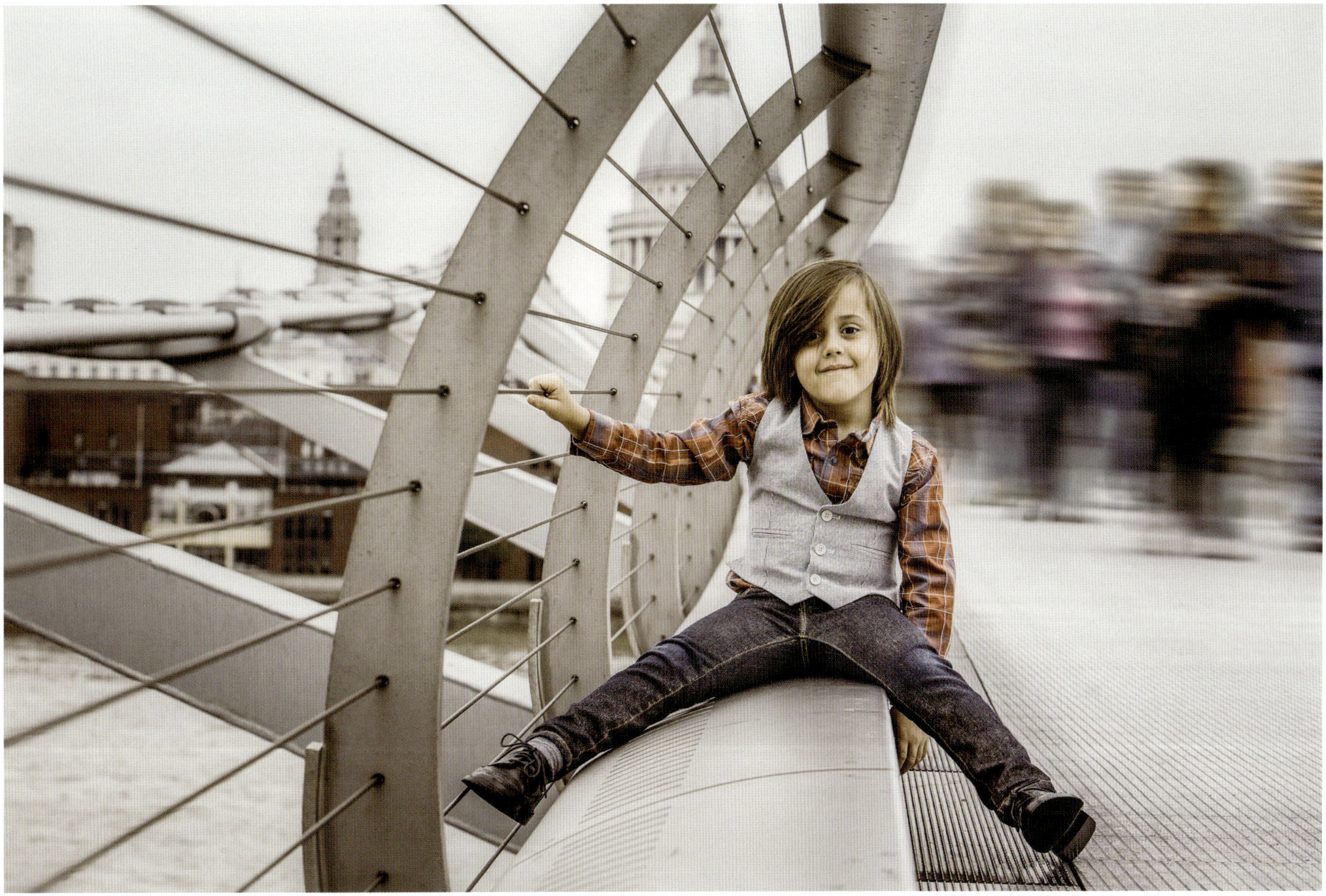

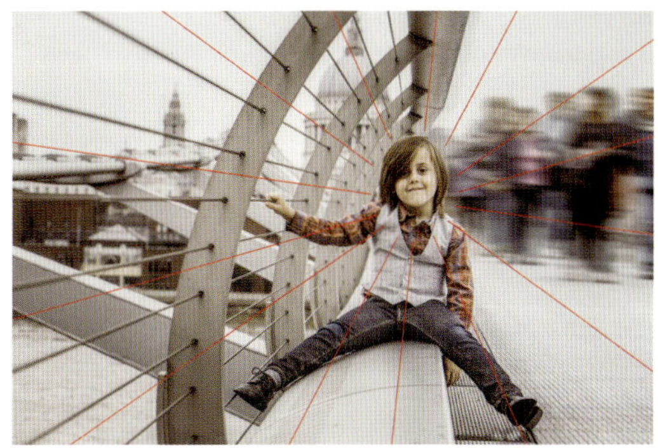

It would be a boring world if every image we captured had to be central or on an intersection of thirds, but there are plenty of different devices we can use to carry the eye around a scene. The idea of leading lines is a very useful tool. Train yourself to search out leading lines within a location, such as fences, roads, lines of trees, and so on, and then position yourself in relation to the subject so that all the lines lead to the "hero" in your shot. You can use this principle in many different ways

Above & right: Leading lines are designed to "lead" the viewer to the focal point of the image.

Focal length: 70mm

Aperture: f/5.6

Shutter speed: 1/320 sec.

ISO: 640

and at almost any point within the frame: the lines will draw the eyes of the viewer to the subject, no matter where they are.

The Golden Ratio

The "Fibonacci curve" or "golden ratio" is regarded as the ultimate expression of the rule of thirds. Named after the man who spent his life studying its effect—the 12th-century Italian mathematician Leonardo Fibonacci—a Fibonacci curve describes a perfect curling line that is always decreasing in angle, forming a spiral that ends one-third into the scene.

This mathematical sequence was used extensively by Leonardo Da Vinci and many artists after him, and seems to appear repeatedly in nature; in the way that most flowers grow their petals, the ammonite shell, and even the way a hurricane forms as seen from space, for example. Because of these factors, the Fibonacci sequence is often regarded with magical reverence: all points lead to the center of the spiral, and at that point all things are complete.

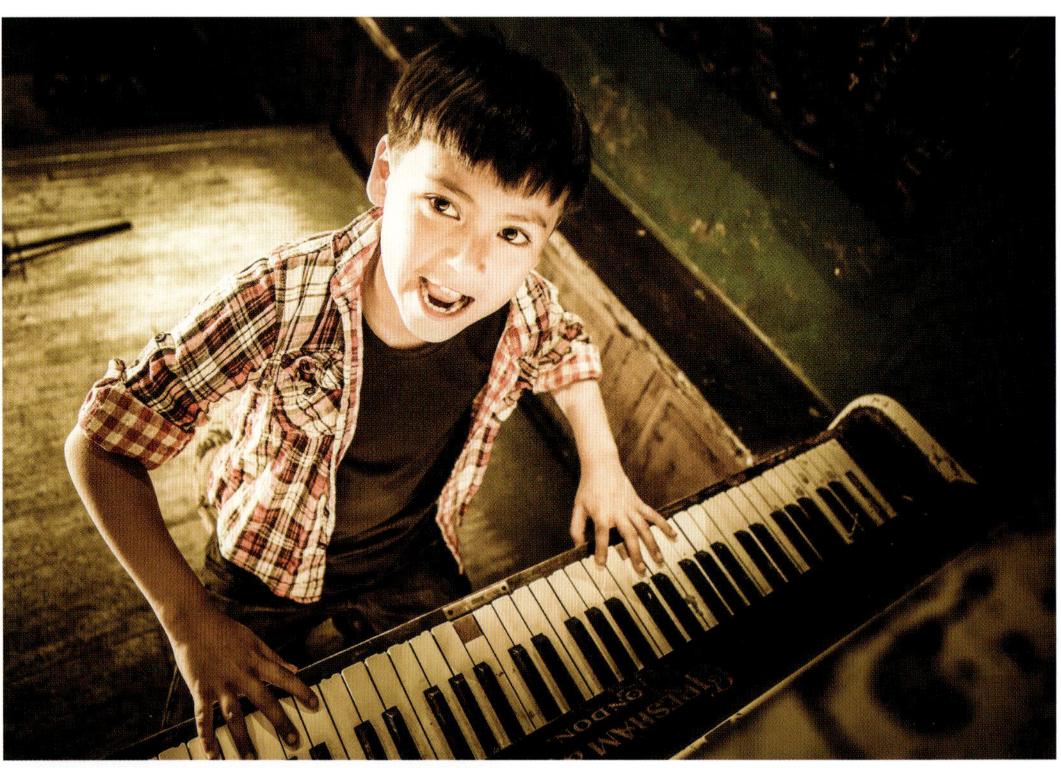

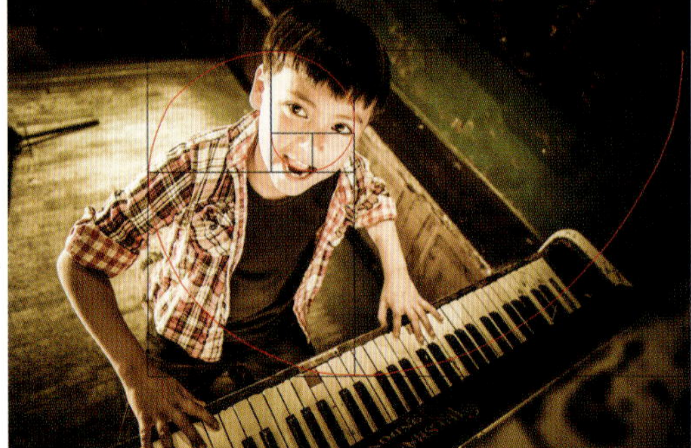

Above & left: The spiral form seen in nature can be used in the composition of a portrait as an expression of the golden ratio.

Focal length: 24mm

Aperture: f/2.8

Shutter speed: 1/30 sec.

ISO: 4000

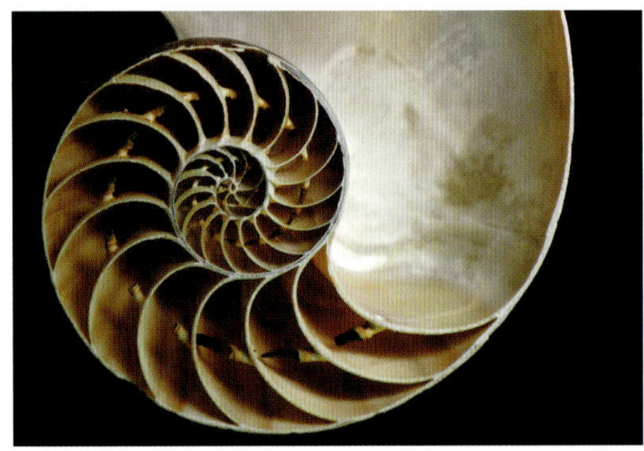

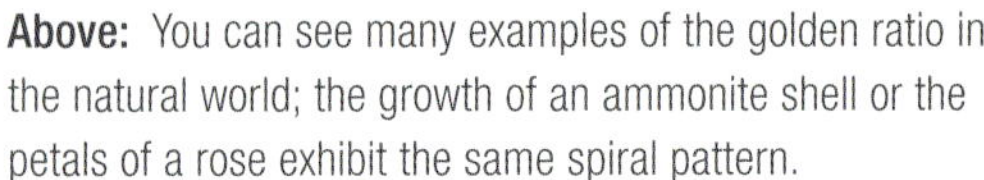

Above: You can see many examples of the golden ratio in the natural world; the growth of an ammonite shell or the petals of a rose exhibit the same spiral pattern.

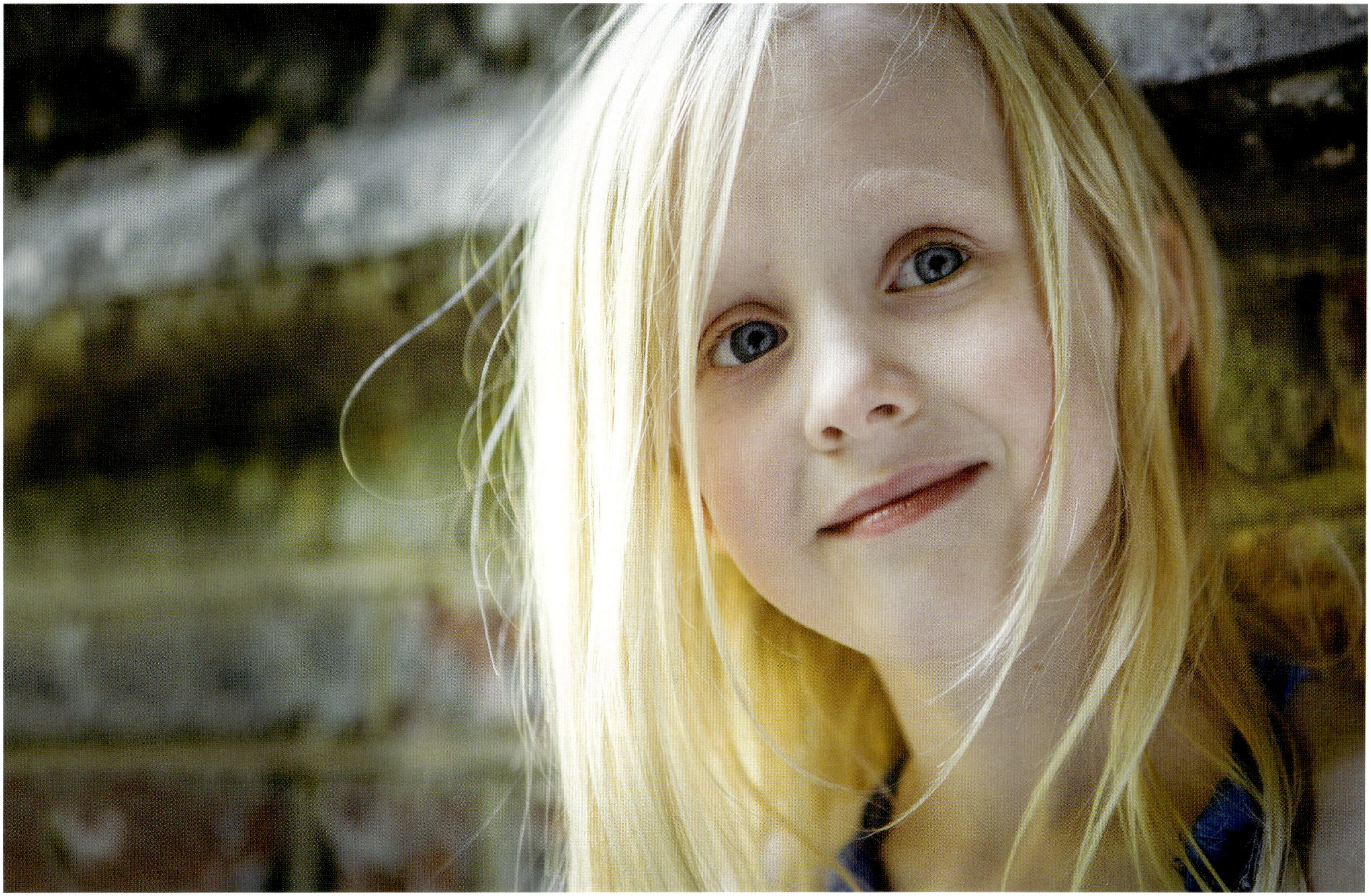

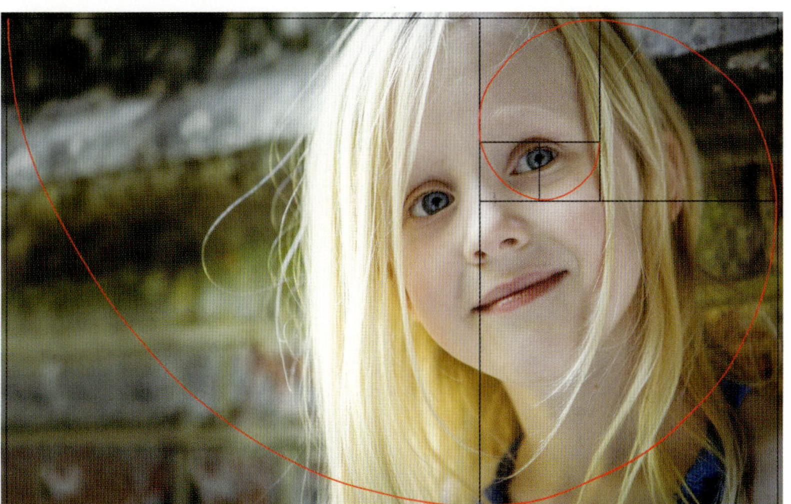

Above & left: An image plotted within the Fibonacci curve creates a naturally pleasing result that is powerful and meaningful.

Focal length: 70mm

Aperture: f/2.8

Shutter speed: 1/60 sec.

ISO: 500

Natural Framing

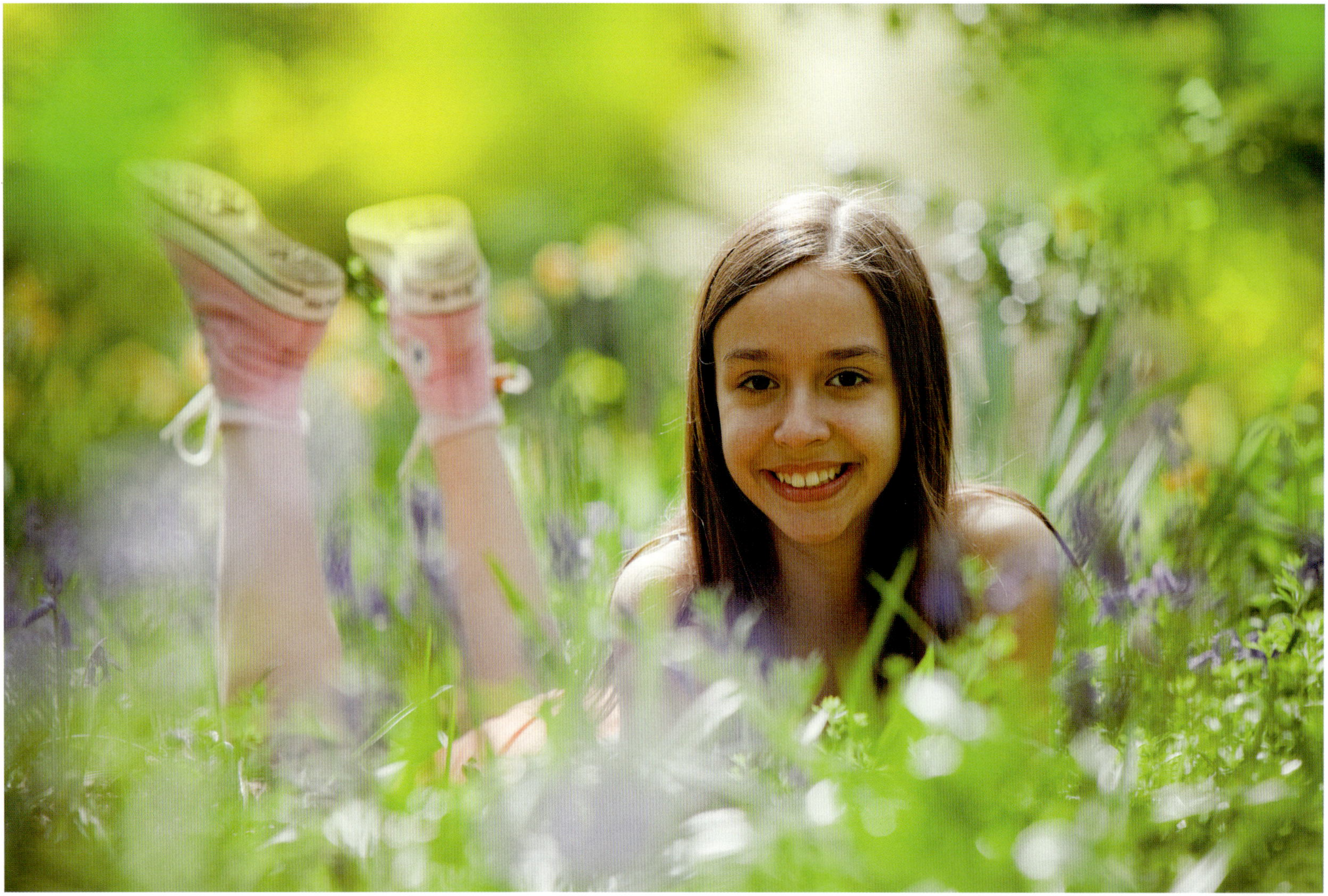

The choice of framing is a big decision for an image, and for good reason: an image without a frame has to rely on the space around it to show it off. If you cannot control that space you are not necessarily going to see the image in its best light.

Because of this, it is always pleasing to the eye if there is a natural frame within the image itself. It can be square, rectangular, oval, circular, or a more complex shape, but by encasing the subject you are controlling the way the viewer sees the picture, regardless of whether it then has a physical frame or not. Look for trees, rocks, and doorframes and use them to encircle your subject.

Another location-framing technique involves embedding yourself within the available plant life. Allow the plants close to the lens to form a blurred frame of foliage around the child. This is also a great way to add a natural, candid feel to the image, creating intrigue and a sense of secrecy.

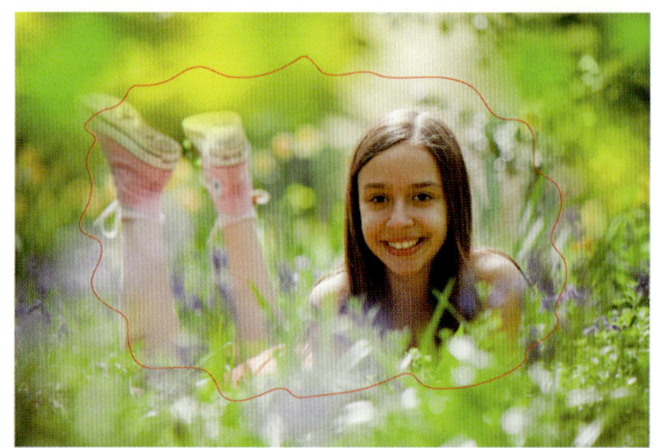

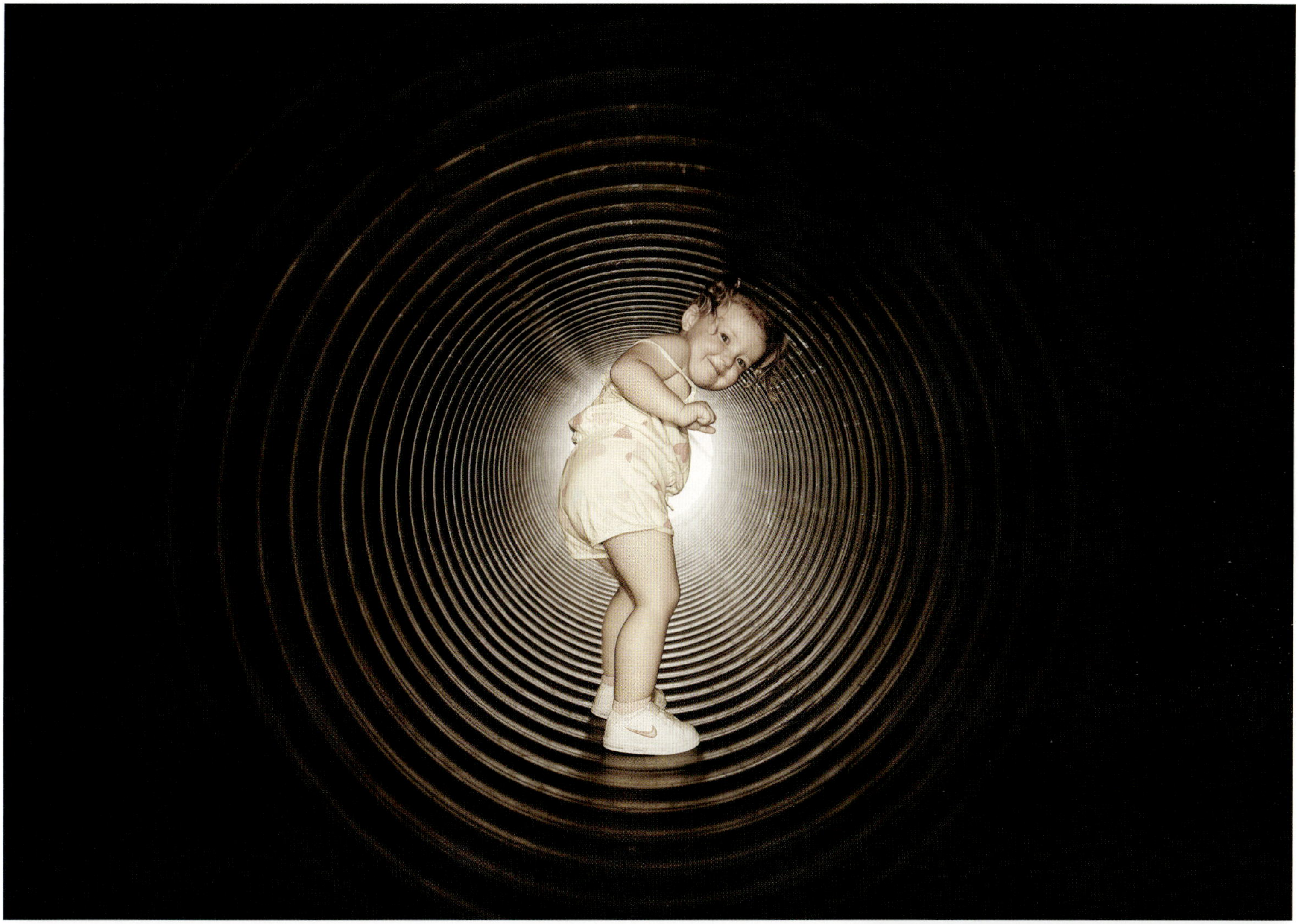

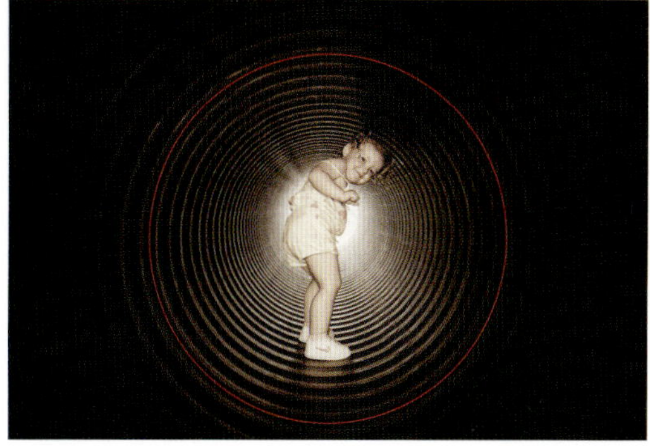

Opposite: Blurred foliage can create a natural frame that focuses attention on the subject. This can be exaggerated by applying a vignette during postproduction.

Focal length: 200mm

Aperture: f/4.5

Shutter speed: 1/1000 sec.

ISO: 640

Above & right: Unconventional framing features can be sought out and used to great effect.

Focal length: 28mm

Aperture: f/3.5

Shutter speed: 1/60 sec.

ISO: 400

Patterns

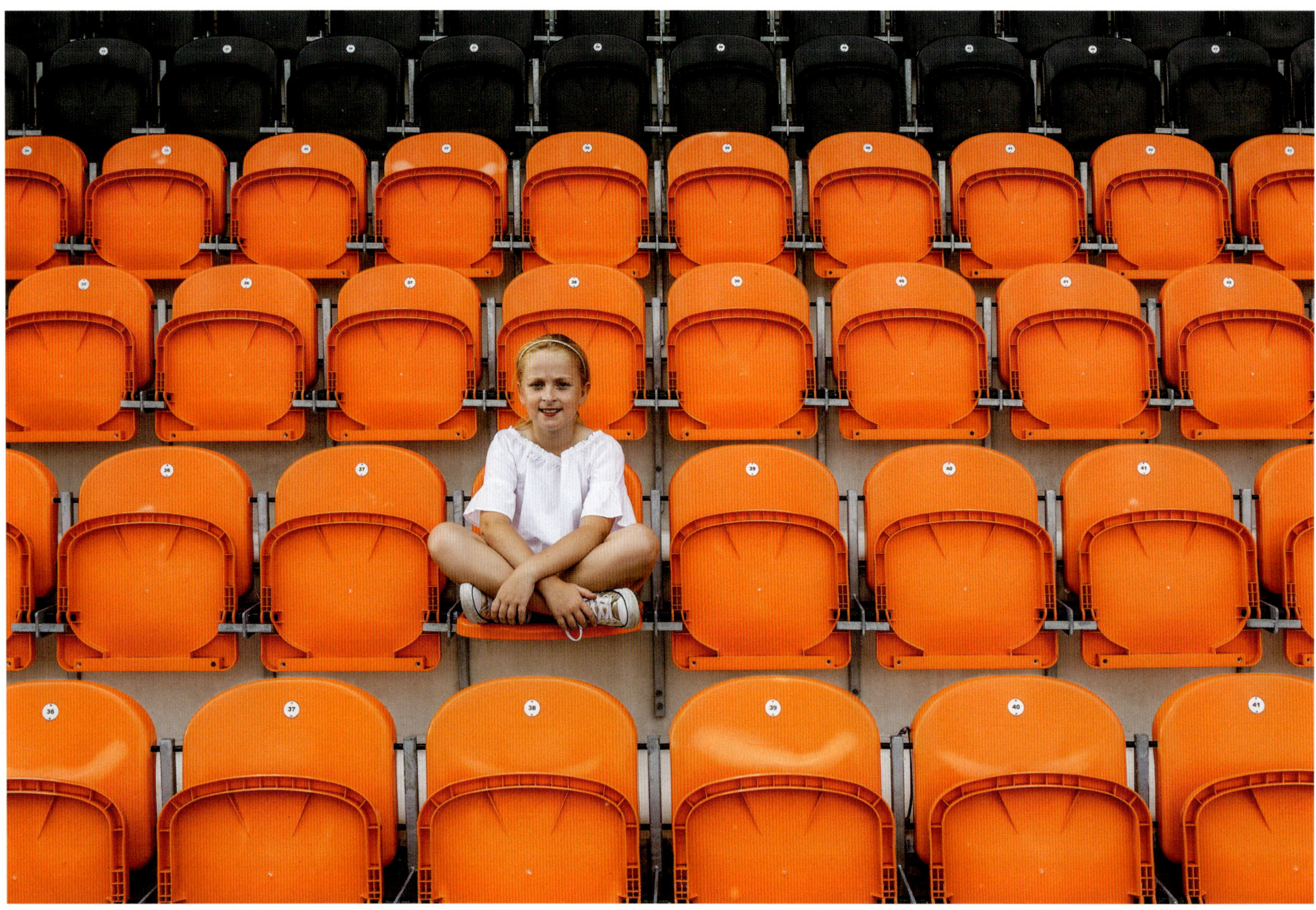

We are all attracted to patterns. People like to see repetitive forms in nature and in life, as they give us a sense of security, familiarity, and consistency. We can use this principle to create interesting and intriguing images. By placing your subject within a repeated pattern you can make them the one thing that stands out from the crowd.

You can often use this principle in an ironic way and it can look funny and cool. Think about a line of deckchairs, a number of window frames in a building, repeating floor tiles, or even the railings of a fence. Place your subject at a point where they may not be expected to be and the eye will be drawn to them with graphical precision.

Above: The eye is naturally drawn to a subject that breaks the regularity of a patterned environment.

Focal length: 40mm

Aperture: f/8

Shutter speed: 1/250 sec.

ISO: 800

Shooting Loose

Many of the compositional guidelines we have looked at can be applied retrospectively at the postproduction stage. This is very useful, because you will often find when photographing children that you have only a few seconds to capture a particular moment and that does not always let you carefully consider every aspect of the composition. Because of this, it is often a good idea to deliberately "shoot loose," which means purposely leaving a bit of extra space around the subject so you have cropping options. For this reason it is not advisable to place your subject too close to the edge of the frame, even if you feel that it's the "correct" position for the composition. Although it may well be right, it restricts your creativity and leaves you with limited options.

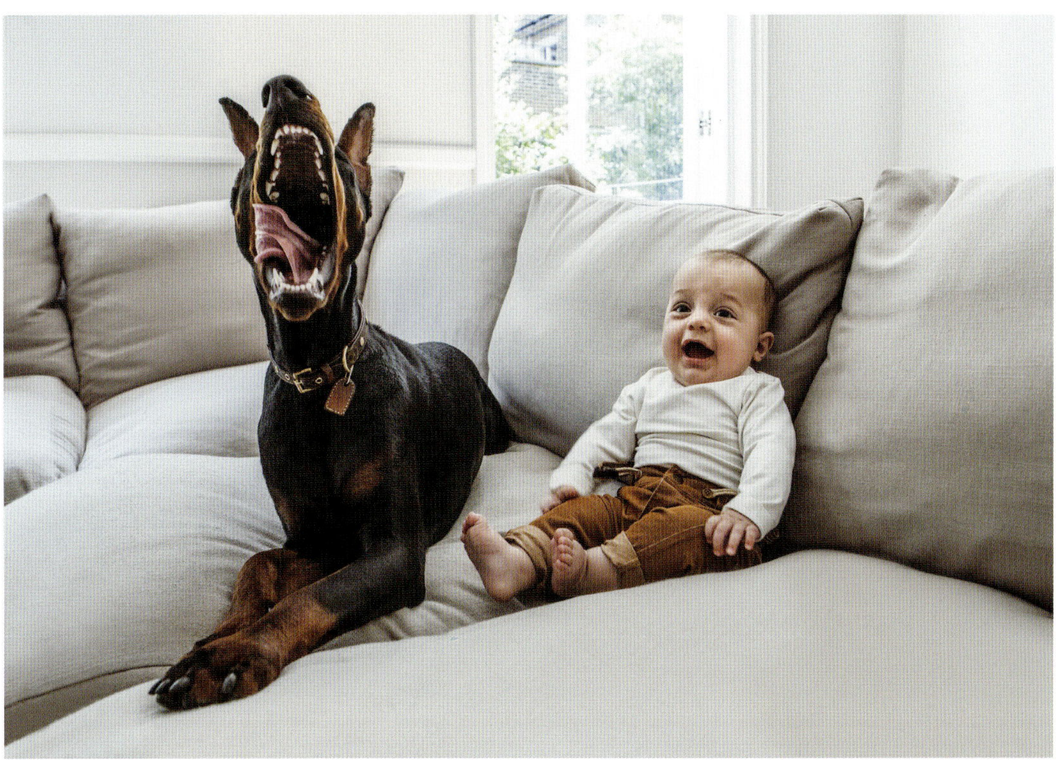

Tips

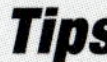

- Full-frame digital cameras shooting high-resolution files make "shooting loose" all the more desirable, as the quality of the final image is rarely affected.

- Used creatively, composition is often responsible for transforming a good image into a great one, so master the rules and then break them. Build your own visual vocabulary around the basic principles, but never be afraid to try something new.

- Improving your postproduction skills will also enable you to create the perfect composition by removing distracting elements from the frame and enhancing the detail of key subjects.

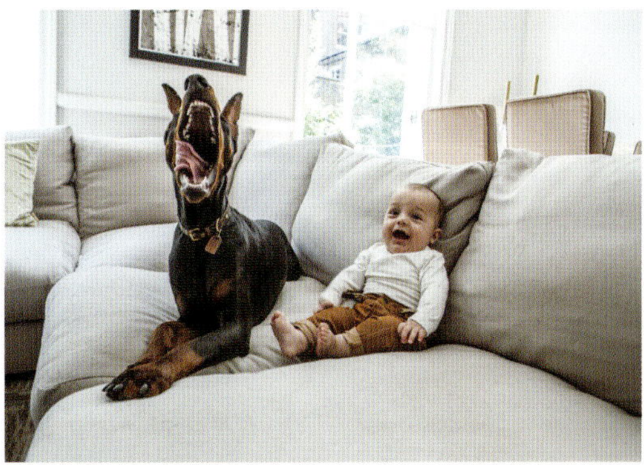

Above & right: Here, the original composition (right) has been cropped and the distracting features have been removed, drawing the eye to the subjects with greater impact. Although this could have been done in camera, shooting a "loose" composition allows more options at the postproduction stage.

Focal length: 27mm

Aperture: f/5.6

Shutter speed: 1/160 sec.

ISO: 1600

Profile: Helen Bartlett

BIOGRAPHY

Helen is a family portrait photographer and Canon Ambassador with an international reputation. She shoots exclusively in black and white and this is what first strikes you about her work. You can see a "philosophical" approach to photography that is evident in the naturalistic style that shines through all of her images, and if you look deeper you will notice that she has an enviable ability to catch a particular moment that will have meaning for parents and children for many years to come.

www.helenbartlett.co.uk

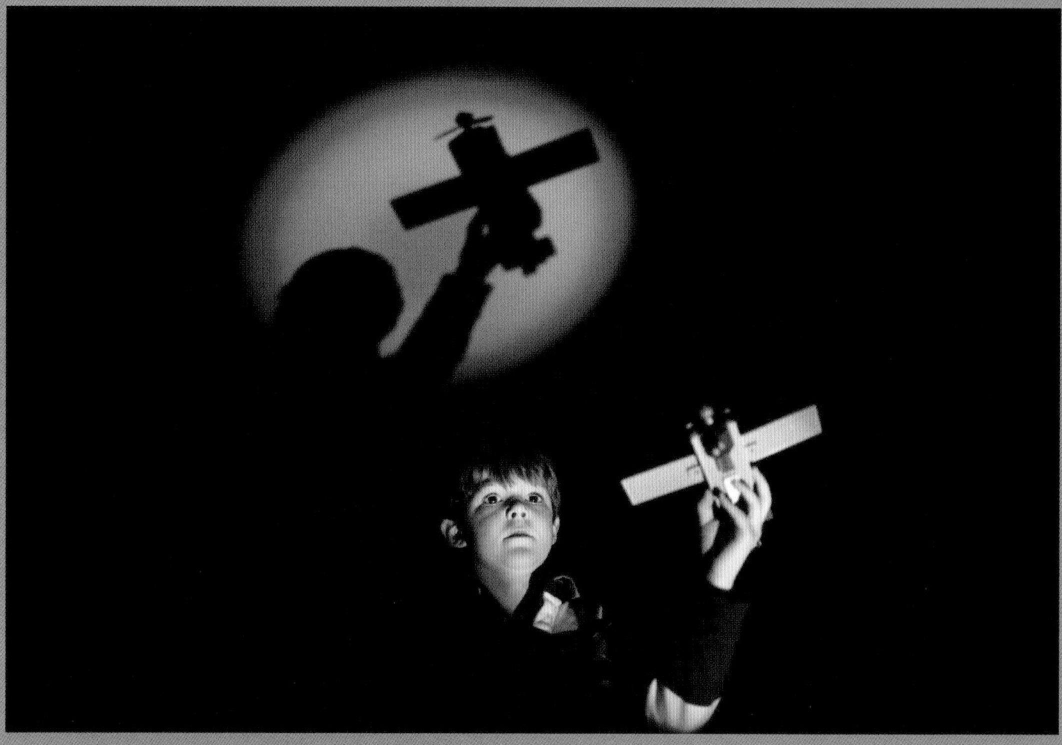

Q) What equipment do you use regularly?
A) I'm currently using two Canon EOS 1DX MkII cameras and a mirrorless EOS R and usually shoot with prime lenses. My standard lens choices are 35mm, 50mm, and 85mm focal lengths, but I will occasionally use other lenses if the situation requires it, such as a 100mm macro for newborn work, or a 70–200mm zoom on the beach.

Q) Why do you shoot black and white?
A) I work in black and white because I feel this is the most timeless medium for family photography. I want my images to be about the relationships between the people in the pictures, about emotion and interaction, and also about the graphics and light in the composition. I find that color is a distraction and its absence allows us to focus on what is important. I also think that black-and-white images better stand the test of time: they will look as good in 50 years as they do today, which is important with family photography, as images increase in emotional value over time.

Q) How do you go about setting up a session and preparing the client?
A) My sessions are child-led, so we do the things that the children want to do and go to the places they want to go. I shoot primarily in a documentary fashion, watching and observing the action, and then finding the best shots as the children play and enjoy themselves.

Q) Who are your favorite photographers/ artists and how did they influence you?
A) My biggest influence photographically is my father, whose black-and-white pictures of my brothers and I growing up form the cornerstone of everything I do. I hope to create images that my clients will cherish as much as I cherish the pictures of my childhood. I also love the work of Sally Mann and return regularly to her book *Immediate Family*.

Q) How important is postproduction and do you do your own?
A) Postproduction is important for any photographer. I always do my own because I know how I want my finished images to look.

Q) What is your top tip for child portrait photographers?
A) Have fun and don't panic! If you enjoy yourself and make it fun for the kids then you will get the pictures you need.

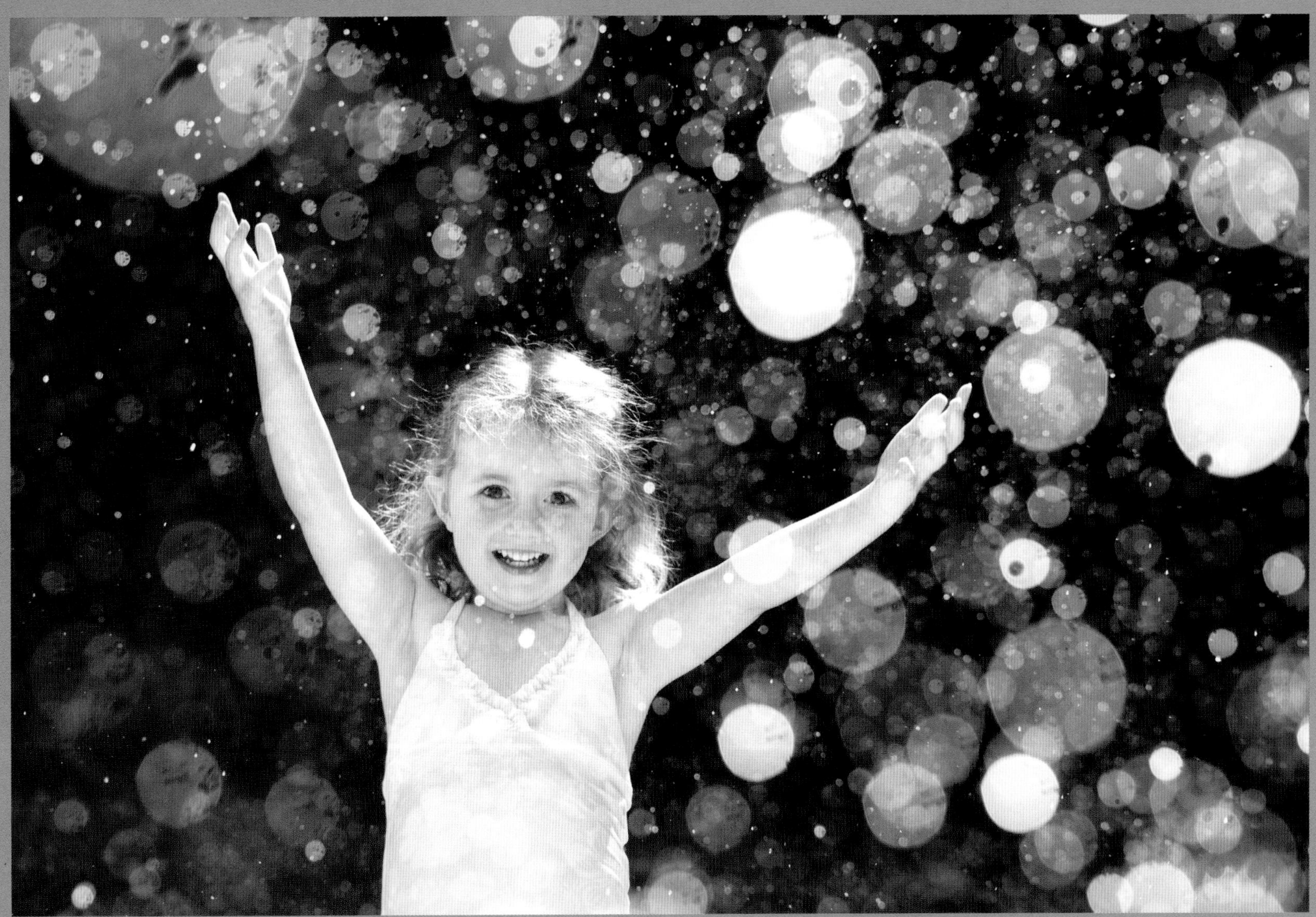

Left:

Focal length: 35mm

Aperture: f/1.4

Shutter speed: 1/250 sec.

ISO: 8000

Above:

Focal length: 50mm

Aperture: f/2.5

Shutter speed: 1/2000 sec.

ISO: 400

Chapter 4
Location Portraits

Location portraiture is the mainstay of many child portrait photographers. I have completed more than one thousand child portrait assignments in the past few years and the majority of these have been done on location. By choice I like to shoot in an environment that is familiar to the child and I usually find that a studio is just too restrictive. The great outdoors presents you with an unending supply of photographic opportunities: parks, forests, beaches, street corners, and even backyards can be perfect places to shoot, while more exclusive locations such as sports grounds, theaters, and historical buildings can add drama and a sense of "occasion" to the day.

Right: The right location should be a good fit, enhancing your child model's natural personality. Look for interesting angles and positions that tell a story.

Focal length: 24mm
Aperture: f/2.8
Shutter speed: 1/1250 sec.
ISO: 1000

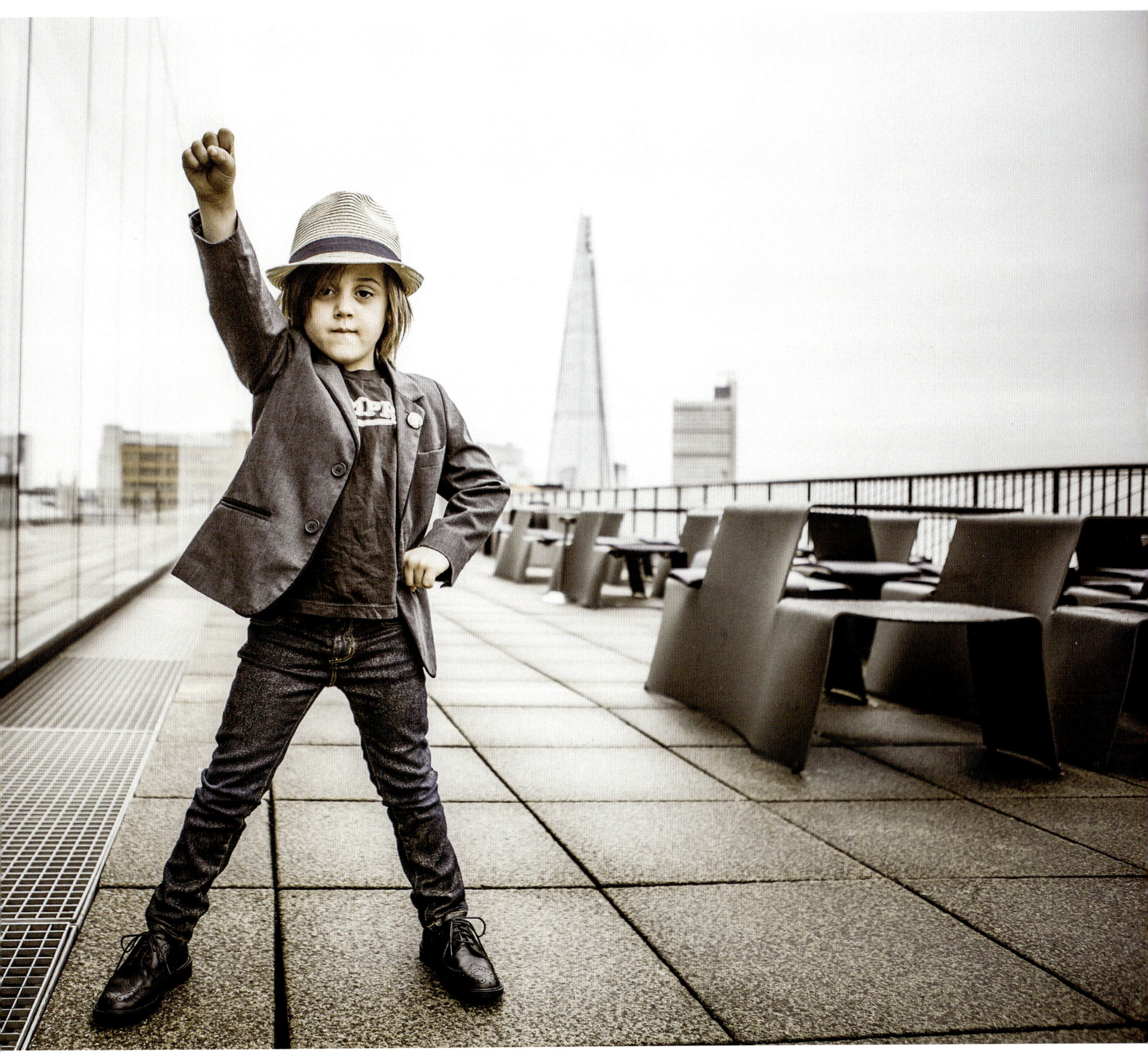

Location Kit

Establishing the perfect kit for your child portrait sessions will always be a work in progress, as times change and equipment gets better and more advanced, so there will always be a newer and better version of your favorite gadget. Your ability and your influences will also change, so you may need a different lens or accessory to give you a different look or help you achieve better results. I have had plenty of time to refine the equipment that I need when I go on location: you may want to use the accompanying lists as your baseline and then develop your own individual kit list as you go.

Location Flash

Location portraits place less emphasis on artificial lighting, as the majority of your images will be shot outdoors. However, when it comes to complex child portraits you might want to use battery operated flash units. Most lighting manufacturers now offer "location flash" units, which work from a large battery pack, but the type of image that requires this sort of lighting is pretty rare, so there is no need to dwell on location flash units (it is also similar to studio flash, as outlined in chapter 6).

If you want to try out some location flash techniques, a good place to start is to use off-camera flash units or "speedlights." Set them to their slave mode, attach them to lighting stands, and you have a very effective way of trying out some dramatic location lighting.

BUDGET LOCATION PORTRAIT KIT	ADVANCED LOCATION PORTRAIT KIT	OPTIONAL ADD-ONS
Pro DSLR or mirrorless camera body	*Pro DSLR or mirrorless camera body*	
28–105mm f/3.5 lens	*24–70mm f/2.8 lens*	
	70–200mm f/2.8 lens	
	Extension tubes	
TTL flash	*TTL flash*	
30in. (75cm) double-sided reflector (silver/white)	*30in. (75cm) double-sided reflector (silver/white)*	
16GB memory cards (x2)	*16GB memory cards (x4)*	
128GB memory card (x1) as backup card in second card slot	*128GB memory card (x1) as backup card in second card slot*	
Spare camera batteries (x2)	*Spare camera batteries (x2)*	
Spare flash batteries (x2 sets)	*Spare flash batteries (x2 sets)*	
Plastic refuse sack (to sit on when the ground is wet)	*Plastic refuse sack (to sit on when the ground is wet)*	
Compact shoulder camera bag	*Compact shoulder camera bag*	
		Additional camera body
		6–35mm f/2.8 lens
		85mm f/1.8 lens

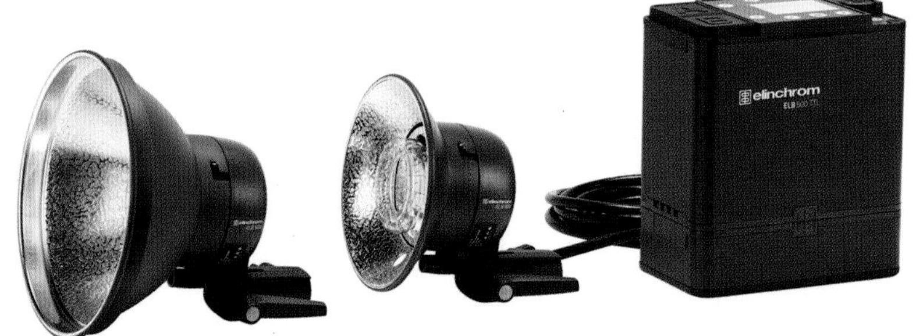

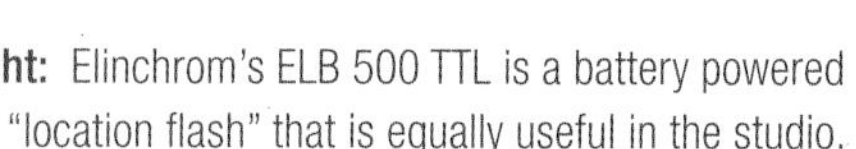
Right: Elinchrom's ELB 500 TTL is a battery powered "location flash" that is equally useful in the studio.

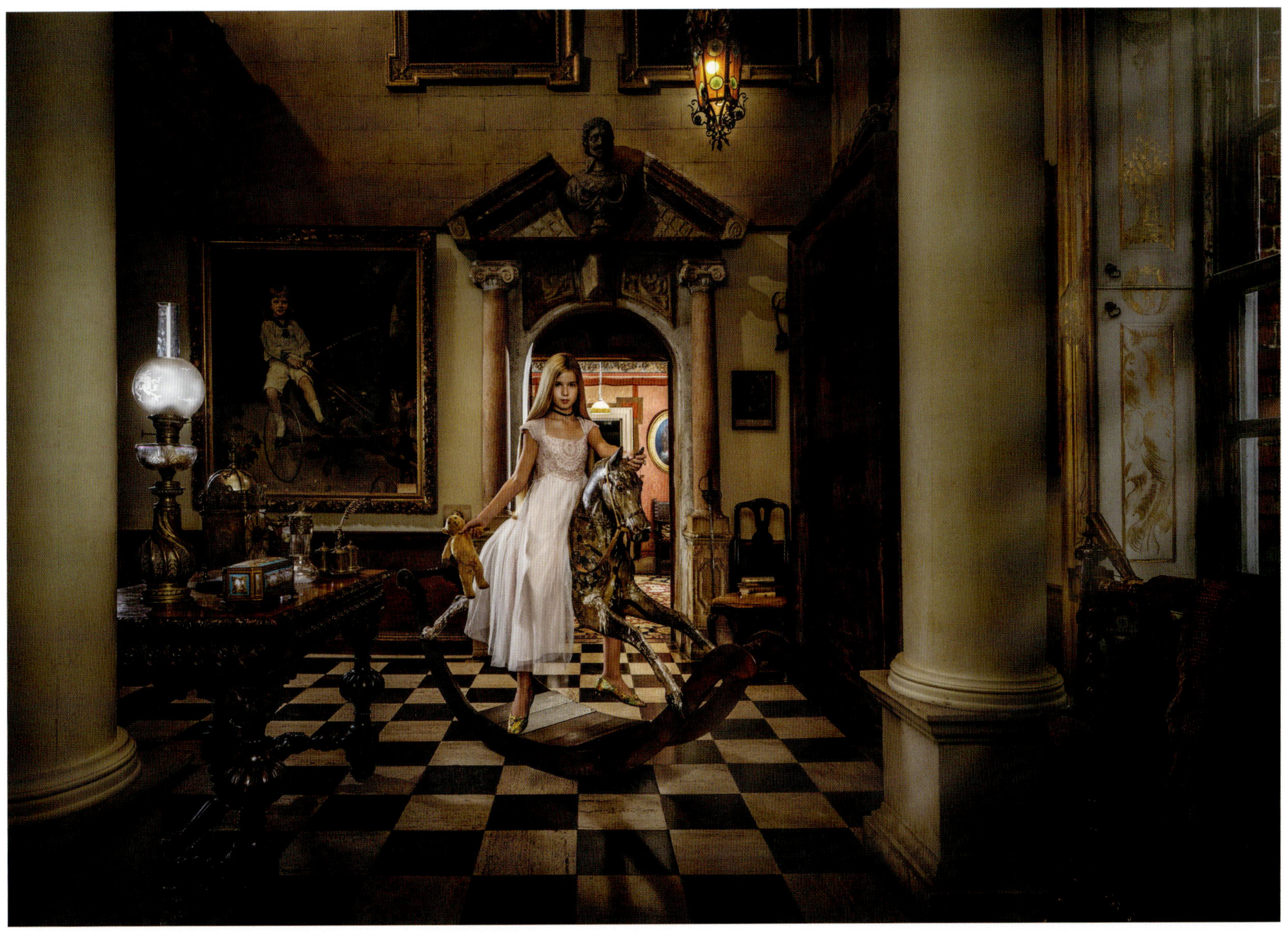

Above: If you want to control every aspect of your location lighting then you need to think about shooting with location flash units. For this shot I used a combination of three Elinchrom ELB 500 TTL location flash units, daylight, and regular interior lighting.

Focal length: 19mm

Aperture: f/13

Shutter speed: 1/60 sec.

ISO: 400

Location Portrait Techniques

There is no better way to capture the essence of a child's free spirit—their joy, their happiness, and even their cheekiness—than to photograph them on location. For my child portrait sessions I insist that the child chooses where they would like to be photographed (albeit with a little help from their parents). In this way it is the child that sets the scene and—to a large extent—the theme of the shoot. A studio shoot can never offer the same possibilities when it comes to backgrounds, lighting, and action that you find with environmental portraiture, so photographing children on location provides a sense of joy and freedom that is unmatchable.

The technical requirements thrown up by different environments can be very challenging, and I always shoot child portrait sessions alone, without an assistant. The key to success is to stick to a clear set of rules and apply them as required to every different situation, taming what can otherwise be a rather chaotic event. You need to develop a technique that will guide you through every situation and guarantee consistent quality, which is how G.L.O.W. was born…

Below: Sometimes it is a good idea to let the model choose where they would like to be photographed. A little bit of color co-ordination is always helpful.

Focal length: 34mm

Aperture: f/7.1

Shutter speed: 1/200 sec.

ISO: 500

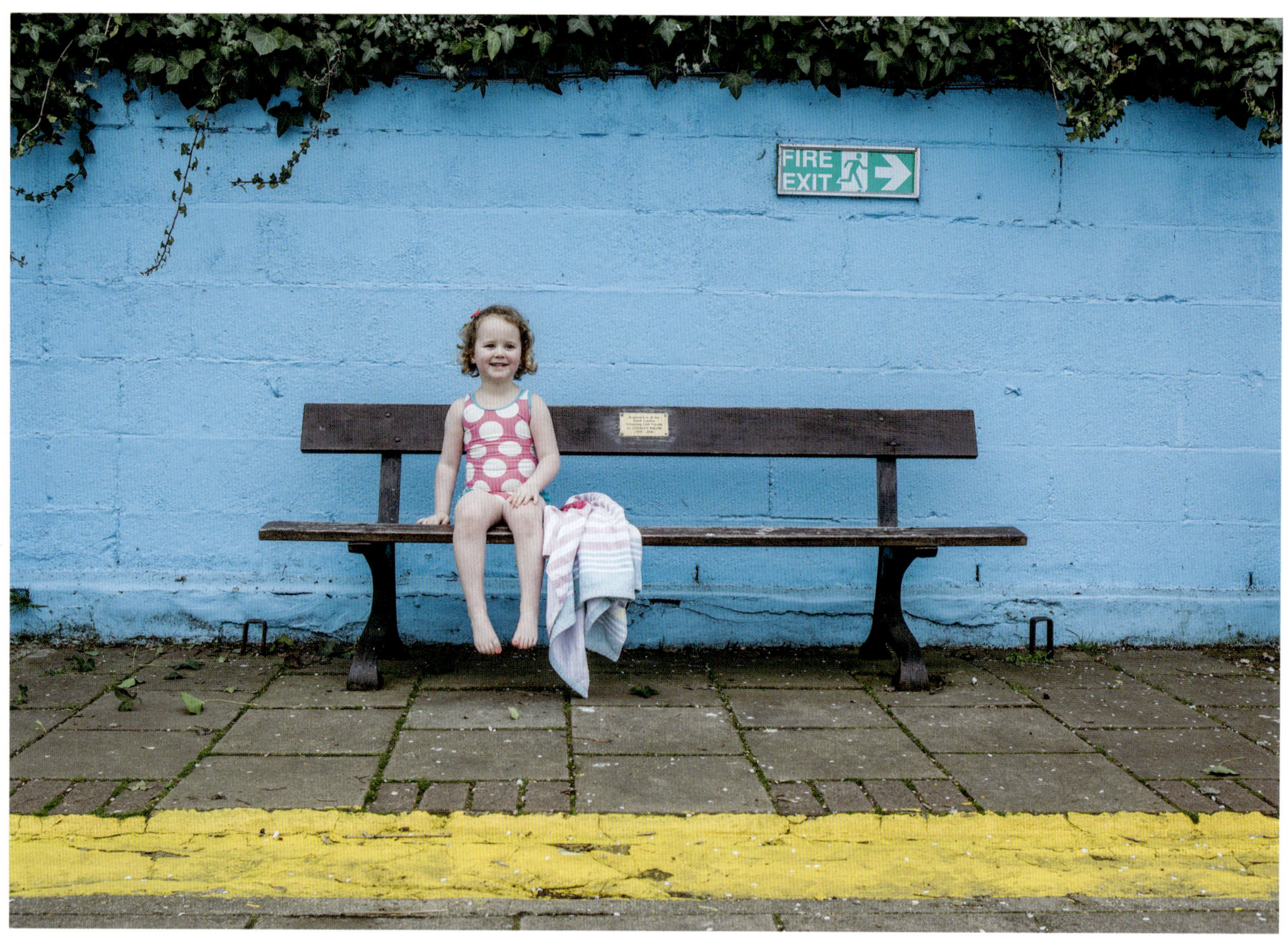

G.L.O.W.

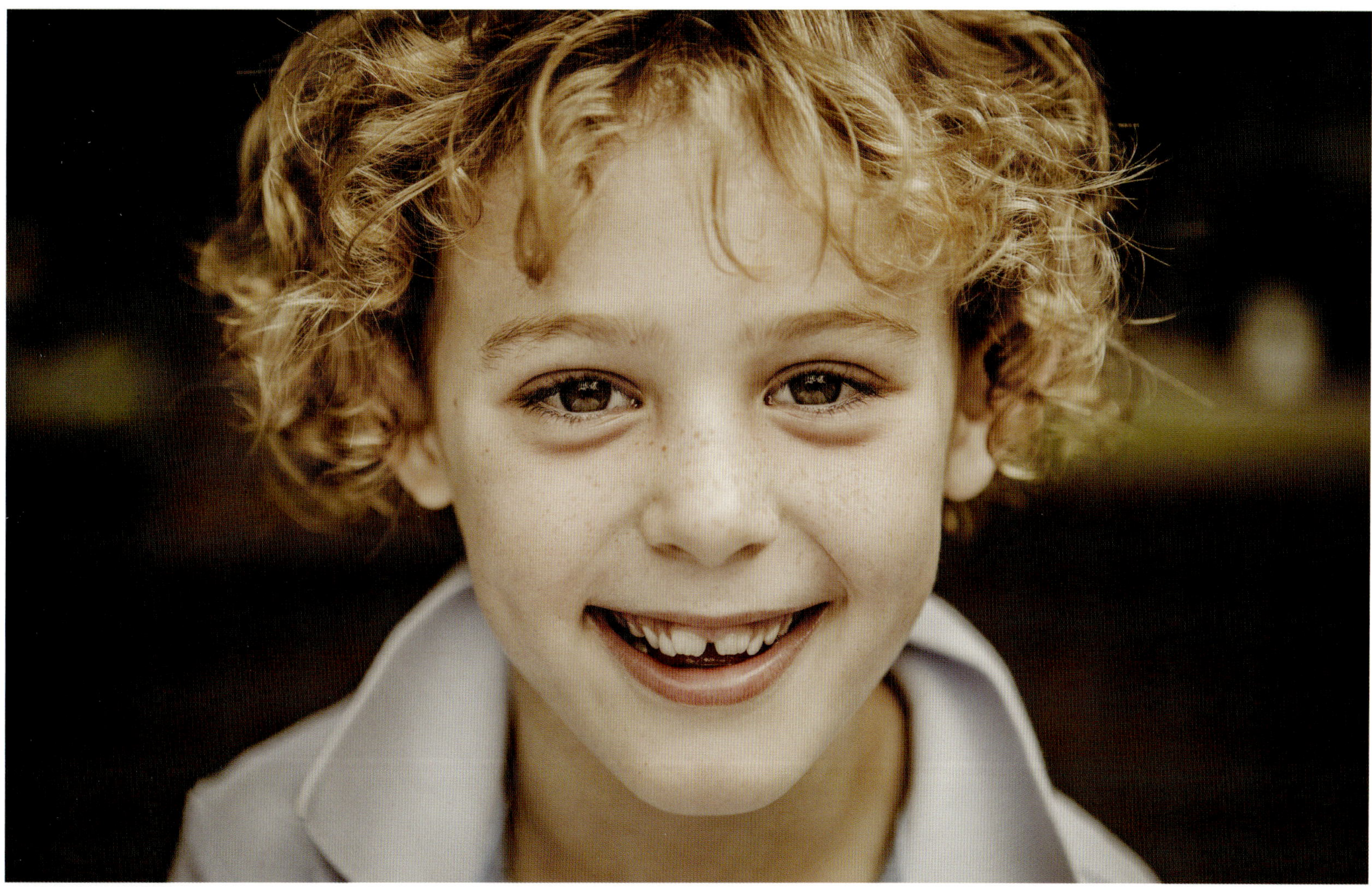

Above: There is nothing quite like the "glow" of a child's face shining through the perfect portrait.

Focal length: 70mm
Aperture: f/2.8
Shutter speed: 1/1000 sec.
ISO: 500

G.L.O.W. is a basic set of guidelines that remind you what you always need to do, no matter what the day throws up. It stands for:

Get down low
Light from behind
Open the aperture
Work the subject

Before I go on, I want to make one point crystal clear: in my opinion there are no absolute rules in photography. I say that because the art world is peppered with examples of people who broke all the rules and produced astonishing work.

So what I am about to describe on the following pages is a set of guidelines that I have perfected over years of photographing children. They work for me, but they may not work for you, so don't feel you have to follow everything to the letter. Find your own pathway: you will know when it is the right one.

G: Get Down Low

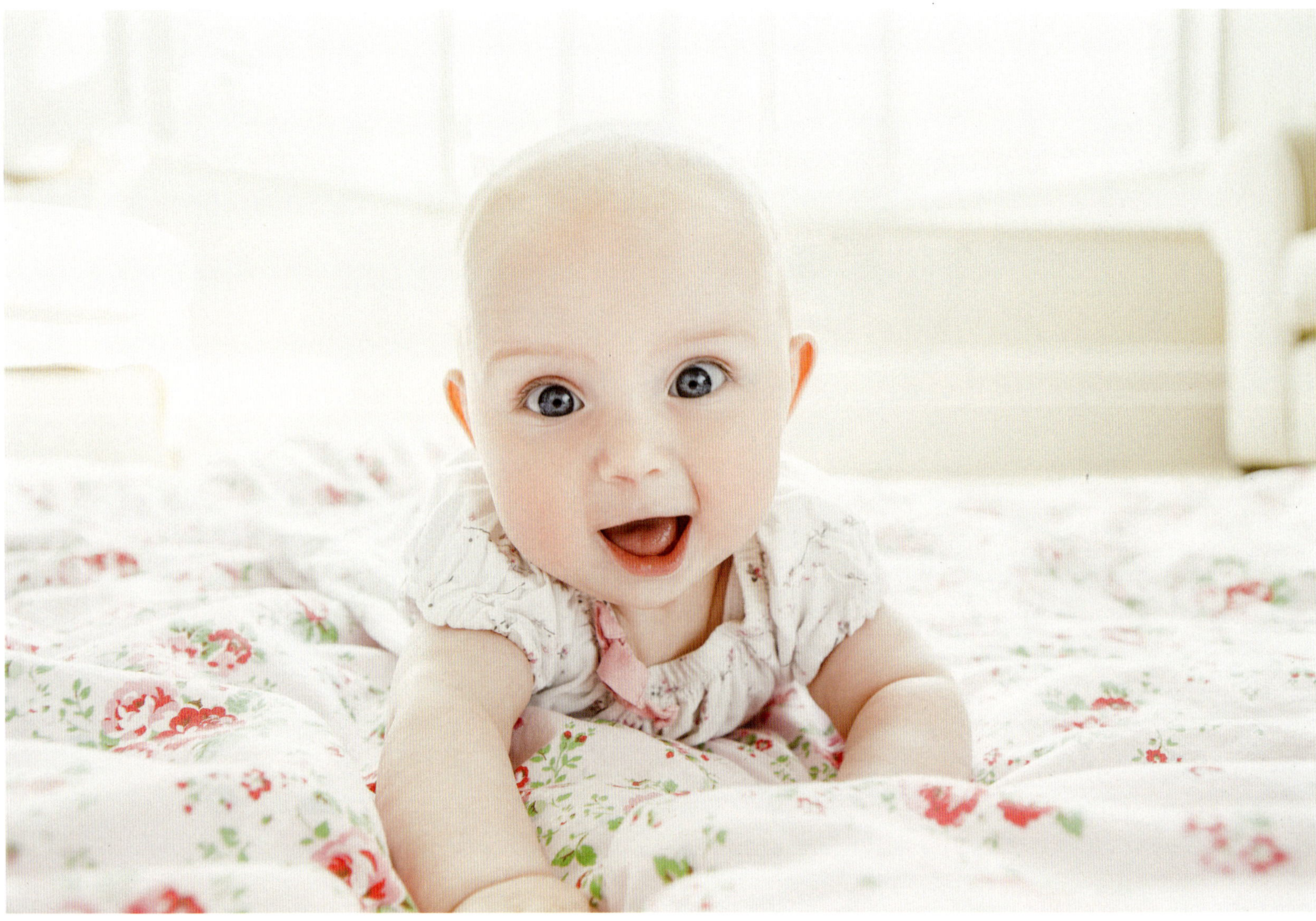

In simple terms, children are small and adults are tall. If you stand up straight for every shot you take you will be photographing children's heads from the top down. As animals, we are all programmed to understand a hierarchy, and the hierarchy here is that dominant animals look down on the less dominant.

With children, this is an everyday occurrence: teachers, parents, and just about every other authority figure in their lives looks down on them. In most portrait sessions you will have 60–90 minutes to make a child do what you want them to do, so this means you need to become their best friend very quickly. The best way to do this is to ensure that you are on their level: seeing eye to eye is essential for any good relationship.

At first, you may find it a little unnatural to be squatting, sitting, or even lying on the grass

Above: A low viewpoint brings you face to face with your subject for a more personal image.

Focal length: 30mm

Aperture: f/4.5

Shutter speed: 1/80 sec.

ISO: 640

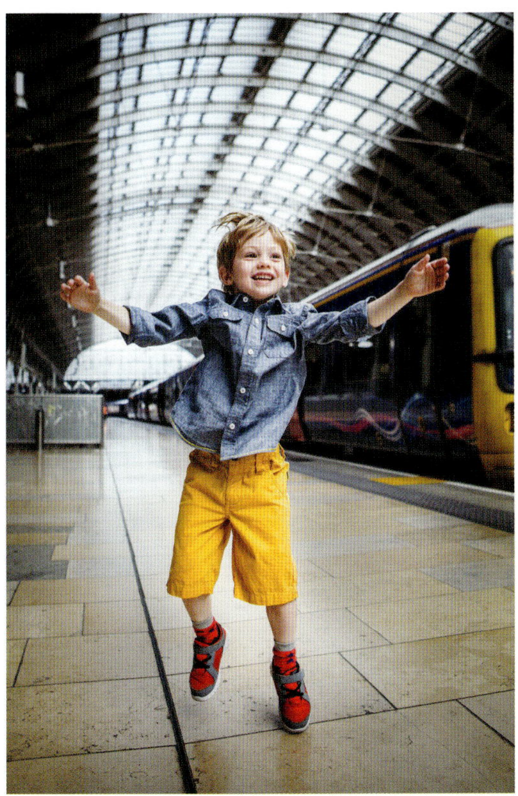

Above: A low viewpoint can give your images a spontaneous, candid feel.

Focal length: 28mm

Aperture: f/3.2

Shutter speed: 1/1000 sec.

ISO: 1600

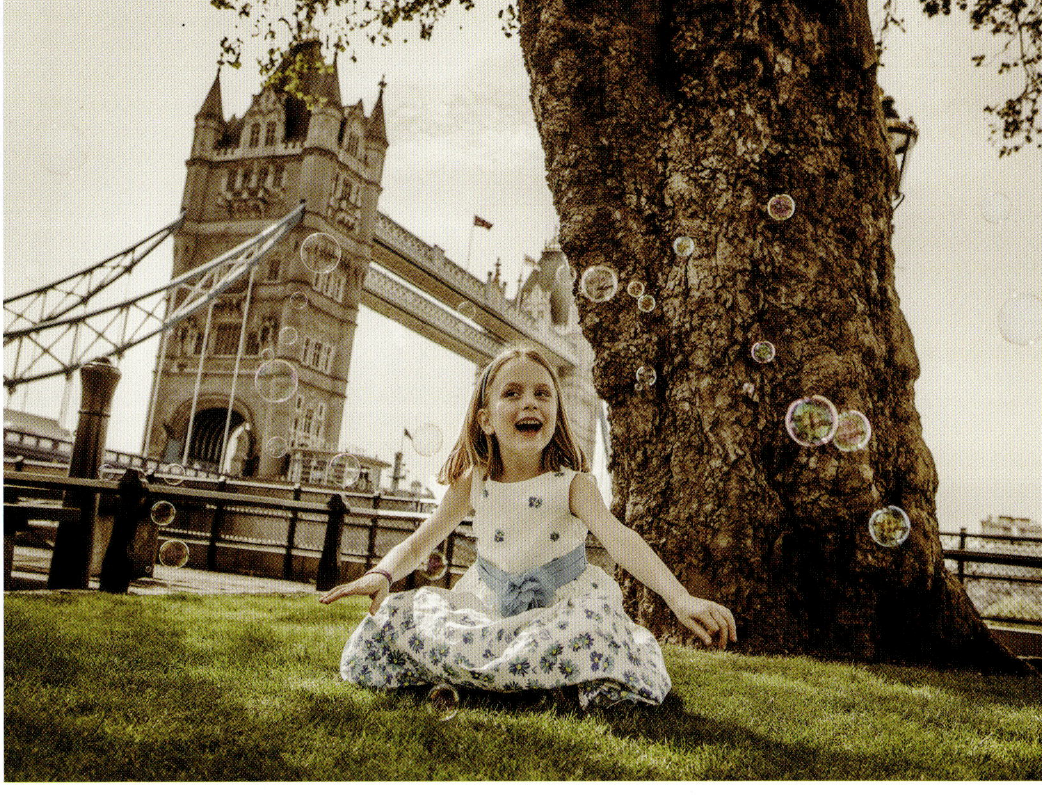

Above: Shooting from a low position enables you to include the backdrop, giving context to your portrait.

Focal length: 35mm

Aperture: f/4.5

Shutter speed: 1/1000 sec.

ISO: 400

of your local park, but I can assure you it will pay dividends. Once you are at eye level with your subject you can see the world from their perspective. Your shots will have a distinctive look that parents will not have seen before, and the child will more readily accept you as an equal.

The majority of children will look for their parent in most situations. If you have not managed to get their attention, you at least want to ensure their eye-line is consistent, so before every shoot, ask the parent(s) to stand behind you throughout. Have them join you low down—rather than standing over you—and this will guarantee the children will be looking toward the parent and/or camera, and not over your head. I sometimes also quietly invite the parent to make fun of me behind my back, which generally gets a laugh from the child and another great shot!

Shooting from a low position is also a great way to get beautiful textural ground-level views, including out-of-focus grass and interesting "view-throughs." Low-angle shots often have a candid feel due to the unusual viewpoint and this is also a great way to include the background, especially if it is an important landmark that's adding context to the shoot.

L: Light From Behind

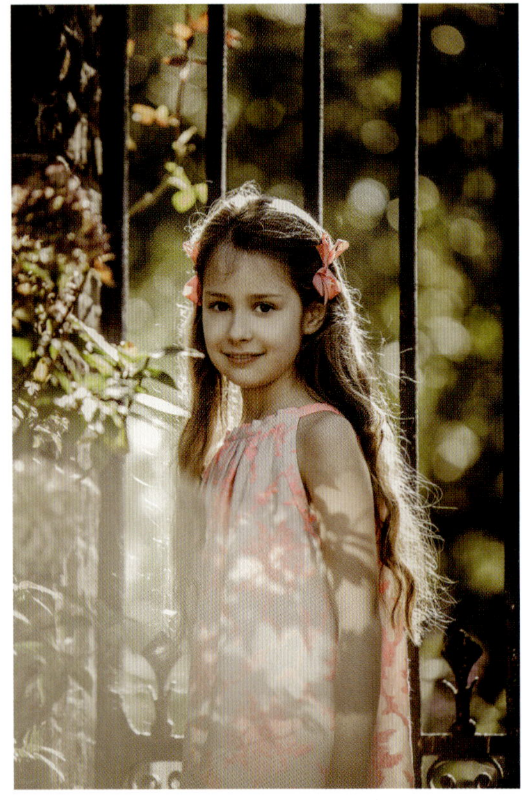

Above: Lighting your subject from behind adds a romantic frame. You can control the lens flare to enhance this effect.

Focal length: 200mm

Aperture: f/3.2

Shutter speed: 1/1000 sec.

ISO: 640

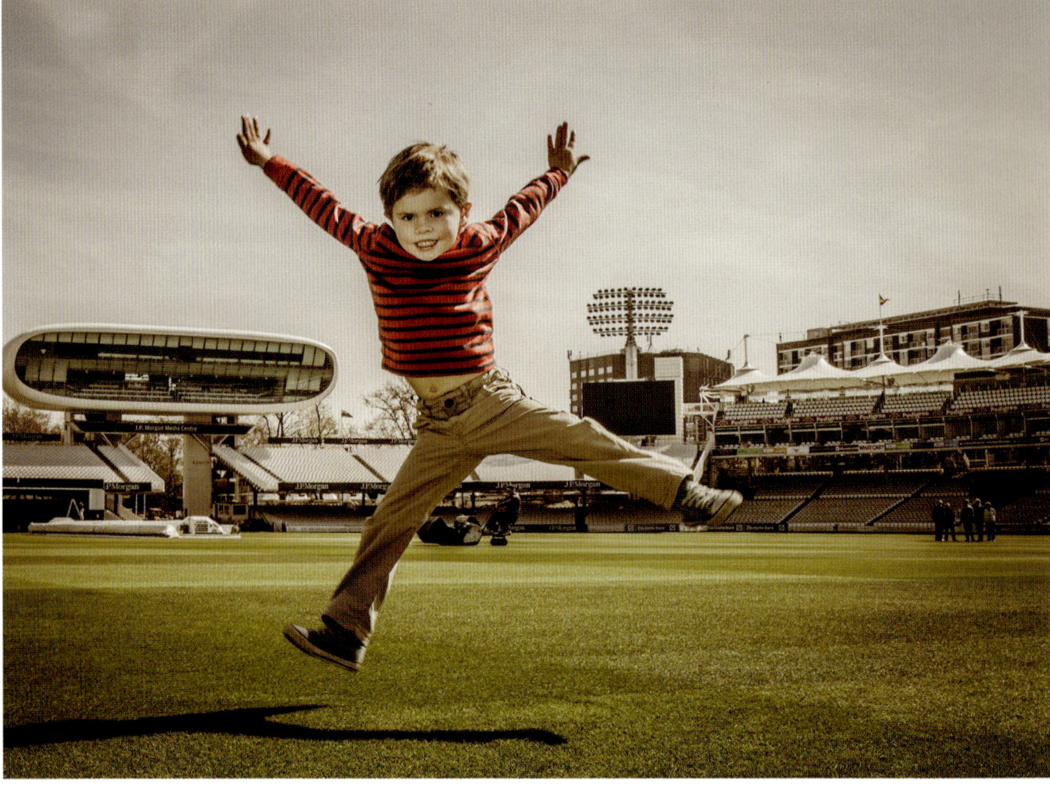

Above: A backlight does not always have to come from directly behind your subject.

Focal length: 42mm

Aperture: f/16

Shutter speed: 1/200 sec.

ISO: 500

When Kodak launched the Box Brownie (the first camera for the "common man"), it came with a set of instructions that stated you should stand with your back to the sun, place the subject in the middle of the frame, and shoot. In the early 1900s this was the way to get sharp, well-exposed photographs every time, but if you want to shoot truly beautiful images today you need to apply a different set of rules.

When you arrive at a location you should immediately look for the position of the sun. Back light is without doubt the most beautiful direction of light, as it frames and distinguishes your subject in a manner that is simply unbeatable. All you need to do is place your subject between yourself and the sun, fill in the resulting shadow with a reflector or flash and you have the ideal setup for incredible portraits.

Back light does not mean that the sun is directly behind the subject, though—it can come from the side or from above, and as long as it is further back than the body line it will give a gorgeous "clip light." This is where your bounce reflector really comes into play and you can use either the silver side for a hard bounce or the white side for a softer bounce to "fill in" the shadow areas, creating soft shadows and stunning reflections in the eyes.

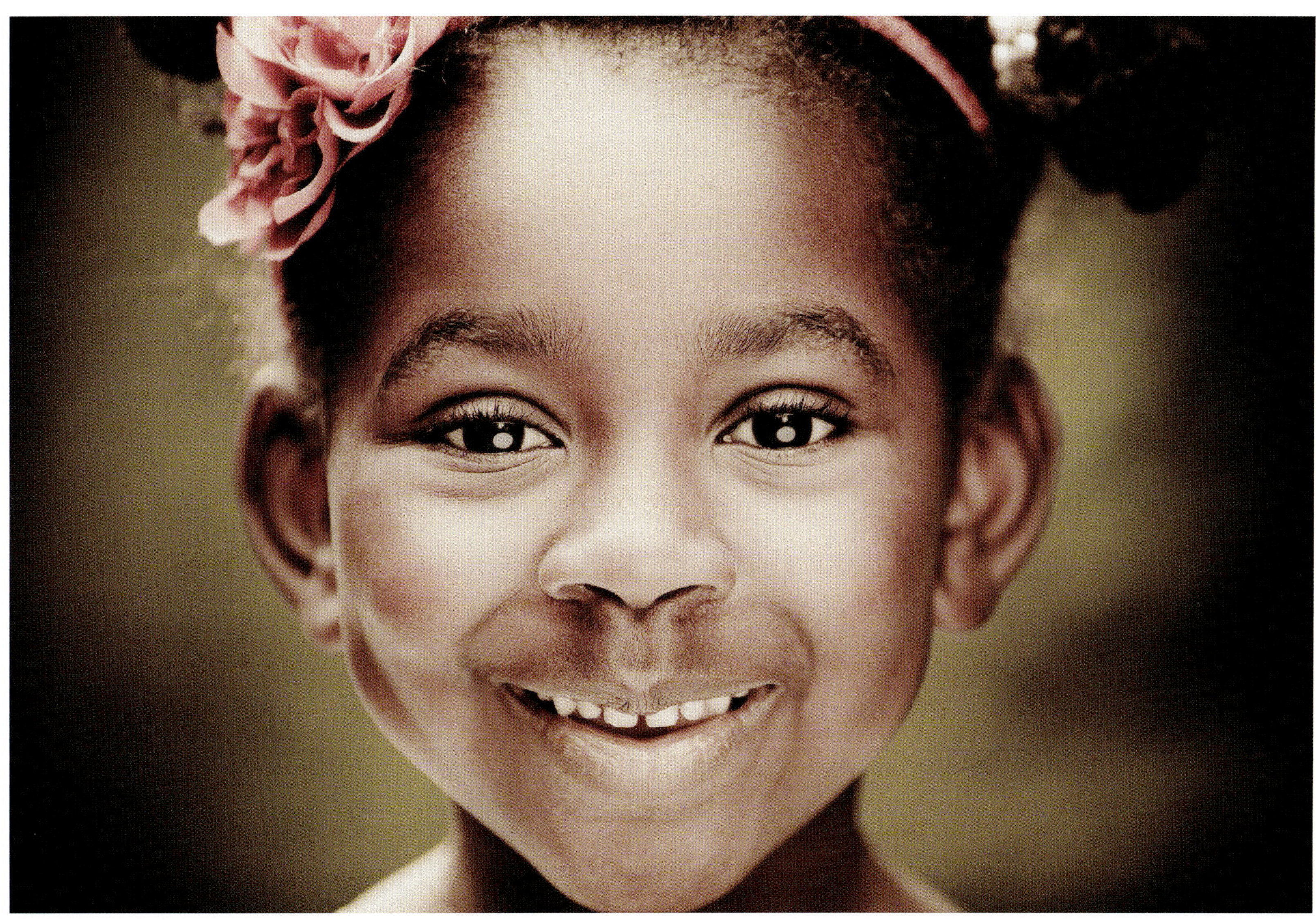

At a greater distance you can employ a flash to do the same thing as a reflector: practice setting the flash at low levels and see the difference it makes as a "fill" light. It is worth noting that light works in mysterious ways and it will always fill in the shadows before it washes out the highlights, so you won't need much.

If you don't have a flash, and cannot get a decent reflection from your bounce reflector, simply open up the exposure and expose for the shadow areas. The background will start to blow out and you will get a super-bright overexposed backdrop with the child at the center.

Above: Use a bounce reflector to brighten your subject's face and create beautiful highlights in their eyes.

Focal length: 175mm

Aperture: f/3.5

Shutter speed: 1/250 sec.

ISO: 400

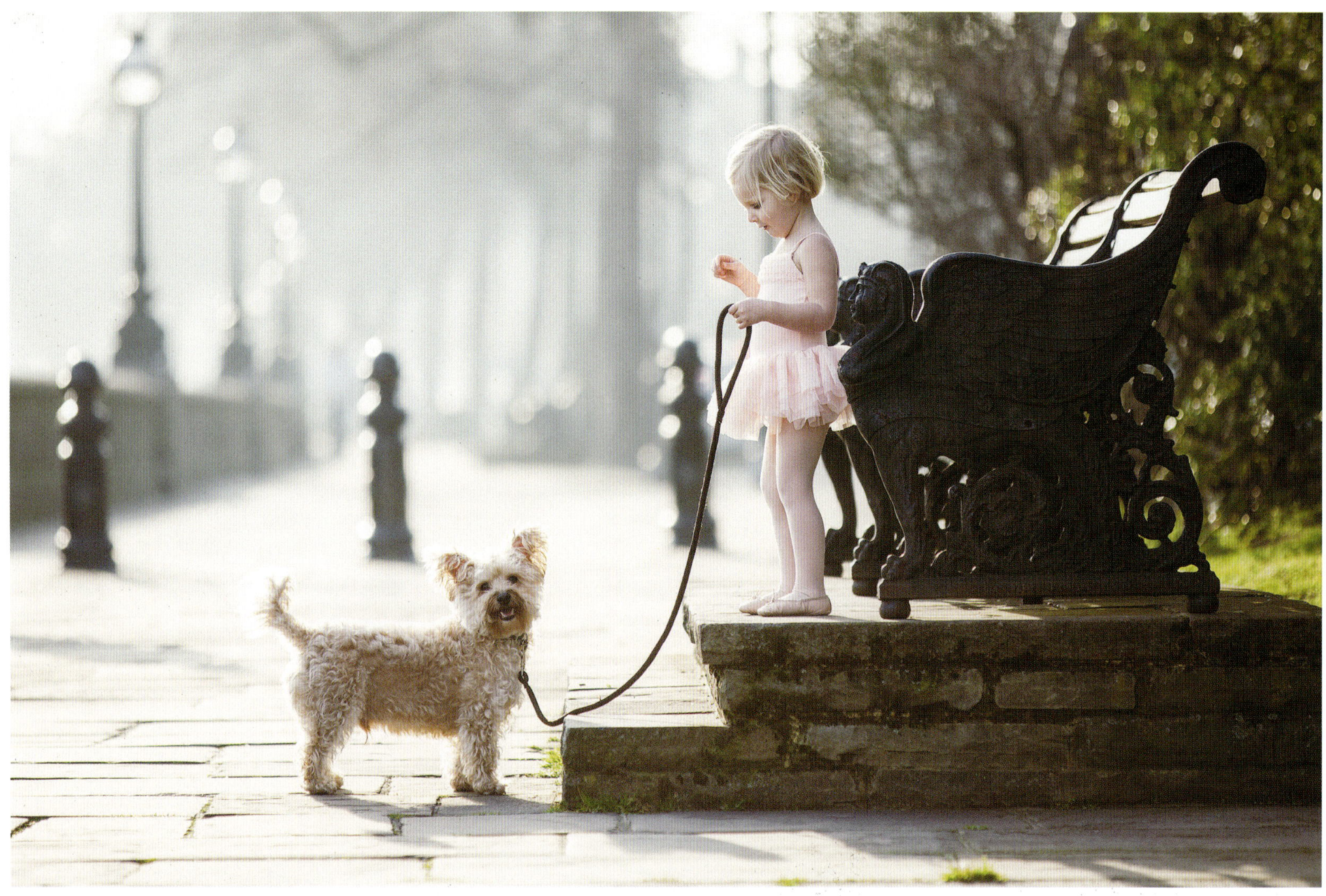

We have already looked at the "bokeh" effect created by using a wide aperture, especially in conjunction with a long or telephoto lens. Some lenses are now designed with this effect in mind and will give stunningly consistent, soft, circular points at a distance, acting as a subtle backdrop to your model. Look for locations where the effect can be used: long lines of trees work extremely well, as do long fences and walls to prop the child against. A wide aperture also has the effect of cutting the subject out from the background, or can be used to highlight the eyes, while the rest of the face remains softly blurred.

The bokeh effect also works in the foreground of a scene, and out-of-focus objects in the foreground often add interest and drama to images. Find areas where you can embed yourself in undergrowth with plants or flowers between you and the child. Locate a small gap through the leaves to shoot through and allow the rest of the leaves to encircle your model, taking care not to obstruct the model's face with any defocused branches. The reason this works so well is because we have all enjoyed the experience of watching a child playing when they do not know you are there. It is a wonderful thing to see as a child creates stories and imaginary situations in their private world. The camera allows you to capture these moments and the memory of them will be something that parents will cherish forever.

Left: A wide aperture has the effect of isolating the subject from their background.

Focal length: 200mm

Aperture: f/2.8

Shutter speed: 1/250 sec.

ISO: 500

Right: A strong bokeh effect produces beautifully controlled blurring in the background.

Focal length: 50mm

Aperture: f/3.5

Shutter speed: 1/1000 sec.

ISO: 800

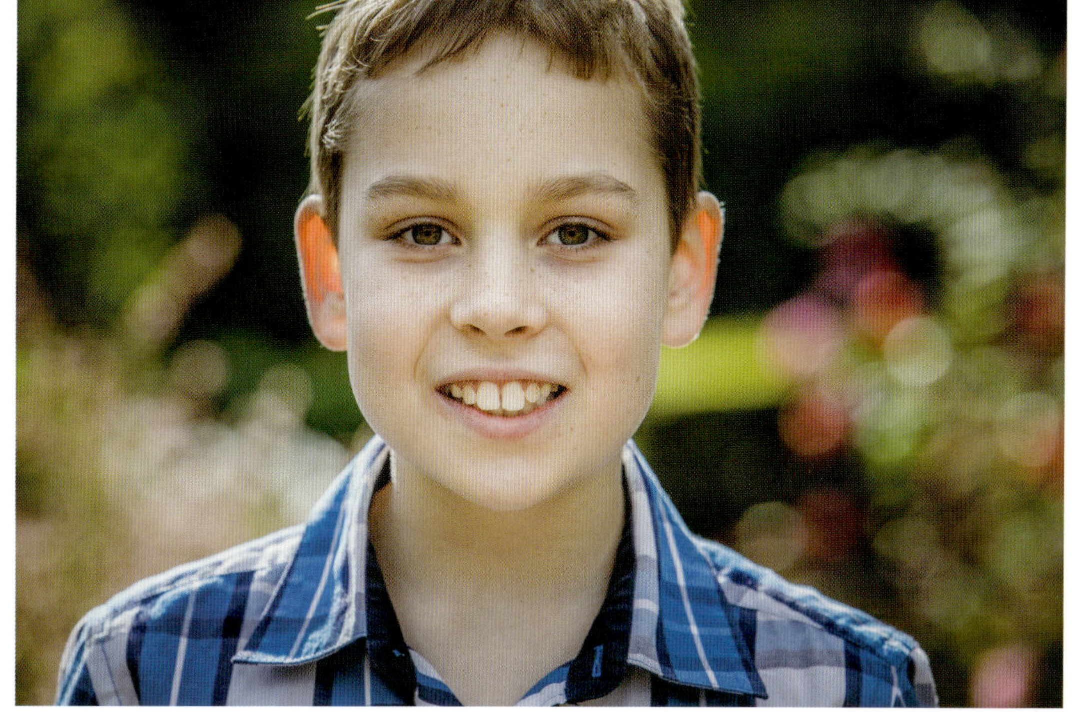

Right: Blurred objects in the foreground can often add interest to your images.

Focal length: 120mm

Aperture: f/3.5

Shutter speed: 1/800 sec.

ISO: 1600

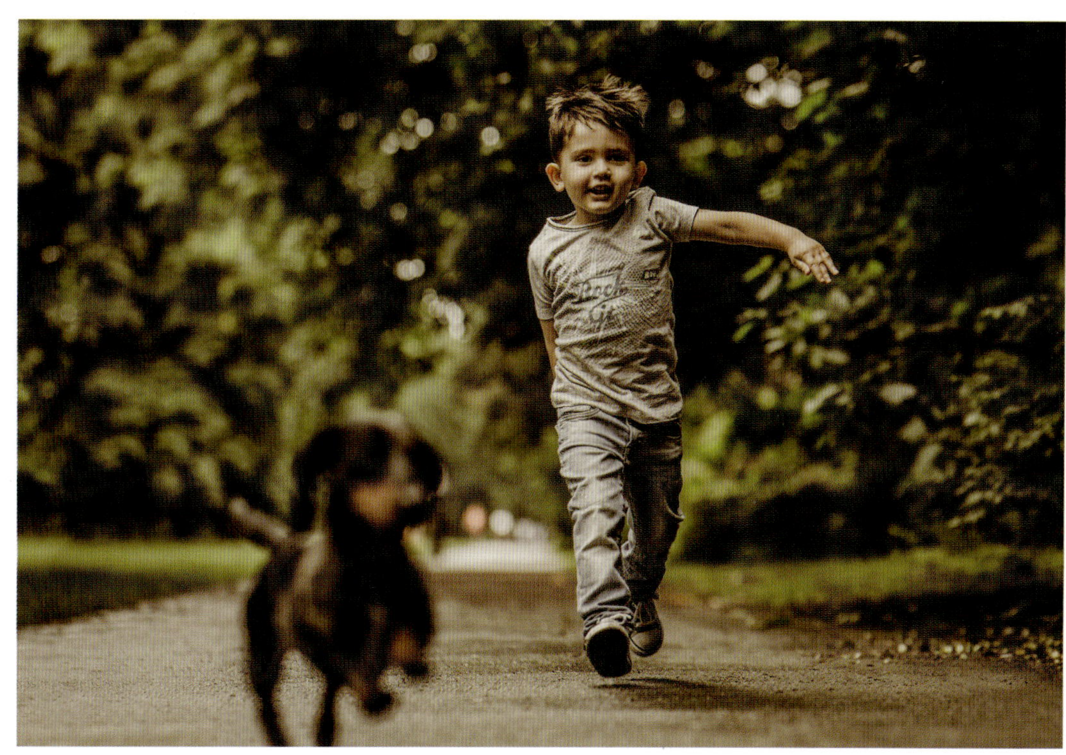

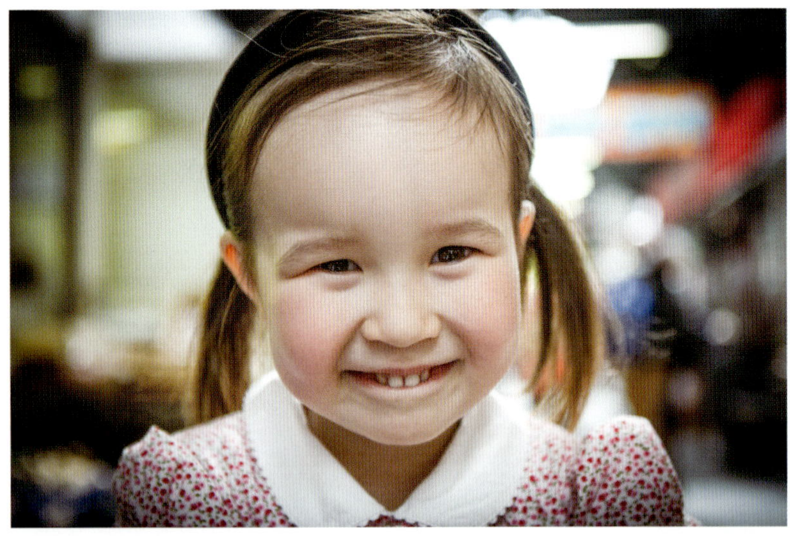 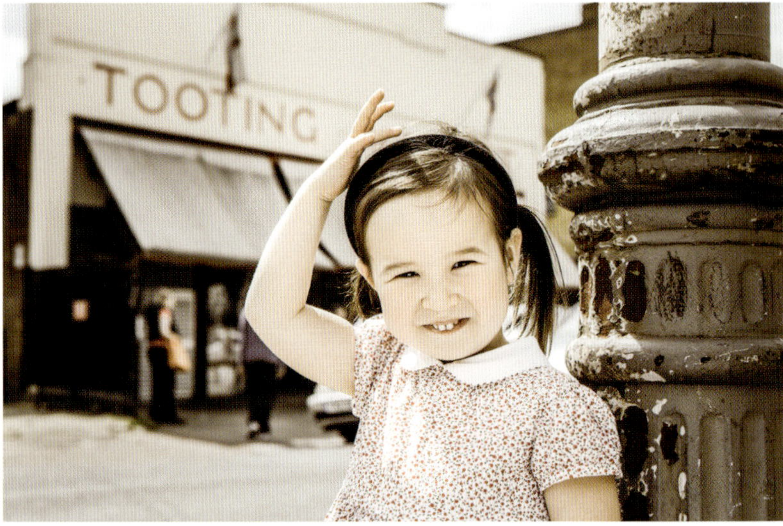

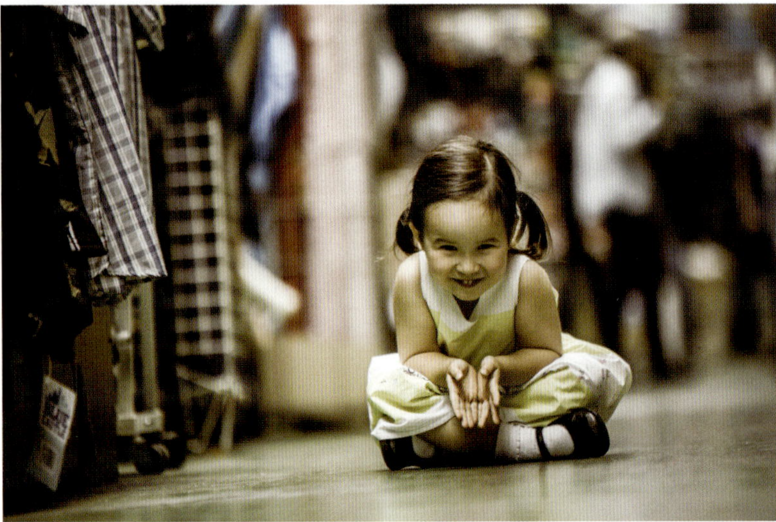 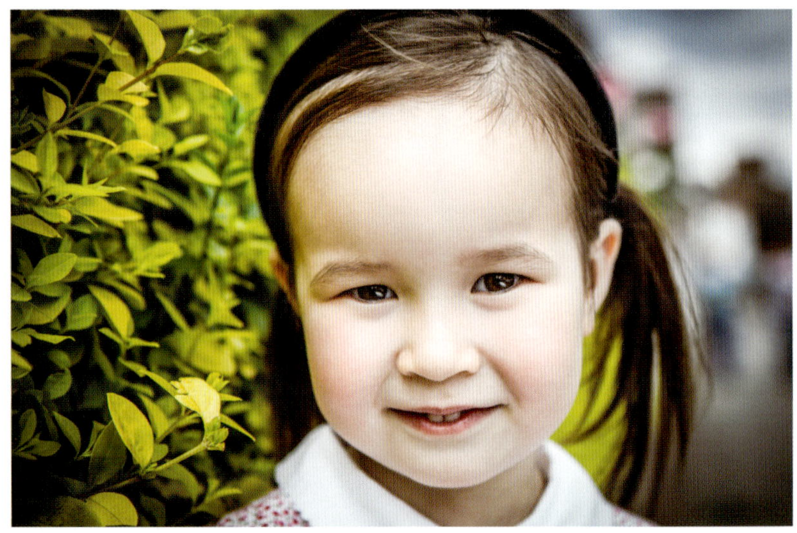

Working the subject is the final ingredient for the perfect child portrait session. This can sound a little brutal, but this principle is based on something that was very difficult to do until the digital age. In days gone by (when we all shot film), you always had to be aware of how much you were shooting because film and processing is expensive. Fashion shooters were quick to realize that one way to get great pictures was simply to shoot a lot of film, which is great if you have a commercial client who is prepared to pay for it, but portrait photographers have always been expected to cover their own costs. However, with the switch to digital it is now possible to use the fashion photographer's trick.

In simple terms, use all of your skill, psychology, and talent to get your model to the perfect position and then shoot plenty of images. Children move, they blink, they sneeze, they pull faces—they are not like adult models, so you can never fully direct them. Therefore, working your subject is a vital ingredient to a successful child portrait shoot: capture every nuance of every situation so you have plenty of shots for your final edit.

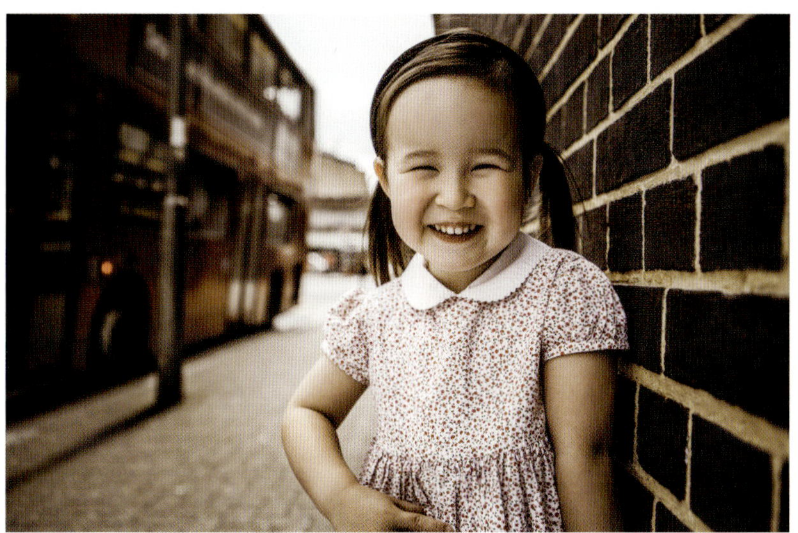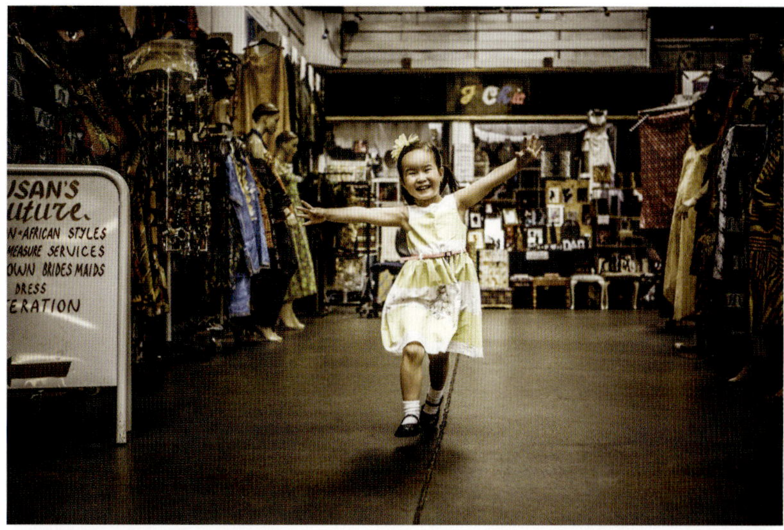

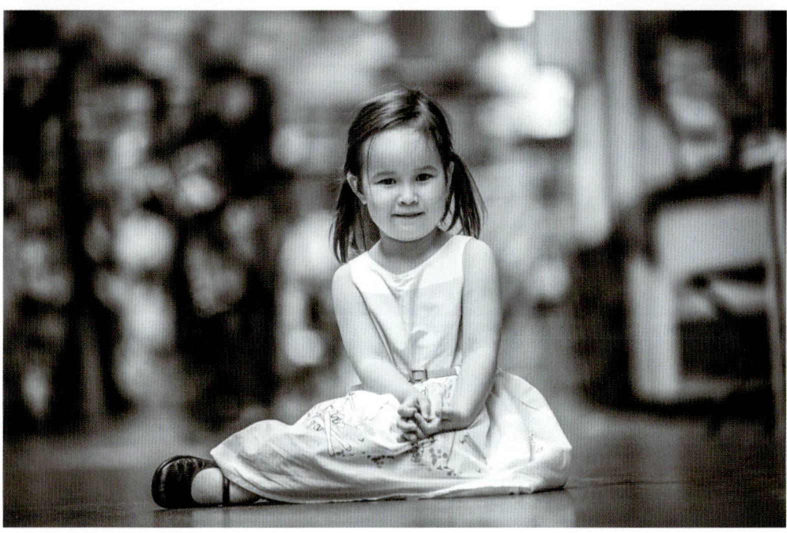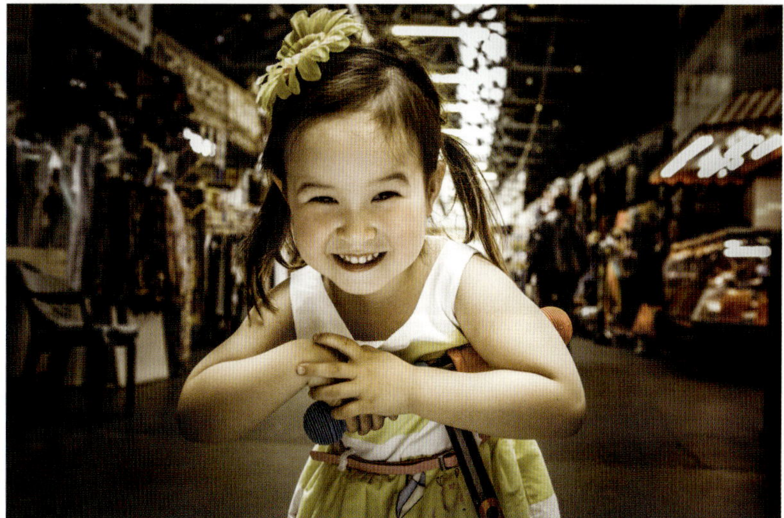

Opposite & above: Once you have established your subject within the location, work hard to get as many images as you can from the situation.

Variety

The best child portrait sessions are always those that have great variety. Most children are happiest when they are moving around, so try to capture that. I often choose to do running shots when I first meet the children. This is because they can be a little hesitant about doing a photo shoot, and are likely to have only a formal school photo for reference: hours of standing in line and then being perched on a stool and asked to smile can be very intimidating for some children, and downright boring for most. So when you arrive and say "OK, lets do some running around!" they just love it.

You also need variety in the child's outfits, so get the parent to bring at least three different outfits—and use them. This is all part of your preparation work, so don't forget to tell the parent what you want them to bring. You want the outfits to be as different as possible, so think

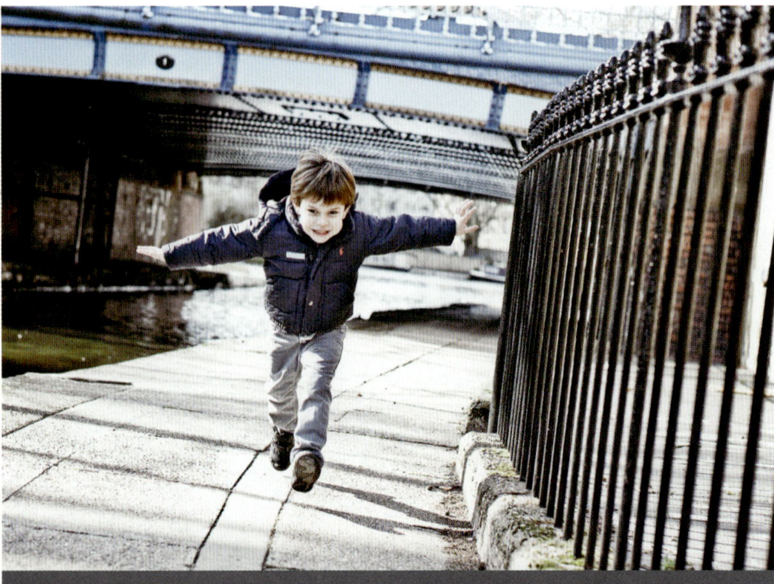

AIRPLANE RUN

I often tell my subject that mommy has told me what a fast runner they are, and this is a great way to get them to prove their speed. Normal running sometimes looks too serious, though, and can also result in flailing hands covering up their face by mistake, so use the "airplane run" instead.

Ask them to stand on a pathway about 60ft (20m) away and tell them you want them to run straight toward you, as fast as they can. Show them how to run with their arms outstretched and maybe ask mom to stand with her arms out to receive the running child. Do this and the shoot will start off with a bang; the child will be happy; they will have warmed up; and mom will feel involved as well. I set my camera to 1/1000 sec. (in Shutter Priority mode or Manual) and the shots look incredible.

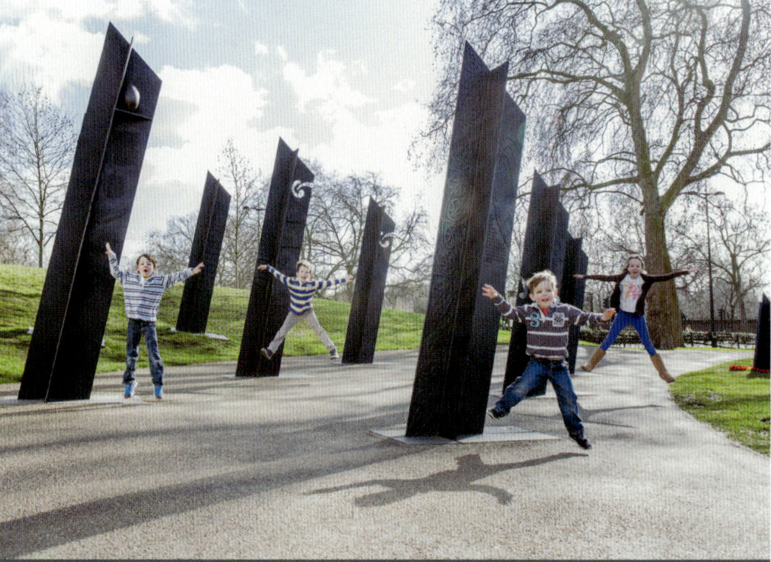

STAR JUMPS

Next we do "star jumps," often in front of a wall, as this works well in an urban setting. Check your frames, as it is easy to get strange facial expressions doing this: cheeks can rise up awkwardly and create an ugly image when the final shot is blown up. Take a close look at the faces on your preview screen and work the subject until you are happy you have the image. I sometimes do jumps off park benches or low walls as well, but make sure they are safe before you try this.

Some children might be able to do gymnastics, and handstands are great— preferably with bent legs (like a scorpion). I tend to steer clear of cartwheels, though, as even if the child loves to do them, they are rarely successful: the face is never in quite the correct position to be photographed when in full flight. In general, the star jump is a good "go to" action that most children can do well and it looks great in the final photographs.

about something formal, something casual, and something fun. Children will often adopt a completely different persona in different clothing, which can be a real asset to the shoot.

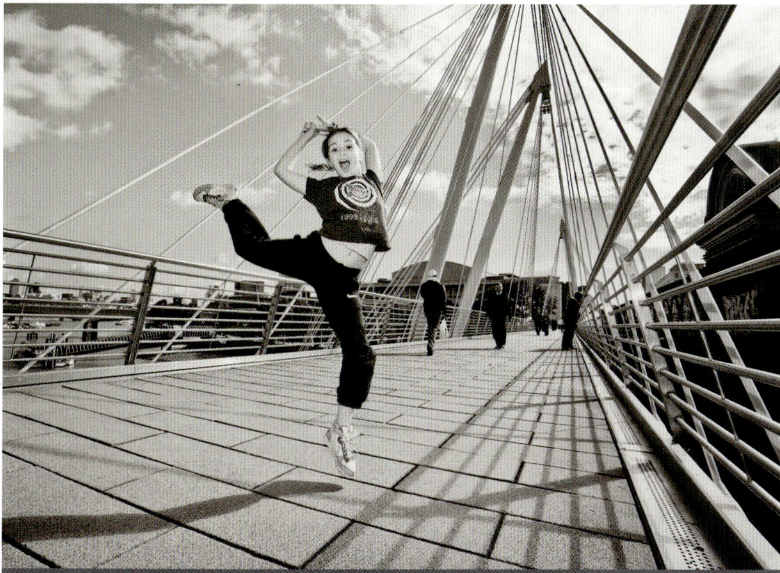

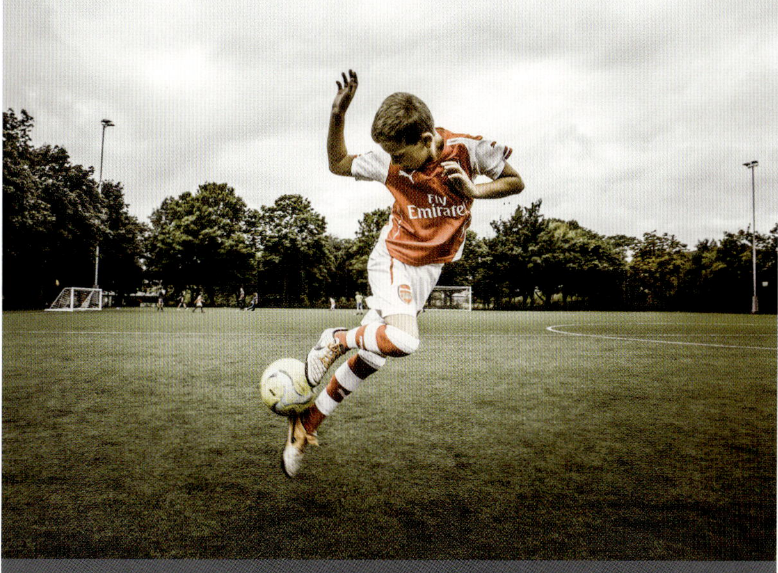

DANCING

Dancing is another brilliant way to bring out the talent of a child and this can vary from formal ballet poses to wild street dancing or just spinning. Spinning requires plenty of patience, but don't be afraid to guide the child to keep repeating the dance until you get the right image. When they are spinning you are looking for the moment when they turn and look directly at camera, while their hair and clothes are still moving. Use a shutter speed of 1/1000 sec. for super-sharp images, but try some slower panning shots as well, to get a stronger sense of movement.

In low light or indoor locations you will probably have to increase your ISO to achieve a fast shutter speed, but grainy images are well suited to movement shots and can give very artistic results. If your final image is not super-sharp, consider changing it to black and white in postproduction: there is a strong tradition of monochrome press images that work very well even if they are not tack sharp, so slight softness is more acceptable.

SPORTS SKILLS

Most children love sports, whether it's football, basketball, baseball, golf, or even walking on stilts: I did a shoot where the boy loved archery, so we made that a feature of his portraits with wideangle images of the arrow leaving the bow. So use balls, bats, bicycles, scooters, and even include the pet dog in running shots if they have one. If some of these actions get a little out of hand, enjoy the laughter they bring and don't take anything too seriously.

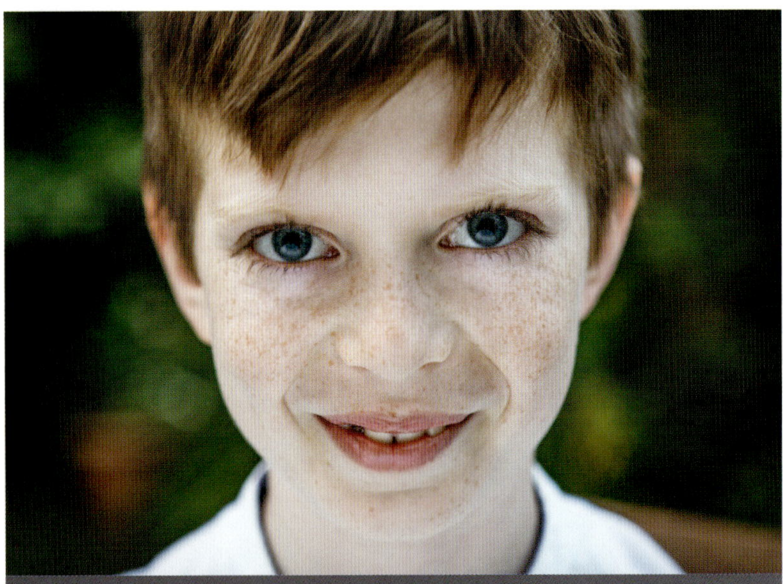

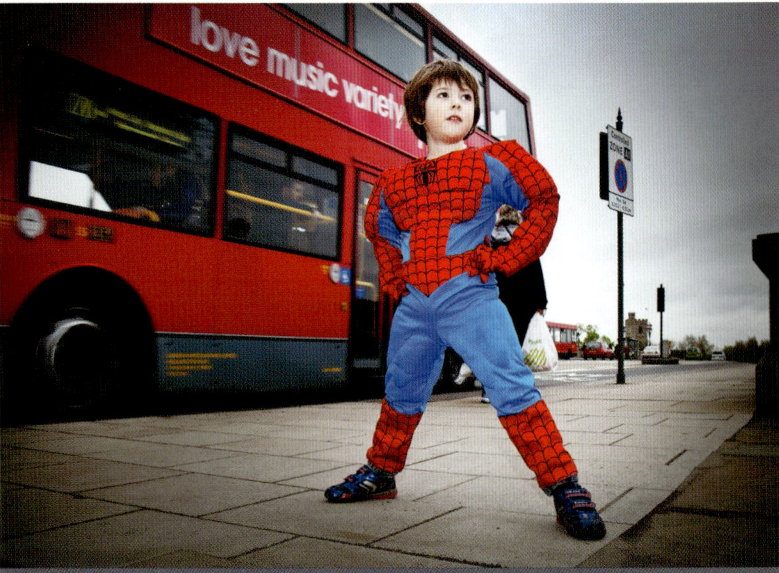

CLOSE-UPS

It is always a good idea to intersperse action shots with still shots to change the mood. You have to keep your subject entertained, so talk to the child and keep them interested in you. Sit them down in front of you and place your bounce reflector on their lap to give some beautiful reflected lighting. Use a 24–70mm zoom to get close and then move back for a variety of looks in just a few minutes.

There are several different close-up shots you can try. A very simple, straight-at-the-camera shot tends to look very contemporary and modern, but the moment a child tilts his or her head or looks over the shoulder or to the side it becomes more traditional. Play on these techniques to get both effects and create more options.

Remember, your subject doesn't always have to be looking into the lens and the effect of looking off camera is very different to an image with full eye contact. Shoot images that fill the frame with nothing but the face, then shoot head and shoulders; vary the position of the sitter within the frame using central composition and the rule of thirds.

SUPERHERO

One of the things I often do is ask my subject to stand wide-legged with their hands on their hips, as shown here. I call this the "superhero stance" and it is entirely different to standard poses. It usually feels less awkward for children to pose this way and looks amazing in the final portfolio. Use a wideangle lens and stand them three quarters on to the camera for an even more enhanced effect (a Spiderman costume is, of course, entirely optional!).

Have your subject standing side on with their arms behind their back, with their head turned to face the camera; first to the left and then to the right. Shoot these options full length and then from the waist up. Get them to turn away from you and then turn their head back toward you. Keep changing the position and you will create a vast amount of options.

Your subject may feel uncomfortable "posing" in this more traditional way, so keep them moving to distract them and keep talking and encouraging them. Horizontal frames and vertical frames can be added to the mix and you'll be surprised how quickly you can build up a large number of images and compositions in just one spot. Lean them against walls and bushes to capture the texture of the surface and then move them into open ground for a different feel altogether.

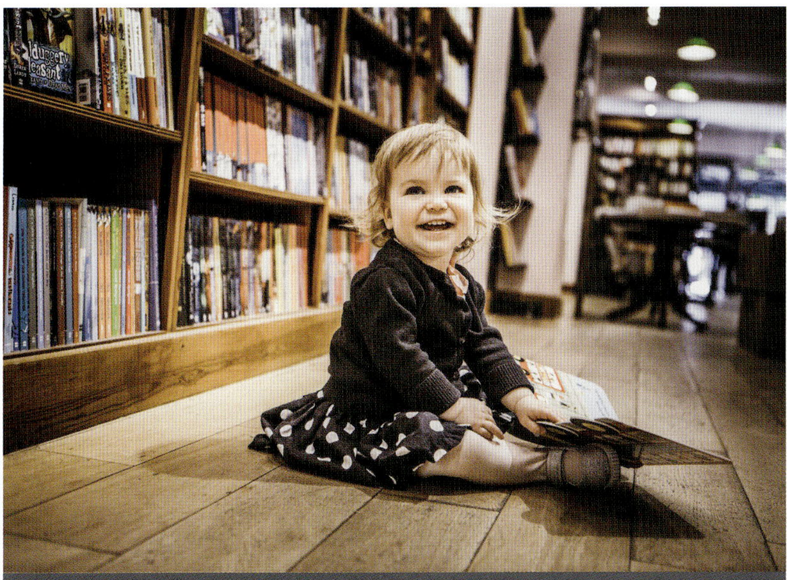

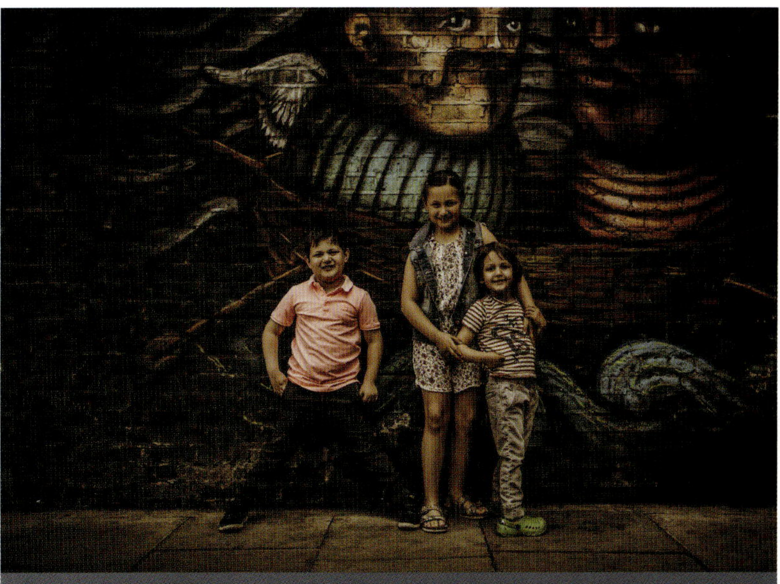

SITTING DOWN

You can get great shots if you sit your model on the ground, up a tree, on a wall, or even have them lying down, but in each case you need to be aware of the positioning of their arms and legs. Hands can be forgotten and appear in unnatural-looking positions, so always take a last-minute look at all the details. In general, avoid having their legs coming directly toward the camera, as foreshortened legs rarely look good. Instead, ask them to kneel or sit cross-legged or with their legs out to the side (but always be aware of the modesty required for skirts and dresses, as a lack of attention to underwear can ruin an otherwise great image).

The most important thing is that they look comfortable and natural. Children will sometimes try really hard to please you, so you need to make them understand that all you want is for them to be natural. The best way to show how you want your subject to position themselves is to show them: your subject will find it a lot easier to mirror your body position, rather than trying to understand a verbal instruction, so show them how to sit and then change your position if you want them to change theirs.

GROUPS

Another way to add variety to your session is to include group shots in your routine. With families with more than one child, parents will expect at least one group shot so don't disappoint them.

Handling groups of children—or even just a pair of children—can be very tricky, and you shouldn't forget the family pets as well. In some ways, groups are almost a different discipline, so there is a balance to be struck. On the one hand, groups can be some of the best images you will ever get and you know that parents will always want to buy them. On the other hand, don't underestimate how long it can take to get just one good group shot: you can spend over half an hour trying desperately to get all the children to smile at the same time, look in the right direction, and look beautiful together at the same moment!

The rule of thumb is that it will take the same amount of frames per person for a group shot that it takes to get each person individually. So if it takes you 10 frames to get one image of a child on their own, it will take you at least 30 frames to get one image of a group of three. Try to manage the expectations of your client so you aren't forced to spend the entire time shooting groups; your client will love you for it when they see the final images, even if they don't realize that at the time.

Don't forget that all of the shot types we have looked at so far can also apply to group shots: groups can run, dance, spin, sit, and so on.

Mix It Up

All of the situations I've outlined so far can be shot in a variety of ways: close-up or far away, vertically framed or horizontally framed, and with a number of different compositions. You should also try to get images that show different expressions, so it's not always a child with a big smile, and not always a child looking straight into the lens.

Always bear in mind that you are telling a story with your photographs, and the location and the immediate background are part of that. Out-of-focus buses in the background or a passing train can be a wonderful addition, and can add interest and subtext to the shoot.

Ultimately, there are numerous ways of creating variety in a shoot, even in a relatively dull location. It is up to you to mix and match positions, poses, lenses, compositions, and lighting to create a wide selection of final images. If you have the opportunity to take some indoor shots as well as some outdoor shots, this is a brilliant way of adding completely different images to your final selection.

The list at the right is the variety of images I try to get with *every* shoot I do. It pays to learn this list and even write it down and have it in your camera bag as a reminder. Your list can be as long as you want it to be, but you should try to cover all of these with every location shoot you do.

You can also mix up the items on the list to create even greater variety, so you might have "leaning against a wall; close-up and far away; straight faced and looking away, then smiling."

SHOT LIST

Running ("airplane run")
Jumping
Star jumping
Spinning
Dancing
Climbing trees
Hanging from trees
Cycling/scootering
Sitting with legs out
Sitting cross legged
Sitting on benches
Sitting on walls
Sitting on tree branches
With pet(s)
Squatting
Kneeling
Lying
Leaning against a wall
Leaning against a tree
Standing straight
Standing sideways
Standing, looking back
Standing open legged ("super hero")
Telephoto
Wideangle
Close-up
Ultra close-up
Far away
Semi-close
Three-quarter length
Full length
Looking toward camera
Looking away from camera
Smiling
Laughing
Straight faced
Funny face
Vertical crop
Horizontal crop

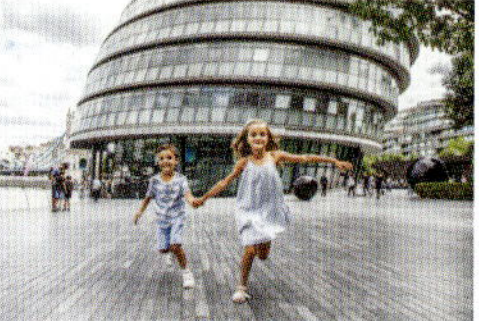
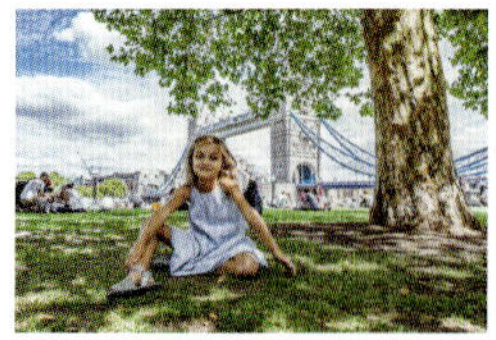
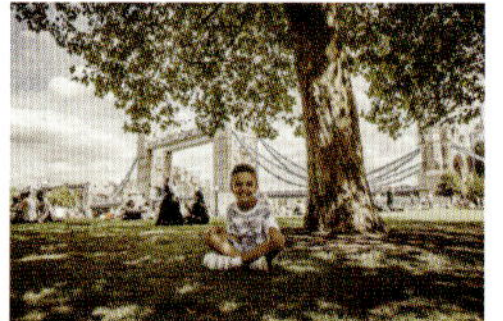
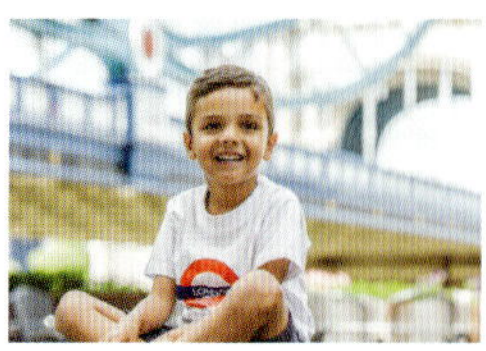
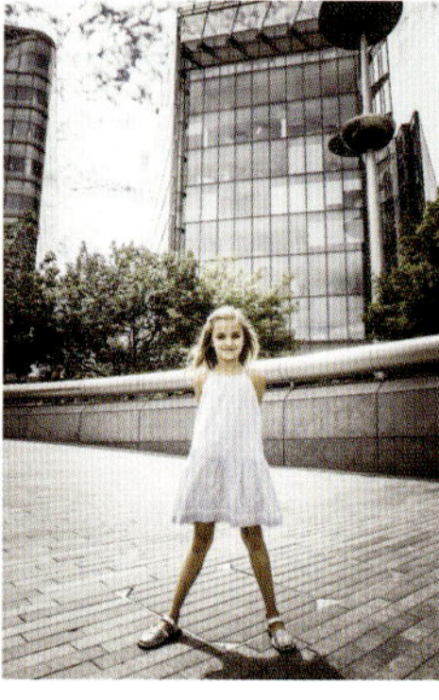
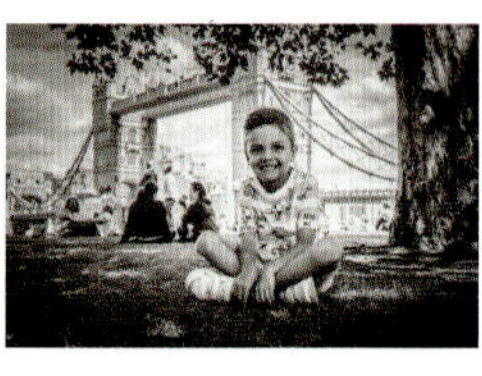
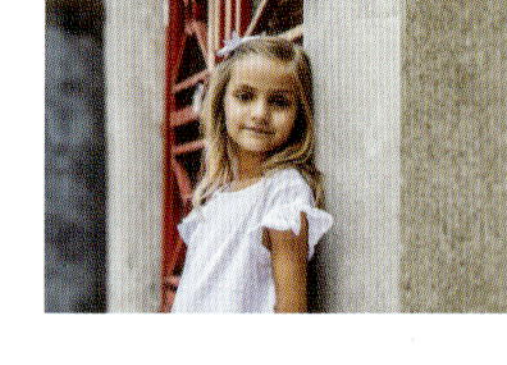
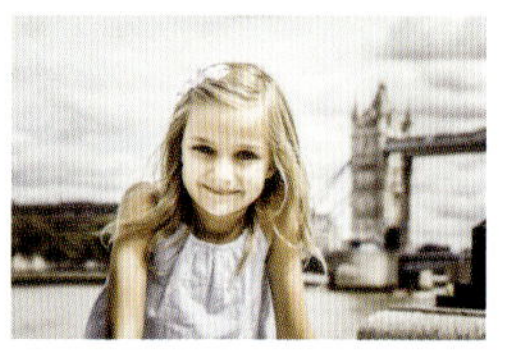
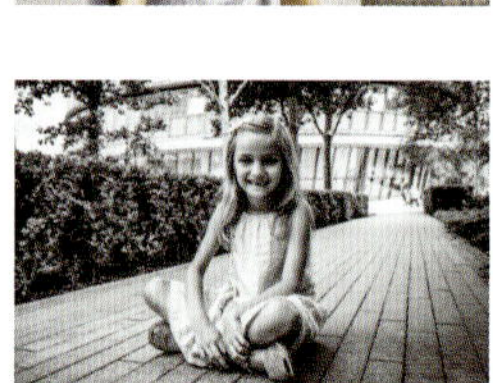
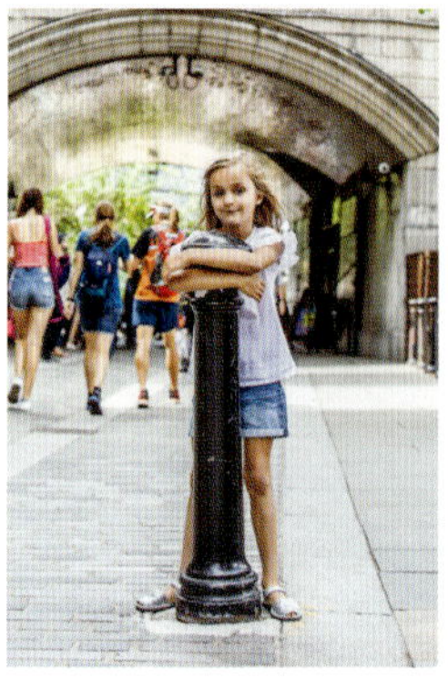

Above: I present each of my clients with a final selection of 40 images from a shoot, as seen here. While it may seem that I have a long shot list, this is essential for ensuring there is plenty of variety when it comes to choosing the final set of images.

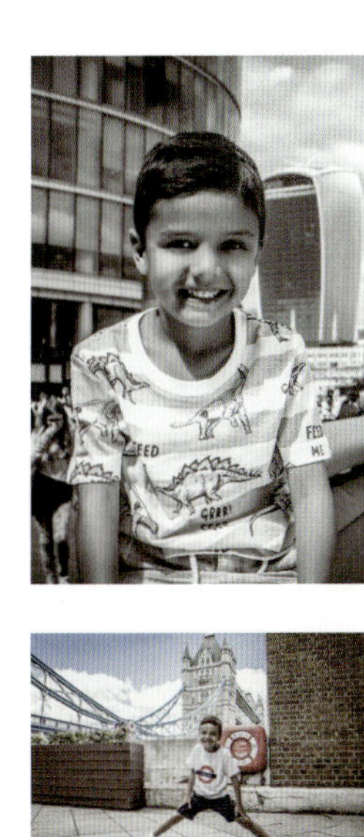
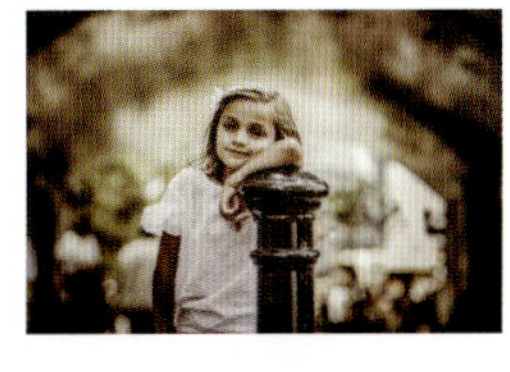
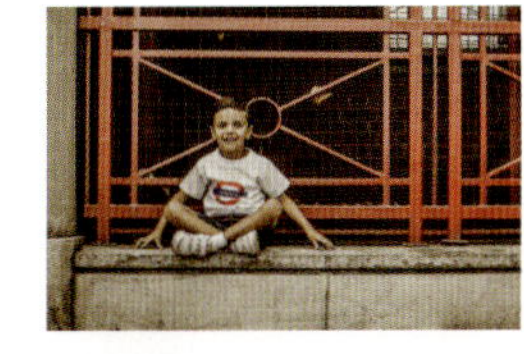
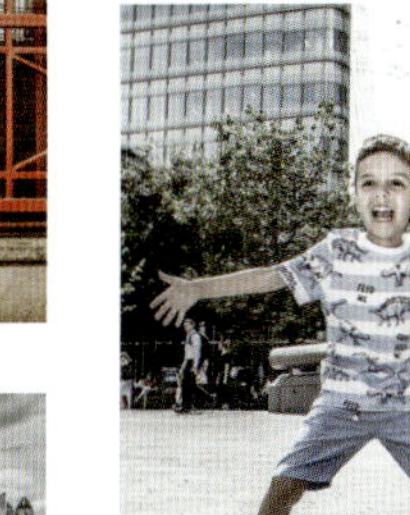
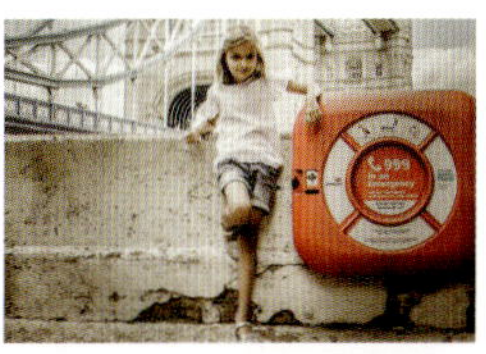
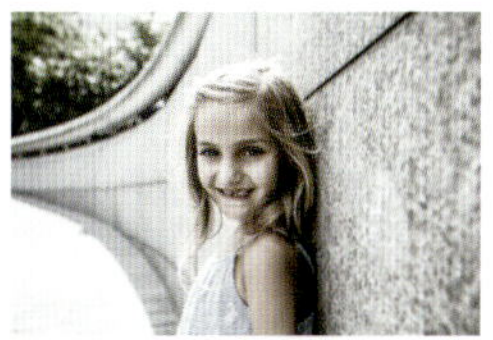
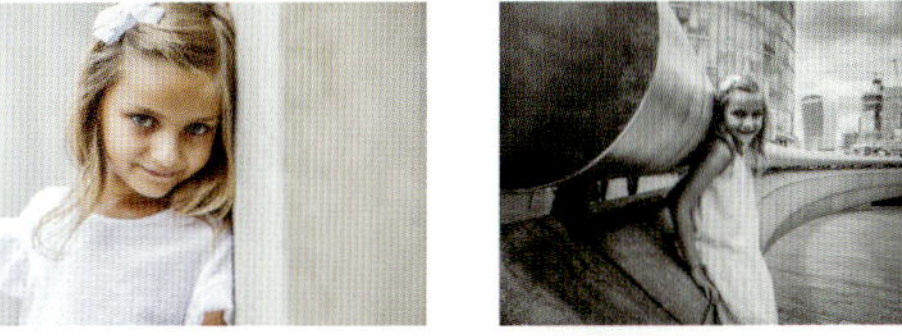
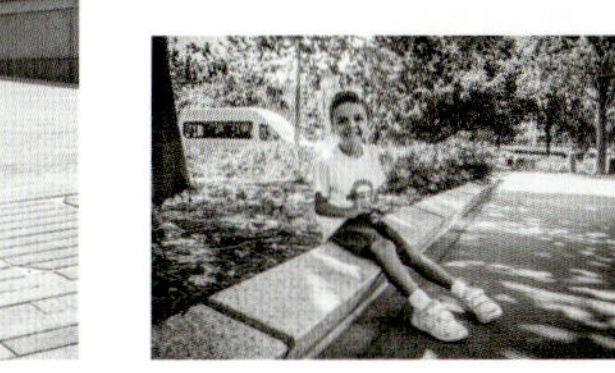
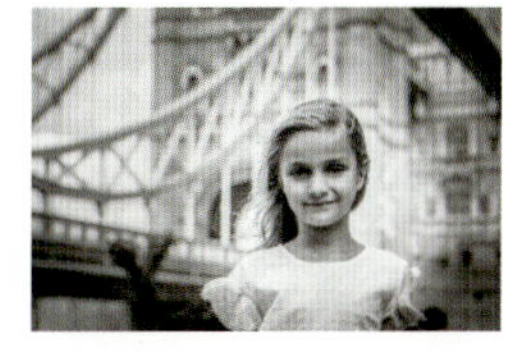
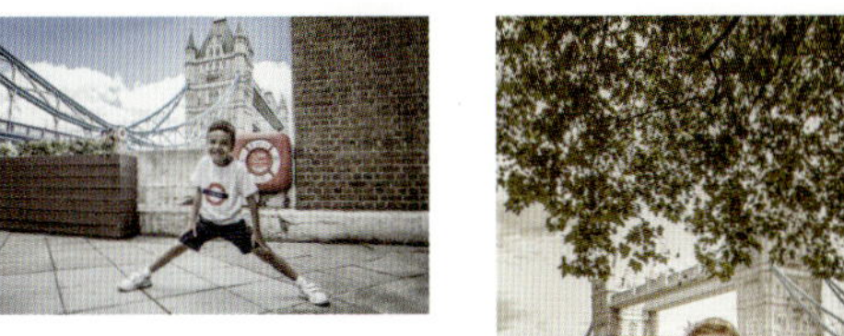
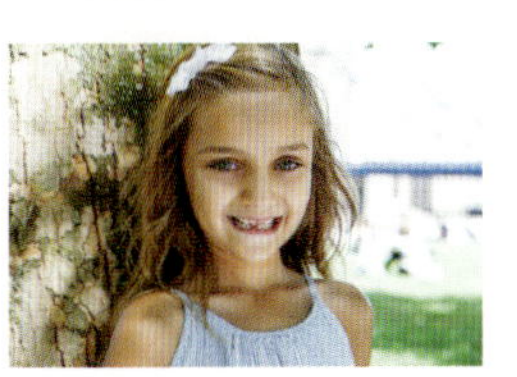
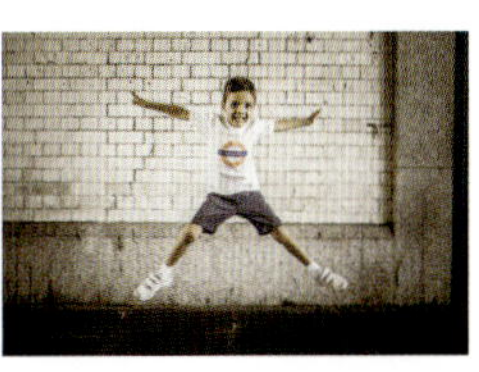
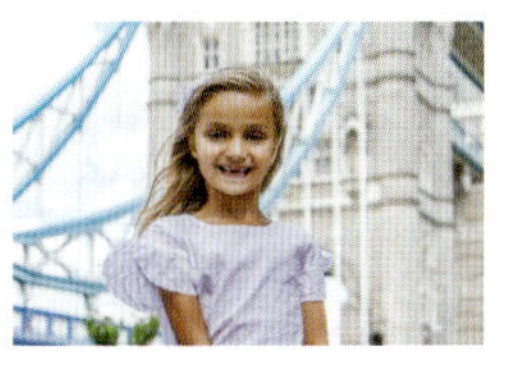
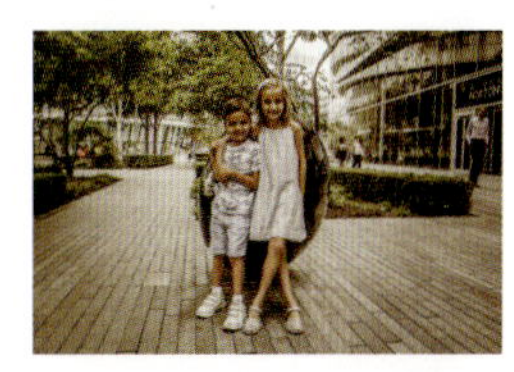
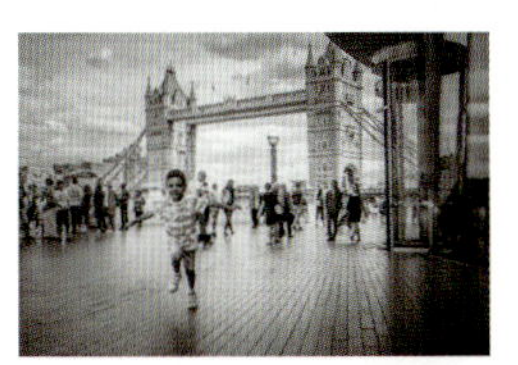
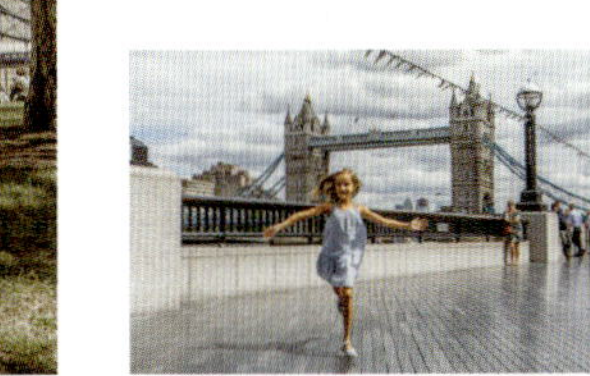
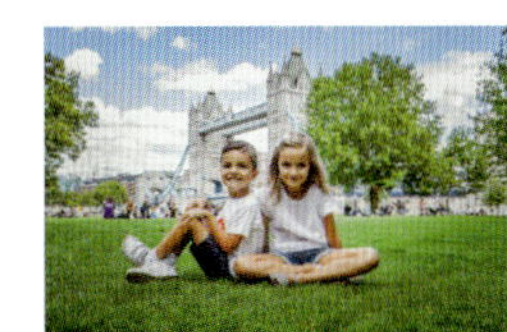
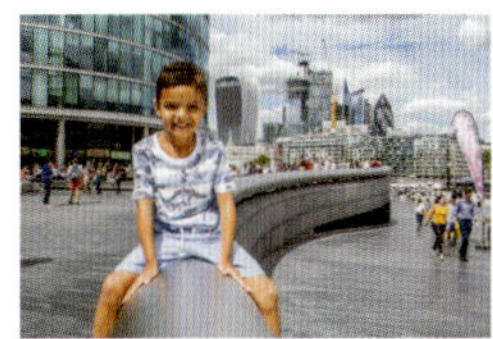
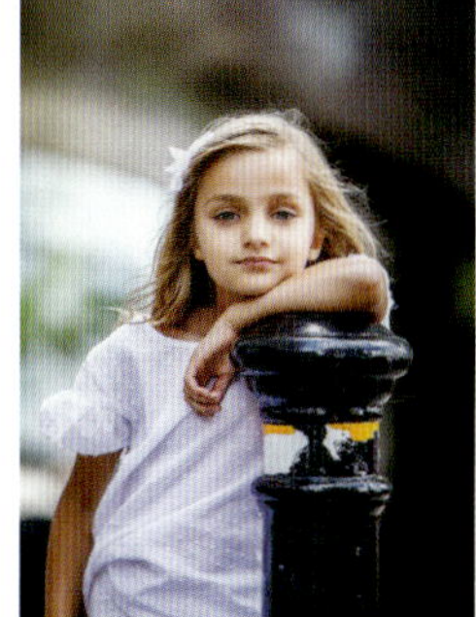
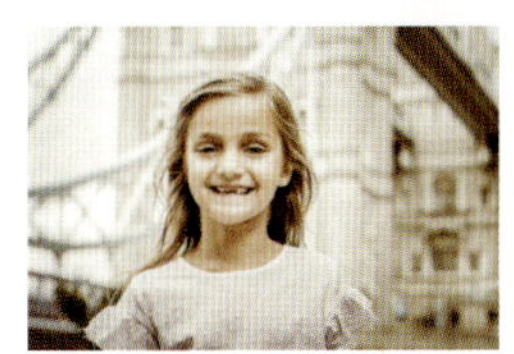
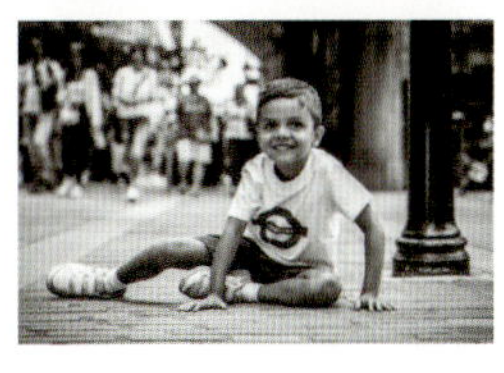
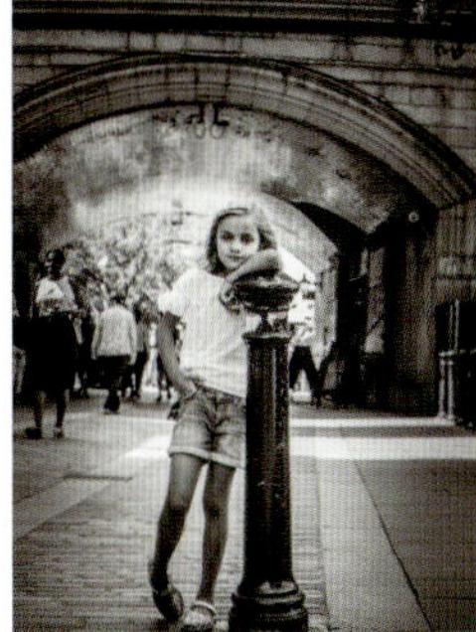
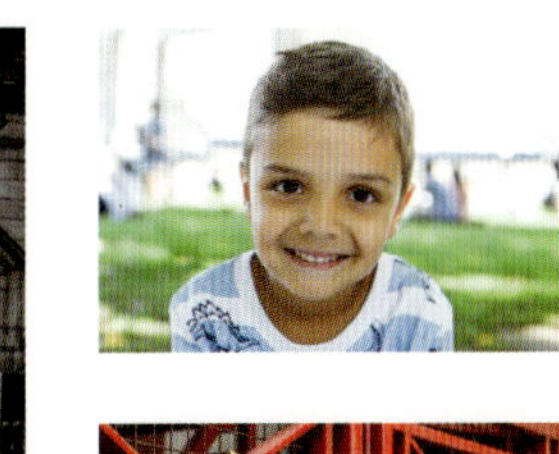
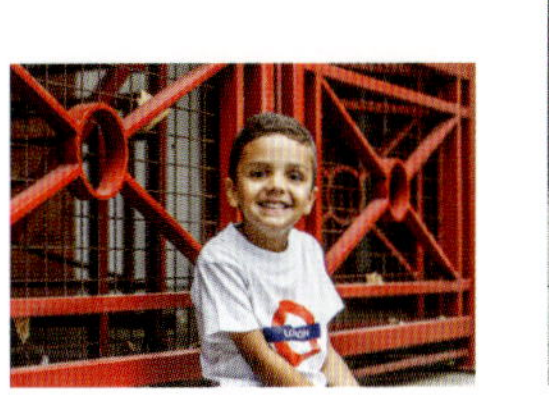
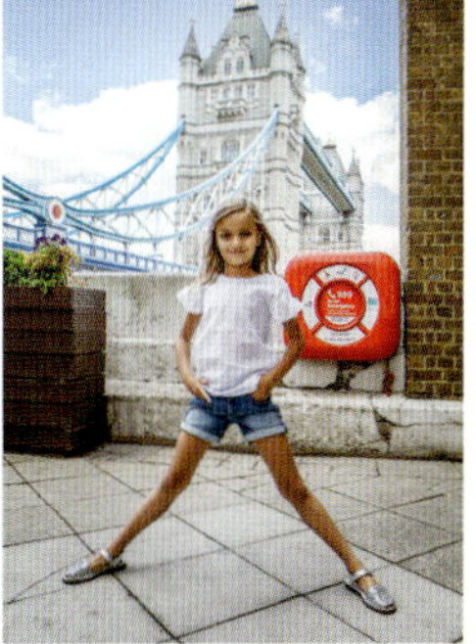
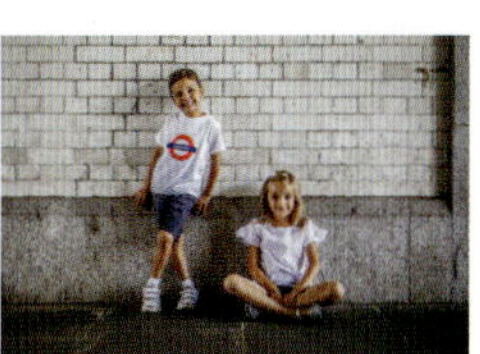
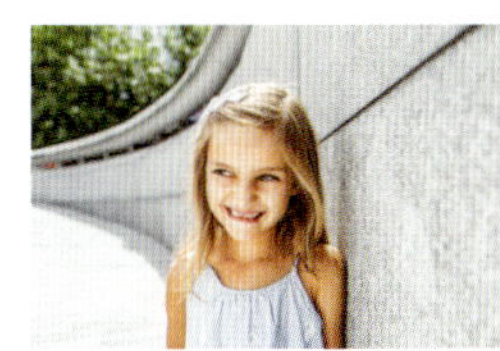

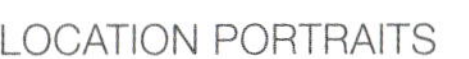

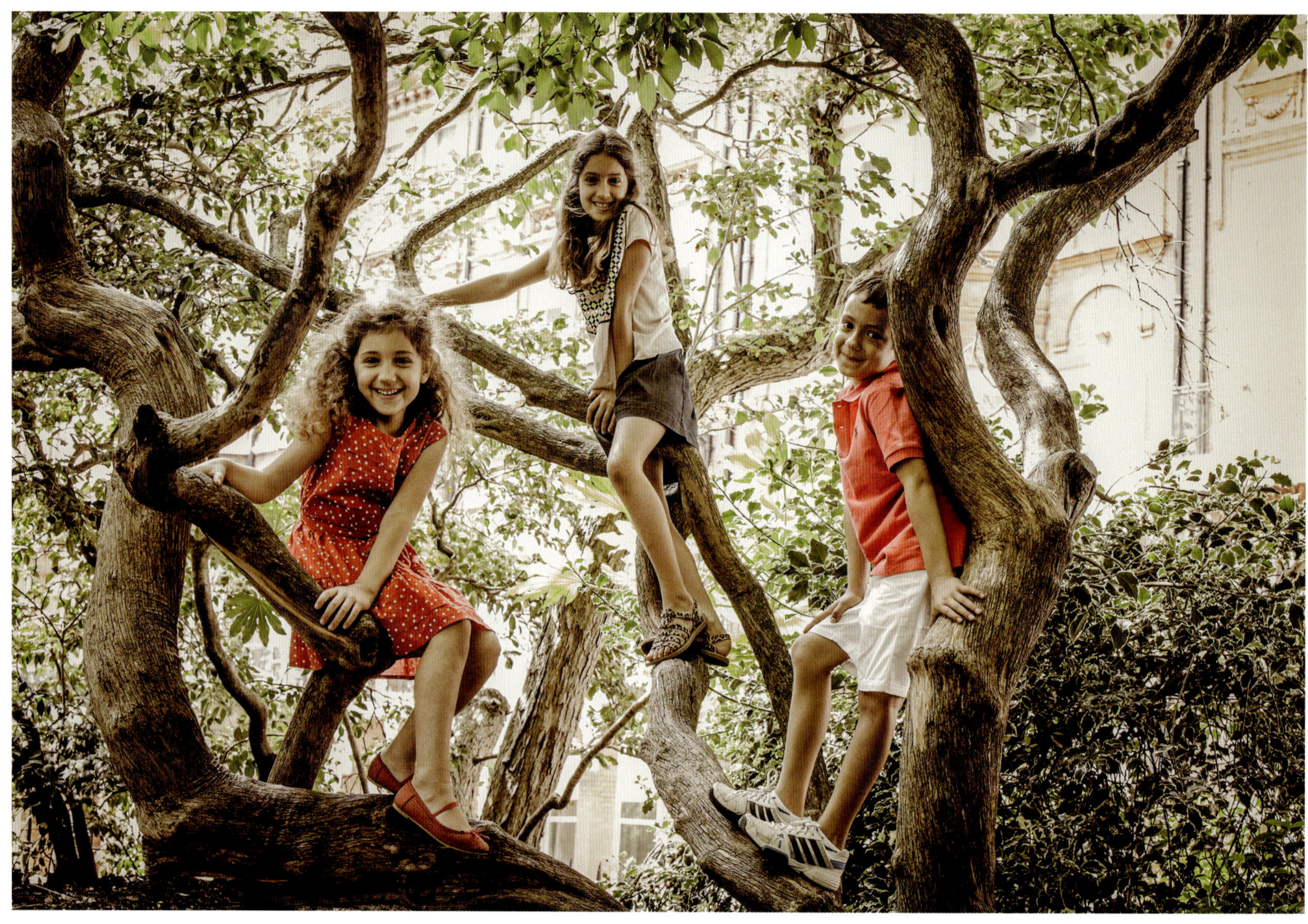

Above: Use your creativity to think of new and interesting
ideas for group shots.

Focal length: 70mm

Aperture: f/9

Shutter speed: 1/40 sec.

ISO: 2000

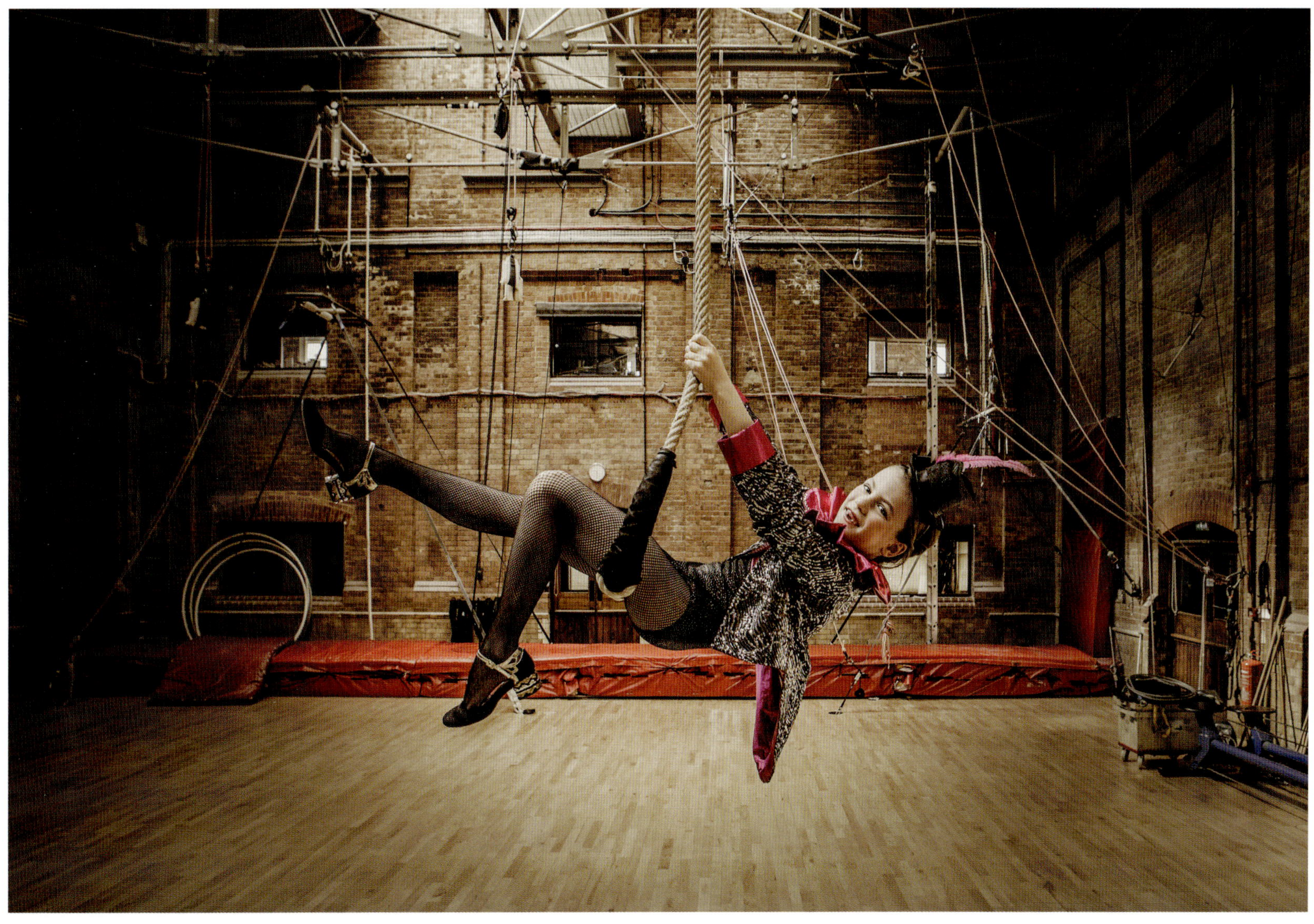

Above: Use every aspect of the environment to enhance
your final image.

Focal length: 24mm

Aperture: f/5

Shutter speed: 1/100 sec.

ISO: 800

Special Locations & Props

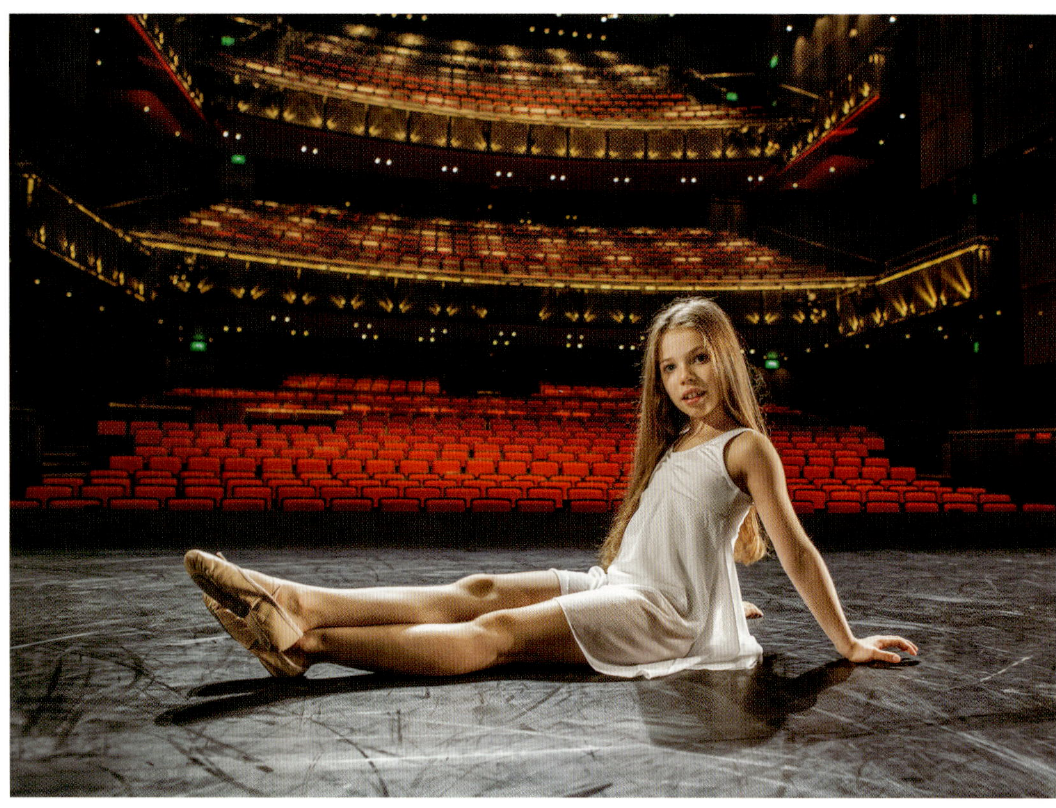

Above: Access to private locations can sometimes be restrictive, but don't be afraid to ask for special permission. Contact the location in advance and be persuasive.

Focal length: 24mm

Aperture: f/3.2

Shutter speed: 1/40 sec.

ISO: 4000

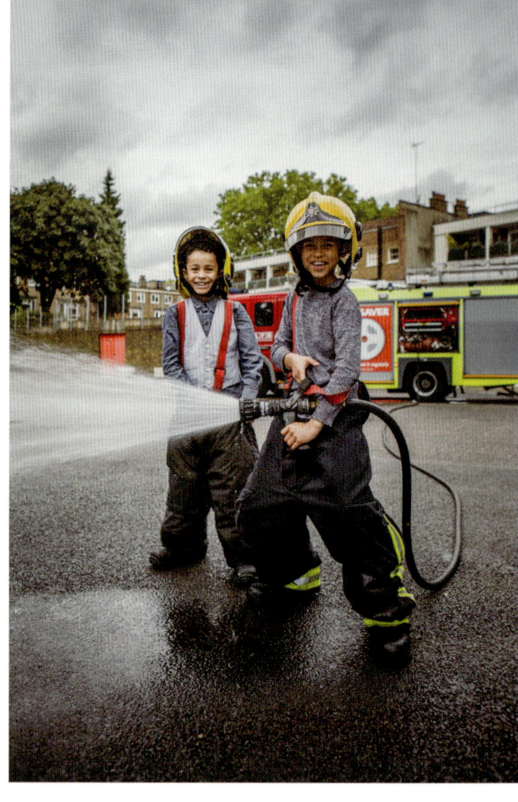

Above: A special location can make a real difference to your portraits.

Focal length: 28mm

Aperture: f/3.2

Shutter speed: 1/640 sec.

ISO: 800

Often, a client will ask if it is possible to shoot at a special or private location: sports grounds, museums, theaters, and historical buildings are all quite common. If this is requested, it is essential that you have all the required permissions and that you are very clear about what you can and can't do at that location. Try to get as much access as you can, but without being too pushy. A permit may be required, so find out in advance and make sure you have all the details to hand of the person you are dealing with on the day.

If approached beforehand, most locations that are open to the public will normally give permission to shoot, as long as they know you are not going to be arriving with a team of professionals and a van full of lighting. They will sometimes require insurance—and may even charge a fee—so discuss any extra costs in advance with your clients to avoid embarrassing situations.

You also need to be aware that copyright laws apply to locations as well as people. If you are intending to use an image to promote your services then you may need a property release form. This is the same as a model release, and needs to be signed by the relevant authority before images featuring the private location can be published. It is generally accepted that personal portraits do not fall under this category, as they will only be displayed in the home, but if you are not sure, check!

It is also worth familiarizing yourself with what is and what isn't a private place. Don't just assume you can take photographs at your local park or

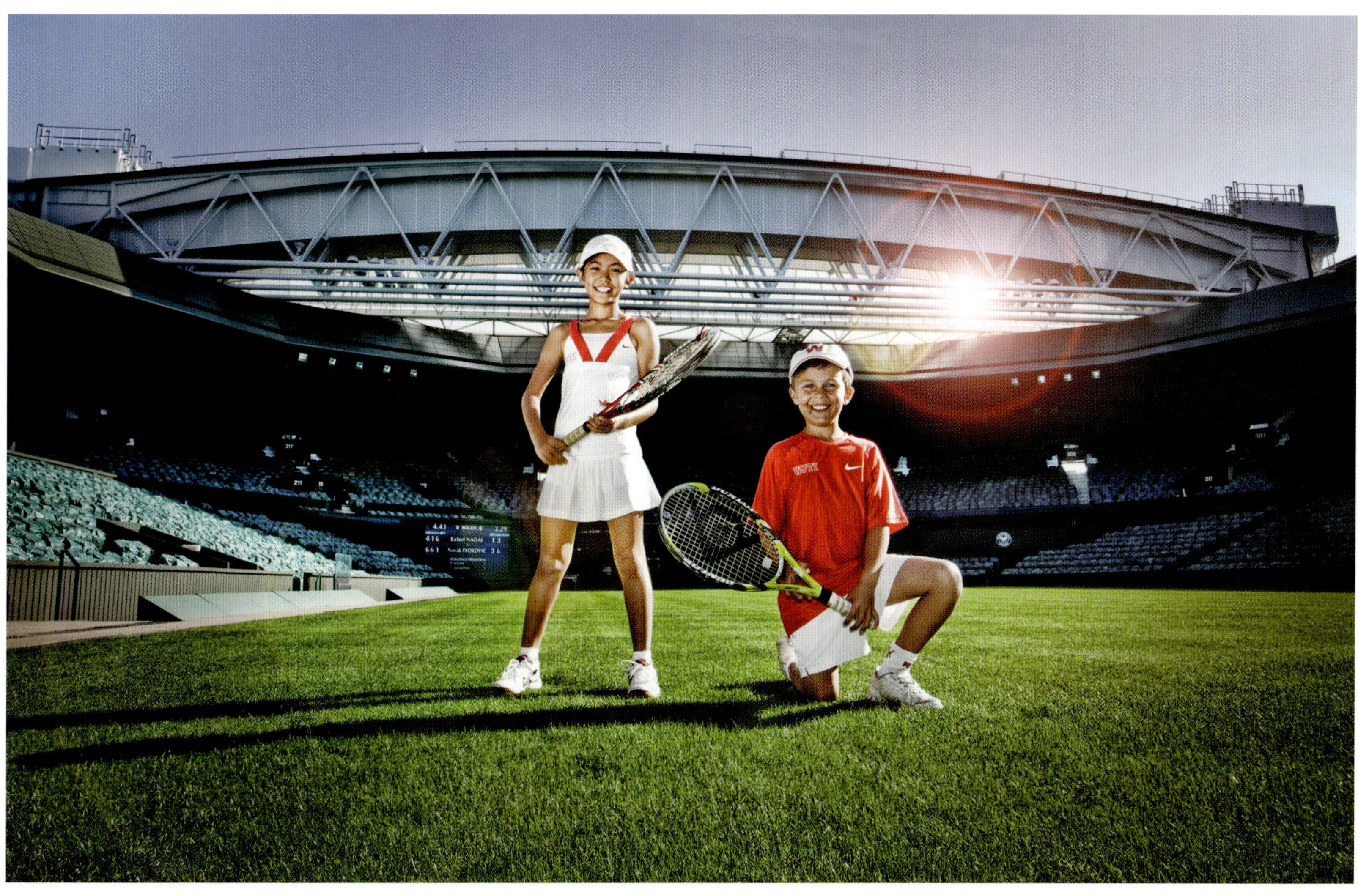

other public space without permission: you may be stopped by a park ranger if you are making it too obvious that your shoot is more than a few family snapshots.

You (and your client) also need to be wary of being so impressed by the special access you have been afforded that you spend too much time enjoying the location. You will probably only have a limited time allotted to you, so make sure you keep a strong hand on the shoot. You need to include elements of the location so the client is getting the most out of it, but don't forget that the location is always just a complementary factor: it is not the subject, the child is!

The same goes for props in a shoot. Props can be a great way to show diversity within a set of images—especially if that child has some special ability that they want to capture. However, make sure that all of the props are suitable and esthetically pleasing, as you don't want to be cornered into including their favorite, horrible plastic toy in every single shot.

Above: World-class sports facilities can be very fussy about access, so check before you step out onto the turf.

Focal length: 23mm

Aperture: f/18

Shutter speed: 1/200 sec.

ISO: 640

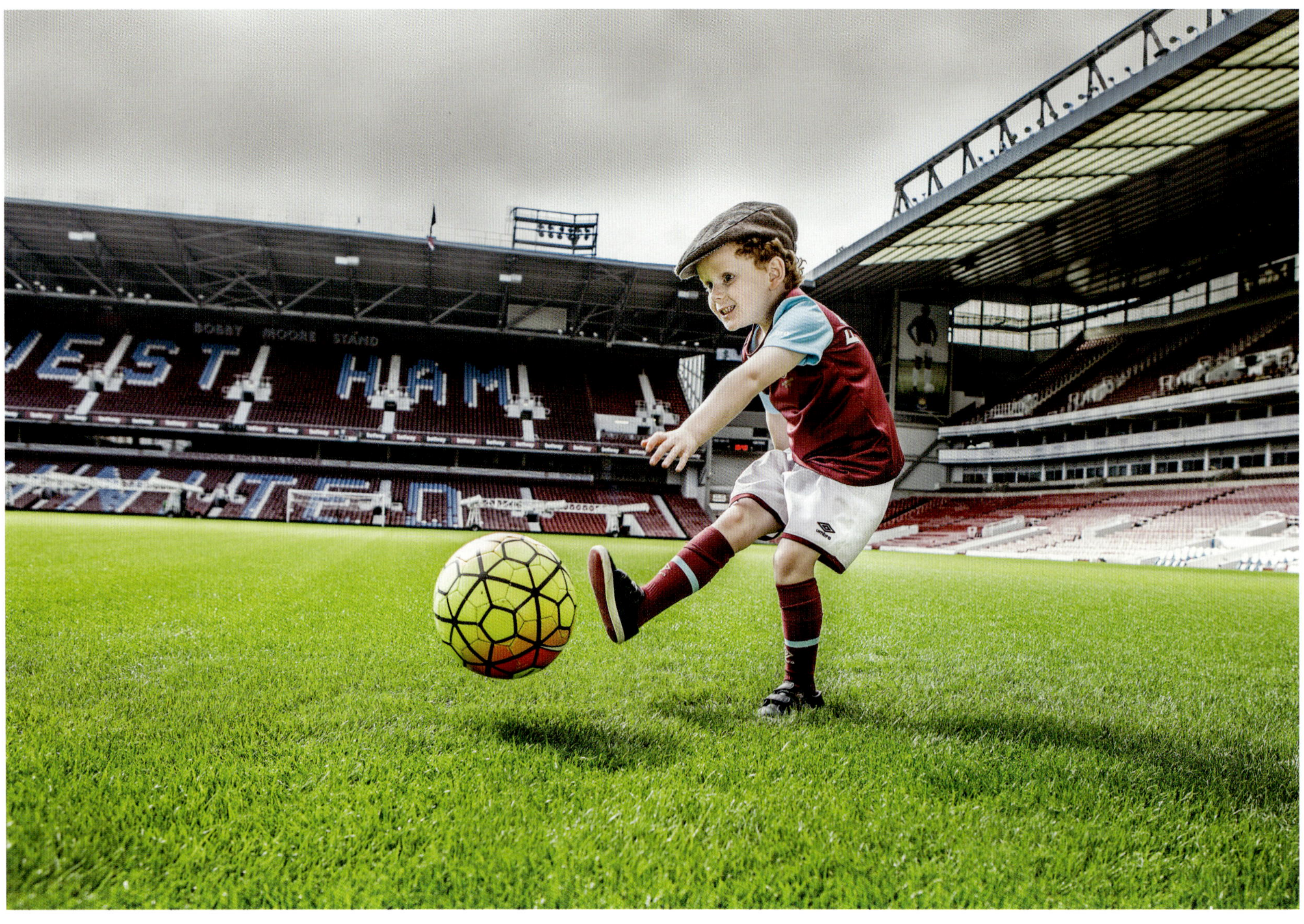

By all means include props that the child feels are important in some of your shots, but don't be a slave to them. If the family brings along their dog, then clearly you will want to include it in some of your shots (and they will probably expect and want you to as well). But don't start to think that it has to be in *every* image. You should be able to read from the child just how important the pet (or the bicycle, or the football, or other item) is to them, but don't let them lead you. At the end of the day, you should always be the one to make the final decisions on a location shoot.

It may sound like a lot to take in and remember, but nothing creates a successful shoot and healthy print sales more than variety. I can assure you that when you look through the images from a shoot you will always wish you had more options. The greater the variety of images you shoot, the more choice you have, and the better your final selection will be, so work the subject.

Above: No matter how impressive the location is, the child should always be the star of the show.

Focal length: 28mm

Aperture: f/5

Shutter speed: 1/1000 sec.

ISO: 800

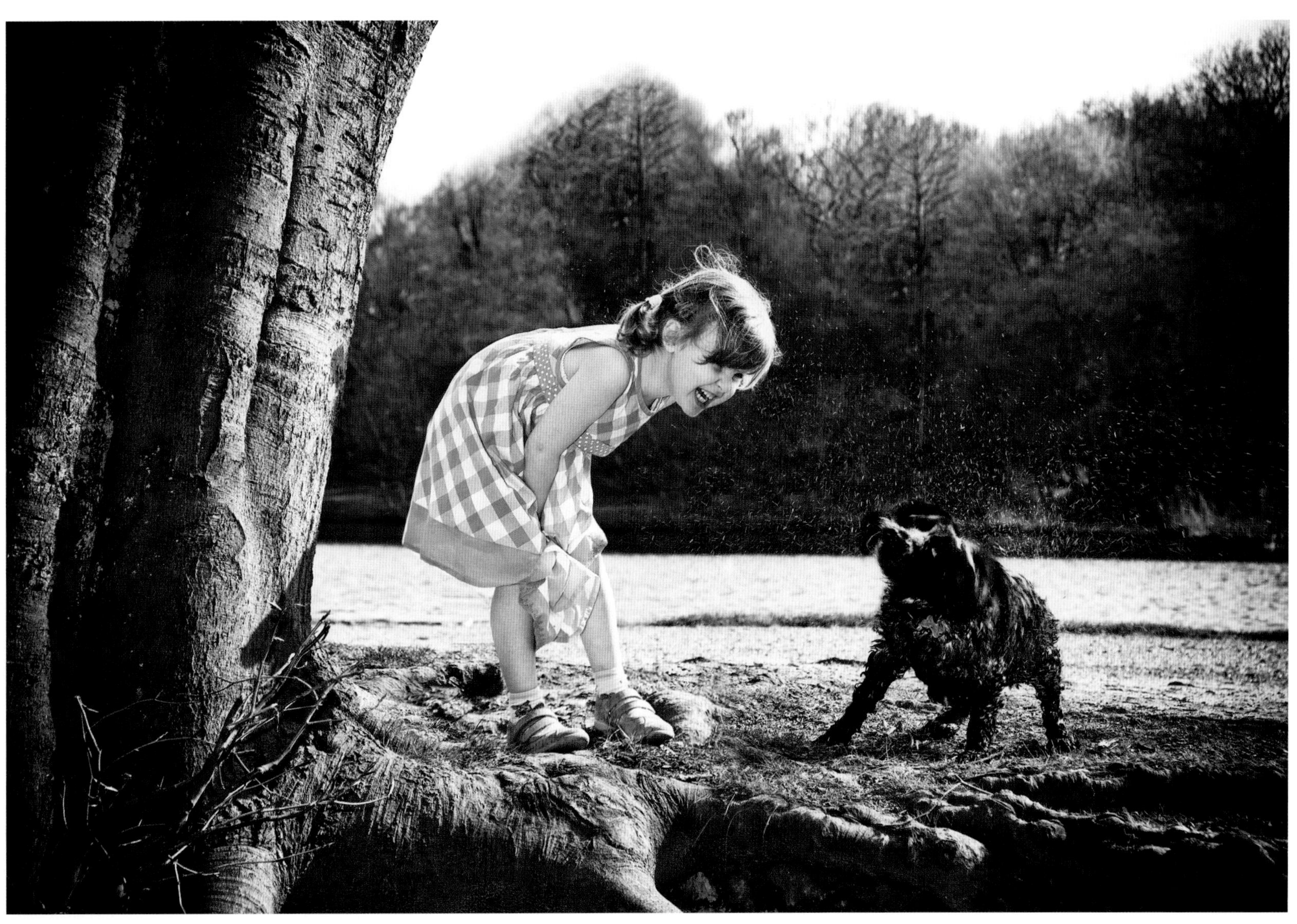

Above: Using family pets in a shoot is a great way to make the day very special for everyone involved.

Focal length: 70mm

Aperture: f/7.1

Shutter speed: 1/200 sec.

ISO: 200

Chapter 5

Lighting On Location

If the environment you choose to shoot in is your canvas, then light and lighting is your palette of paints. If you want to extract the very best from your child portrait session you need to master every aspect of lighting and understand its strengths and nuances. Few elements will affect the quality of your photography in the same way as the lighting, and it is often the one thing that defines you as a unique photographer. As you will see in this chapter, there are four aspects of light that concern photographers, and they apply both indoors and out, on location or in a studio. These aspects are: quality, strength, color temperature, and direction.

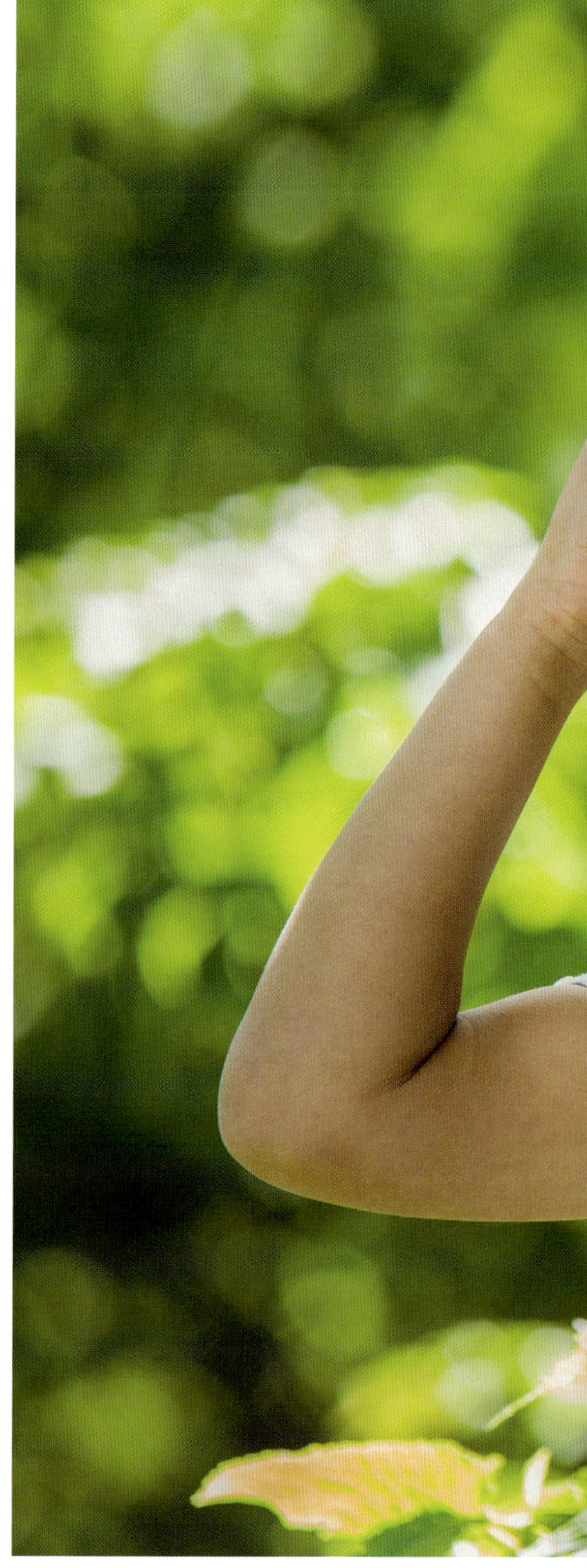

Right: You can have the best model, the best camera, and the perfect location, but unless you master the art of lighting it will all come to nothing. Lighting is at the heart of every great portrait.

Focal length: 200mm

Aperture: f/5

Shutter speed: 1/640 sec.

ISO: 800

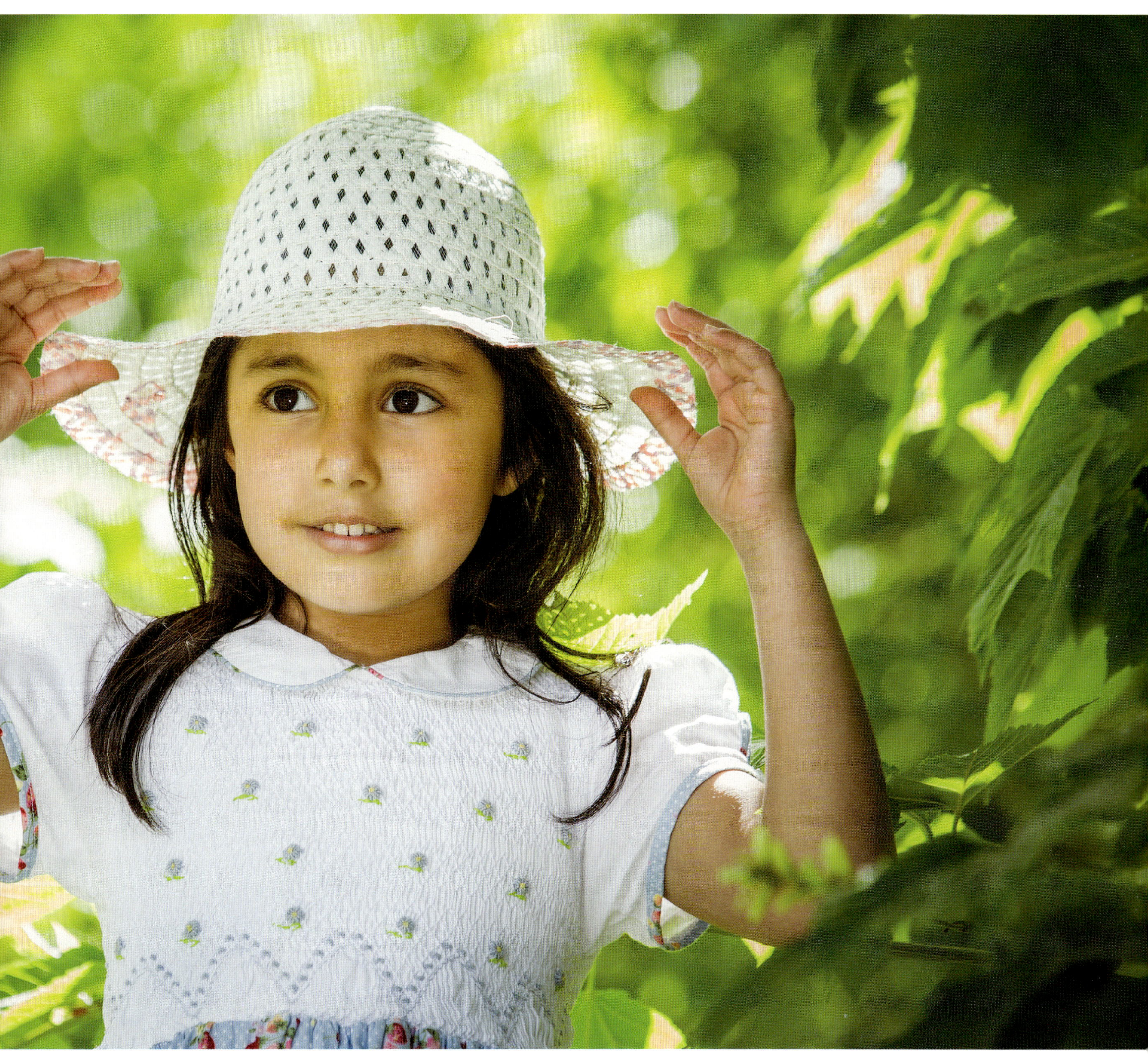

Quality & Strength

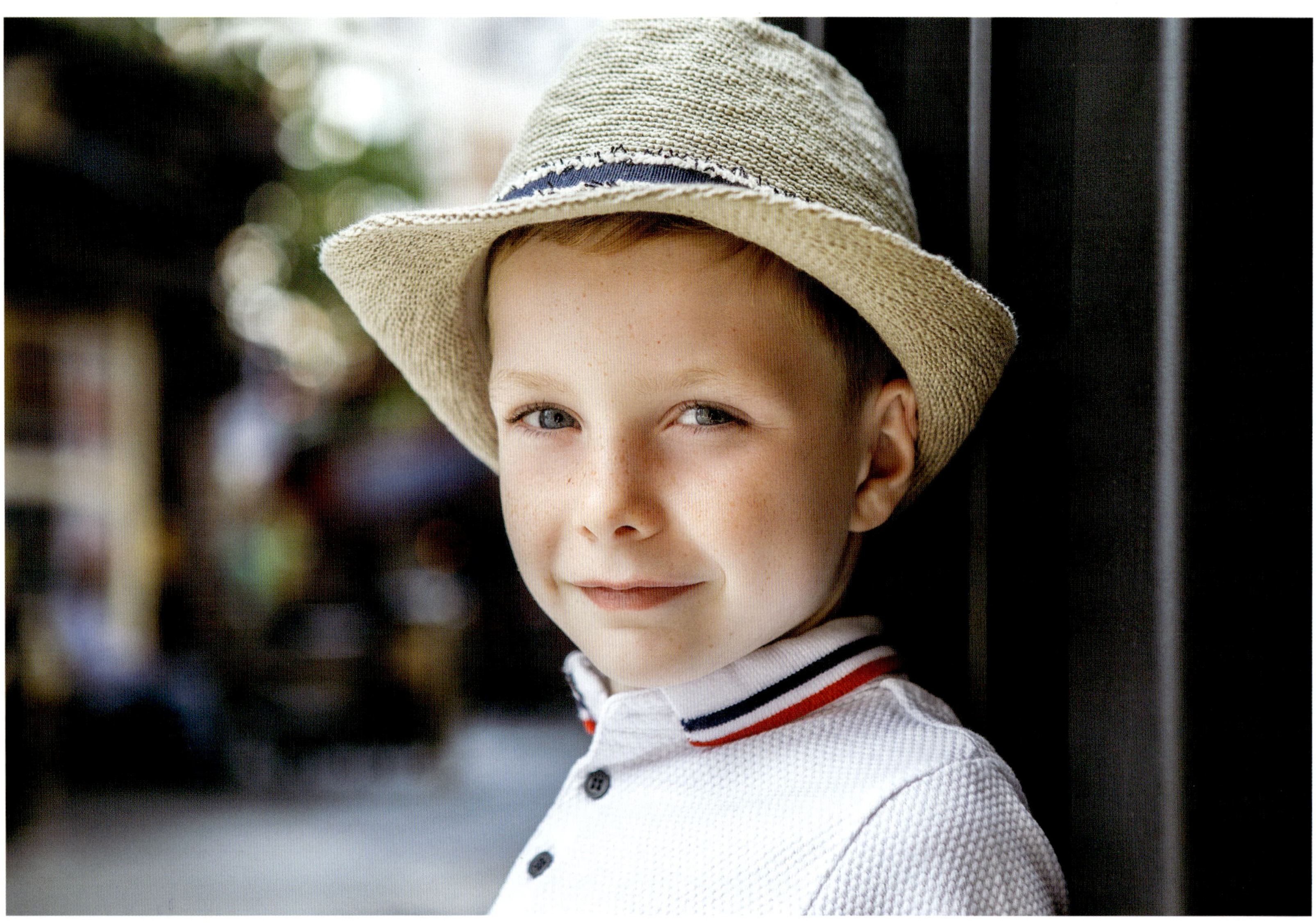

Understanding the "strength" of a given light source is simple: it is determined by the power of the light's output in relation to its distance from the subject. The "quality" of light is a little harder to define, as it is measured on a less tangible scale from "hard" to "soft."

I have grouped these two aspects together because they are connected by size and distance. The farther away a light source is, and the smaller

it is in relation to the subject, the "harder" or more "direct" the light will be. Conversely, "soft" light sources are created when a large light source is very near to the subject in relation to its size.

The popular misconception is that placing some sort of diffuser between the light and the subject, such as a softbox over a flash, automatically creates a soft light source. This does work, but only if the light source is close to the subject and

Above: Controlling both the strength and the quality of the light is the key to a well-balanced image.

Focal length: 70mm

Aperture: f/3.5

Shutter speed: 1/500 sec.

ISO: 800

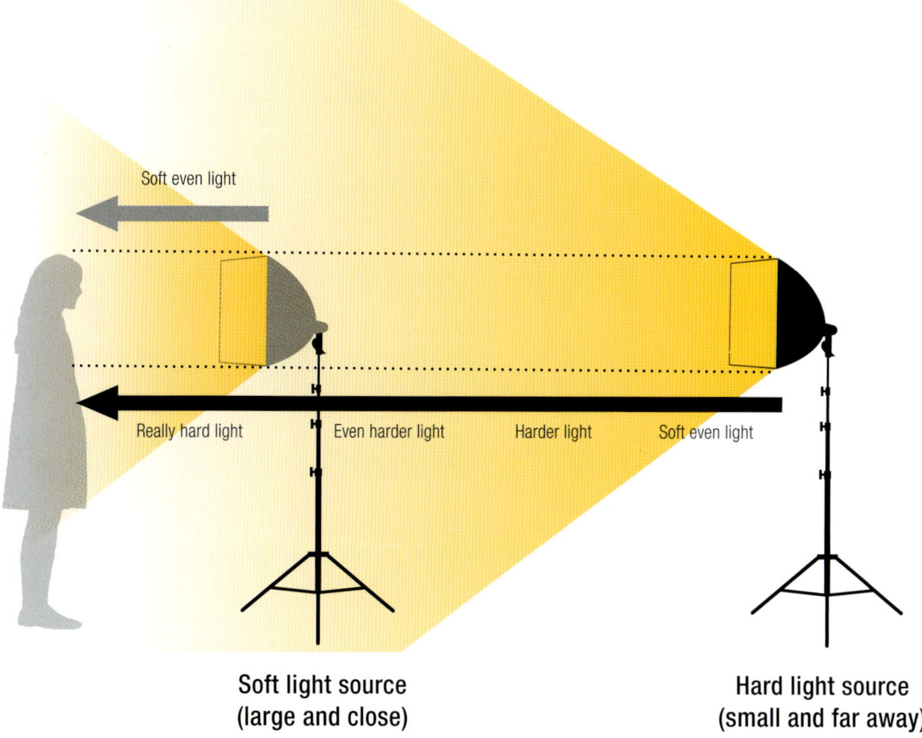

Above: The same light source can produce hard or soft light, depending on its size and distance from the subject.

the subject is smaller than the soft box: if you stand the same softbox 60ft (20m) away from your subject it will be a hard light source.

If you're shooting outdoors, the sun is your main light source. Because it is so far away it appears small, so on a clear day it is a hard light. However, cloud will diffuse the sunlight, so on an overcast day you will get soft light, while a hazy day gives you light that is somewhere in between.

COLOR TEMPERATURE

We have already looked at how different situations will have different color temperatures. When working outdoors this will normally be around 5500K, and most of the time you can set your camera to auto white balance and let it do its thing. The problem comes when you have a cloudy or misty day, or there is street lighting in the shot, or you are working indoors in a lit barn or warehouse. Your camera's auto WB should generally give you a pretty good idea of the correct setting, but remember to keep checking your results as you shoot: mixed lighting can be a challenge at times and it is much easier to fix any problems in-camera, rather than trying to correct them in postproduction.

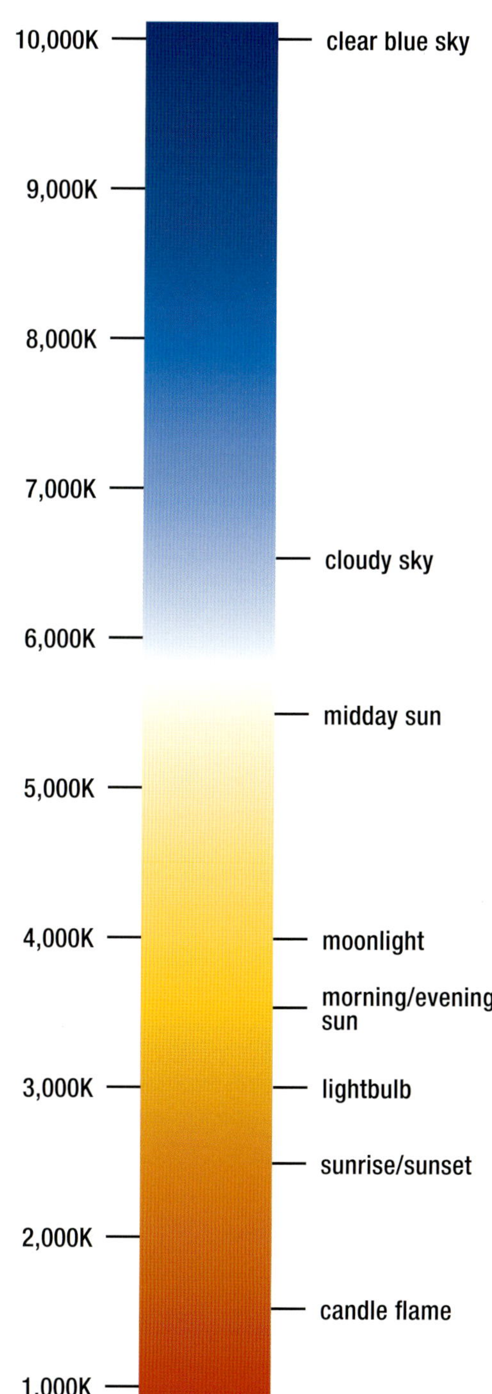

The Direction Of Light

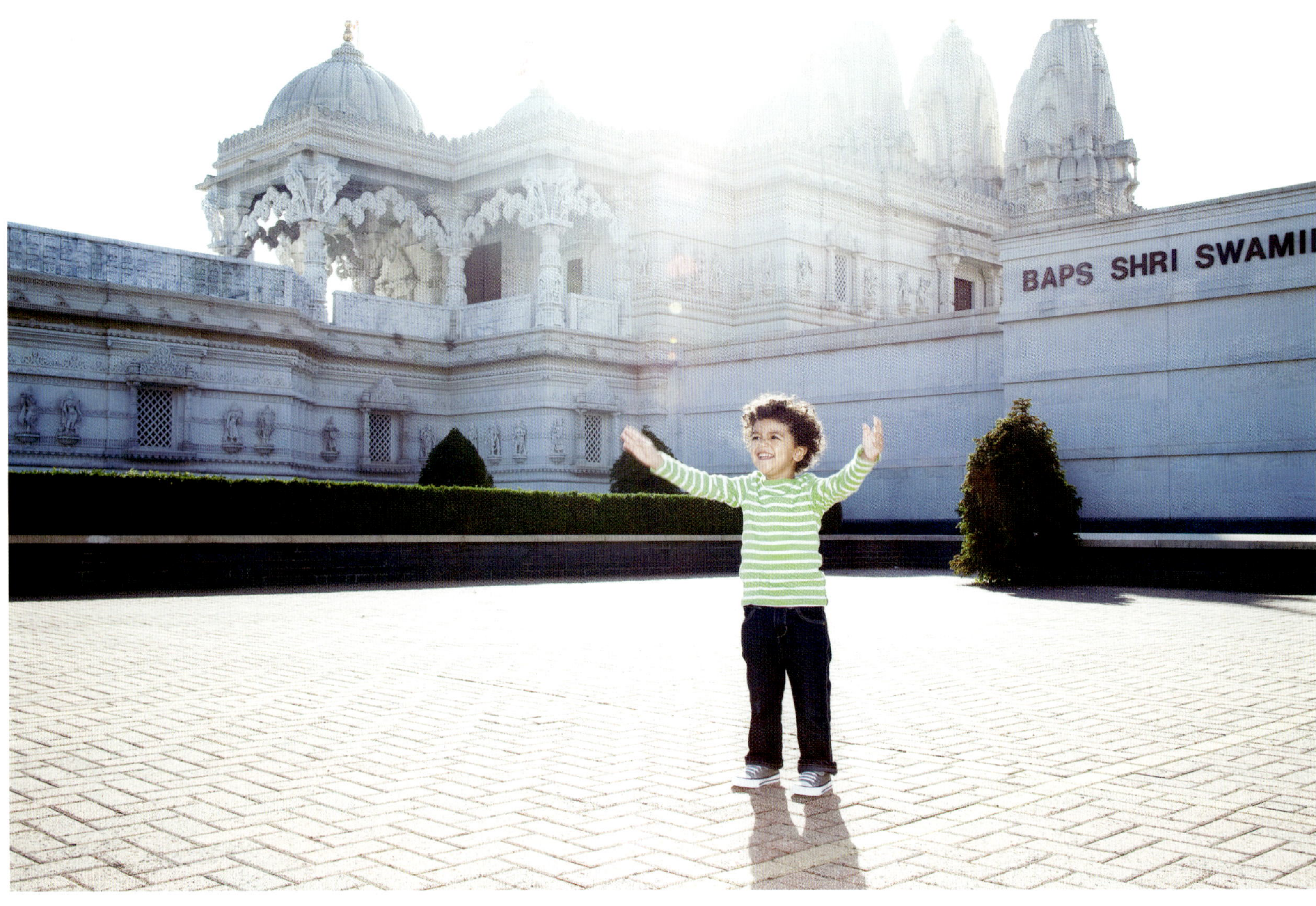

The direction the light comes from has a huge part to play in the look of your images, and there are four basic directions to be aware of.

Backlight

"Light from behind" is one of my basic rules (see page 60), because it creates a beautiful, romantic, and often dramatic look. But there are a couple of points to be clear about when it comes to your lighting options.

For a start, using backlight does not mean that every setup has to have the main light directly behind the subject's head. Backlight can come from the side or from above; providing the light source is positioned behind the line of the subject then you will get different levels of rim-lighting.

The farther the light source is behind the subject, the more dramatic the effect will be.

Above: Extreme backlighting is dramatic, but needs to be handled carefully to avoid unwanted flare.

Focal length: 38mm

Aperture: f/13

Shutter speed: 1/200 sec.

ISO: 400

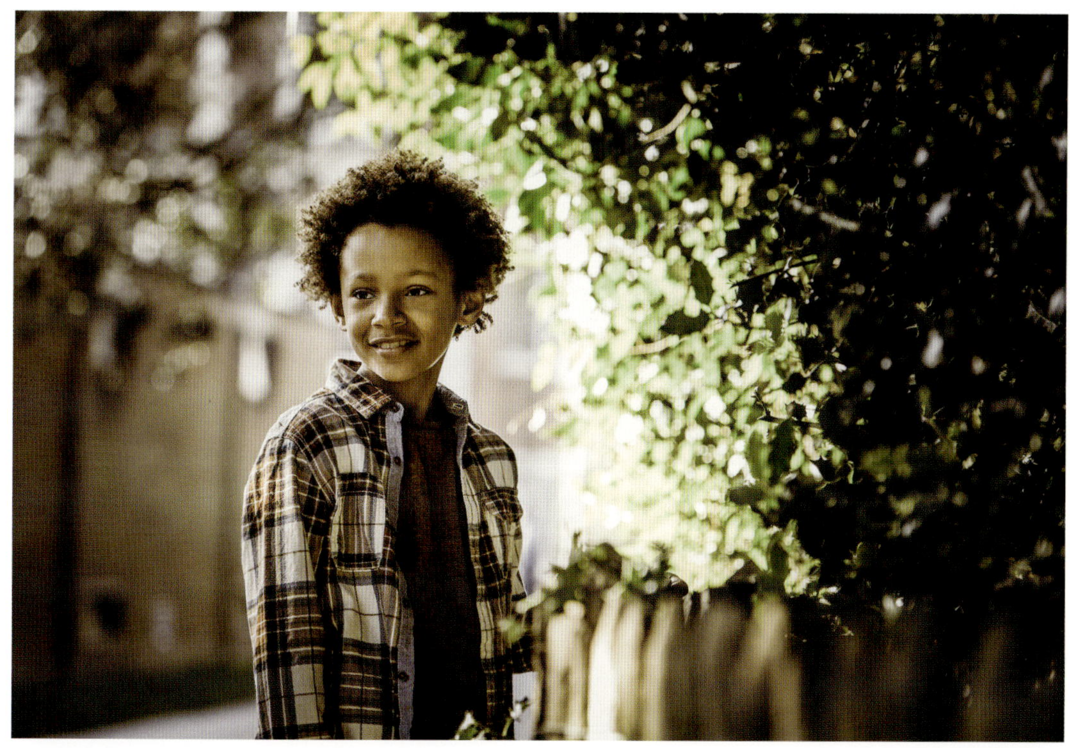

Left: A backlight does not need to be hard light. Shoot into pools of soft, reflected light for a gentle, naturalistic look.
Focal length: 115mm
Aperture: f/3.5
Shutter speed: 1/160 sec.
ISO: 500

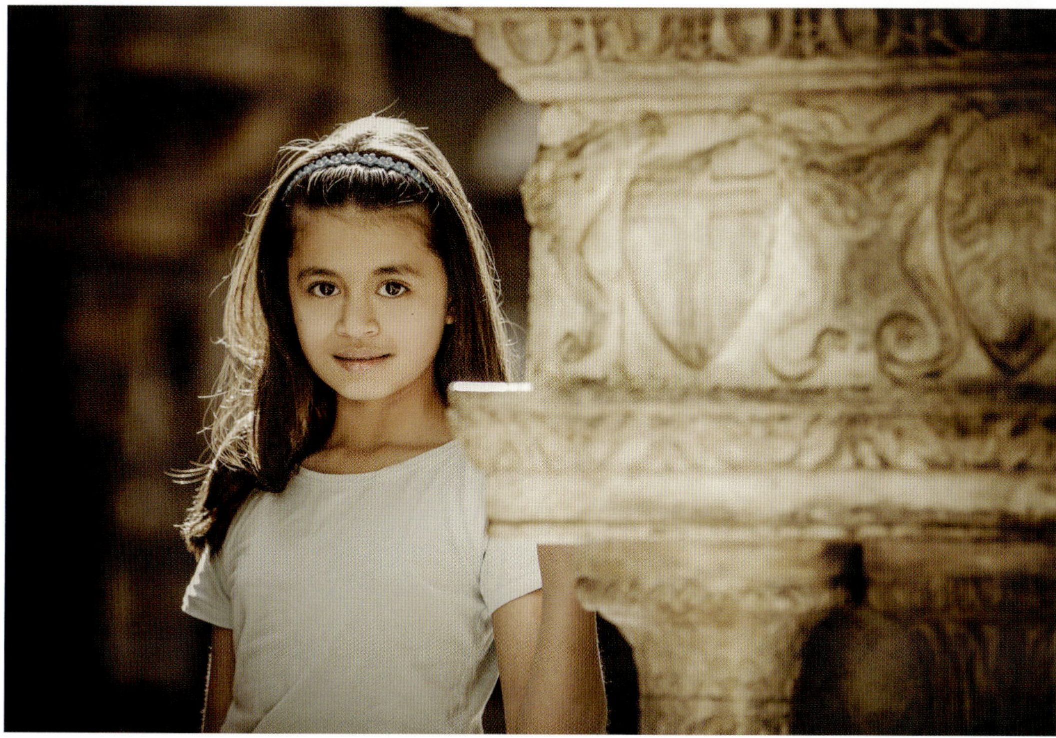

Left: Position your backlighting to create a beautiful rim-light around your subject.
Focal length: 130mm
Aperture: f/2.8
Shutter speed: 1/160 sec.
ISO: 800

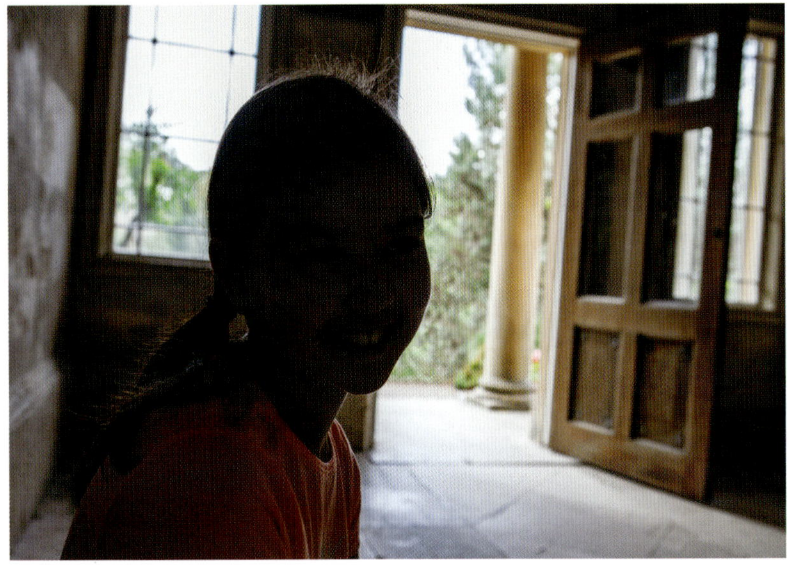

Above: With the camera set to Shutter Priority the subject appears dark against a light background.

Focal length: 34mm

Aperture: f/5.6

Shutter speed: 1/60 sec.

ISO: 500

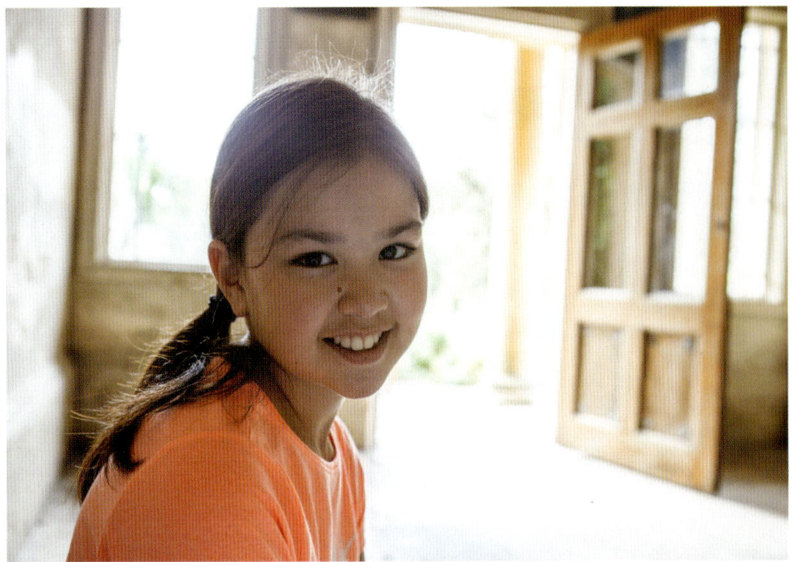

Above: Using +1 stop of exposure compensation lifts the subject and makes them appear correctly exposed.

Focal length: 34mm

Aperture: f/4

Shutter speed: 1/60 sec.

ISO: 500

Filling In The Shadows

If you place the sun directly behind the subject's head on a clear day (so their head "blocks" the sun) it is possible to create a rim-light that encircles the subject. This can be almost surreal in its appearance, and can sometimes be a little too much, but try it and see for yourself. As the angle between the light source and the camera narrows, the backlit effect is reduced, but only you can decide what works best for your shots. I recommend trying all options with every shoot so you get lots of variety in your final collection.

When you are using a strong backlight you need to be aware of flare. If the light source appears in shot, or is close to the edge of the frame, it can create blobs or streaks of unwanted reflections in the lens. Using a lens hood is a good starting point, but in extreme situations lens flare can be very difficult to deal with. One solution is to look for a shaded position that you can shoot from, such as beneath the branches of a tree, and then photograph toward the area of sunshine where your model is positioned. That way you can get all the advantages of beautiful backlight, but none of the problems of lens flare.

The next thing to understand about backlighting your subject is that their face or body will be in shadow, and most cameras will be "fooled" by the backlight into underexposing further. When shooting in any of the "auto" modes (Aperture Priority, Shutter Priority, or Program), setting the exposure compensation to +1 or +2 stops (or higher) can help, as this will adjust the overall exposure so that the face is correctly exposed and the rest of the scene will be slightly overexposed.

Although opening up the exposure can give a dreamy, brightness to your image, it also loses all of the detail and richness in the background. If you don't want this to happen you need to "fill in" the shadow areas, so you are balancing the exposure for the foreground and background. This is where your bounce reflector or your flash will help.

On-camera flash can be a fairly blunt tool, so be careful and use it on low power to "fill in" rather than blast your subject with light. However, used subtly, a flash can produce some great results. Simply set it to TTL (Through The Lens) control if you are in changing light and play around with the relative power: you usually need less than you think to add a twinkle in the eye and clean up the dark shadows.

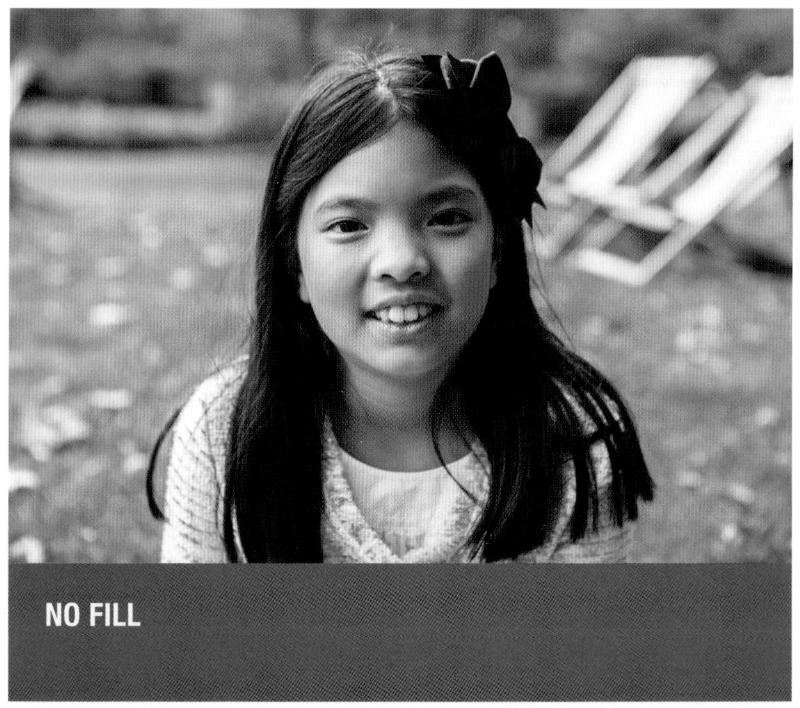

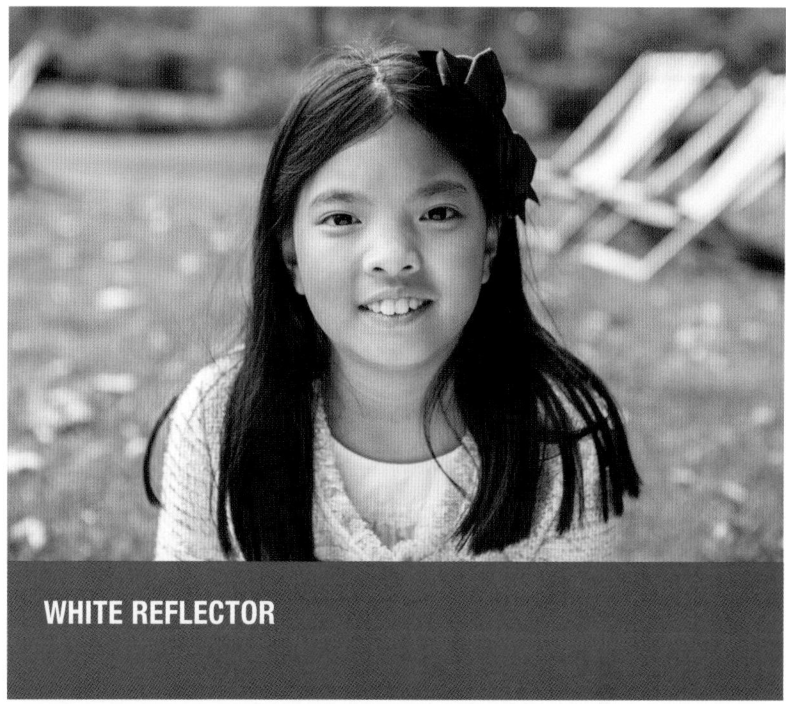

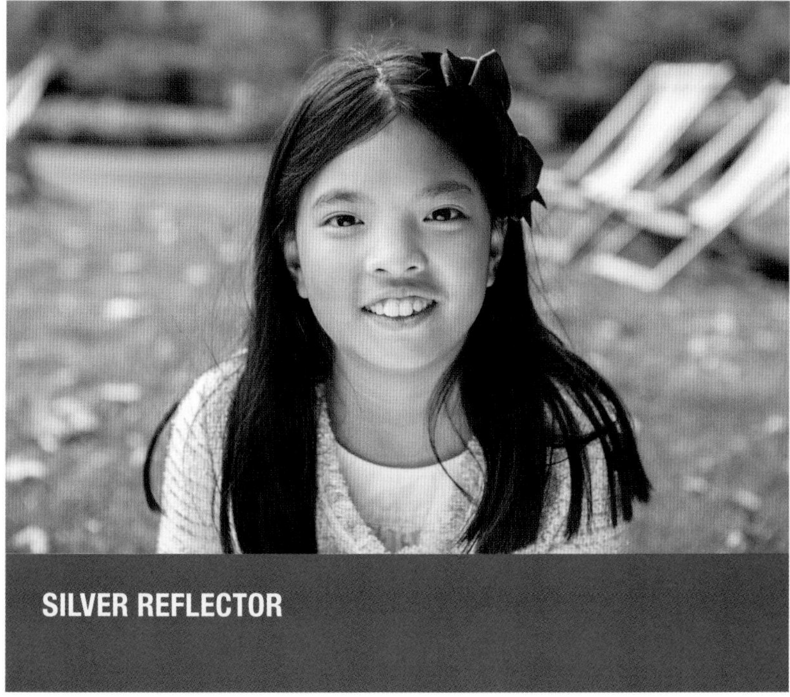

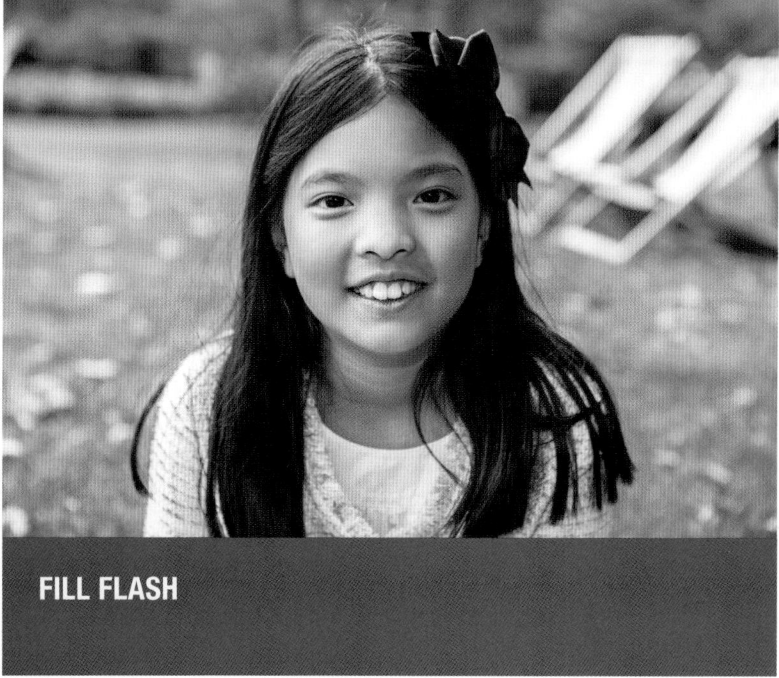

Above: These four shots show the impact that a reflector or flash has when it comes to "filling in" the shadows caused by backlighting your subject. Note the subtle difference between a "hard" silver reflector and a "softer" white reflector.

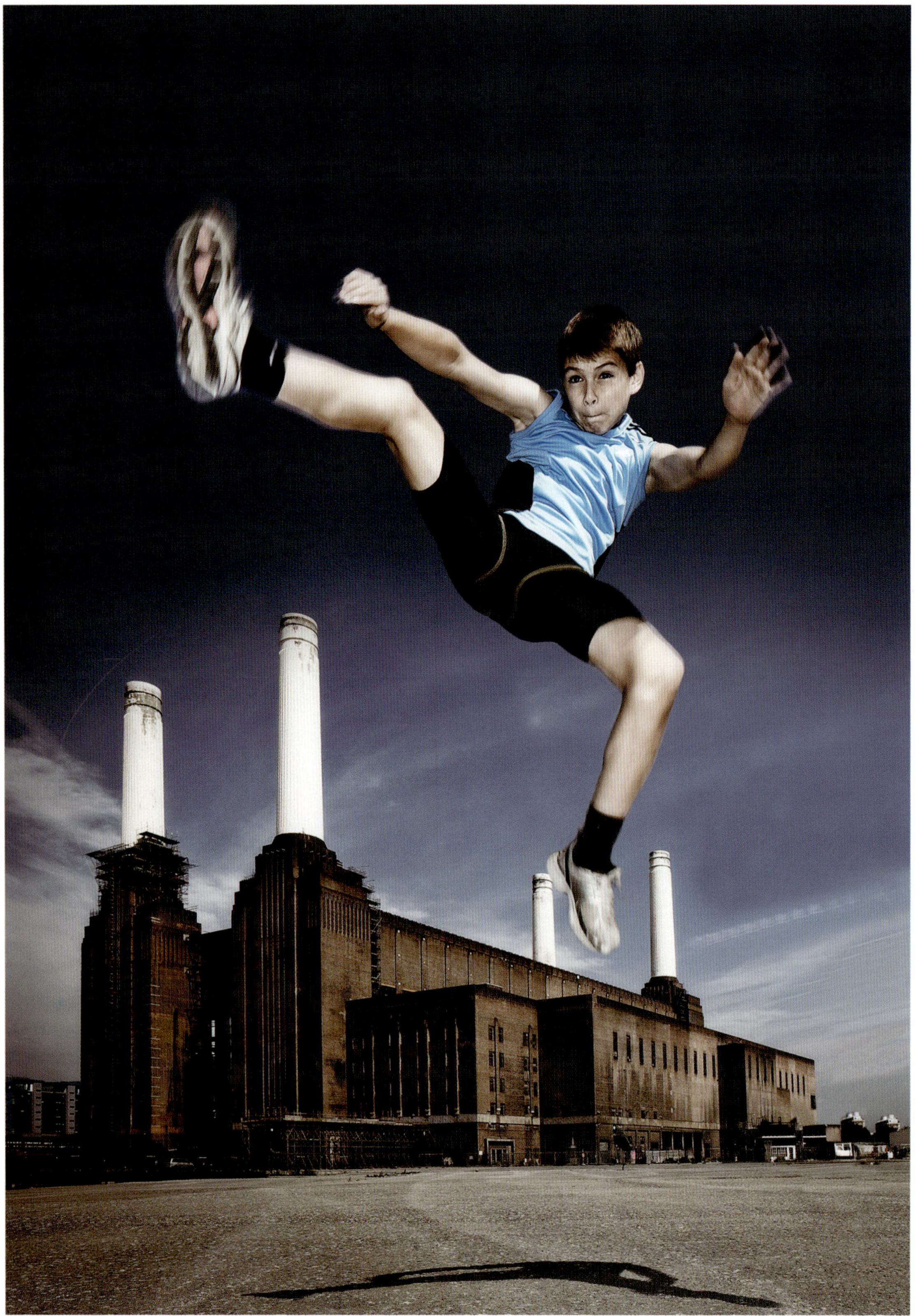

Left: Using flash with a moving subject can create some interesting ghosting effects.

Focal length: 27mm

Aperture: f/13

Shutter speed: 1/200 sec.

ISO: 100

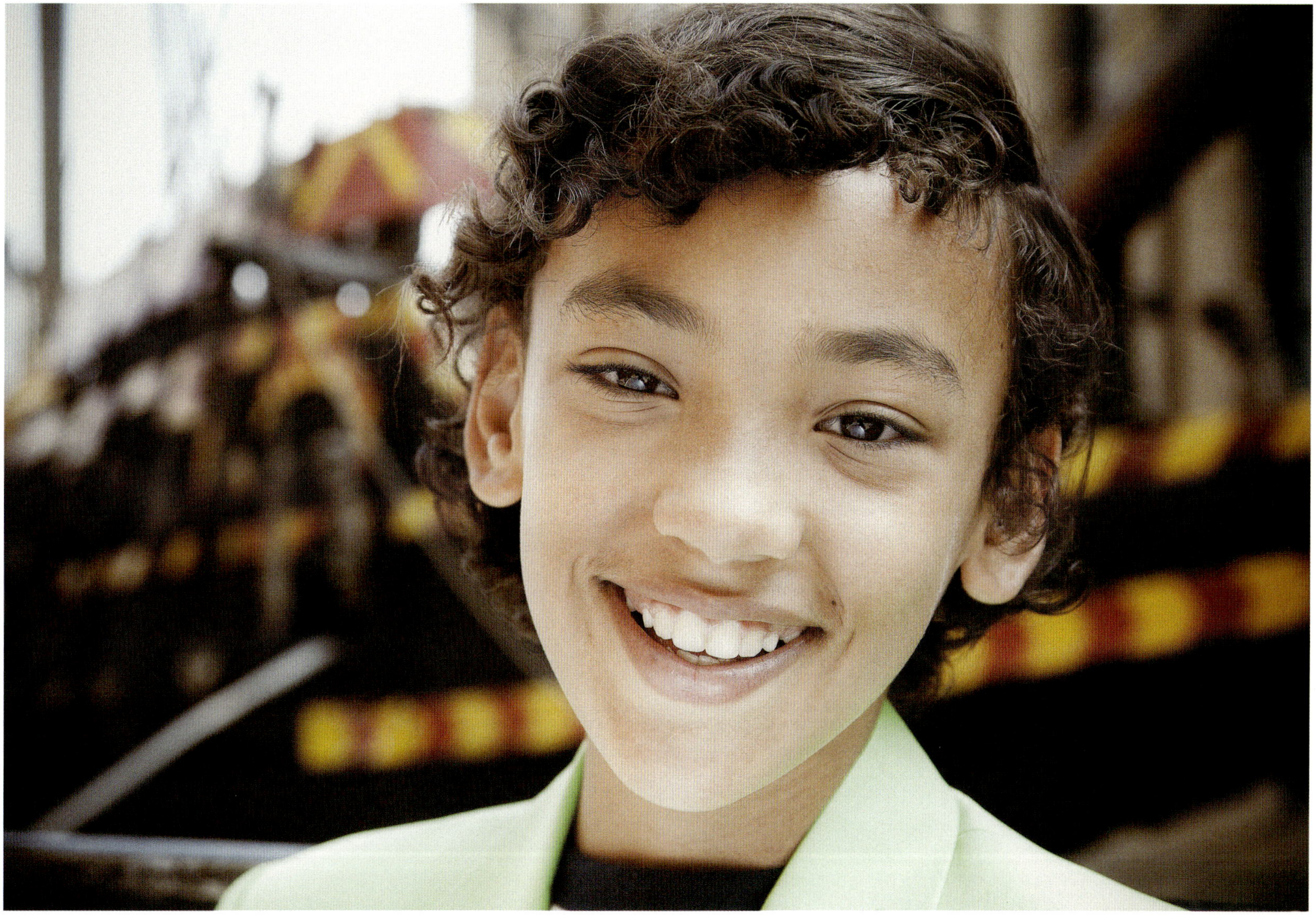

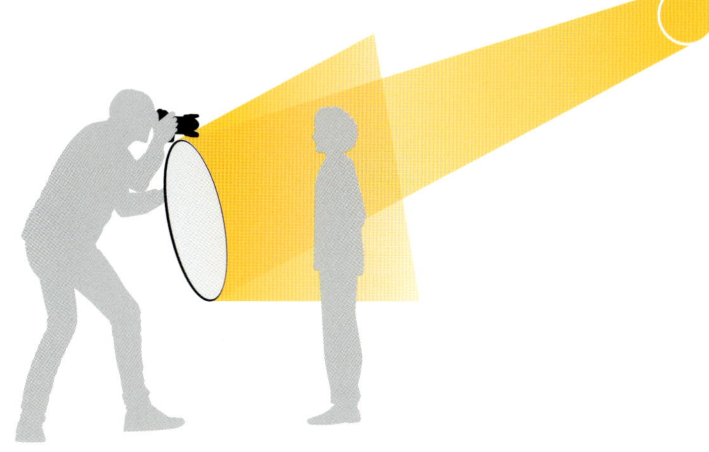

Above: A handheld reflector not only fills in the shadow areas, but also adds a desirable reflection in the eyes.

Focal length: 73mm

Aperture: f/7.1

Shutter speed: 1/200 sec.

ISO: 640

Right: Hold the reflector at an angle to the sun so the light bounces back onto your subject's face.

Sidelight

Positioning the subject so the light comes more distinctly from the side can create a very pleasing effect. This sidelight can come from low down or high up, and can be hard or soft, all of which give a very different feel. In either case, look out for unsightly shadows created by the nose across the face and be aware that cross light will highlight the texture in an image; it is not suitable for spotty teenagers or kids with bad skin.

To control the shadows on the face, this is another occasion where you can involve the parent in the shoot. Position them with a reflector on the shadow side of the child, and have them bounce some light back into the shadows. Another option is to position the child next to a white or brightly colored wall and allow that to naturally bounce light onto them.

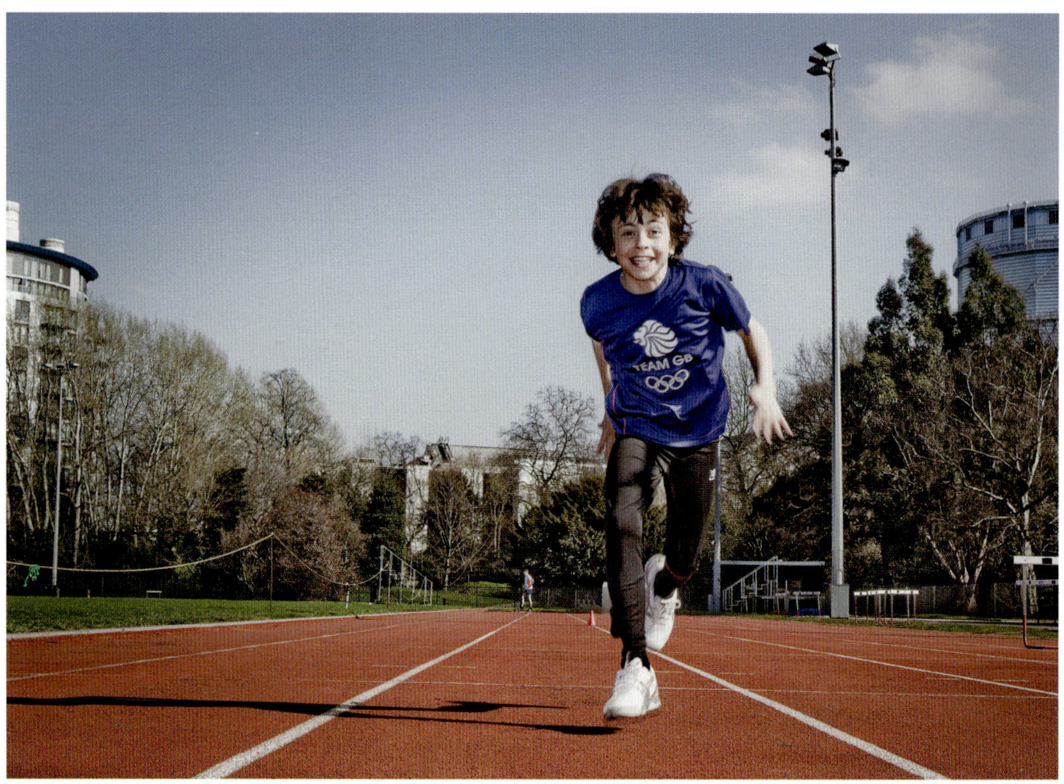

Above: Get the child's parent to hold a reflector off-camera to bounce light and lift the shadows caused by sidelighting.

Focal length: 51mm

Aperture: f/14

Shutter speed: 1/200 sec.

ISO: 400

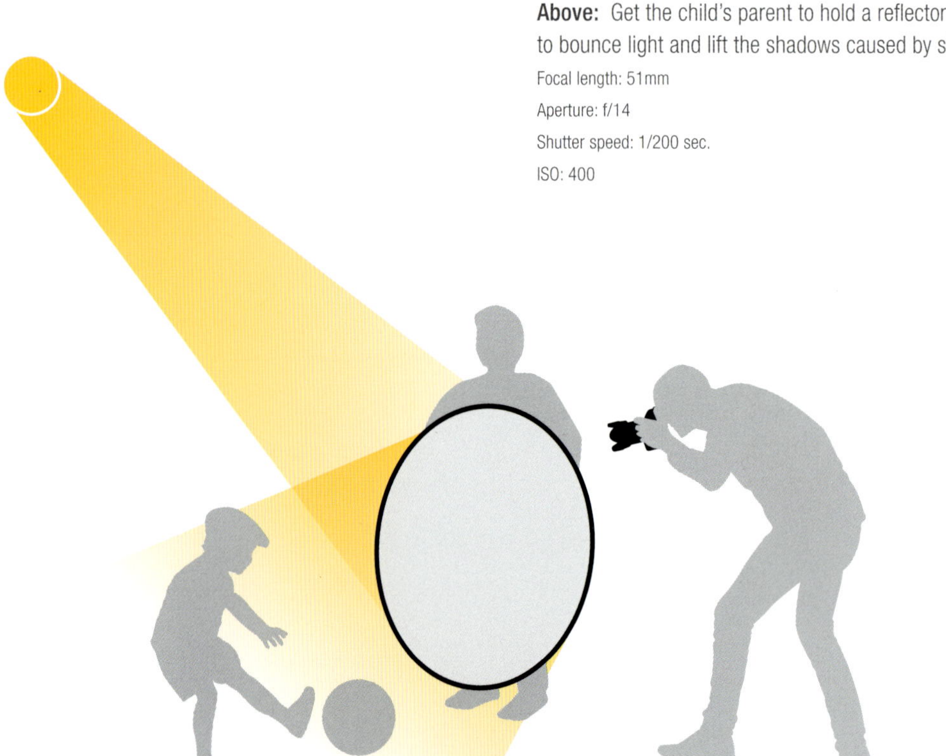

Right: Use an assistant or parent to hold the reflector off camera to the side.

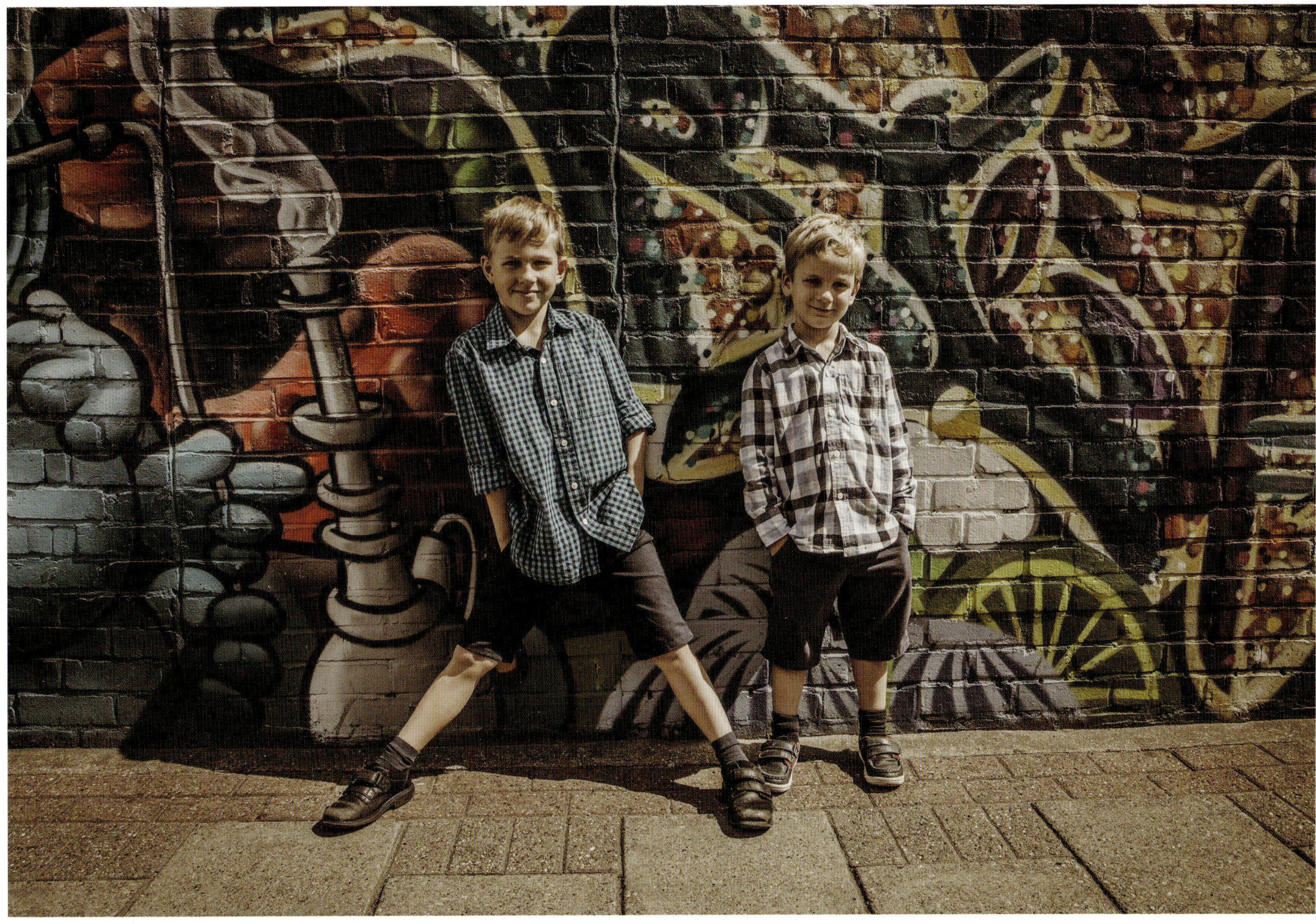

Above: Sidelighting on a brick wall behind the subject
creates a detailed, textural backdrop.

Focal length: 27mm

Aperture: f/11

Shutter speed: 1/500 sec.

ISO: 800

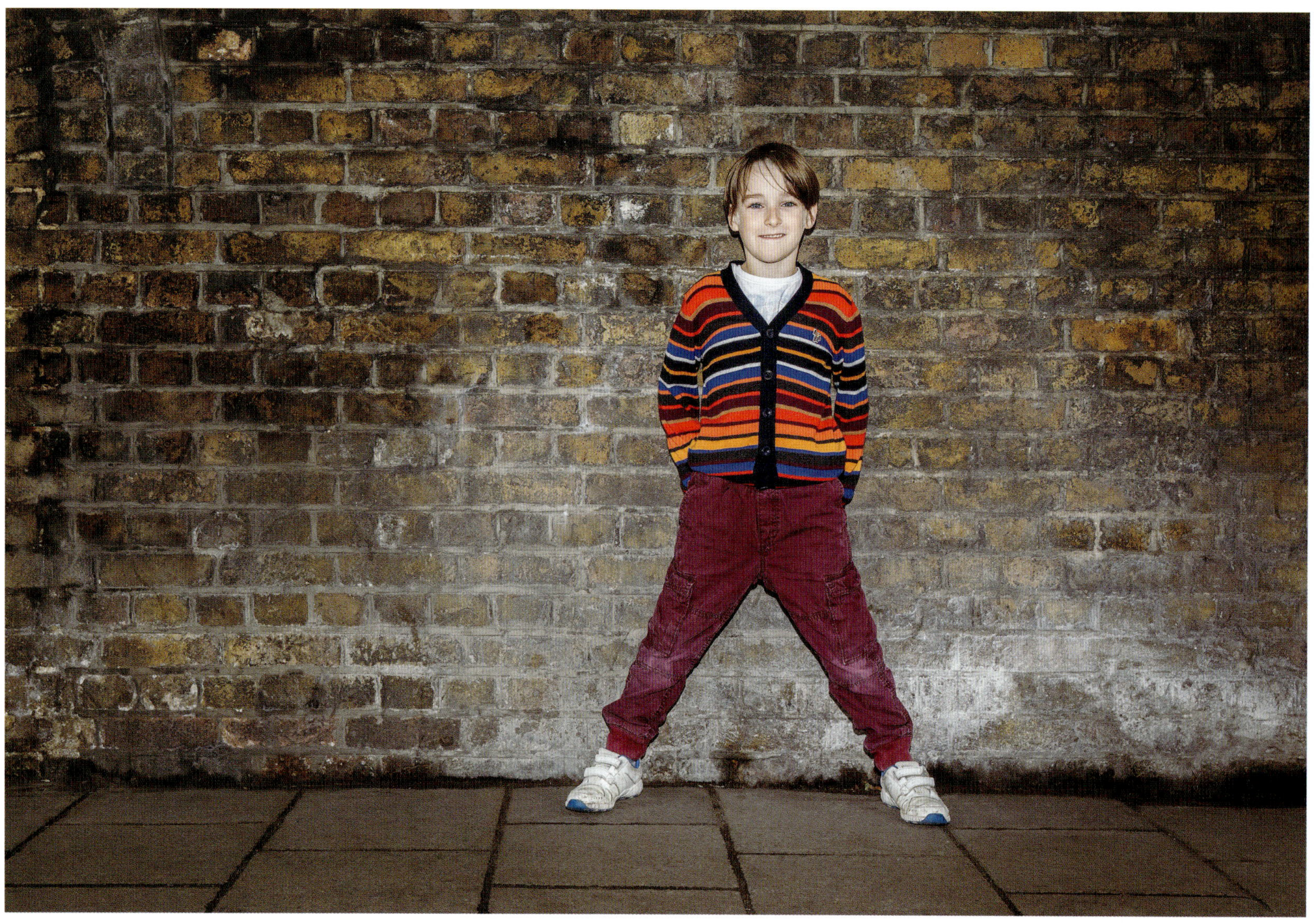

Front Light

Despite my addiction to backlighting, I have to admit that frontal lighting can also provide a very interesting image. Soft frontal lighting from a hazy sun situated at an angle behind the photographer's back is a great way to ensure consistent exposures and softly textured skin.

Conversely, harder front light techniques can give a gritty, contemporary effect that is popular with fashion photographers and can be very cool!

Try this with your flash facing a wall. If you set the flash to a low setting it will mix with the daylight and fill in the shadows, giving a nice highlight in the eye and a clean contemporary look.

If you push the power up you can start to create a "spotlight" feel as you overpower the ambient light—this is very theatrical and can give you some superb images.

Above: A strong burst of flash creates a very contemporary feel to this image.

Focal length: 43mm

Aperture: f/11

Shutter speed: 1/200 sec.

ISO: 1000

Top Light

Side lighting is generally accepted as being better to work with than top lighting in most portrait situations, as it gives shape and form to the subject. However, it is simply impractical to shoot all your child portraits at the end of the day, when the sun is low in the sky, so you have to get used to shooting with the sun directly overhead.

This does not have to be bland; you just have to be clever. An overcast day can provide some of the best shooting situations, as it provides you with even lighting for every image. If you practice using your bounce reflector close up you will quickly learn that you can produce beautifully soft images, with even eye reflections and a backdrop that feels almost painted. Embrace the flatness of the light to create front-to-back consistency in your lighting.

More direct lighting from above is a little trickier, but used correctly it can be theatrical and dramatic. If the hard light of the sun is just too much, then look for an overhang or a tree canopy and head for the shade. The light flickering down through a backdrop of trees can be amazing, so shoot in the shade and use the top light to create shapes and reflections in the background.

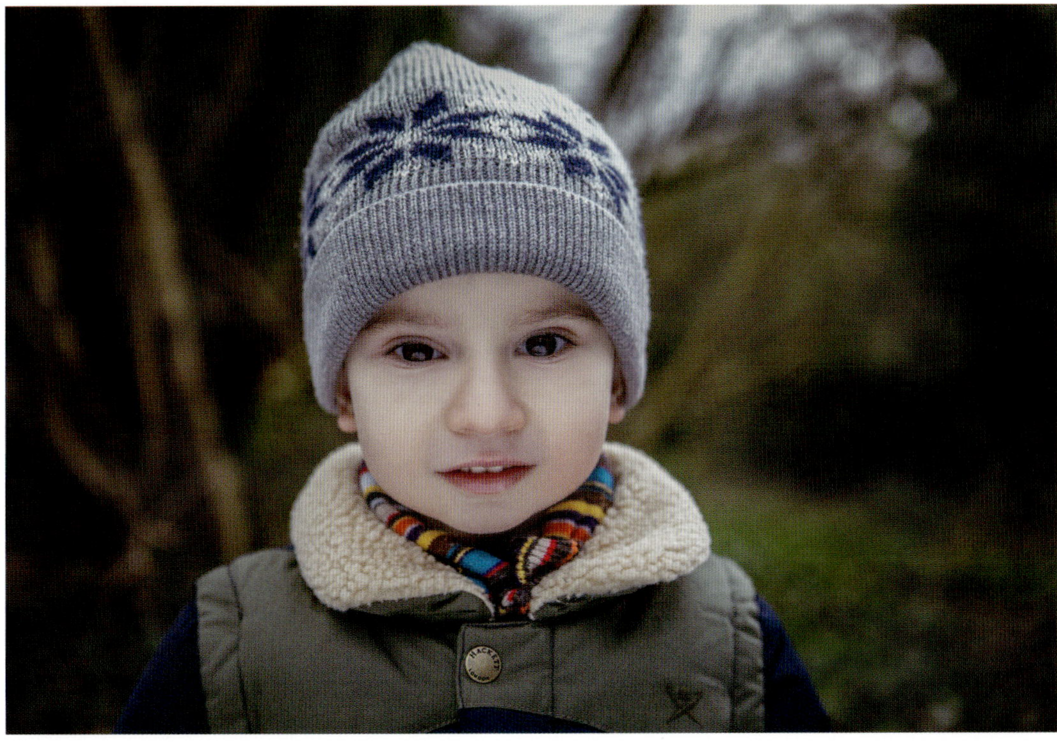

Above: Soft lighting from above gives a very usable and even effect that can be enhanced by using a reflector to add lovely reflections to the eyes.

Focal length: 51mm

Aperture: f/3.2

Shutter speed: 1/1000 sec.

ISO: 1600

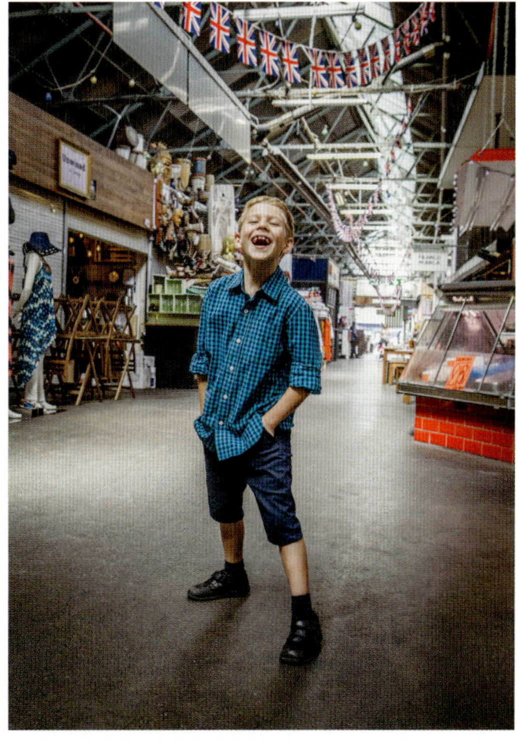

Above: The skylight in a building provides the perfect top light for an atmospheric image.

Focal length: 34mm

Aperture: f/5

Shutter speed: 1/100 sec.

ISO: 800

Types Of Light

The direction and quality of the light you are using can often depend on the location you are in and the options you have around you. Outlined here are some of the specific lighting situations guaranteed to help you with your shots.

Reflected Light

The unique feeling created by reflected light is subtle and detailed, and can produce some of the most beautiful child portrait images. Reflected light is the result of a primary light source hitting a large reflective area; I've mentioned bounce reflectors before, but any surface that is lit can create a reflected light source, whether it's a wall, a body of water, or a road sign. The intensity, shape, and size of the reflection will determine the finished result, but it is not always obvious that the reflected light will be usable, because it is often so subtle.

Look out for white painted walls outside or plastered walls inside. Corrugated metal buildings that seem pretty mundane can create wonderful reflectors, with multiple vertical highlights reflected in the eyes of the subject. Similarly, the whitewash used on some older buildings is another good source, as is white marble. If all else fails you can buy very large reflectors, which are like giant versions of your regular bounce reflector.

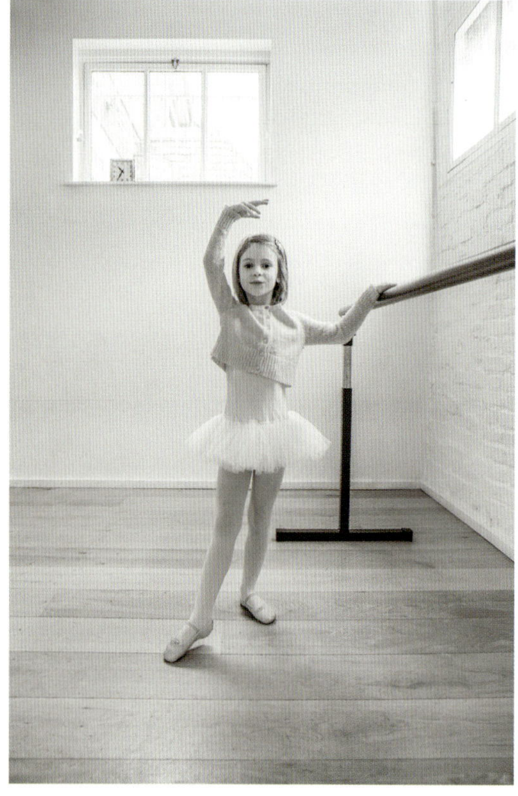

Above: Use reflected light from white walls and light colored flooring for a subtle effect.

Focal length: 24mm

Aperture: f/5

Shutter speed: 1/100 sec.

ISO: 800

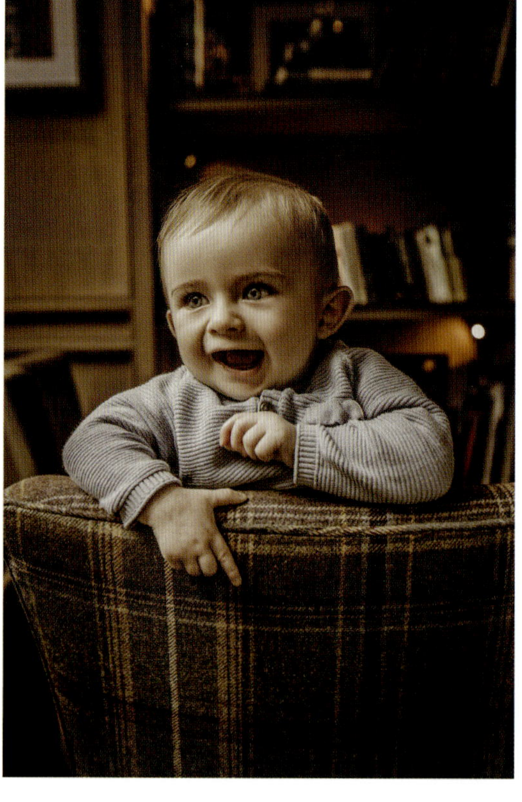

Above: Directional window light can be varied in strength and quality by using net curtains or blinds.

Focal length: 43mm

Aperture: f/4

Shutter speed: 1/80 sec.

ISO: 1250

Tip

When light is reflected it loses a lot of its intensity, so you will need to compensate by opening the aperture, increasing the shutter speed, or choosing a higher ISO.

Window Light

There are few serious child portrait photographers who have not, at some point, used window light as their main light source. A window with sunlight streaming through it creates a natural softbox in just about every building (new or old) at a height that is pretty much perfect for most subjects. As always, the quality of the light is determined by the hardness of the sunlight streaming through it, although hard light can be controlled with a net curtain or diffusion material to give a soft gentle kiss to the side of the face. Ask the child to look partly toward the window to catch reflections in both eyes and then fill in the shadows with a bounce reflector.

Searching For Shade

Shade is much sought after during my shoots.
When you are in a shaded area you have
essentially created your own micro-lighting climate:
everything is controllable, as the light is consistent
and soft, and your exposure measurements
won't be thrown by any sharp highlights or dark
shadows. Because the light is not directional, you
are free to move around your subject, providing
a multitude of options and different backdrops,
be it sunny highlights flickering through trees or
out-of-focus cars, buses, and buildings creating
background interest in an urban setting.

Right: Shaded areas provide soft and even lighting, so
always search for the shade when you're on location.

Focal length: 27mm

Aperture: f/3.2

Shutter speed: 1/1000 sec.

ISO: 400

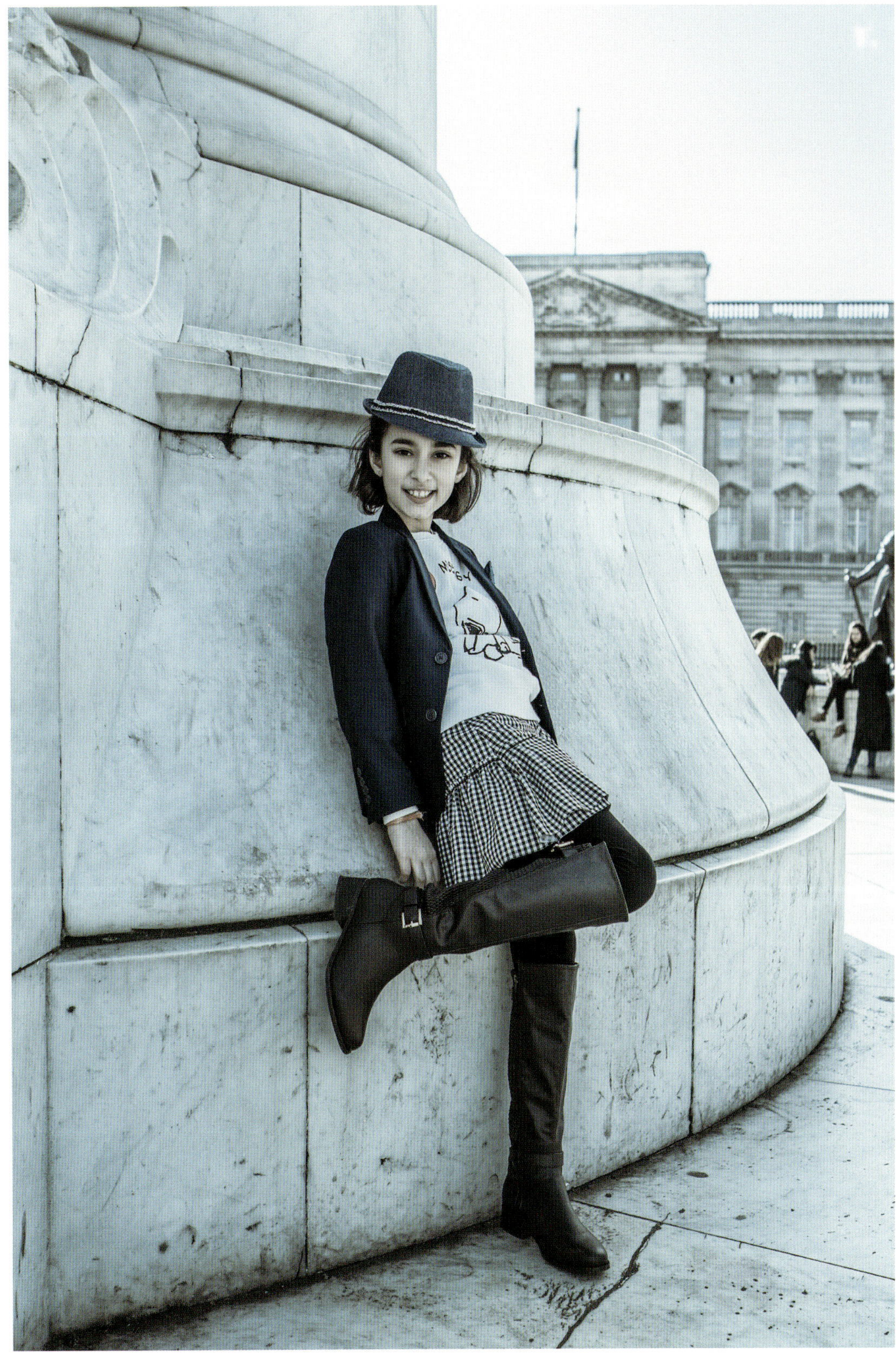

The Canopy Effect

This variation on the theme of shade is something I've noticed and used for countless location portraits. After getting very excited about my "new" discovery I started researching it online only to find there are thousands of photographers already talking about it (nothing in photography is new!).

The idea is simple. In a park or wood, position the child under a tree canopy, while you stand outside the trees and shoot. The lighting effect is simply stunning. The darkened area around the subject creates beautiful, rich detail, while the child is lit by soft indirect light from the sky.

The really beautiful thing about this technique, though, is the reflections that are created in the eyes. The eyes will sparkle with an intense bright highlight; it is like having a huge multi-shaped softbox directly behind the photographer giving a romantic sense of hope for the future in the perfect eyes of a child.

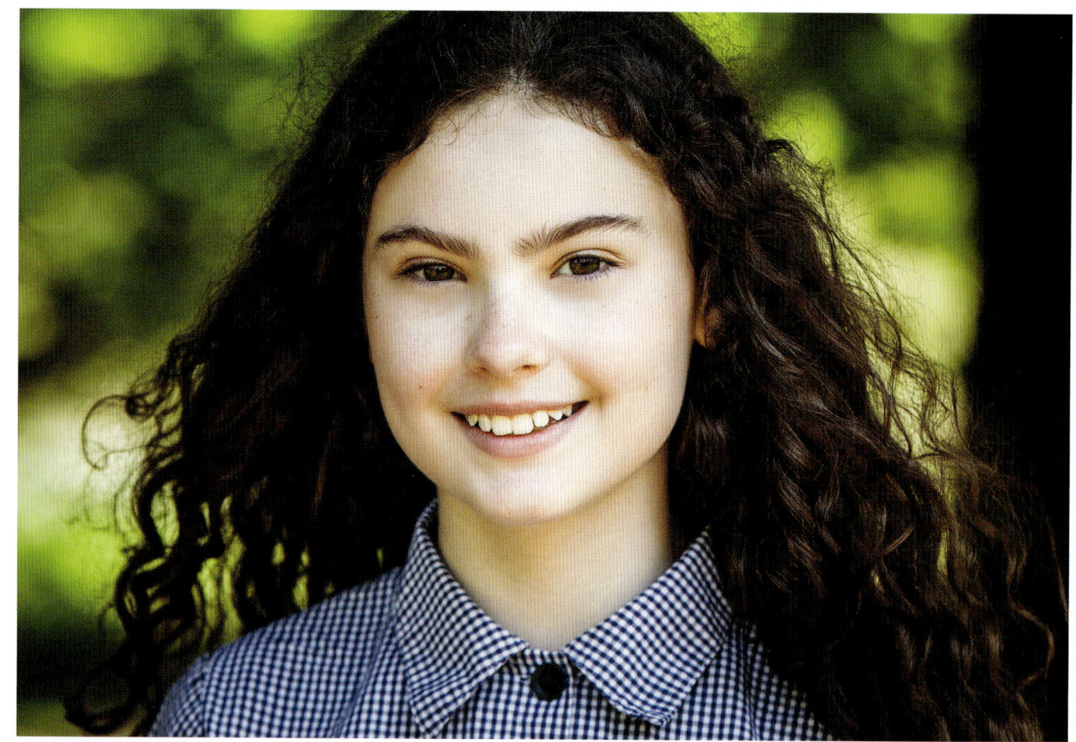

Above right & right: Placing your subject under the canopy of a tree will create fabulous reflections in their eyes.

Focal length: 115mm

Aperture: f/4

Shutter speed: 1/1000 sec.

ISO: 800

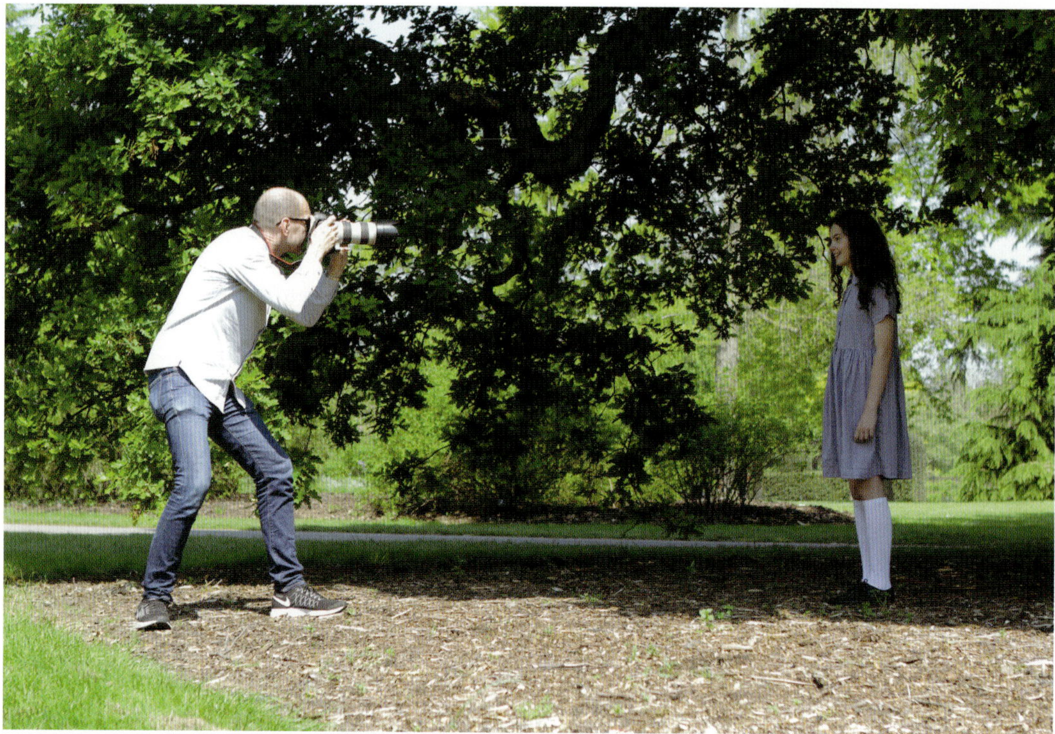

The Golden Hour

You will often hear professional photographers talking about the "golden hour," and it is indeed a wonderful time of day for photography. In general terms, the golden hour is the period after sunrise and before sunset, when the sun is low in the sky, although "hour" is a slight misnomer as the duration changes depending on location and time of year.

In any case, the low sun provides a dramatic sidelight that creates gorgeous highlights and beautiful rim-lighting when positioned behind the subject. The sunlight also becomes beautifully warm, taking on a yellow, orange, and sometimes even red color.

However, the difficulty with shooting in the golden hour is that it doesn't last long and it changes constantly, so you not only need to be ready for it, but have to work quickly. Adding to this, children rarely understand the nuance of a given situation. You can't expect your subject to stand around waiting for that "perfect" moment when the sun kisses the back of their head for about five seconds: in my experience this is asking too much. By all means give it a try and see what you get—and enjoy it when things work out—but don't plan all your shoots around the golden hour.

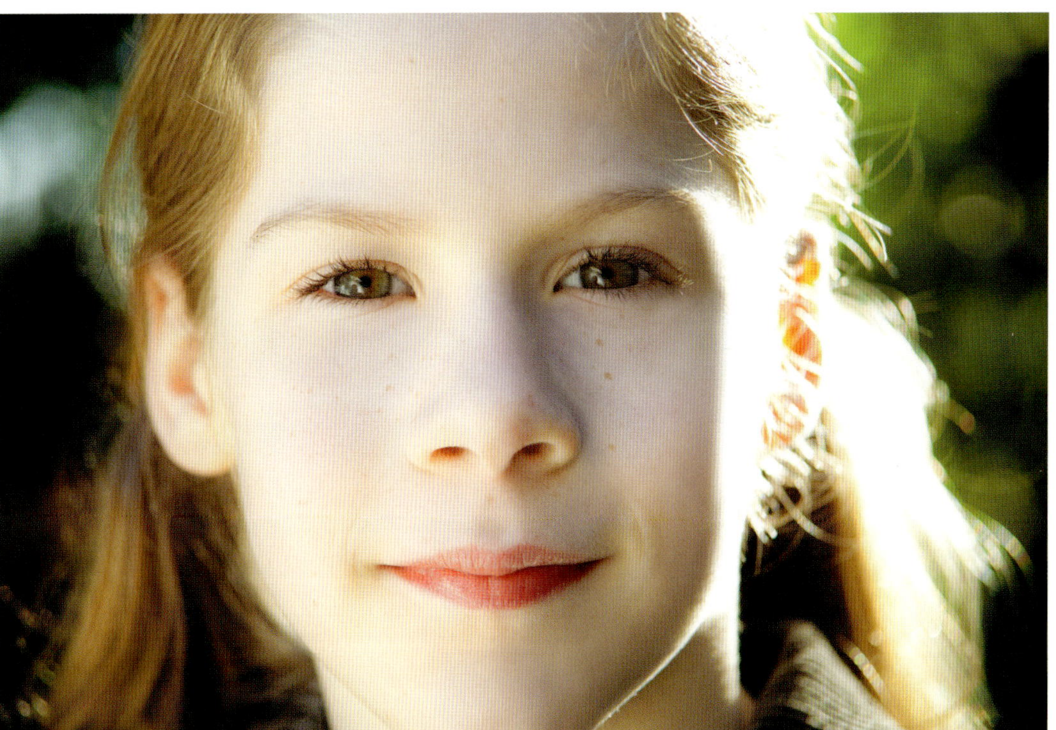

Above right: A unique quality of light is created during the golden hour.

Focal length: 105mm

Aperture: f/5

Shutter speed: 1/125 sec.

ISO: 400

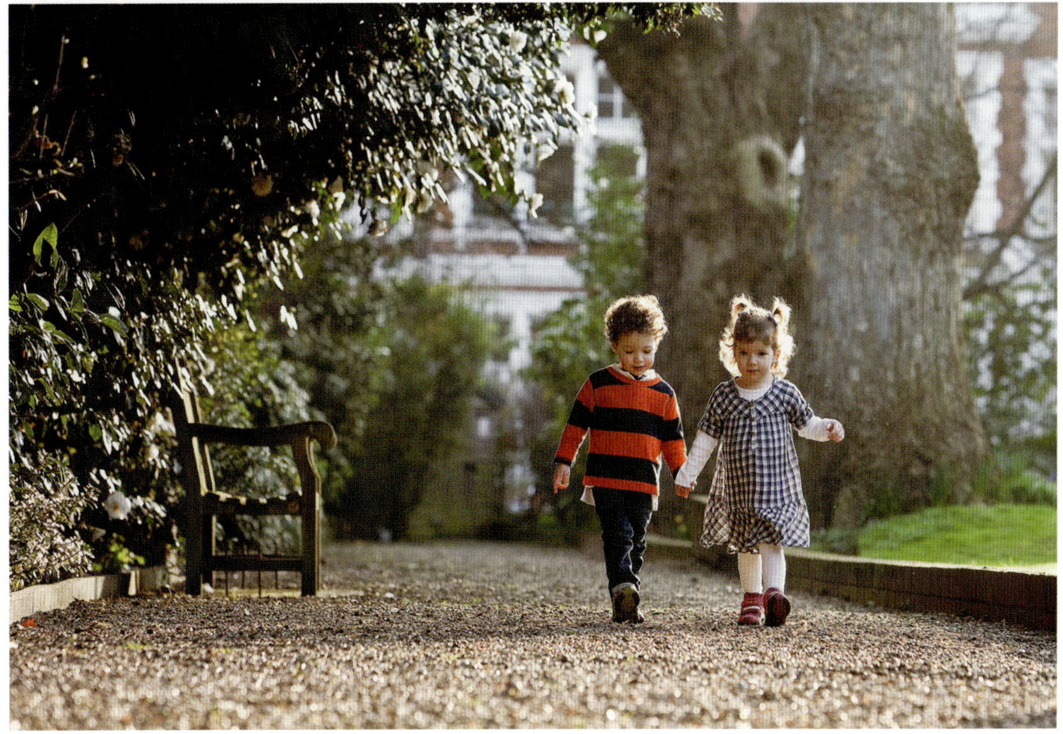

Right: Shooting late in the day or early in the morning is ideal. The sun is low and will bathe your scene in warm, golden light.

Focal length: 130mm

Aperture: f/4

Shutter speed: 1/250 sec.

ISO: 400

Profile: Saraya Cortaville

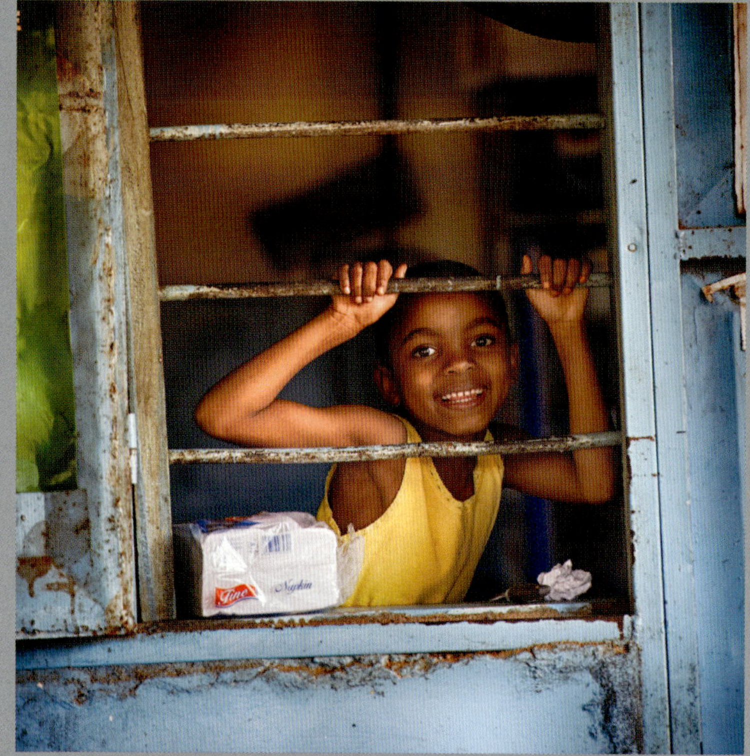

Left:

Focal length: 200mm

Aperture: f/3.2

Shutter speed: 1/320 sec.

ISO: 2000

Q) What equipment do you use regularly?

A) In 2016 I was made a Fujifilm X photographer and currently work with the Fujifilm X-T2 (with an X-T20 as a backup), using 16–55mm and 50–140mm zooms, plus a 90mm prime. This kit covers everything from landscapes through to portraits and is light enough for me to carry on flights and on location. The mirrorless system works well for me, as I can instantly see the results through the EVF. This is especially useful when shooting portraits of children, as any missed expressions are instantly spotted and the shot can be retaken.

Q) Why is it important to you to photograph children in their natural environment?

A) For me, this is a more natural way to capture their personalities. My clients will usually pick a location that means something to them, such as a local park or place of interest that they enjoy visiting together. The children are more relaxed in a location they are familiar with, and the images also have more meaning and are more personal to the client.

Q) How do you go about setting up a session?

A) I always try and find out as much as I can about the client before the shoot. Understanding their intended outcome is vital, as I then know where to concentrate my efforts. I arrive at the location around 20 minutes before I meet them and walk around to pick out suitable spots for portraits; I'll look for textures, colors, natural frames, repeating patterns, and, of course, great light.

Q) What tips do you have for getting the best from a spontaneous location shoot?

A) Work quickly; keep the energy levels high and the momentum of the shoot fluid. This makes a shoot enjoyable and full of fun.

Q) How do you go about lighting your subjects?

A) I only ever shoot in natural light, which has its challenges, especially in the summer months. In bright sunshine I will always look for areas of shade to give softer lighting for the portraits. If I can't find any shade I will shoot into the sun and use a reflector to bounce light back into the face.

Q) How important is postproduction and do you do your own?

A) I do all my own postproduction, but try and edit each image as little as possible, just tweaking the curves and doing a little retouching if needed. Getting the composition and exposure correct at the time of the shoot enables me to do this.

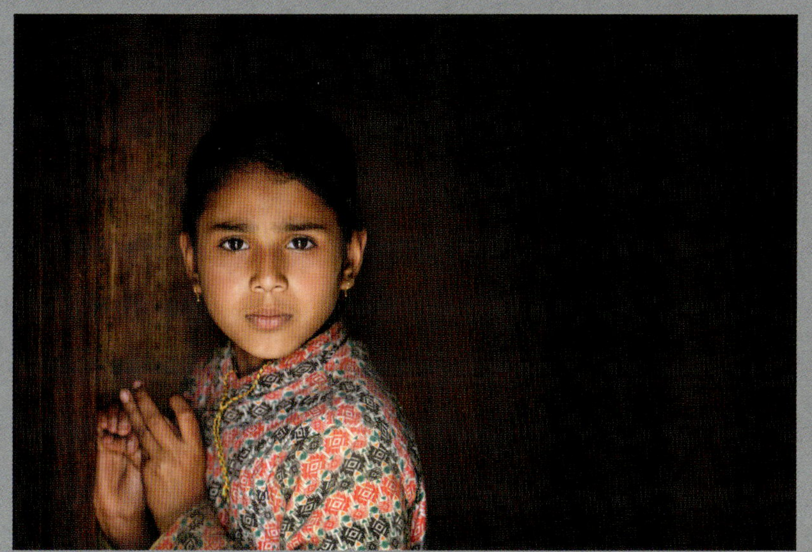

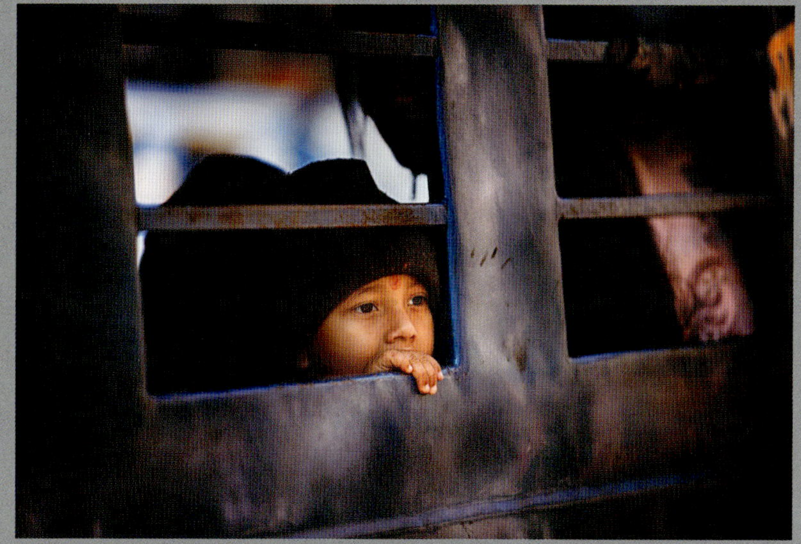

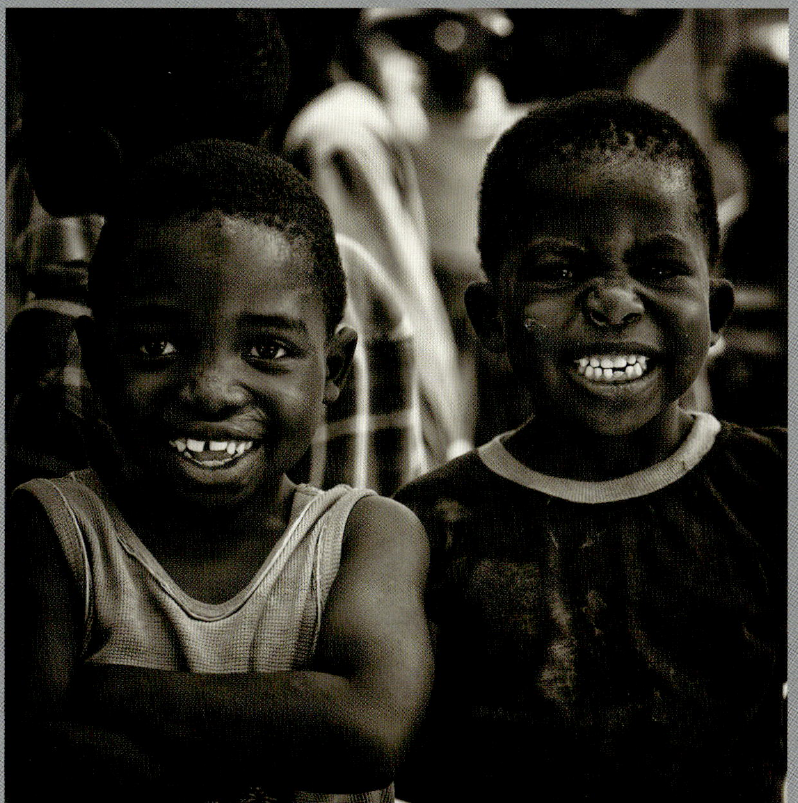

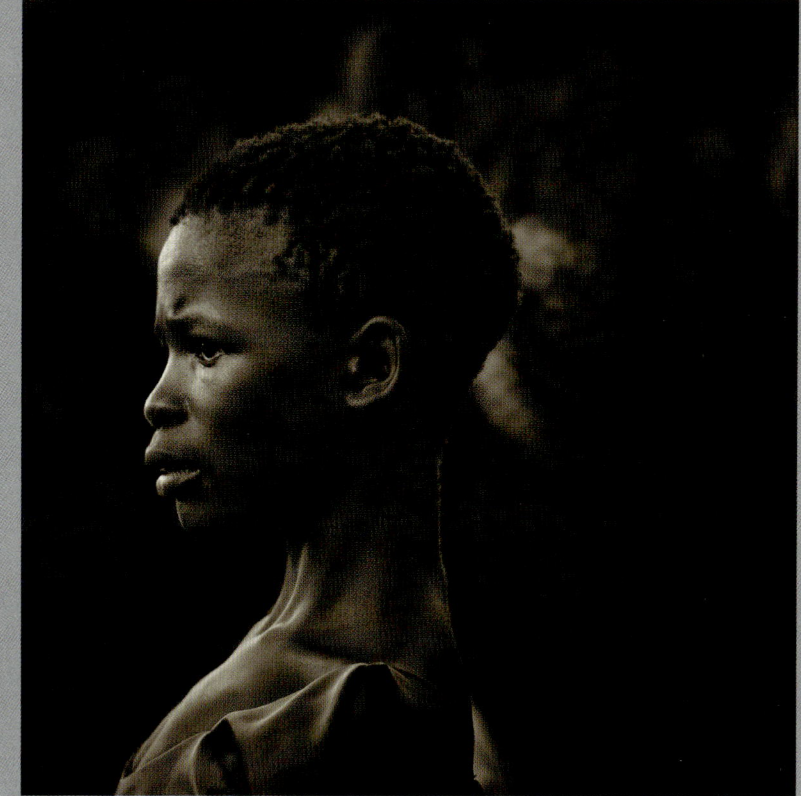

Top left:

Focal length: 163mm

Aperture: f/2.8

Shutter speed: 1/250 sec.

ISO: 1250

Bottom left:

Focal length: 70mm

Aperture: f/2.8

Shutter speed: 1/250 sec.

ISO: 100

Top right:

Focal length: 200mm

Aperture: f/2.8

Shutter speed: 1/250 sec.

ISO: 100

Bottom right:

Focal length: 200mm

Aperture: f/4.5

Shutter speed: 1/320 sec.

ISO: 250

Chapter 6
Shooting In The Studio

There is a great tradition of studio portraiture within photography and child portraits have always been regarded as some of the most beautiful images in any portfolio. There are countless photographers who specialize in photographing children in the studio environment: school portraits have been produced in this way for decades, and many portrait studios produce work ranging from delicate baby images to high-key, fun-packed shots. There are plenty of options and many different ways to approach child portraiture in the studio, and it is up to you which path you take. In any event, you will need to invest in some suitable equipment and there is of course another vital requirement—a studio.

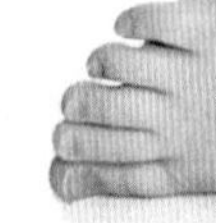

Right: High-key studio portraits are the biggest sellers for many portrait studios.
Focal length: 48mm
Aperture: f/6.3
Shutter speed: 1/125 sec.
ISO: 200

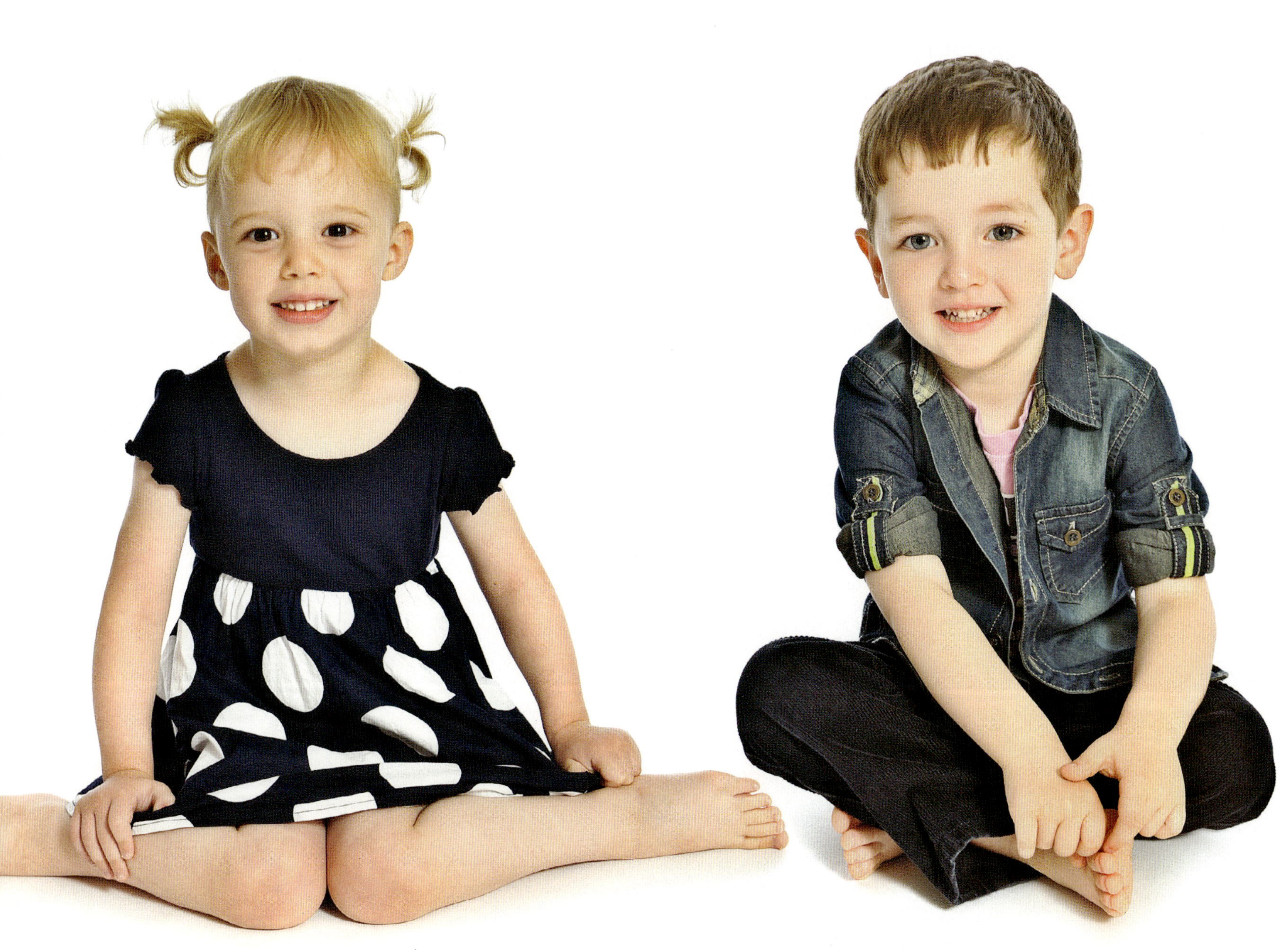

The Perfect Studio Space

In reality there is no such thing as the perfect studio, there is only *your* perfect studio. You really want to have a space that is as large as you can get and with a good ceiling height—you will often want to have lights above the subject, so you need headroom if possible.

Most commercial studios start at around 500ft² (45m²) with a ceiling height of at least 11ft (3.5m). This is regarded as a fairly small space, but luckily, children are smaller than adults, so some savings can be made if you stick with just photographing children.

A studio measuring around 17x15ft (5x4.5m) makes for a reasonable starter studio, so a double-garage-sized room is ideal. However, many photographers work in makeshift studios that are smaller than this, so don't be put off; just learn to work with the space you have available.

A "daylight" studio is one that is setup to use natural light as the main light source, with large windows and skylights positioned strategically for the best available light. Daylight studios can be fun to work in, and can lead to some great shots, but as they are reliant on ambient light you might not be able to work all the time.

The alternative is to create a controlled studio that uses artificial lighting. An outbuilding can often be converted into a suitable space, providing it has a good power supply and you can control the daylight with curtains or blinds. If you have outdoor space available, an alternative option is to buy an easy-build outbuilding and use that as a studio.

However, check with your local authority before you start construction to make sure there aren't any building restrictions.

Inside, your studio's walls should ideally be a neutral color, as they will reflect light. Black, white, and gray are all perfectly acceptable, but my preference would be white so you are getting as much reflected light as possible. The ceiling should also be white so you can bounce a flash.

Not all of your walls need to be painted, though: a "raw" brick wall can make a great backdrop. Many professional studios will also have an infinity curve or "cove" that is easy to light and produces a totally white backdrop. Although you can create a similar effect with seamless white background paper, a well-constructed cove is more robust.

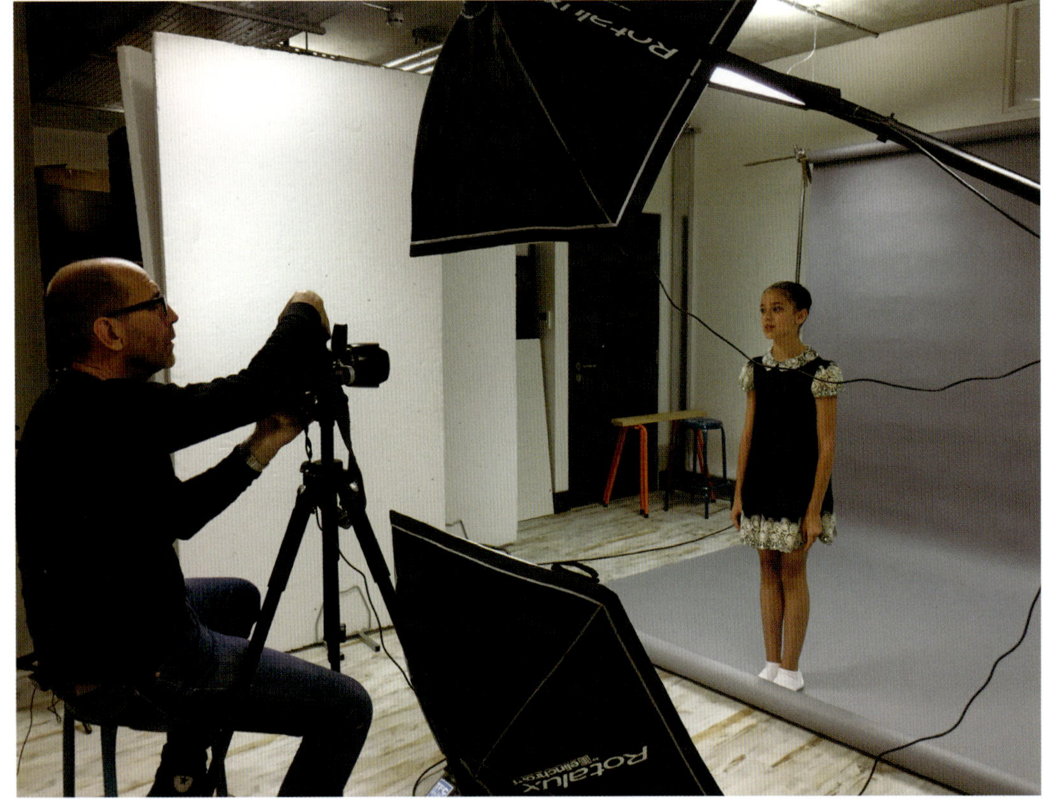

Left: There is no such thing as a "perfect" studio: it is up to you to find a space that you feel is right for you. However, a good studio space will be as large as you can find, with a high ceiling to allow for top lighting, and painted in a neutral color.

Lighting

Setting up your first studio can be complicated, as there are so many options available and countless styles and influences that will define the look of your shots. The camera and lenses you use will generally be similar to the kit you use on location, although as the parameters of a studio are more clearly defined, you may wish to invest in fixed focal lengths rather than zooms. Generally these give slightly better image quality and have faster maximum apertures.

Lighting is, of course, the defining feature of any studio and there is plenty to choose from. I'm going to concentrate on studio strobes here because they offer the greatest flexibility when it comes to different lighting setups. Flash is also the most powerful type of light available and is daylight balanced, so mixes readily with daylight.

The main alternative to flash is LED lighting, which is increasingly popular as it offers "what you see is what you get" continuous lighting. LEDs are still lacking in power, though, so unless you spend a lot of money on powerful units they can create problems when it comes to freezing action.

Studio Flash

Just like smaller flash units, studio strobes work by continuously charging up capacitors in the unit, which then release their power in the form of a super-fast, super-powerful flash of light. There will be a brief recharging time in between flashes and the flash head should indicate when it is ready with a bleep or a flicker of its modeling light.

There are two types of studio strobe: monobloc heads that have the power pack and controls built into the flash head itself, and "pack and head" systems that have a separate power pack and simpler flash heads.

For child portraits, monoblocs are a good starting point, as they are usually cheaper than packs and heads (although also have a lower power output). Choose a brand that has plenty of accessories, such as different reflectors and softboxes, as you may want to change your lighting as your ideas and ability develop. Ideally, you want to buy a monobloc unit that uses the same accessory fitting as the more powerful units, so you don't have to replace all of your accessories if you upgrade your lights.

Most modern flash units (monoblocs and packs/heads) have built-in radio or infrared receivers so they can "talk" to each other, or they have optical slave cells that detect the flash from one unit and immediately fire in sync. In a small studio a basic three-light kit will cover most requirements, although you can never really have enough lights.

BOUNCED LIGHT

As well as multi-light setups, there is another clever technique that is often overlooked, but can be used in a studio or even on location in someone's home: bouncing light off the ceiling. A lot of ceilings are painted white and are usually clean and uncluttered, which makes them the perfect giant reflector. Simply point a flash up at the ceiling to create a large pool of light and you will have a large, soft light source. The same technique can be used with white walls or even large reflectors, so experiment with different reflective surfaces to create different lighting effects. If necessary, use a piece of card to prevent any light from spilling directly onto your subject.

Portable Home Studio

Setting up studio flash in a home environment is challenging, as it tends to take up a lot of room. However, there are several clever options available to the keen home studio photographer. For a start, you can purchase compact white fabric background units that can be set up and folded away with relative ease; there are even some easy to use pop-up backdrops, which can be transported to your client's home in the back of a car and set up quickly.

When it comes to lighting, monoblocs and packs/heads can be used, but an increasingly popular option is location flash units. These strobes run off batteries, which means you can work literally anywhere: in a house, in a forest, or even up a mountain. Location flash is more expensive than its mains-powered cousins, and you will need spare batteries so you don't run out of power mid shoot. An increasing number of these units now have TTL (Through The Lens) control, which makes them as easy to use as a hotshoe-mounted flash.

Regardless of the lighting you choose, it's a good idea to ask your client to clear a space for you before you arrive, as few homes have a large, clear space already available. A garage is often a good option, so suggest this before you arrive for the shoot. Kitchens can also be good areas to set up in, but be aware that you will need to minimize the natural daylight in the room.

Tethered Shooting

When you're shooting in a studio you are working in a very controlled environment, and having access to shelter and power means there are a few new options to be considered. Tethered shooting is a great way to record and view images as you shoot, and can be helpful for both you and your client, as you can see each image on a computer screen as it is captured.

"Tethering" your camera is simply the process of connecting it directly to a computer, either wirelessly or with a cable, so you can save your shots directly to the hard drive, rather than the camera's memory card. Most pro-spec cameras come with their own tethering software that you can use, but there are also a number of popular independent software packages designed specifically to do this: the two most popular are Phase One's Capture One and Adobe Lightroom.

Once tethered, you shoot as normal, and your images appear on the computer's screen as you go. You can also apply standard profile settings to the images as they are captured, so you can see the effect on your final developed images before you fine tune them at a later date. It is also possible to tether your camera to other external devices, such as tablets and cellphones, so you can see the images when shot.

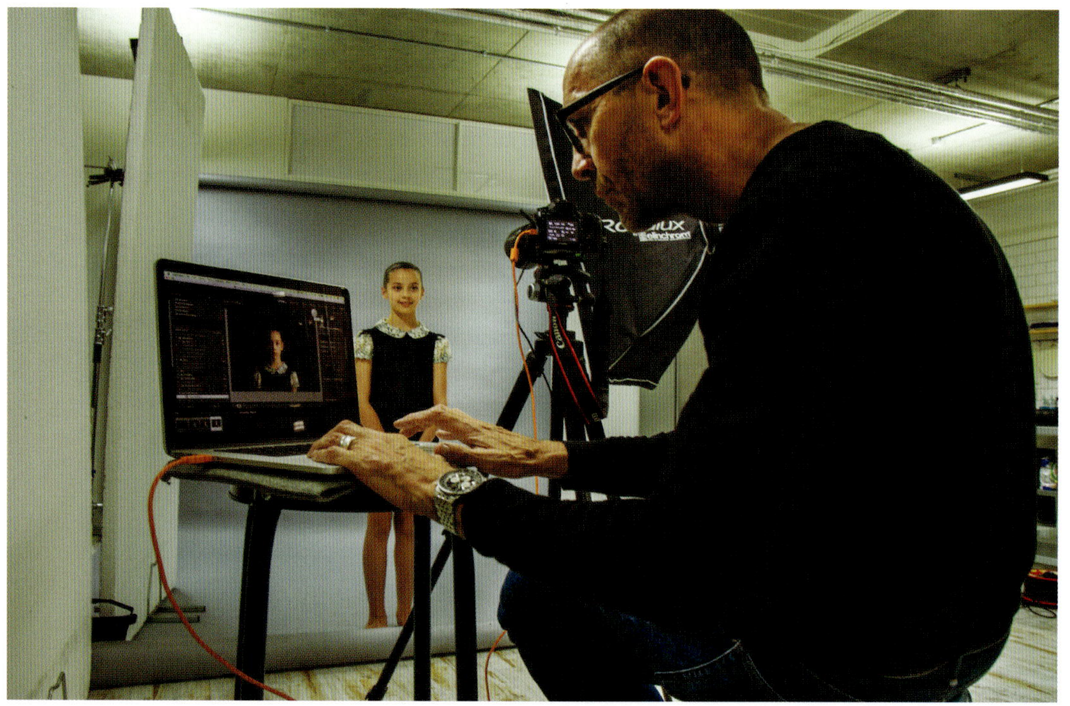

Above: Shooting tethered in a studio has a number of advantages, including the option to save files directly to the computer's hard drive.

Flash Exposures

Setting up your camera to shoot with studio flash is something that you need to become familiar with. It is not difficult, as long as you understand the limitations of what you are doing.

In normal circumstances, all cameras with a focal plane shutter (which includes DSLRs and mirrorless cameras) have a maximum shutter speed at which they can synchronize (sync) with flash. This sync speed is usually around 1/200 sec. As most studios have no windows, or have limited natural light, the ambient light in the room will not be enough to affect the exposure, so the shutter speed setting on the camera is fairly superfluous: you simply need to set the camera to Manual and choose a shutter speed at or below its sync speed.

However, your camera's metering system cannot help you set the exposure for studio strobes, so a dedicated flash meter will be useful. Set the flash meter to your chosen shutter speed and ISO, and ask your subject to hold it (usually in front of their face) with the meter's white dome facing the camera or the light source, depending on the effect your require. Ask them to press the flash button and when you fire the lights the meter will give you the aperture that you need to set on the camera for the correct exposure.

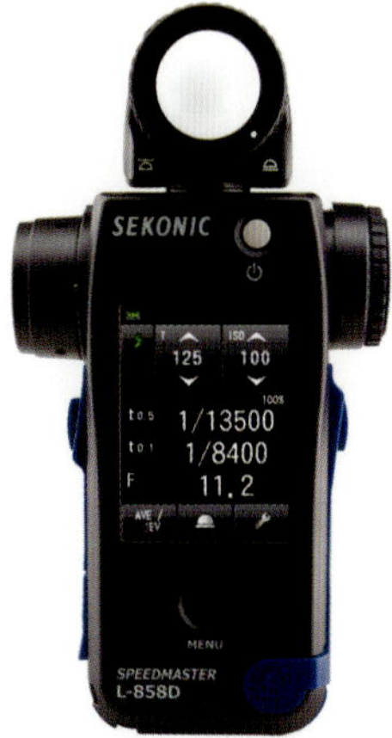

Above: Sekonic's flagship L-858D light meter lets you take both flash and ambient light readings.

Inverse Square Law

There are certain basics that apply to all lighting, such as the closer and larger the light source is, the softer its light will be; the more distant and smaller the source, the harder it will be. There is also one piece of math that is worth being aware of when shooting regularly in a studio: the "inverse square law."

It is logical to think that if you moved a light closer to your subject, halving the distance between the two, the power of the light would double in intensity. But this is not the case. In physics, any force that spreads its influence equally in all directions (as light does) will obey the inverse square law.

What this means is that it will increase in power inversely proportionate to the square of the distance from the original source. Or, put simply, if you halve the distance between the light source and the subject you will increase its intensity by four times. If you have a light meter you can measure this, but it is enough to understand the basics so you know what effect a light will have on the exposure if you move it.

The other important aspect of the inverse square law is the effect it has on how the light "falls off." The power of any light reduces as it moves away from the source, but because of the inverse square law it does not fall off in a linear fashion.

For example, if you are lighting someone's face from the side there will be a difference between the brightest side (nearest to the light) and the darkest side (farthest away from the light). This difference will be greater when the light source is closer to the subject, so if you want a softer fall-off, the light source needs to be farther away from your subject. This is very useful to remember when you want to maintain detail in the shadow areas, allowing you more options when you edit your images.

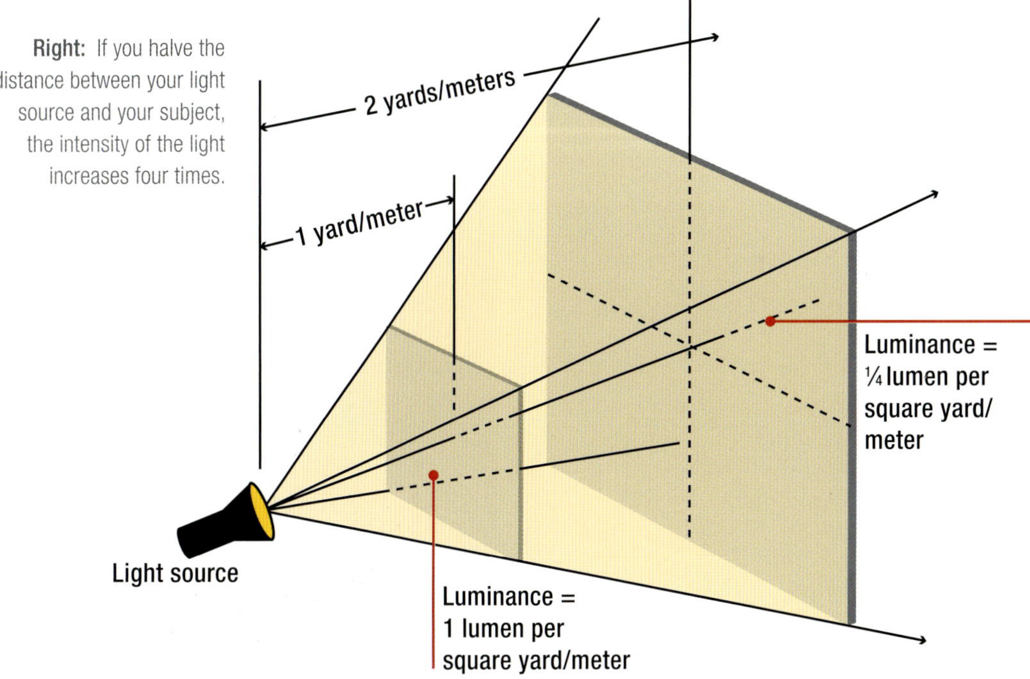

Right: If you halve the distance between your light source and your subject, the intensity of the light increases four times.

Lighting Setups

If you want to control every element of your child
portrait session then there is no better place to
be than in a studio. In this section we will explore
some basic lighting setups using one, two, and
three lights. These are some of the most popular
setups, which should form the basis for lighting
in any child portrait studio. It may help to start
with just one or two lights and then add more as
you gain experience, but there are no "rules"—try
these setups and then adapt them to suit the look
you are after. This is how new lighting techniques
develop—through trial and error.

In many of the lighting setups shown here you
can use a white or silver reflector to maintain detail
in the shadow areas. The same rules that apply
to flash in terms of size, distance, and fall-off also
apply to reflectors, so experiment and see what
works for you. It is worth noting that light will affect
shadow areas more than highlights, so the addition
of a white reflector will add subtle detail and clarity
to the shadows without washing out the highlights.

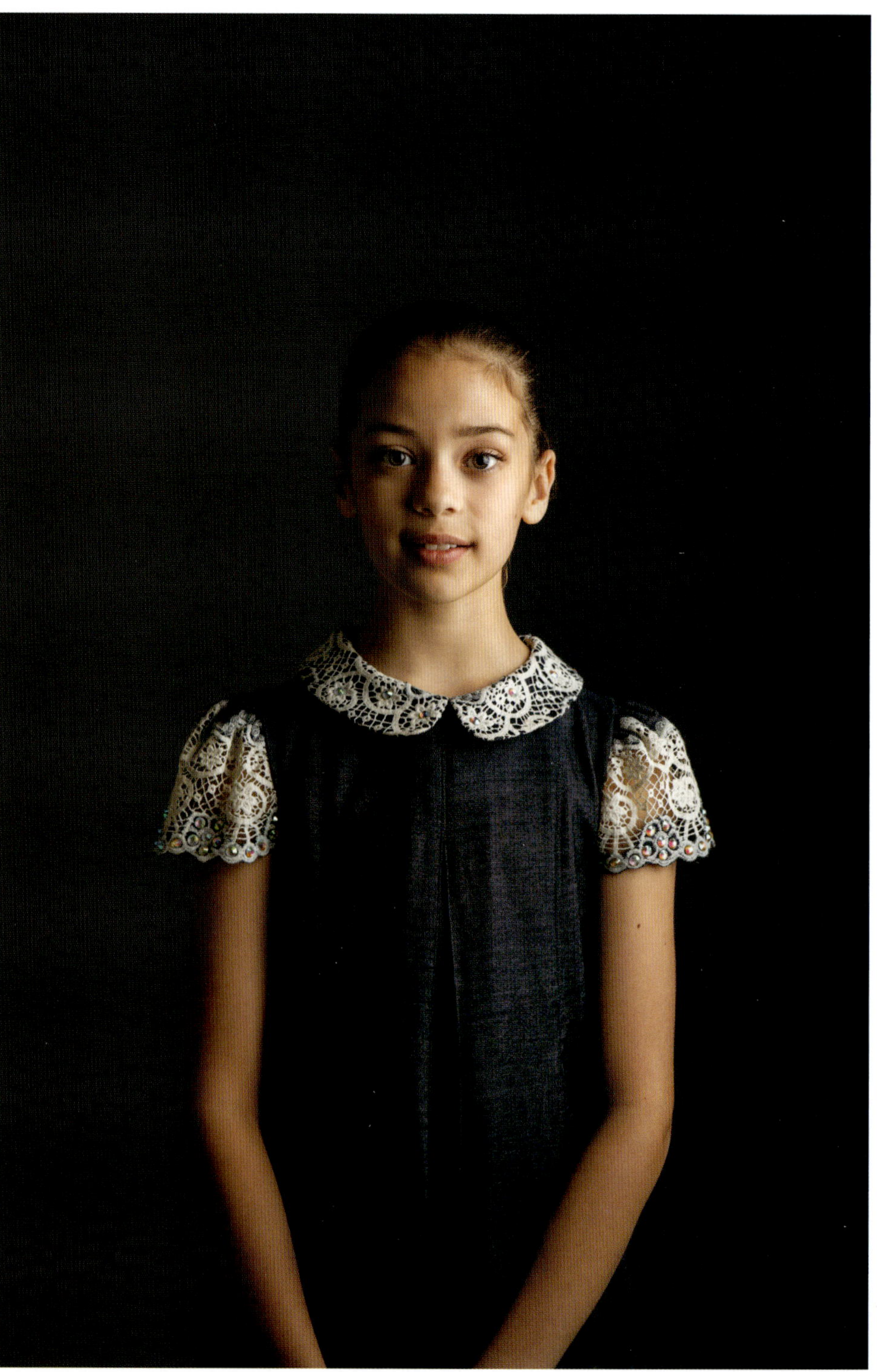

One Light: Version 1

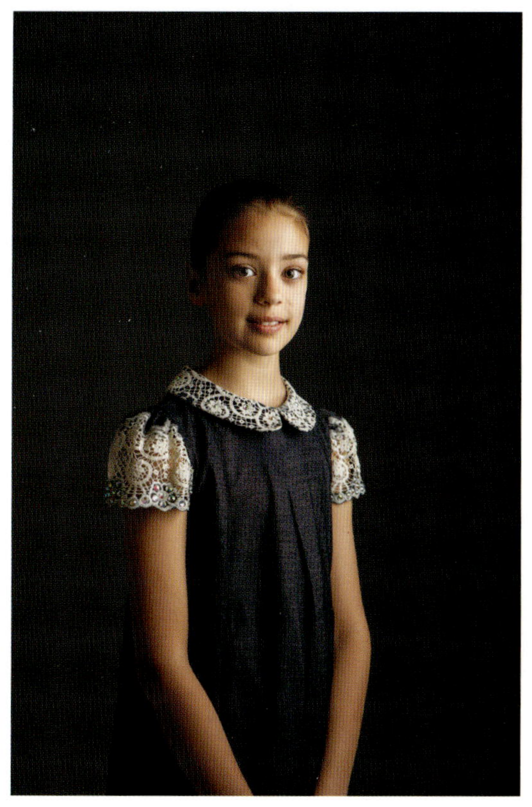 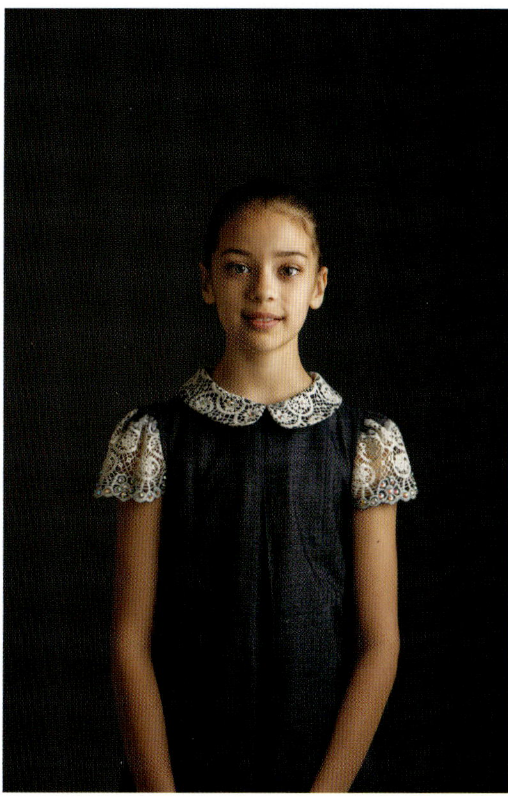 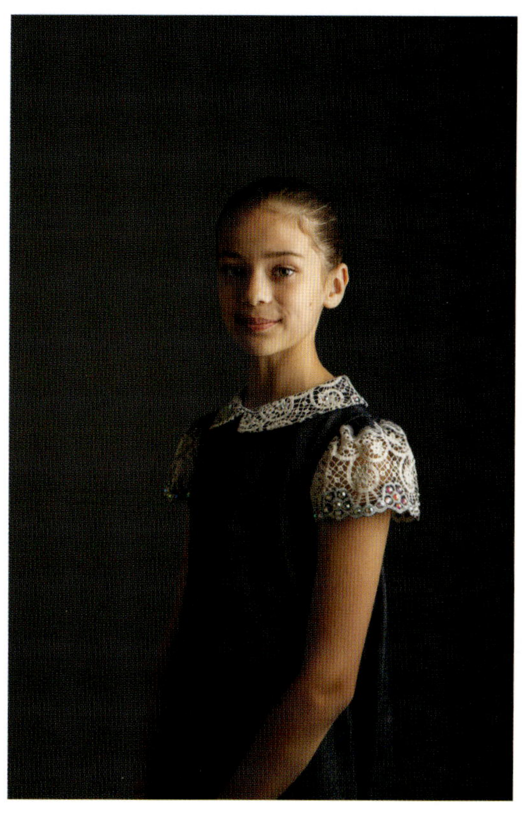

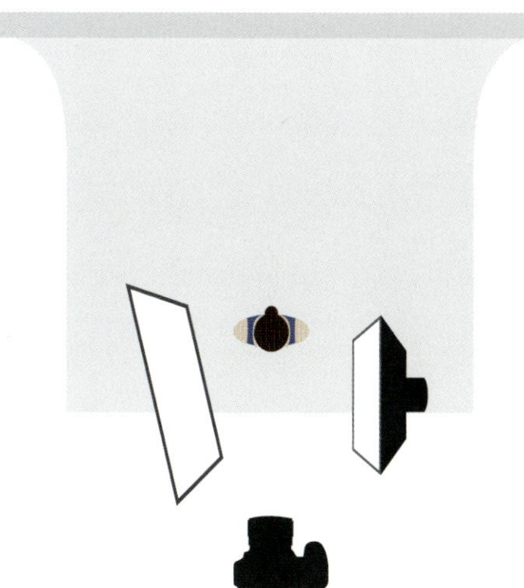

One front side perpendicular soft light, plus reflector.
Every studio portrait photographer should be able to create a beautiful image
with just one light. There are many ways to use this light, especially when you
add a large reflector to fill in the shadow side of the subject. There are many very
successful top portrait photographers who only ever shoot with a single light.

One Light: Version 2

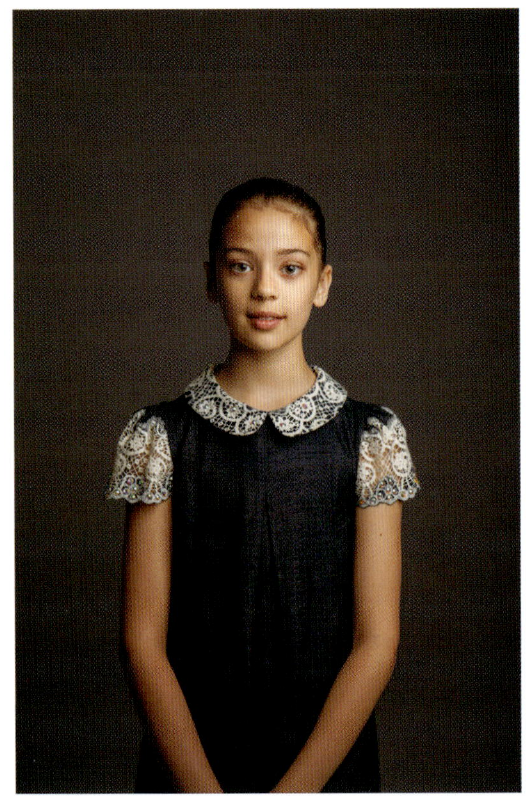 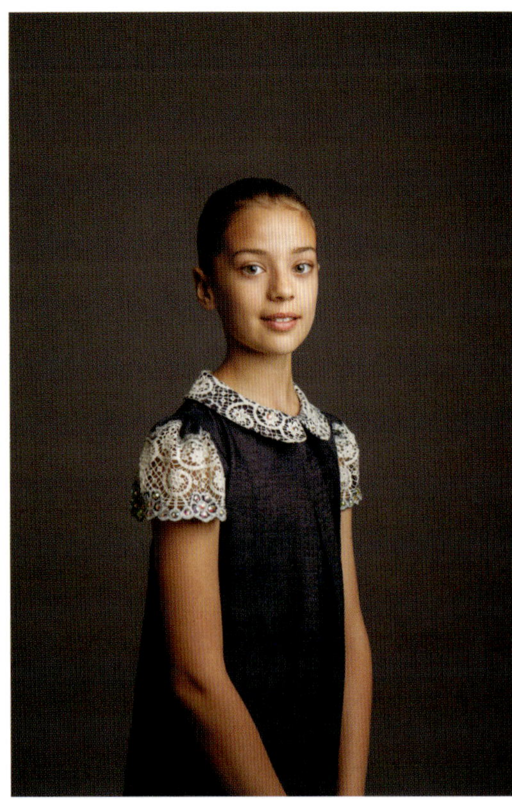 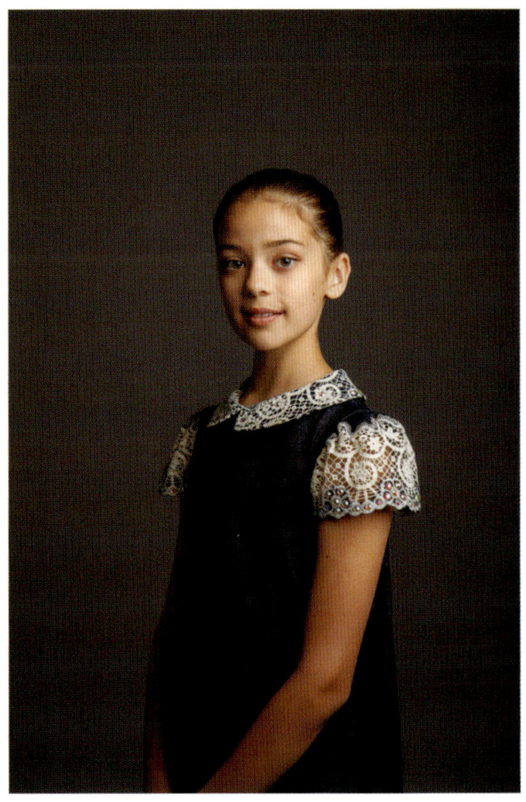

One front side-angled soft light, plus reflector.

One Light: Version 3

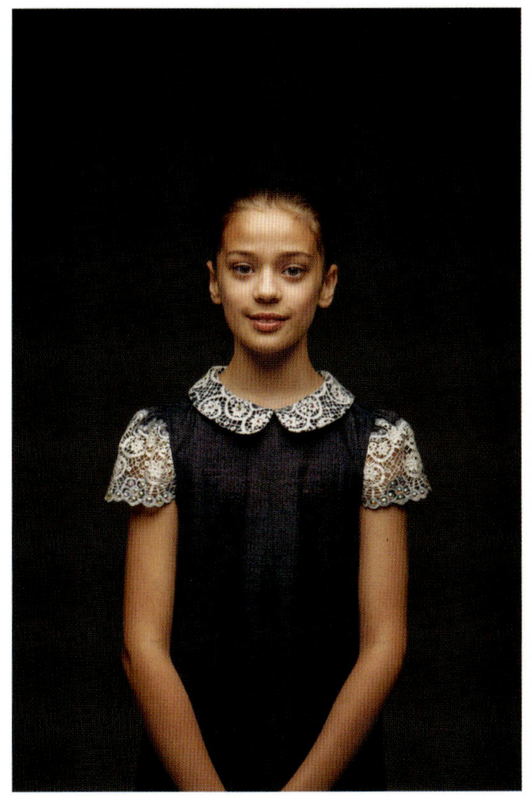 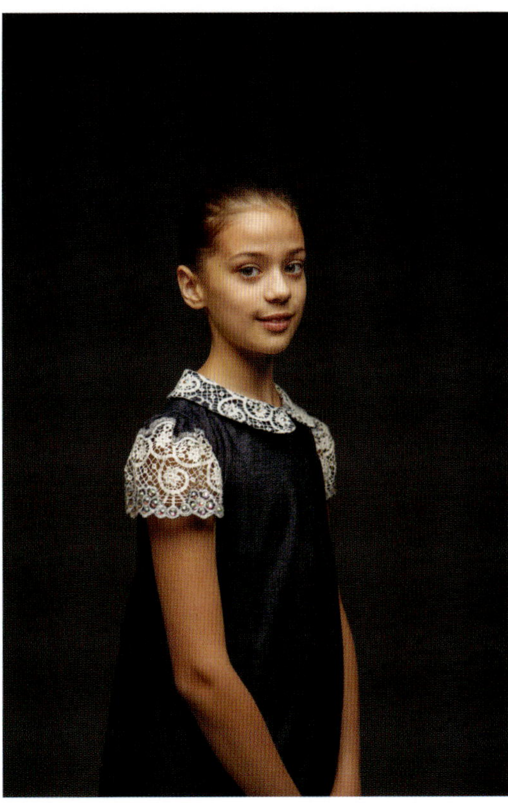 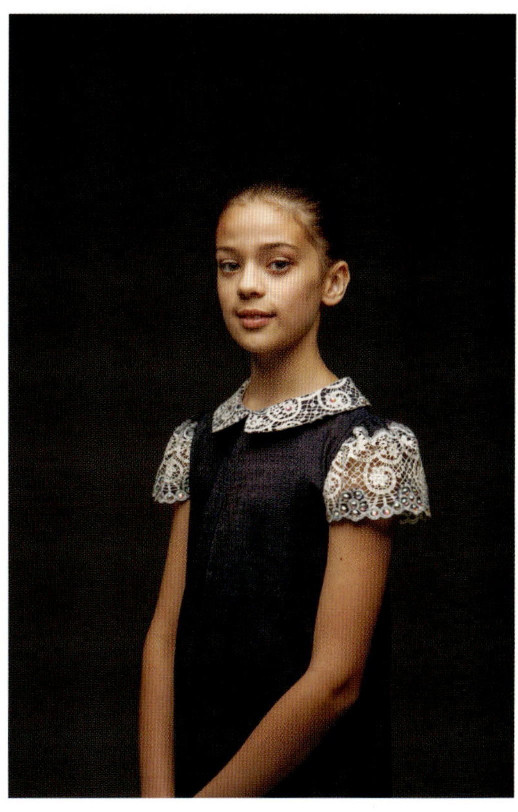

One front top soft light (angled down), plus low reflector.

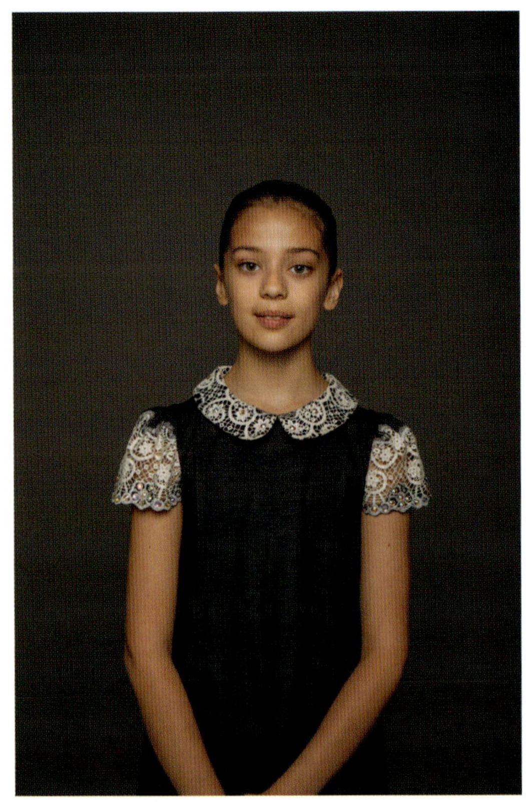 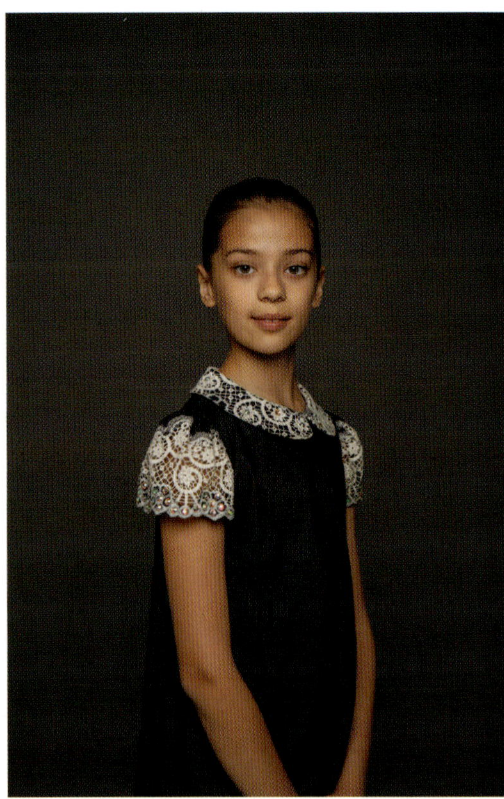 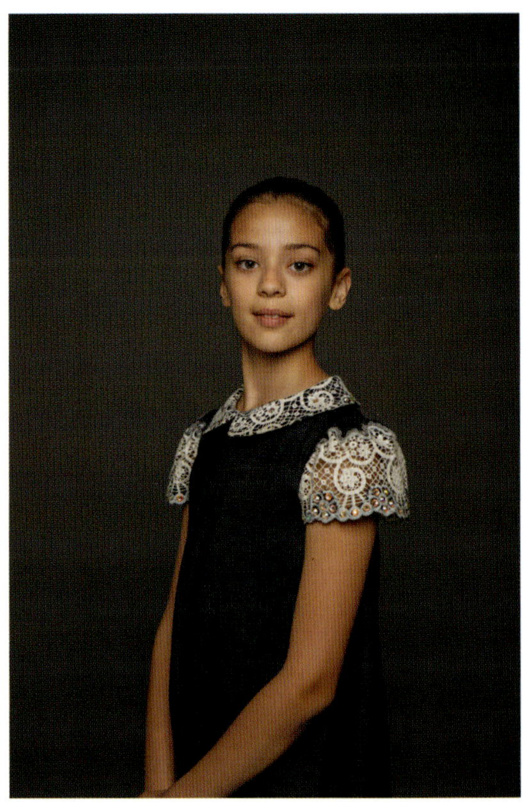

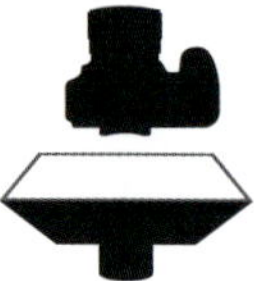

One large front soft light (placed behind the photographer).

Two Lights: Version 1

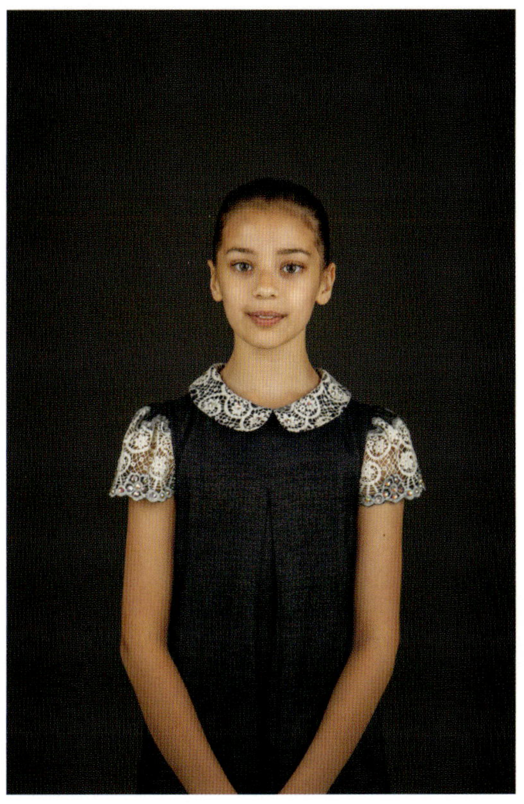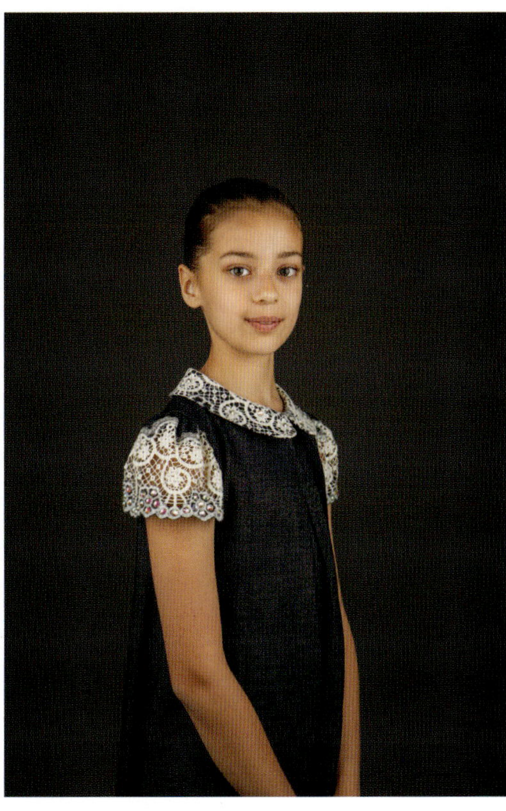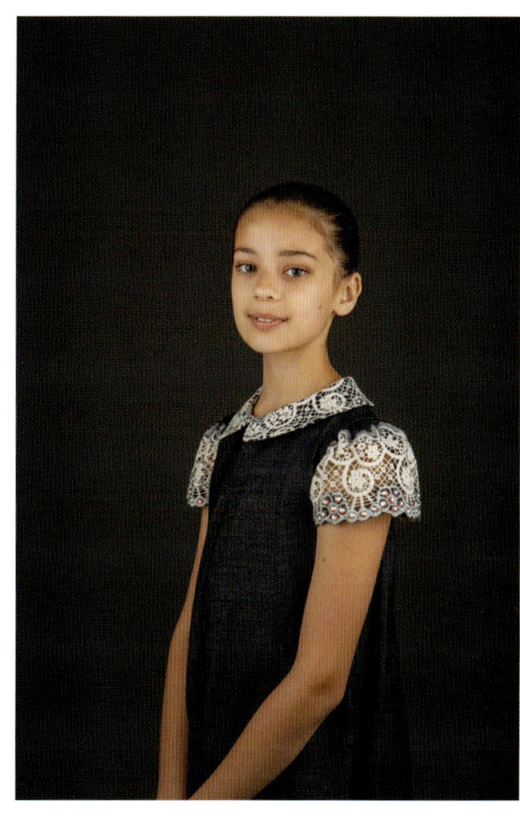

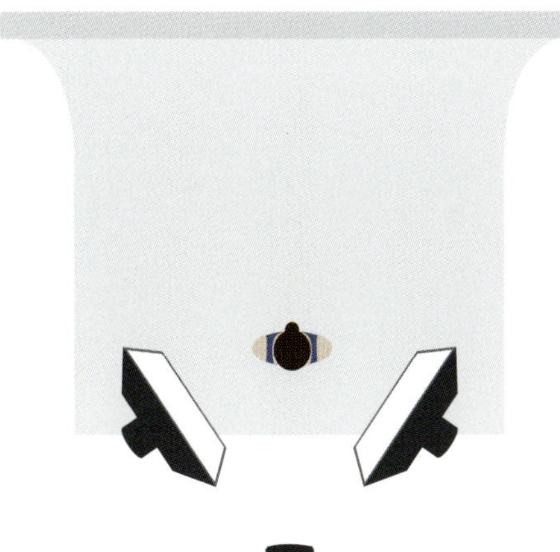

Two front angled soft lights.

Adding a second light will immediately expand the options available to you. You can place your second light in front of or behind the subject to change the character of the lighting: experiment with the lights' positions, distances, and angles to create subtle difference in your final images.

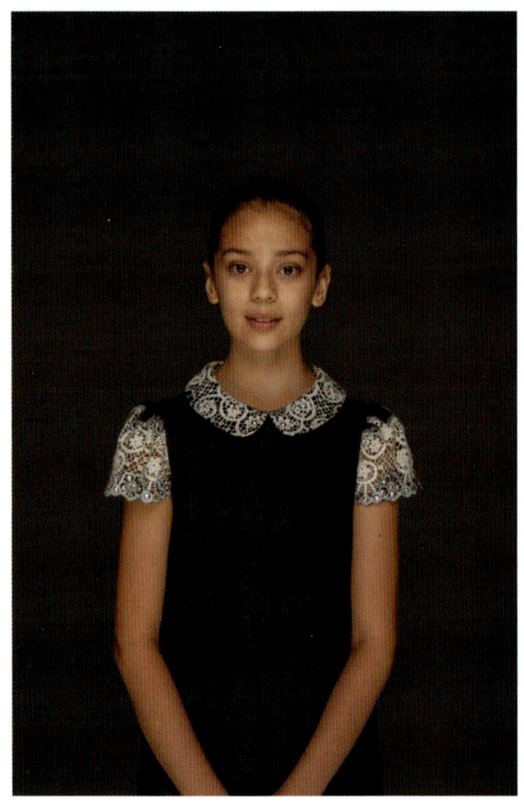 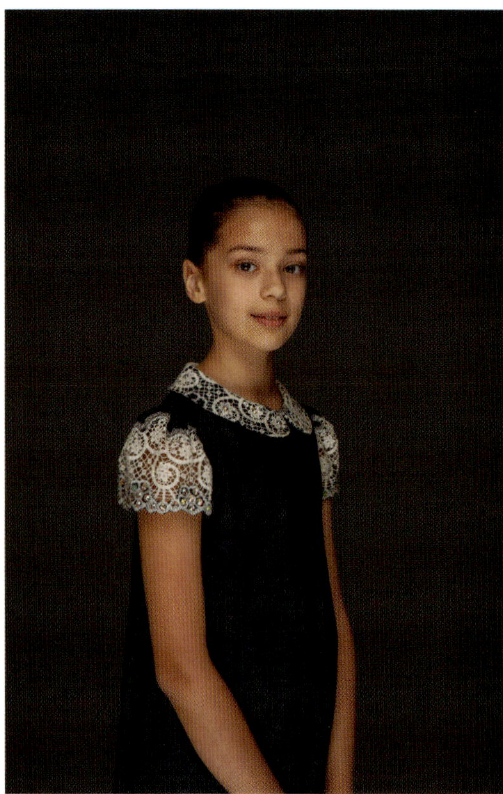 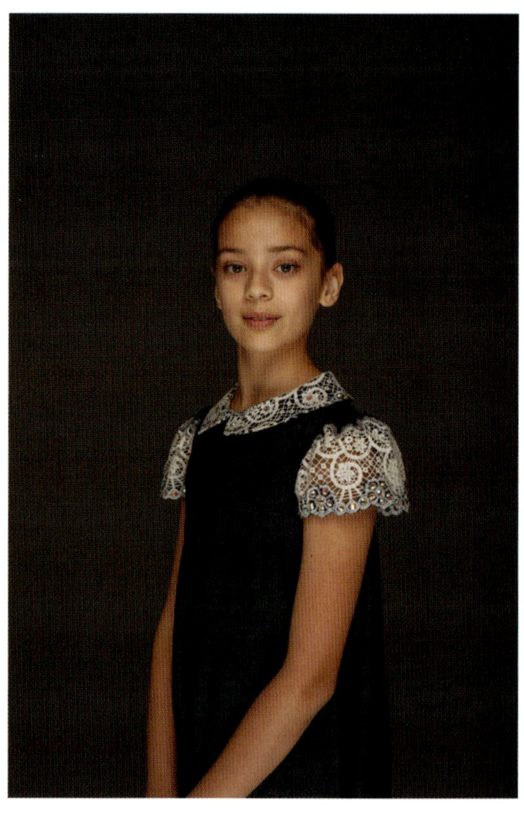

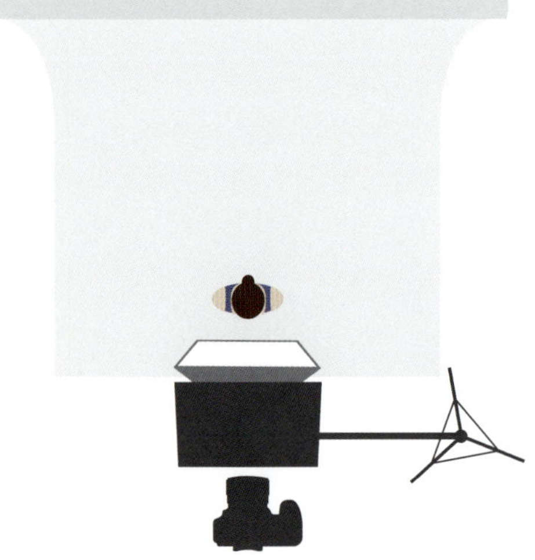

One front top soft light (angled down) and one front bottom soft light (angled up). Often referred to as "clamshell" lighting.

Two Lights: Version 3

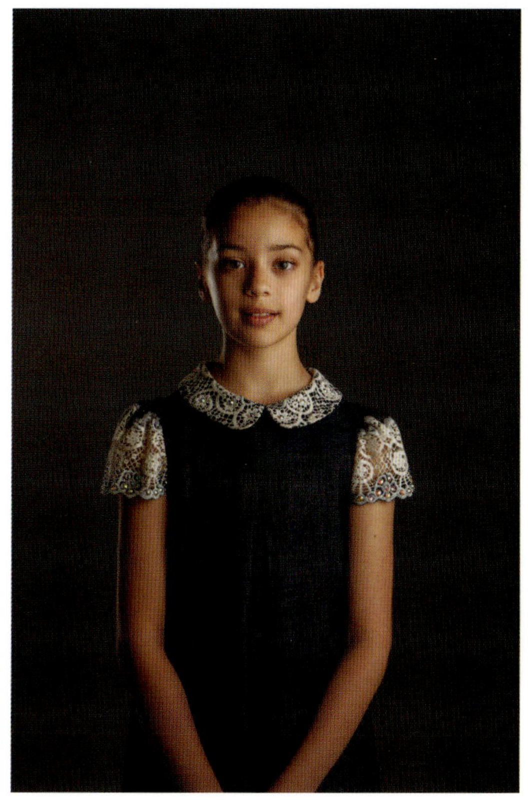 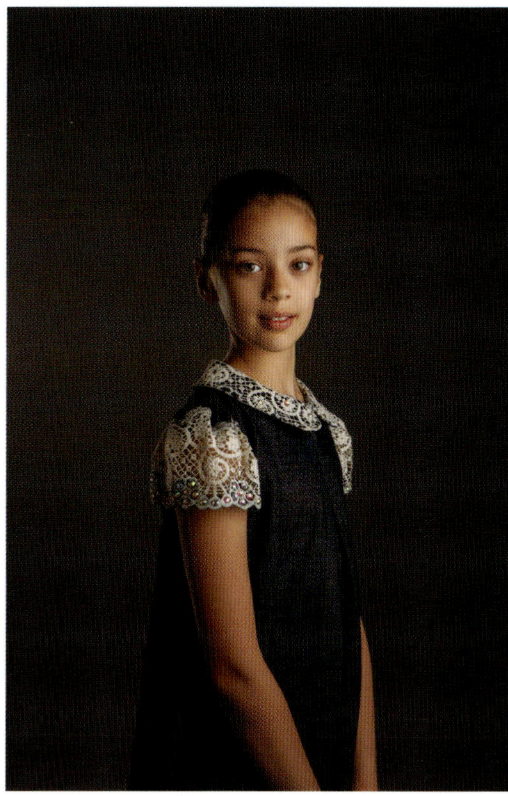 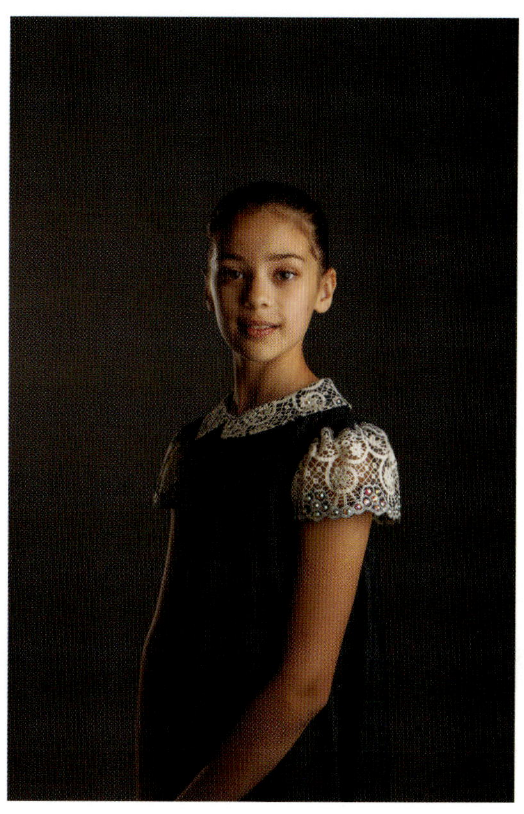

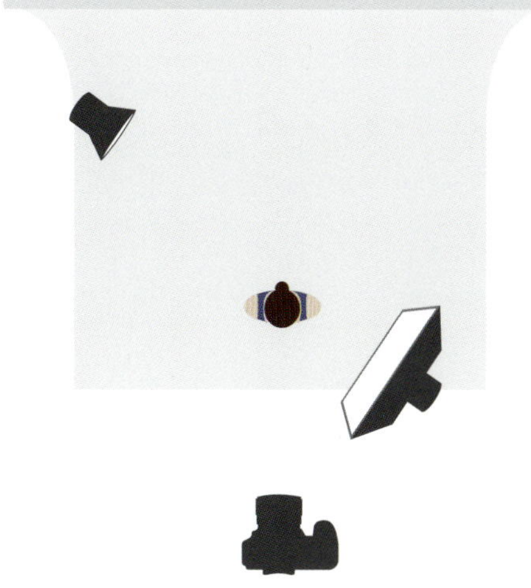

One front side-angled soft light and one back side-angled hard "clip light."

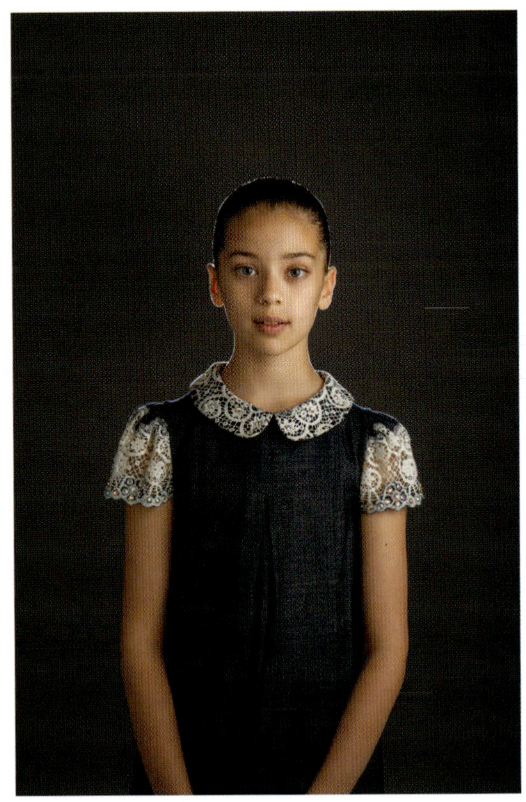
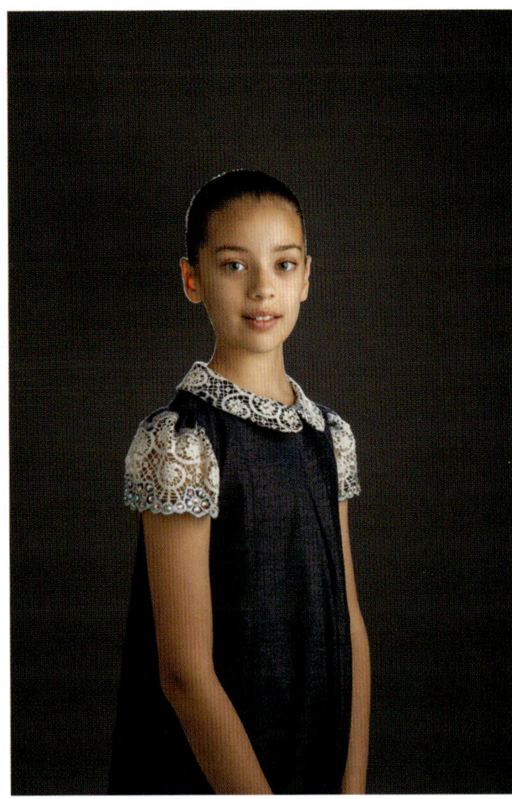
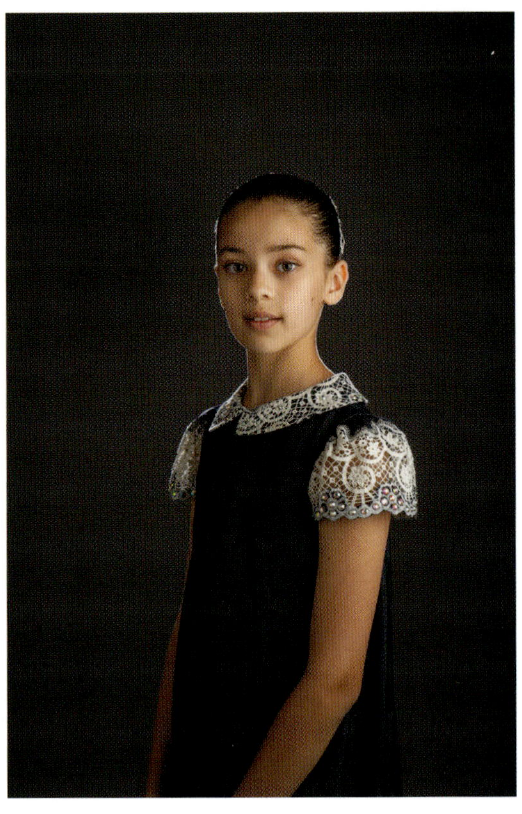

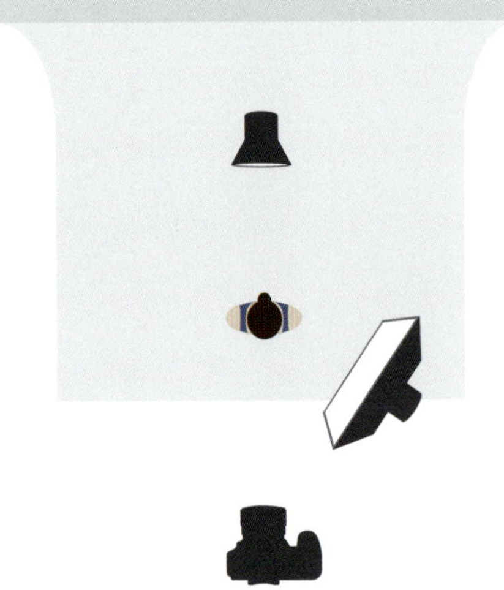

One front side-angled soft light and one back hard light placed directly behind the model's head, facing toward the camera.

Two Lights: Version 5

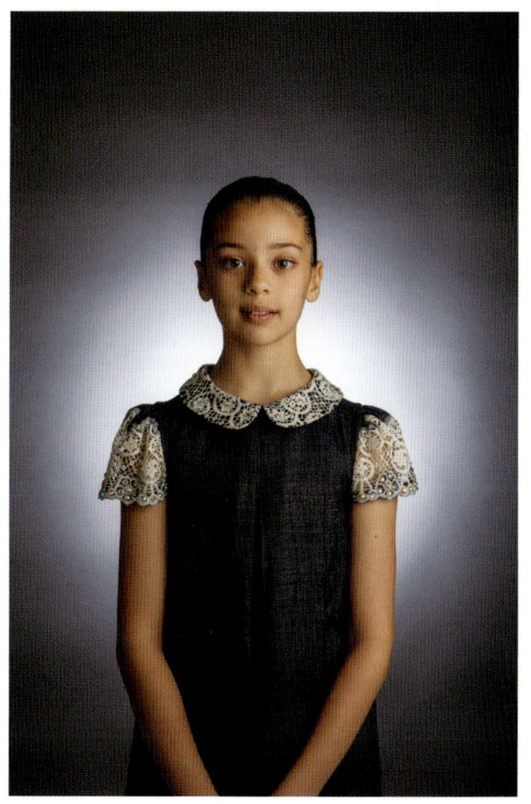 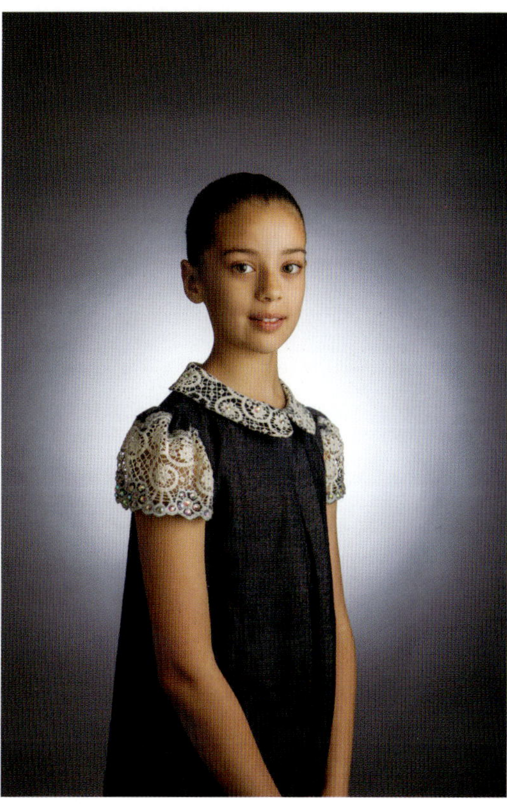 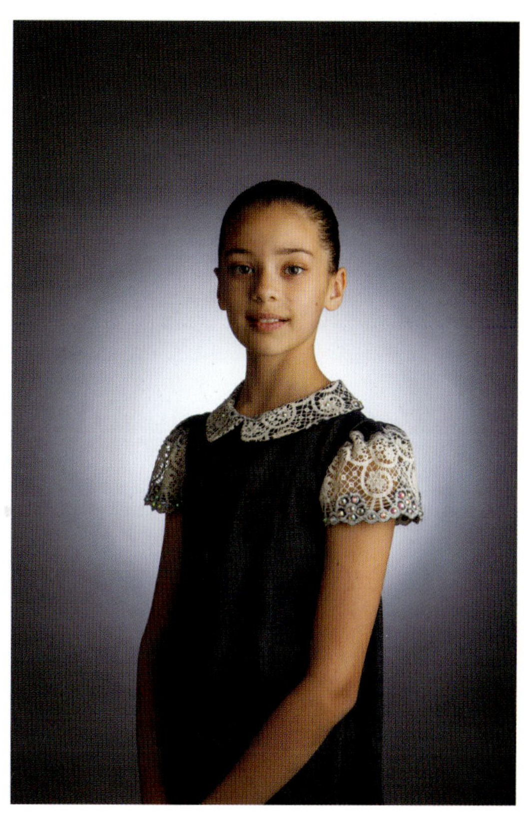

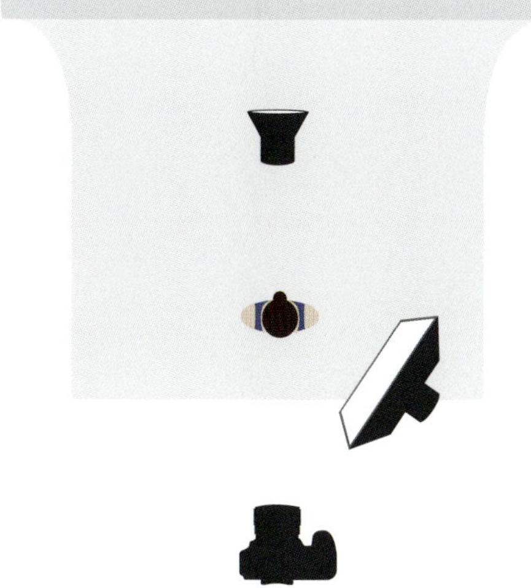

One front side-angled soft light and one back hard light placed directly behind the model's head, aimed toward the background.

Three Lights: Version 1

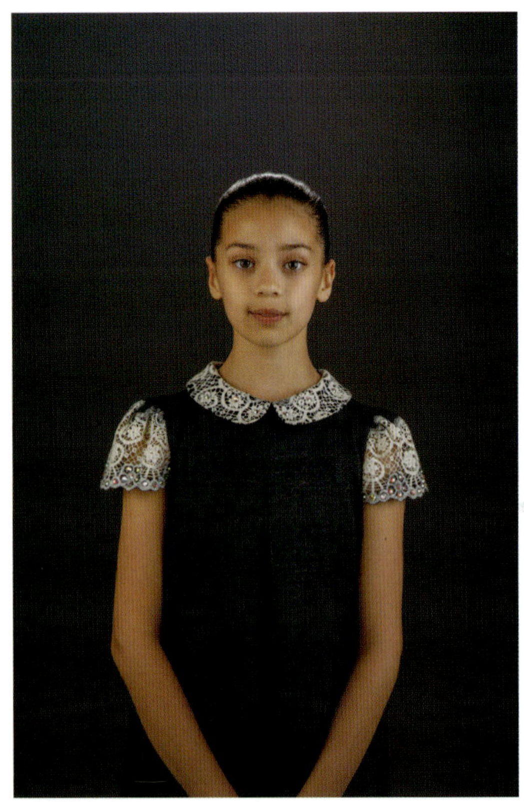
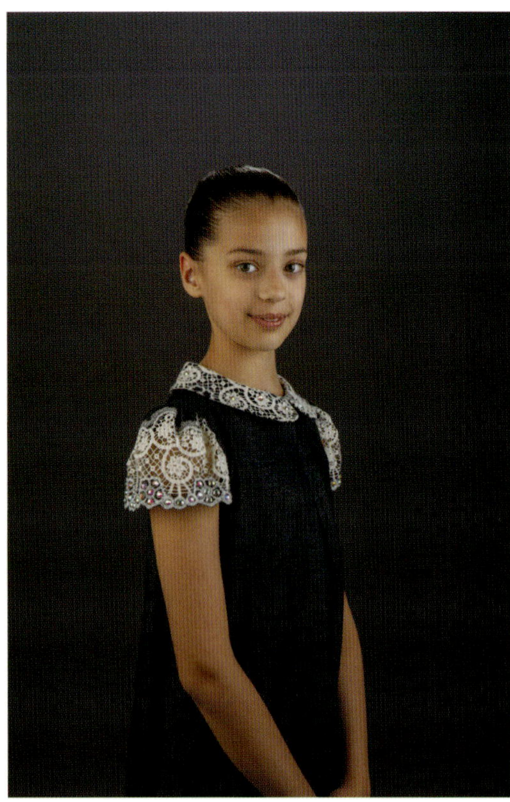
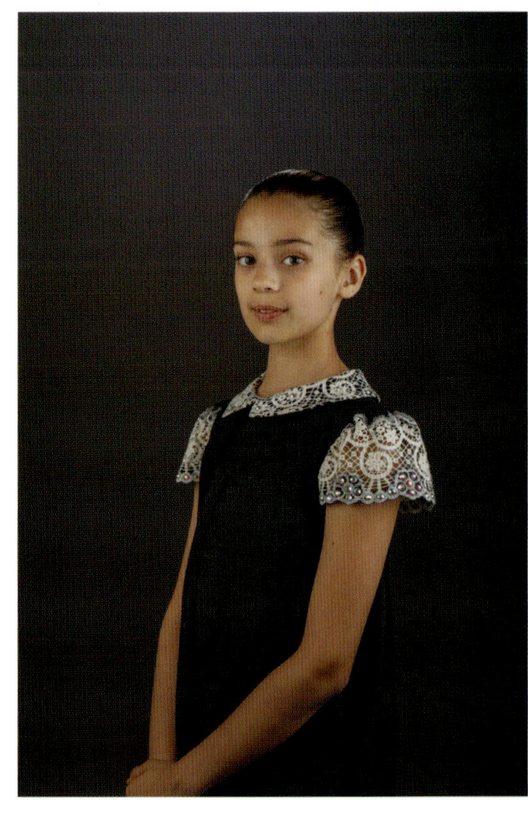

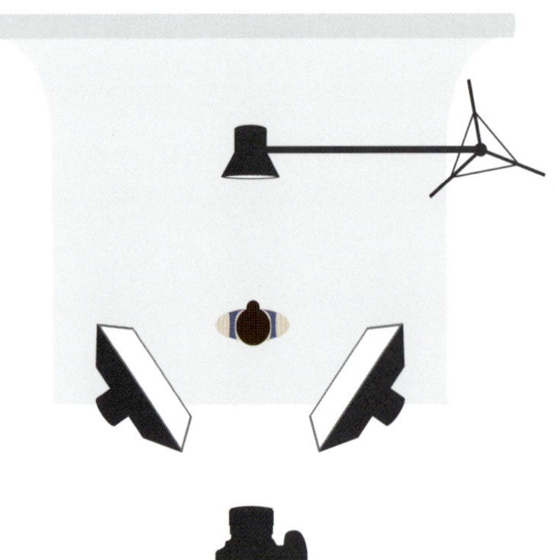

Two front side-angled soft lights and one back hard light placed above and behind the model, aimed at their head.

As you gain confidence in the studio you can add a third light. A backlight (often called a "clip light") will give a beautiful "filmic" effect. You can use your third light to pick out details and help to tell the story of the shoot. Using hard and soft light sources combined opens a whole world of possible lighting techniques.

Three Lights: Version 2

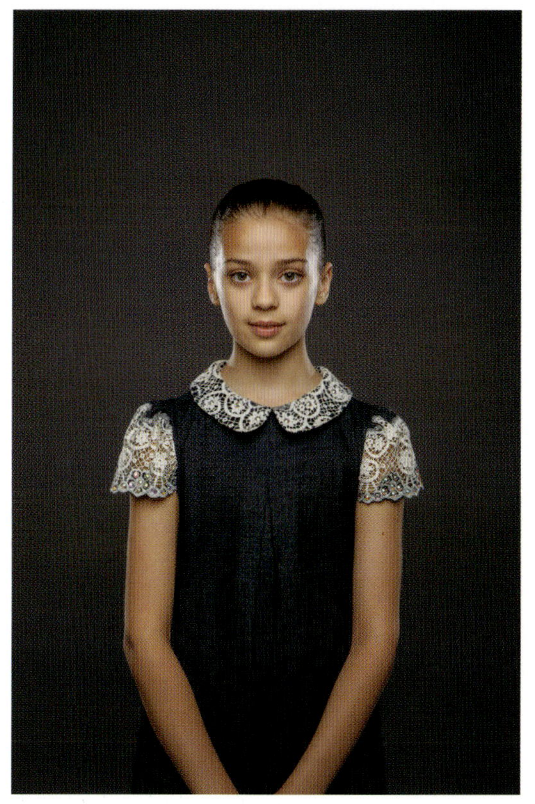 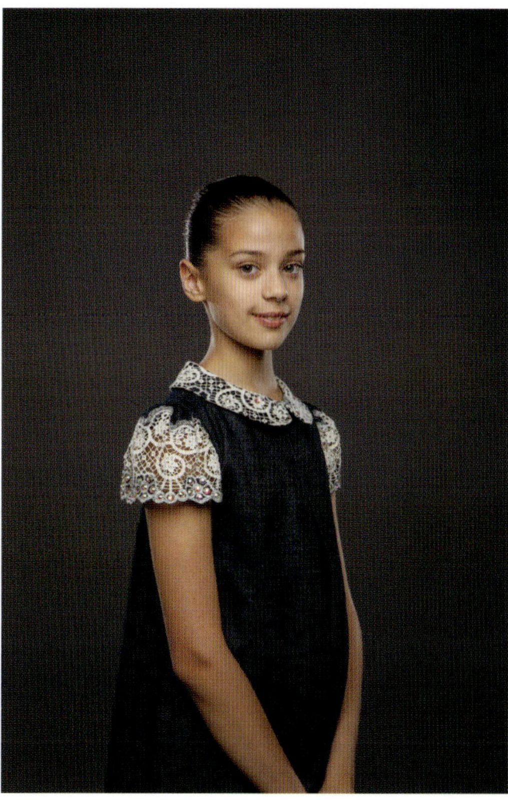 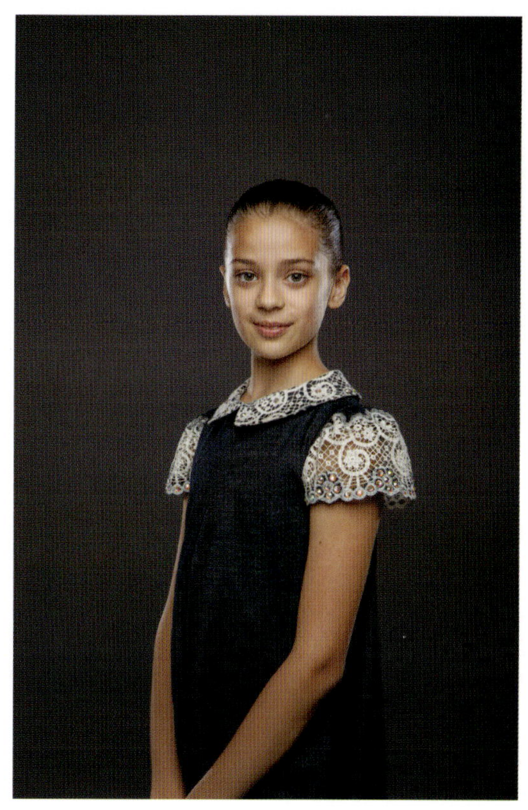

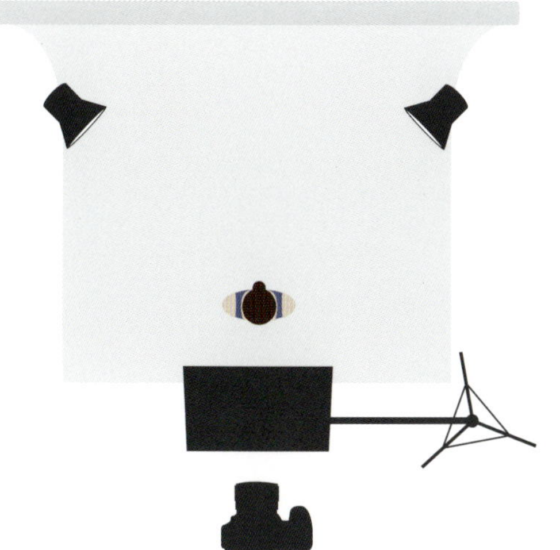

One front top soft light and two back hard lights, aimed toward and clipping the model's head.

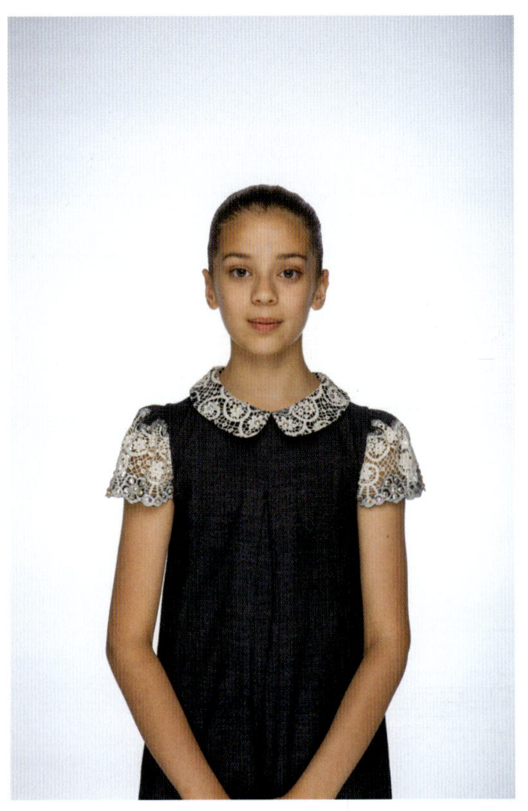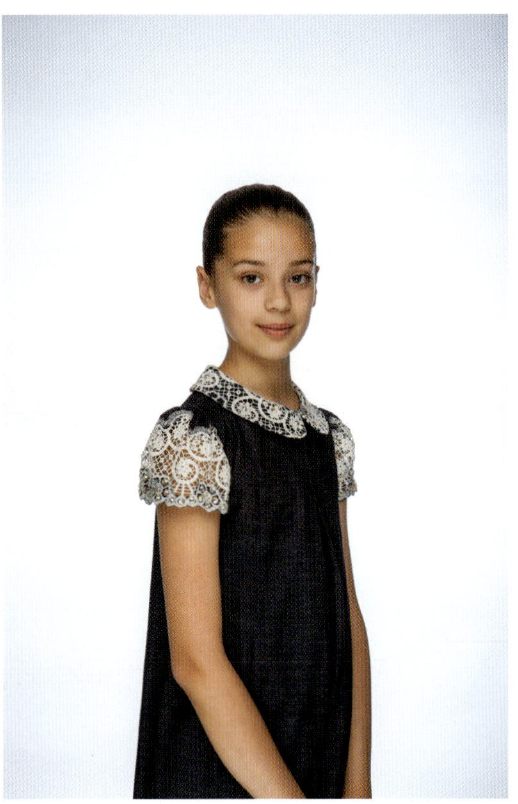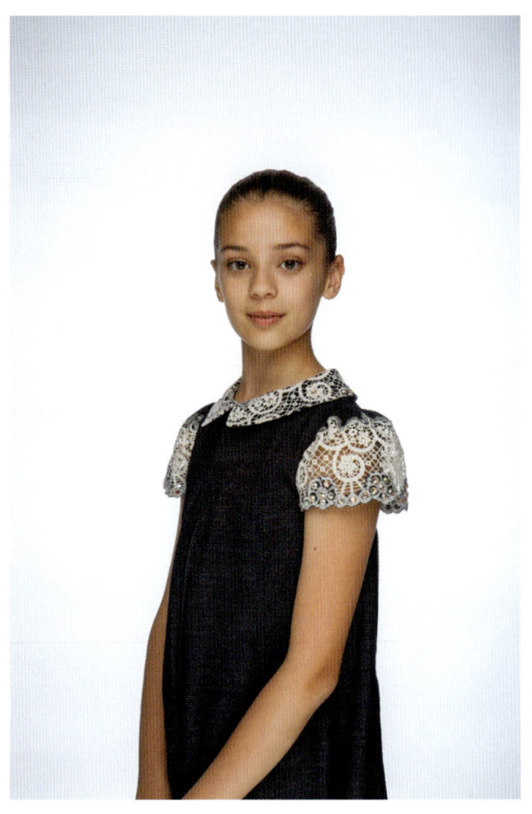

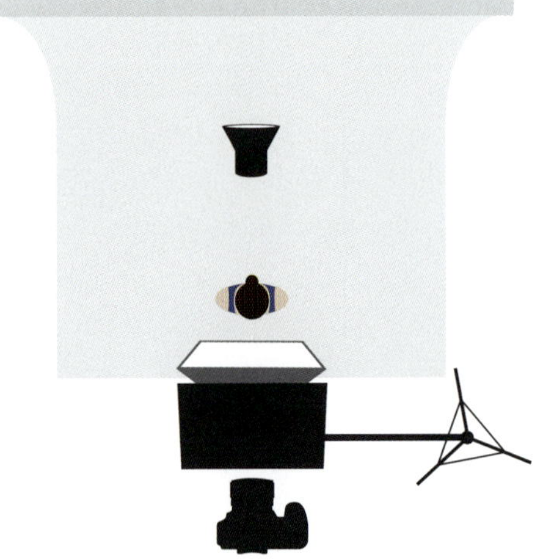

"Clamshell" lighting (see page 110) plus one back hard light aimed toward the background.

Three Lights: Version 4

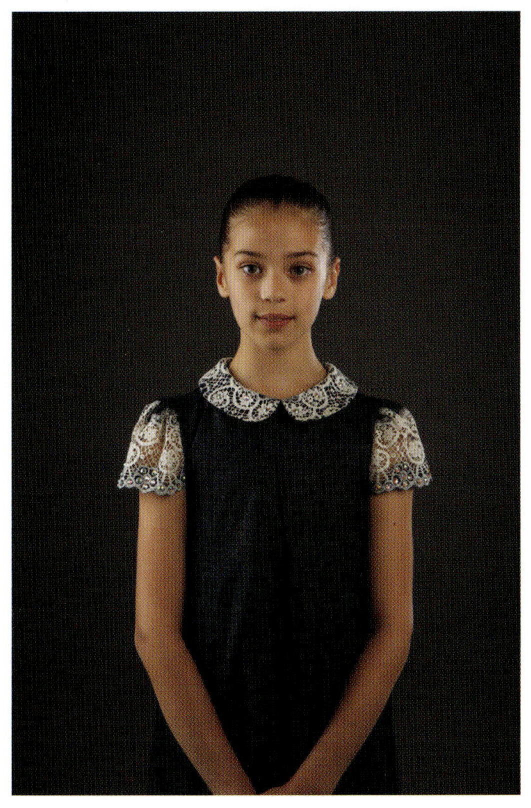 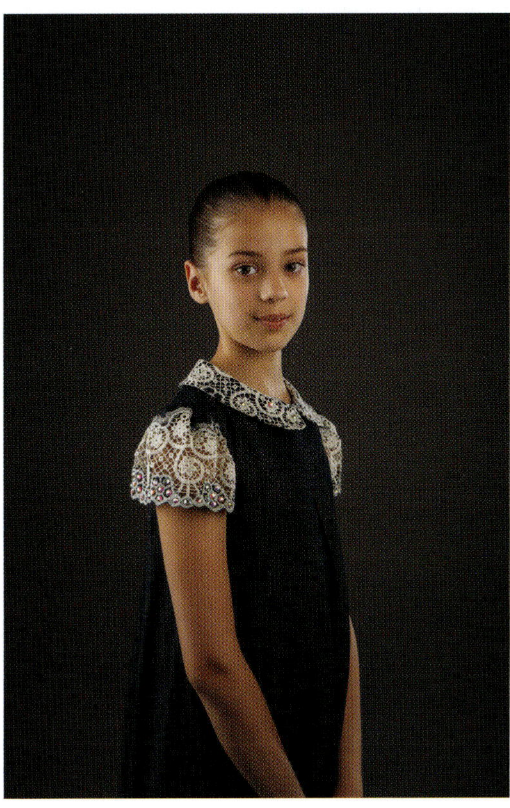 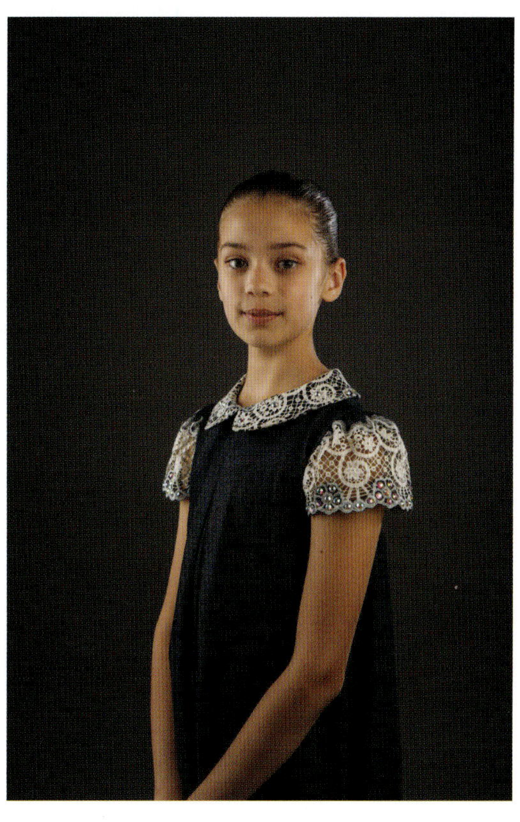

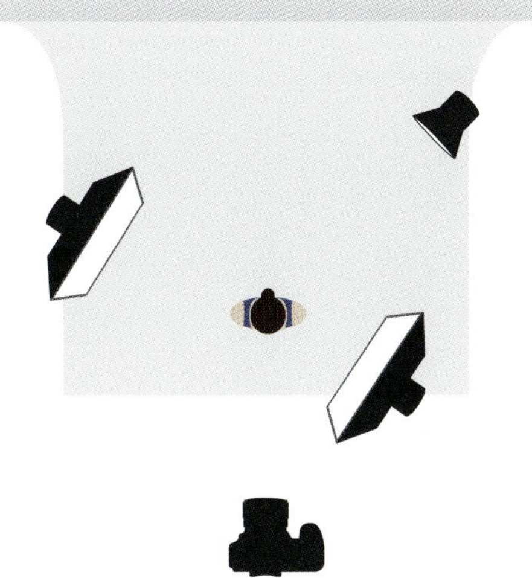

One side-angled soft light, one back side-angled soft clip light (aimed toward the model's head), and one side-angled hard clip light (also aimed toward the model's head).

Capturing Movement

Children like to move about and that is one of the defining features of most child portrait sessions. However, if you want to be in control of any movement it is vital that you understand how flash works in relation to shutter speed.

The burst of light from a flash lasts a fraction of a second. Different flash systems have different durations (and more advanced systems have the ability to adjust their flash duration), but in a studio situation you are simply required to ensure that the camera's shutter is open for long enough for the flash to go off and the sensor to be exposed fully. As you saw on page 103, most DSLRs and mirrorless cameras have a focal plane shutter and will synchronize with a flash unit at any shutter speed up to around 1/200 sec. Effectively this means that the shutter is opening with a long enough window of time for the flash to fire and be registered by the sensor.

If you're shooting in a controlled studio, with minimal ambient light, the flash will usually be so powerful that with a shutter speed of 1/200 sec. and a low ISO (ISO 100–200) the ambient light will have no effect on the exposure. However, if you increase the ISO and/or use a longer shutter speed, the ambient light can begin to play a part in the overall exposure. The point at which this happens will depend on the intensity of the ambient light, but if you set a shutter speed of 1/15 sec., for example, you may find that the ambient light starts to affect the exposure. You can use this creatively, so the flash catches an expression while the longer shutter speed records a blur of movement, but you will need to test this to get the right balance for the flash and ambient exposures. The simple rule is that the shutter speed only controls the ambient light exposure, while the aperture affects both the ambient and flash exposures.

If you set a shutter speed that is faster than the camera's sync speed you will start to see the actual shutter in your shots, as a blurred black line over the image. This is because at faster shutter speeds a focal plane shutter forms a "slit" that scans across the frame, so the sensor is never exposed in its entirety.

Many modern flash units—especially dedicated hotshoe flashes—have a high-speed sync mode that overcomes this by firing the flash repeatedly at a low power setting. However, this is generally more useful outdoors when you want a fill light, rather than in a studio situation.

Tips

- For the most part, if you want to capture movement in a studio setting, you need to turn off all of the ambient lights and rely solely on flash. This will give you the cleanest result.

- Artificial lights can introduce a color cast to your images when they are mixed with flash. Tungsten (incandescent) bulbs will give a yellow/orange cast, while fluorescent lighting tends to create a green cast.

Right: Combining studio flash with daylight will enable you to capture movement in an almost surreal way, so why not try taking your studio outdoors?

Focal length: 40mm

Aperture: f/9

Shutter speed: 1/100 sec.

ISO: 100

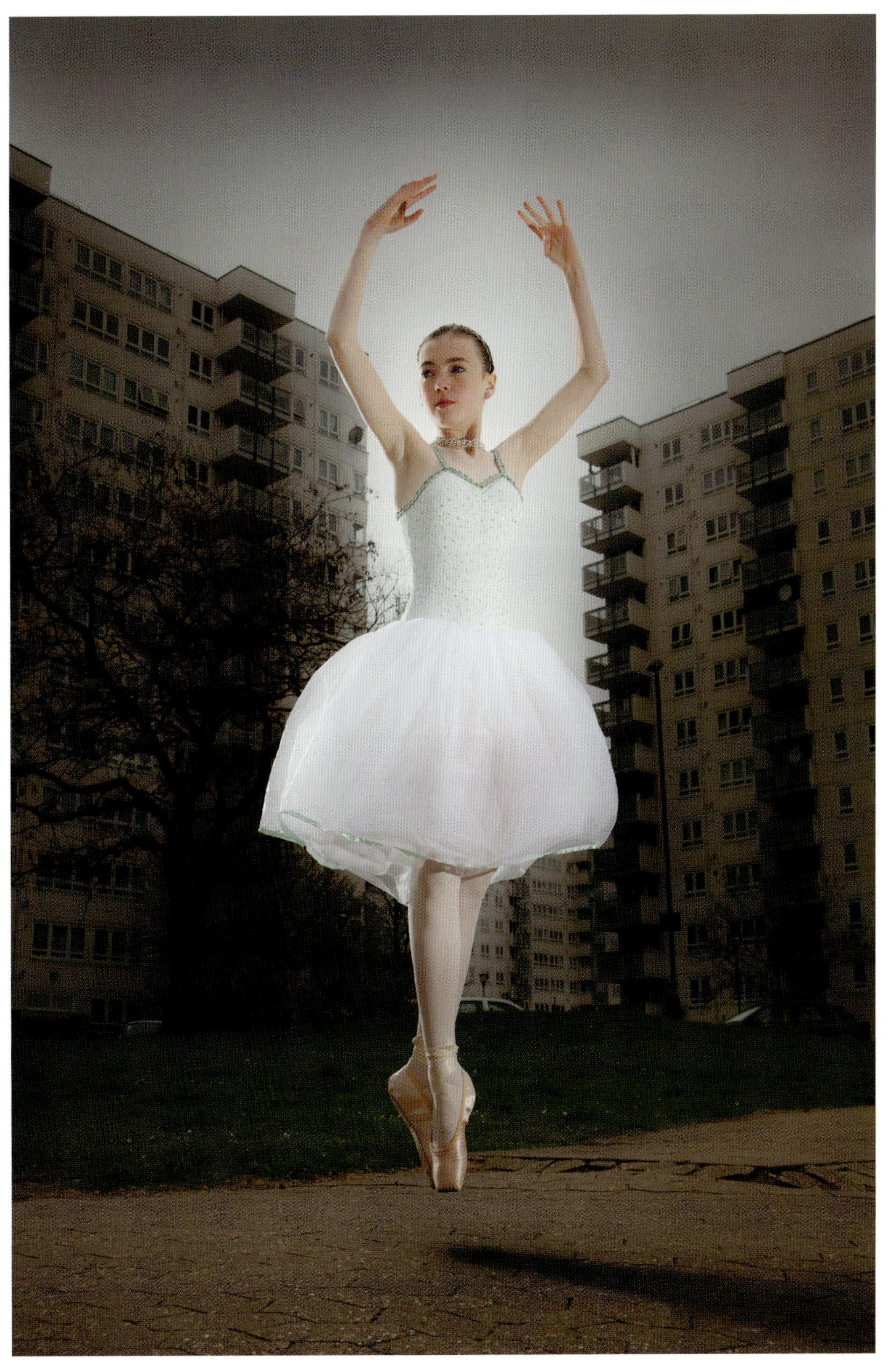

Profile: Lisa Visser

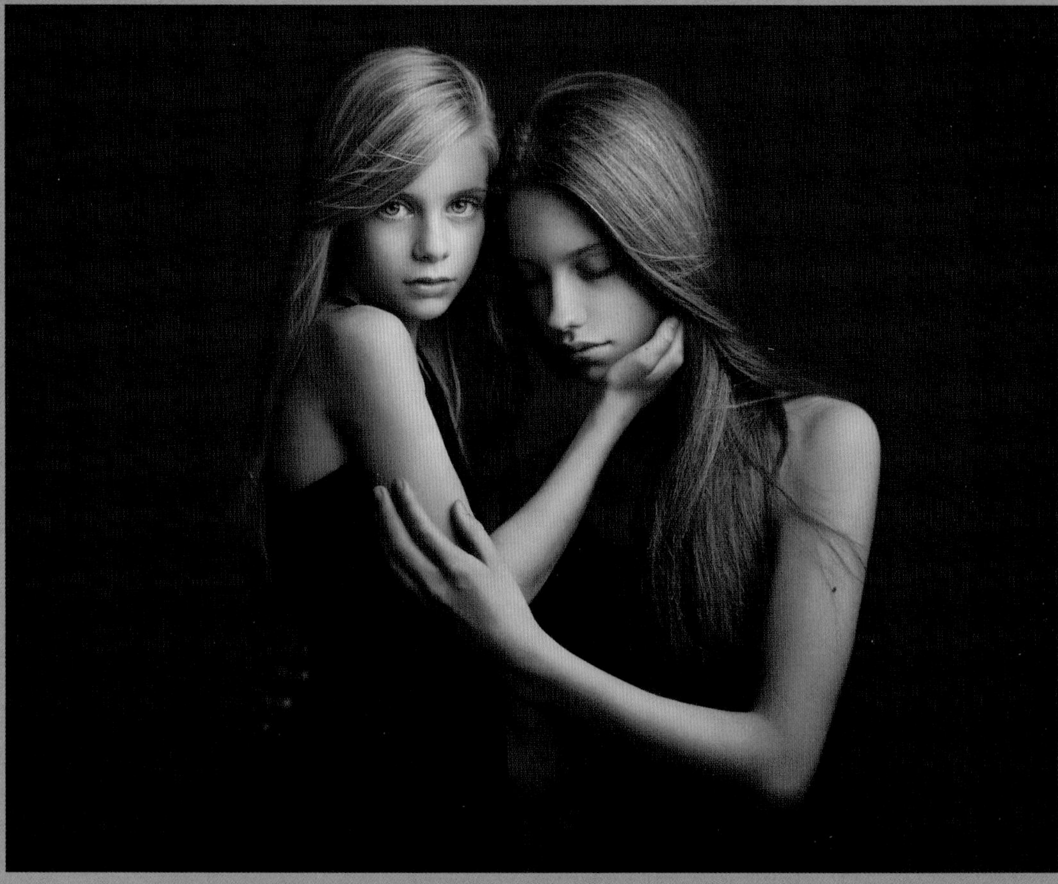

Above:

Focal length: 35mm

Aperture: f/11

Shutter speed: 1/125 sec.

ISO: 100

Q) What equipment do you use regularly?
A) I use a Canon EOS 5D MkIII and 24–105mm lens. In the studio I use Elinchrom monobloc strobes, along with silver and white reflectors.

Q) Why is it important to you to shoot portraits in your distinctive fine-art style?
A) I've been a children's portrait photographer for 30 years and it has been a journey of development and change. When I started out my portraits were photographed in the style of the company that I worked for, but as time passed I started to put more and more of myself into my work. I started to think more about my own style of children's photography and began to get a much greater sense of satisfaction in creating and presenting these images to my clients.

Q) How do you go about setting up a session and preparing the client?
A) Many of my clients book me specifically for my style of children's portraiture and put a great amount of trust in me. Of course, I always check what their expectations are and what type of images they would like, but they are usually happy for me to create images of their child in whatever way I think is best. The things I think about are outfit choices and colors, the background, and what lighting setups I am going to use; hairstyling is also a key consideration to give the right feel to the image.

Q) What tips do you have for controlling and guiding children during a shoot?
A) With children under the age of three I use a lot of distraction techniques, such as toys and bubbles, to grab their attention and get the eye contact and expression I need. With older children who can follow instructions I am watching and assessing them during the session. I am looking

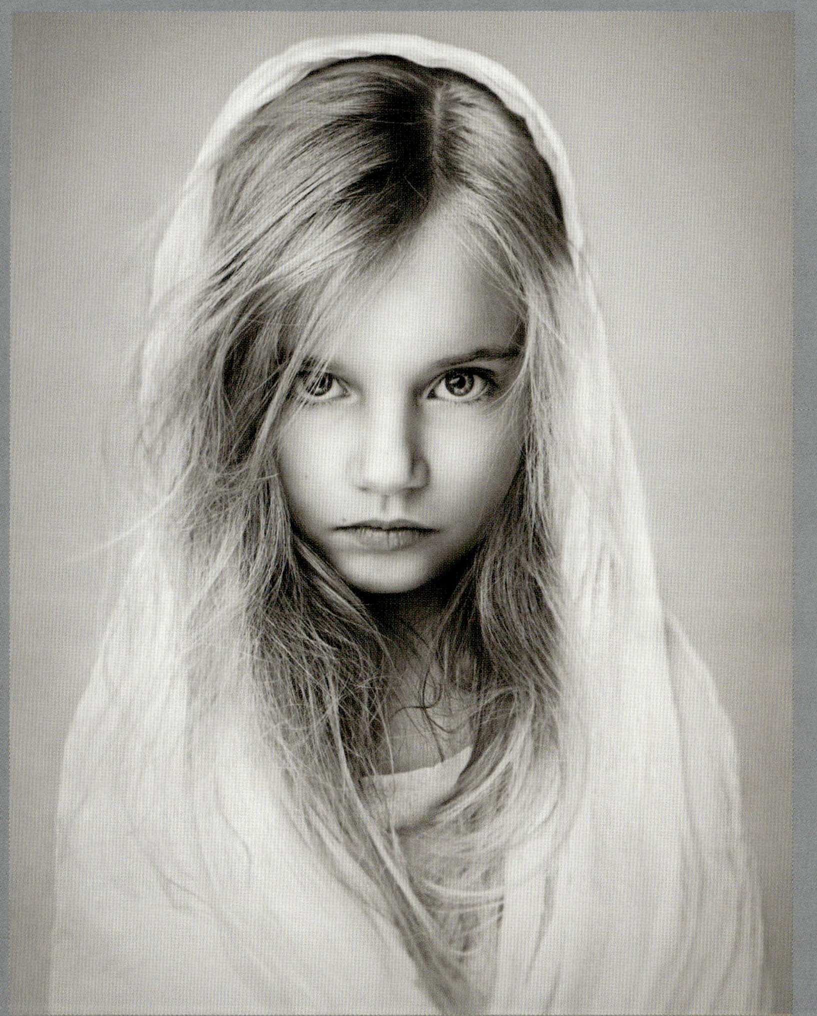

Above:
Focal length: 58mm
Aperture: f/11
Shutter speed: 1/125 sec.
ISO: 100

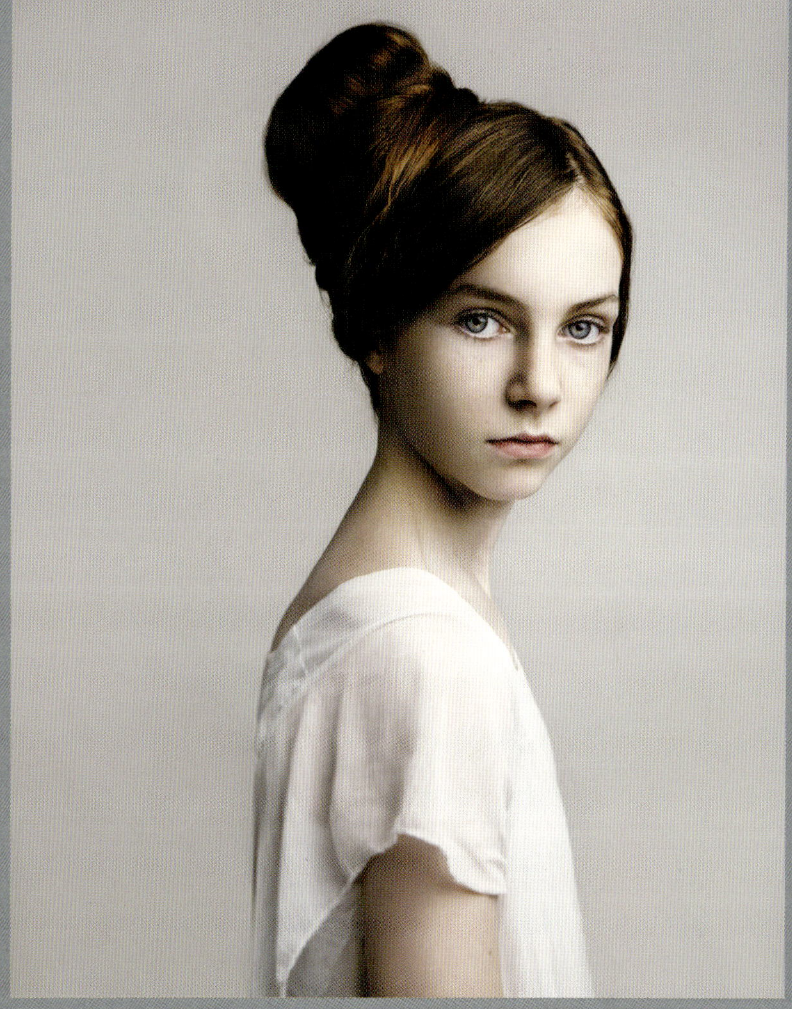

Above:
Focal length: 67mm
Aperture: f/11
Shutter speed: 1/125 sec.
ISO: 100

to see if they are shy, confident, or are losing interest. I watch for all these things and then adapt myself and adjust the session to make sure I get the best out of them.

Q) How do you light your subjects in the studio?
A) I try to keep my lighting as simple as possible. If I have one or two subjects then I usually use one light and a reflector, varying the position of the light to create slightly different lighting patterns.

Q) How important is postproduction and do you do your own?
A) Postproduction is really important to me, as it is what makes a good image come alive and where I can add more of my own style. At the moment I do all my own postproduction, as I like to have control over the final image.

Child Psychology

Even with many years of experience, skill, and training, in the heat of the moment it is incredibly easy to lose track of what you need to do to get that elusive child portrait shot. It is easy to freeze when faced with erratic (and sometimes plain naughty) children who have decided to make it their afternoon's work to wreck your day. Maintaining control through friendship and respect is the basis of every good child portraiture shoot and having a good grasp of the psychology of your models is essential. To the child you may appear mad and clown-like; calm and philosophical; knowledgeable and teacher-like. All of these personas should be perfected and used with different types of children in different situations, but no matter what, you need to stay in control.

Right: The unique challenge for the child portrait photographer is that they need to be part technician, part artist, and part psychologist. Negotiation skills are not optional.

Focal length: 105mm

Aperture: f/8

Shutter speed: 1/320 sec.

ISO: 500

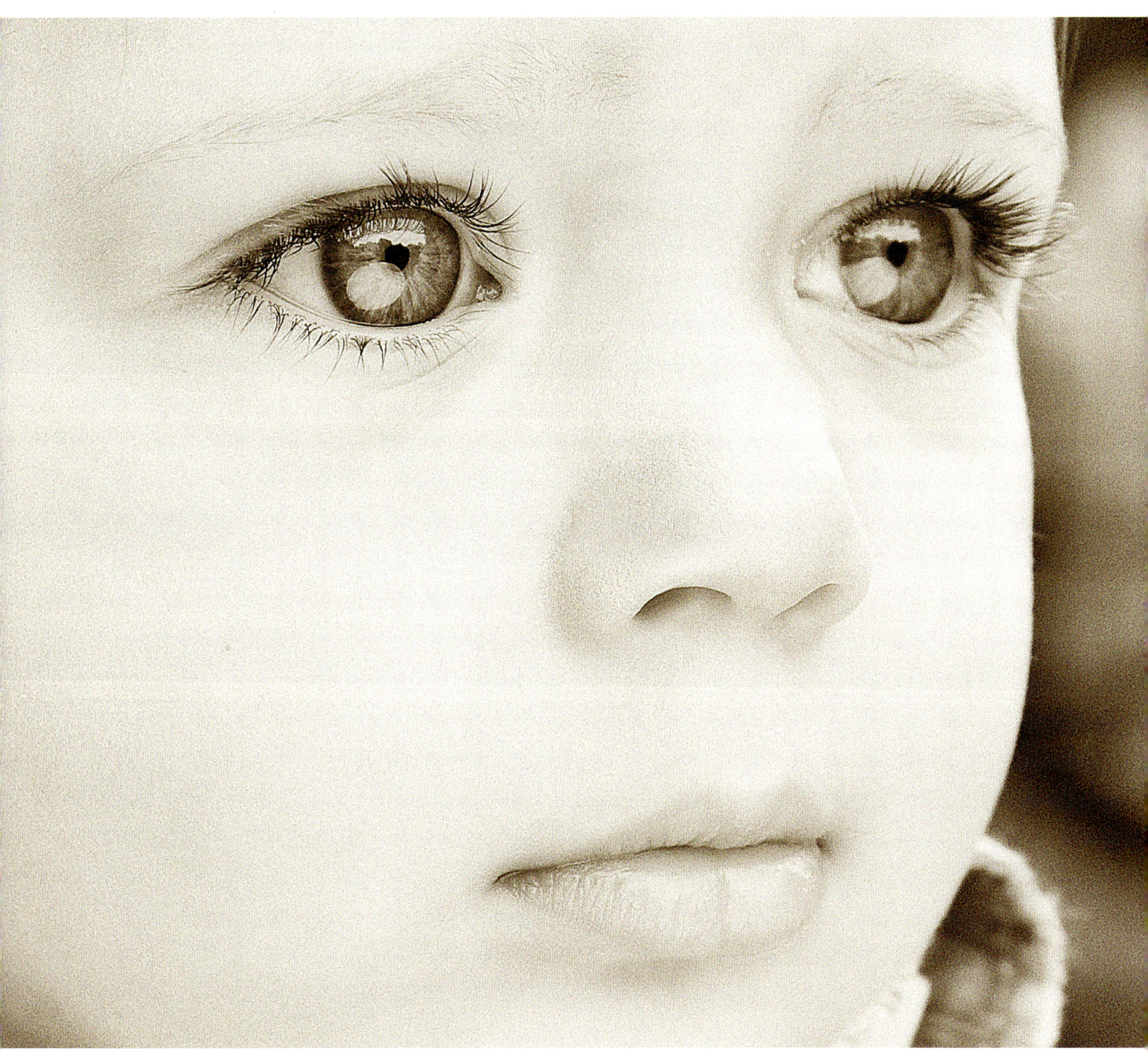

The Unique Challenge Of Children

If portrait sessions were simply a matter of learning how to get the correct exposure, pointing a camera at a subject, and firing the shutter, anyone could be a portrait photographer. But we all know there is more to it than that. For a start, you need to establish a relationship with your subject, even if it is a short-term friendship based on politeness. When you photograph an adult they will instinctively know that what you are doing is to your mutual benefit and will help the process as much as they can. They may be shy or nervous, brash or overly opinionated, but they understand the situation and for the most part will try to cooperate. Children are entirely different!

Firstly, most children will not be as aware of the "rules" that most adults take for granted. Even the best-behaved children in the world do not have the intellectual capability to analyze the nuances of every given situation, so you cannot just supply an endless list of instructions and expect a child to follow them. For this reason, you need to have a strong grasp of what makes a child tick: child psychology is not an option when shooting child portraits, it is essential!

On most shoots with children you will only have around 60–90 minutes for photography, so you need to find ways of engaging with all sorts of children very quickly. Short attention spans, tiredness, and a "stranger danger" upbringing mean that not every child will greet you with the kind of enthusiasm that you'd like to see, so you need to be prepared for any situation.

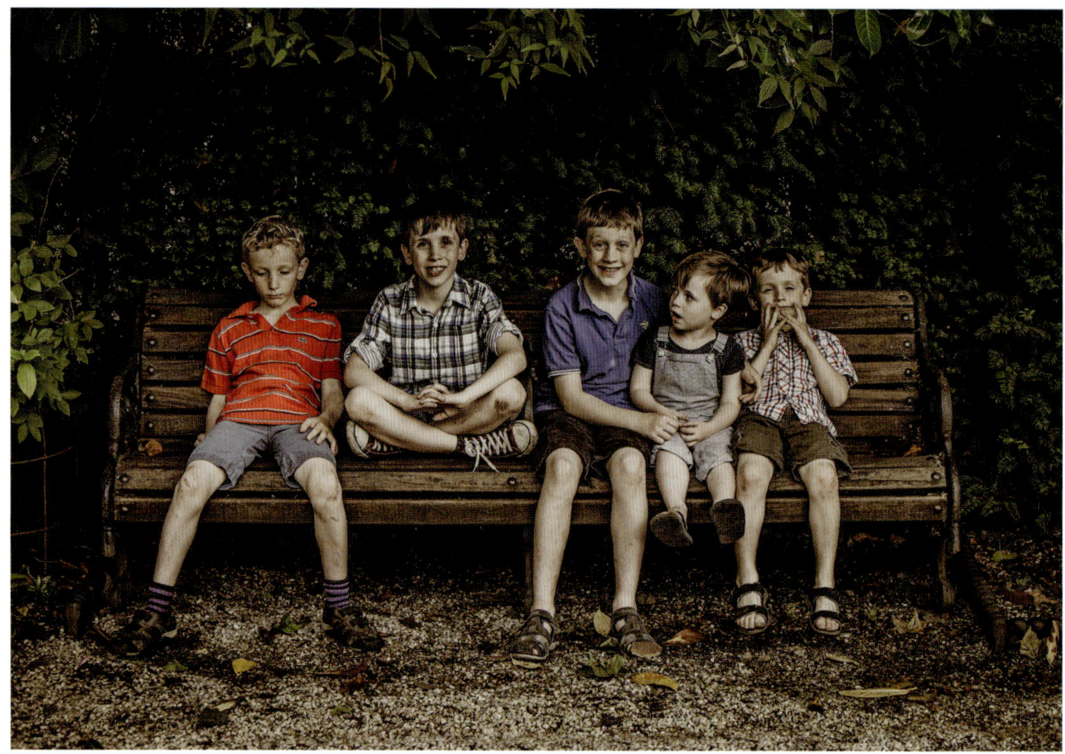

Above: Just like adults, children have different personalities: they are not all the same.

Focal length: 70mm

Aperture: f/4.5

Shutter speed: 1/200 sec.

ISO: 800

Establishing The Rules

Before every portrait session I always spend five minutes having a quick chat with both the parents and the child to establish how we are going to proceed. This is a great opportunity to lay out a set of rules for the child and parent to follow, before launching into the shoot itself.

I have five golden rules and during this initial chat I am looking to create a bond with the child as quickly as I can. I often openly say to the child that "the rules are for mommy and daddy" so they can help me make sure mom and dad follow the rules. In this way I am already siding with the child, so I am one of their friends first; mom and dad come second.

There is also another very effective way to gain a child's confidence quickly prior to a shoot. When

Below: Before you venture off piste with your child model always ensure the parent is happy and you have their permission to try out your idea. Always be safe!

Focal length: 19mm

Aperture: f/13

Shutter speed: 1/10 sec.

ISO: 2000

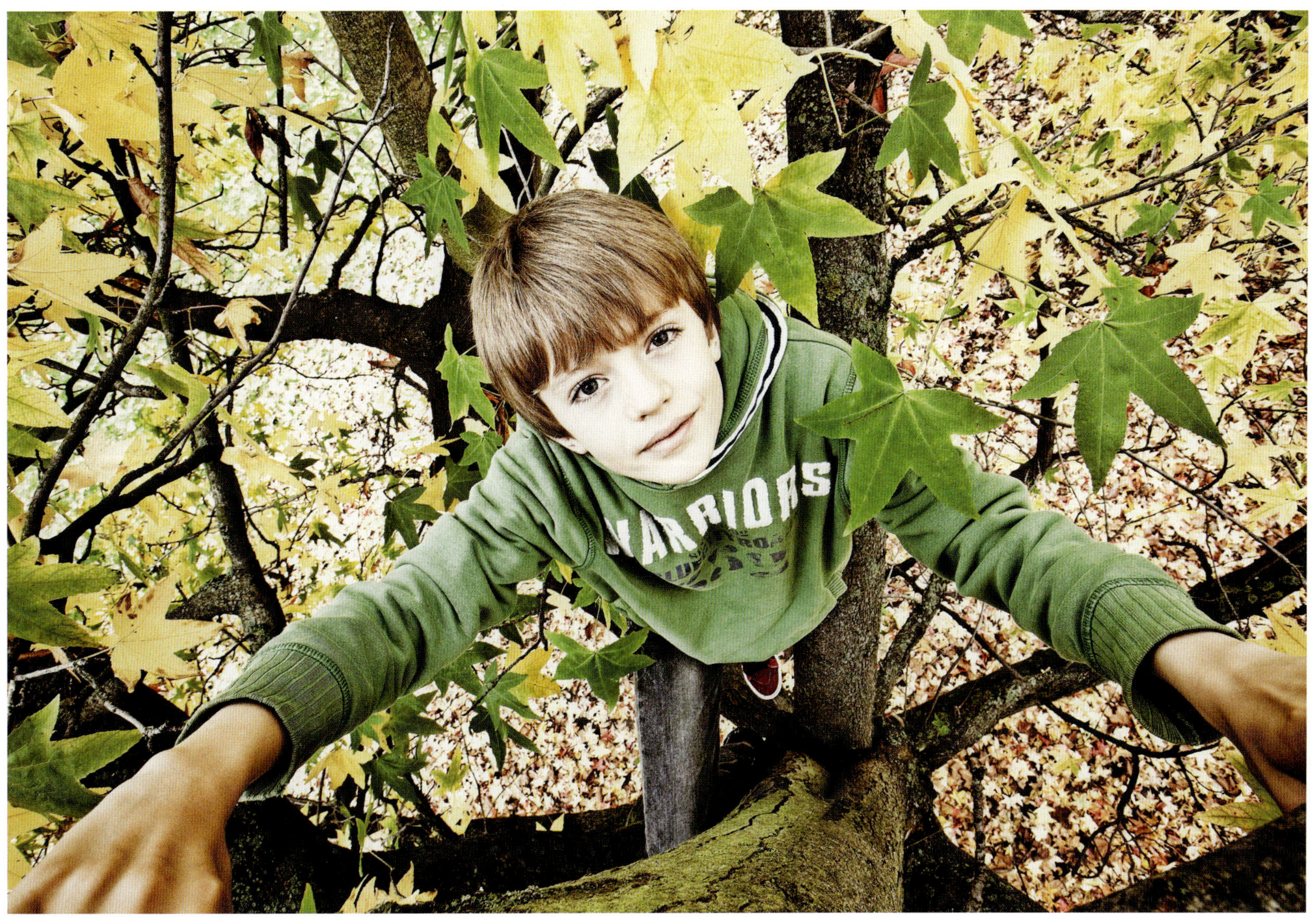

you meet the family on location or at the studio, squat down to eye level and shake hands and say hello to the child first. This is a great way to put the child on a higher level than their parents and at that moment they will realize this is about them, not mom and dad. You need to be a little careful, though, as with shy children this can be a little too much, so assess the situation and make sure you remember their name before you arrive.

What Are The Rules?

I have five basic rules of how a shoot will proceed. Practice them so they are natural to you and don't deliver them like a sergeant major—they should come across with authority, but in a conversational fashion, not as barked orders! Your rules will help to establish you as a professional in the eyes of the parents, and should ensure no unwanted or awkward situations arise due to misunderstandings during the shoot.

Although the "performance" of explaining these rules is designed to get the child on your side, the rules themselves are more about the parent. You effectively have two clients—the child and the parent—and you need to gain the trust and co-operation of both.

RULE 1

It is not for you to decide if the child is safe: it is the parent's responsibility. Therefore it is important to make it very clear to mom and dad that their child's health and safety is down to them at all times. As you get more comfortable shooting child portraits you will take over the situation more and more. The subconscious effect of this for the parent is that you are in charge—much like a teacher is in the classroom—and the parents will often start to let their guard drop. You need to make them aware that you are behind a camera so may not see any hazards that their child could fall off or trip over. I also make it clear that if they are not happy about any situation they must say so and I will change it immediately. If you are working in a studio environment, explain how important it is to be aware of cables and lighting—carelessness can be expensive and dangerous.

RULE 2

Make it clear from the beginning that it is not acceptable for the parents to take photographs while you are shooting, either with a camera or with a phone. This is distracting and most reasonable parents will realize it is also disrespectful. I have had parents turn up with a DSLR kit and then sit behind me shooting throughout the entire session, which is why I introduced this rule.

If you tell someone up front that they can't do something, they will rarely go against your wishes, but if you *don't* tell them and they start to take photos you will have to ask them to stop. In the middle of a shoot this can often seem rude; at the very least it will make them feel a little awkward and create a bad atmosphere. So remember to make this clear before you begin—it makes for a much more harmonious relationship.

RULE 3

This only applies to location shoots and involves asking the parents to be aware of your camera bag. It is all too easy to leave a bag full of expensive equipment in the middle of the park while you chase a child, only to come back and find it has mysteriously disappeared. Photoshoots are like magnets to thieves, so ask the parents to act as an extra pair of eyes and ears. I often ask them to carry the bag or put it on the child's buggy, which gives them greater involvement in the shoot and a sense of "ownership" that often pays dividends when they come to order prints.

RULE 4

I always tell the parents to stand behind me during a shoot, as it not only gives them a clear guideline where they should be, but also means that when I am shooting I can ask the child to look at their parent and by definition that means they are looking toward the camera. The parent needs to be at the same eye height, though, which normally means low down. If not, you can easily find that in all of your photographs the child appears to be looking at the sky as they look at their parents standing tall behind you!

RULE 5

Remember to get a model release form. You can use a standard form downloaded from the Internet, or have your own bespoke form prepared by a solicitor, but you must never photograph someone else's children without a model release form, as it clarifies what the images can be used for and who owns the copyright. If the parents have any issues with any clauses in the form then now is the time to bring this up, not after the shoot. Supply the form to them in advance of the shoot and remind them to bring it with them on the day. Many people will forget, so have some spares and a pen in you kit bag.

Friend Or Authority Figure?

You normally have just over an hour to make a child do what you want them to do, and for that to happen consistently you need to have a range of tools available to you and to be prepared to use them. I always favor the "friend" approach to shoots (as I do in life), but there are occasions when you need to be an authoritarian.

In my opinion, your general approach should be that of a friendly, fun person. This will bring out the best in most children most of the time. There is a chance, though, that the child will misinterpret this as being a play date, and they will start to mess around, pull silly faces, run away, and generally do things that are not conducive to photography.

If this happens, you need to be clear about who is in charge. That doesn't mean shout or be angry; I find the most effective reaction to misbehavior is to act immediately disinterested. "Disinterested" to most children is a clear indication of disapproval.

Sometimes a parent will laugh along with the child when they are being disruptive or difficult, so quietly explain your method and ensure they follow you. In simple terms, if the child is not doing what you want, don't give them any attention. The moment they do the right thing make sure they see your face light up with enthusiastic approval. This way they will quickly understand that the best way to get attention is to respect the rules. Remember, it is not your place to punish or remonstrate with the child. No matter what happens, it is your job to rise above it and be a professional.

I often explain quietly to the parent that I know I am not being a "good parent" and I apologize in advance. I will often do silly things like blowing a raspberry so the child will laugh and then I accuse them of farting. In child terms this is the height of comedy, and rarely fails to get a laugh if done repeatedly and with conviction! As long as I get my laugh, I am happy to continue, but sometimes the child will do the same thing back to me. I have to tell them that is not good and stop them from doing it; if it happens repeatedly I just change

the subject and move on. Essentially a "good parent" would never encourage a child to laugh at something and then tell them off for doing the same thing, but I only have one hour so those rules go out of the window…sorry mom!

The key thing is to be funny and be fun, but not to be a pushover—children can smell fear so make sure you are in control at all times.

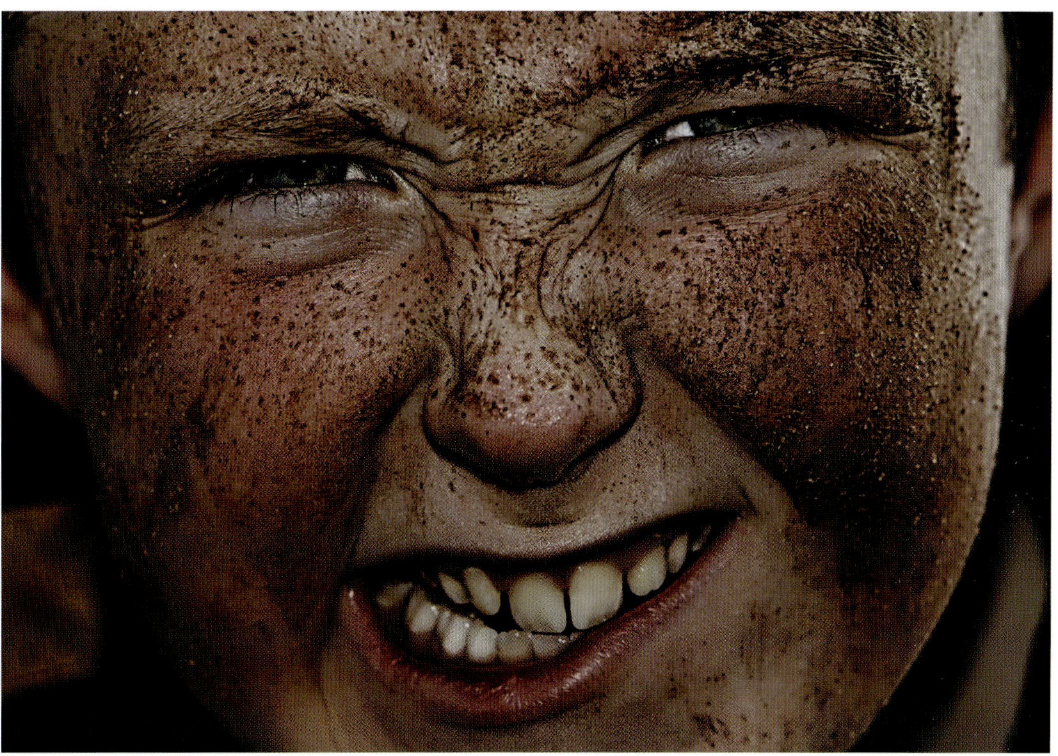

Above: It is essential that you maintain authority throughout a shoot.

Focal length: 200mm

Aperture: f/8

Shutter speed: 1/160 sec.

ISO: 100

Children Are Individuals Too

Having established that children require more detailed attention from the photographer than adults would need, it is worth pointing out that children are individuals. They are shy, they are loud, they are happy, they are morose…just the same as adults. Children are not a different species, although I find it a very common mistake to assume they are.

You need to recognize their individual character traits early in the process and work with them. Outgoing children will sometimes greet you before you even greet them. Be careful of this because they can either end up being naughty, or burn out very quickly once the shoot gets going. I am not saying this will happen every time, just that you need to be aware of it, and watch out.

Some children can be disruptive or bored from the very first moment. It's not always down to bad parenting, so don't make judgments. Engage these children and show them that it's a lot easier to tow the line and have fun than it is to be a pain. Be their friend, but always ensure they operate within your rules.

Shy children are, in my experience, the most difficult to work with. If you have to deal with a naughty or disruptive child, you should normally be able to entertain and distract them into doing what you want them to, but shy children are a lot more complex. They require delicate handling and a careful approach. Let them feel safe by being with mom or dad, but gradually introduce yourself into their world. Try to work close up to them so they get to know you are a friend.

A good tip is to ask them if they want to see a picture of your child or your dog or your motorbike on your cellphone. They tend to forget their shyness and find themselves in close proximity to you. Share a few jokes together, ask them about their hobbies or favorite television shows, and they will gradually come around and grow in confidence, allowing you to gain their trust.

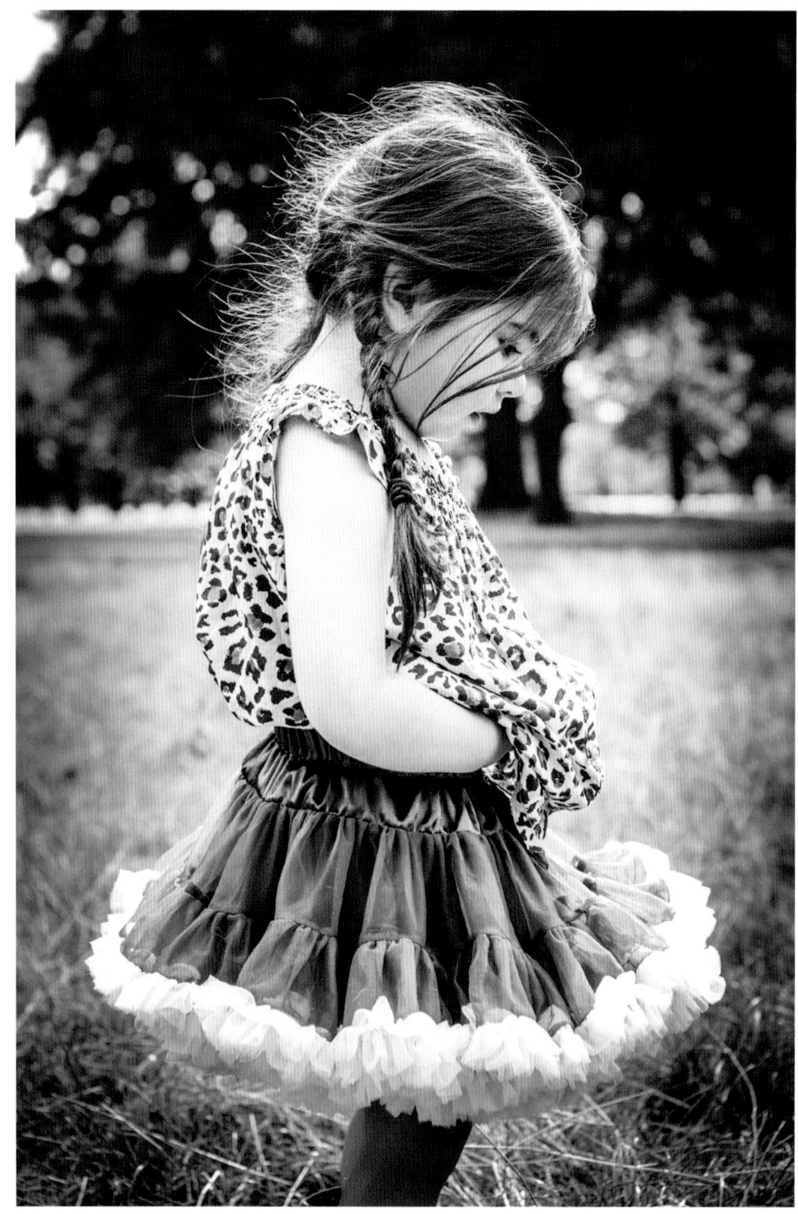

Above: Children are individuals, so you need to learn to deal with shy children as well as extroverts.

Focal length: 70mm

Aperture: f/5.6

Shutter speed: 1/250 sec.

ISO: 800

Distraction Technique

If the child you're photographing falls over and hurts themself or starts to complain about not wanting to carry on, it is time to bring the "distraction technique" into play. This is one of my favorite tricks, which I learned from my mother-in-law who was the vice principal of a school in her younger days.

This technique can feel very alien, simply because to an adult it doesn't seem like it is going to work. It is based on the idea that children generally have a very short attention span and time works very differently for them. A child up to the age of about five or six is only affected by what has just happened. You can see this by the way they cry when they have the slightest problem, and then laugh just seconds later. If this happens while you are on a shoot, don't panic! Just remember that in a very short period they can change their mind, so why not change it for them?

If a child is crying, allow them to do so for a while to give respect to their situation, but then move in close and suddenly bring their attention to a squirrel up in the tree above them; the dog coming down the path; or a big truck that's driving by. Once distracted, they will change in an instant and the shoot can resume. Get mom to quickly dry their eyes without any fuss and carry on with the fun. If you indulge their problem for too long it will just grow, so brush the issue away and bring them back to a happy place. It takes courage and practice to do this, but I guarantee that it works time and time again.

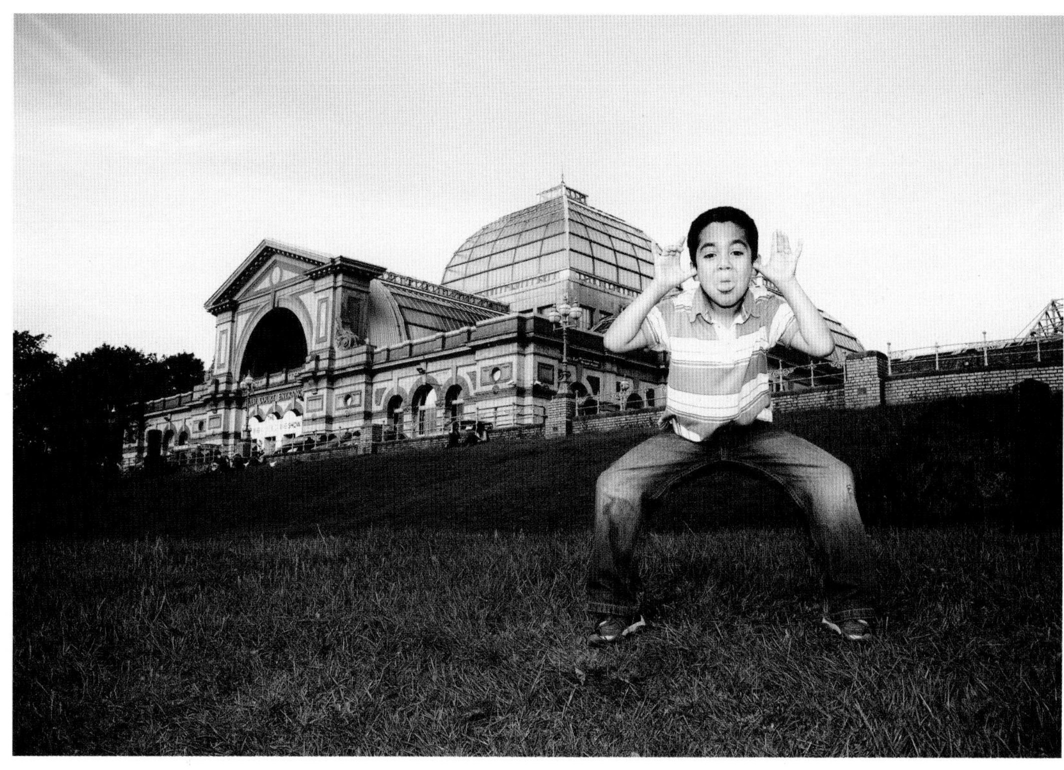

Above: The distraction technique is a great way to make unhappy children laugh.

Focal length: 30mm

Aperture: f/13

Shutter speed: 1/200 sec.

ISO: 400

The End Of The Shoot

When a shoot ends you need to remember that for the child it has been a big thing. Do not just turn to the parent and privately shake hands. Turn to the child first and celebrate: "high fives" are the international expression of solidarity so end with one of those. Let the child know how brilliantly they have done and praise them for all their hard work. Show them some examples on the back of the camera and ask which picture they like the most. Always try to have a moment with the child and the parent after the shoot. In the same way that you needed to start the shoot at a specific moment, you also need to end like a professional.

I usually like to have a coffee with the parent and child in a nearby café before I leave, so we can discuss how much we have all enjoyed the shoot. This is also the time to explain what happens next. I explain how many photographs I have taken during the session and that I will be editing them down to a choice of about 40 perfect finished images. I tell them about the prints, digital files, and storybooks that I offer, and discuss some of my prices. The final process is to agree a suitable time to come back to view the images (preferably with both parents present) and then the sales process begins.

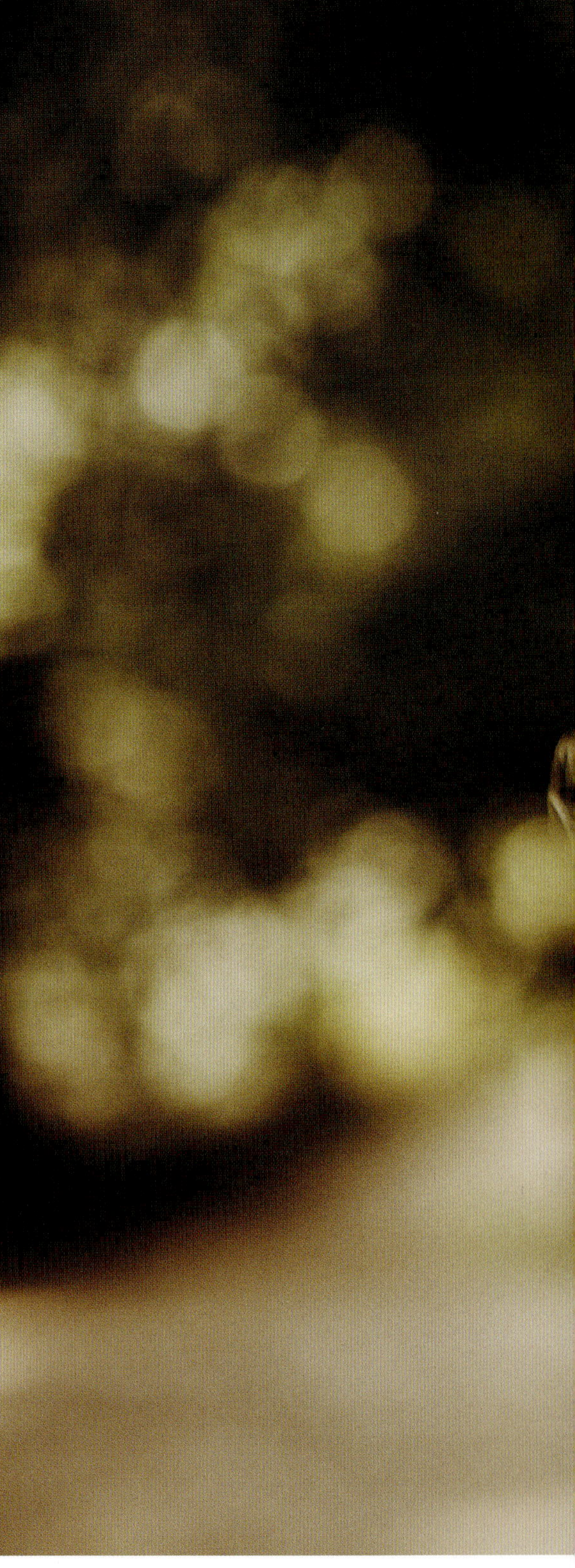

Right: Don't just let the parents walk away at the end of the day; engage with them and create an "ending" that rounds off the shoot.

Focal length: 70mm

Aperture: f/3.5

Shutter speed: 1/500 sec.

ISO: 500

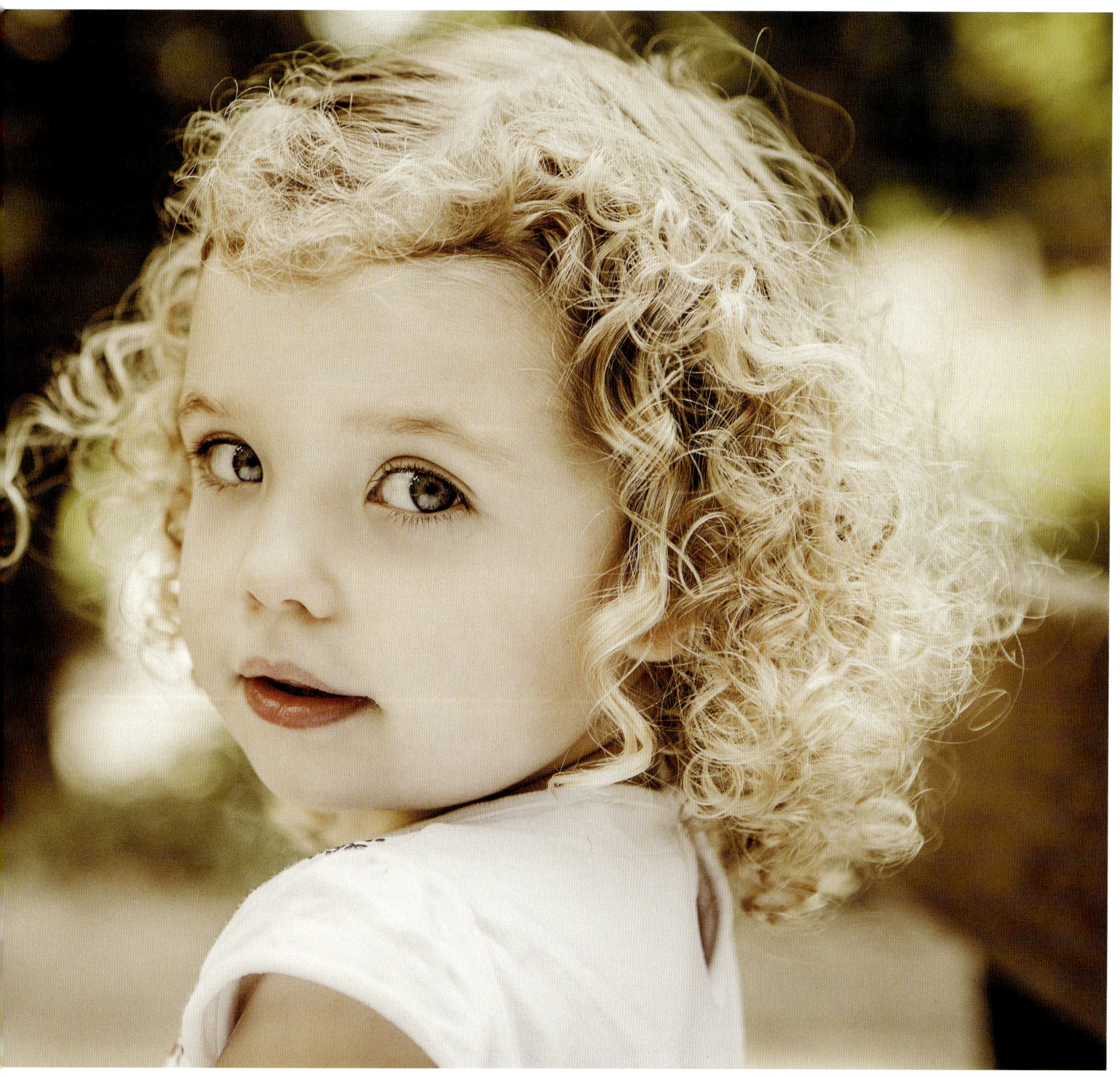

Profile: Imelda Bell

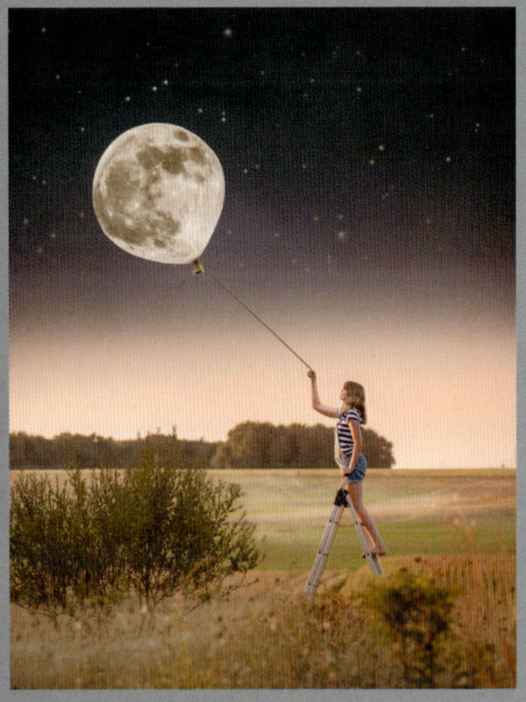 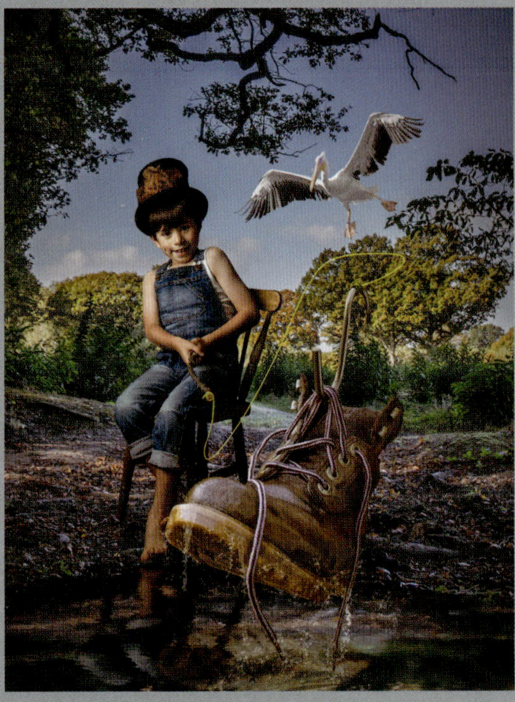

Q) What equipment do you use regularly?

A) I use a Canon EOS 5D MkIII with L-series lenses; in the studio, I tend to use my 24–105mm f/4 lens, and on location I usually use a 70–200mm f/2.8 zoom. I use Bowens monoblocs with a variety of modifiers in the studio, but as I only have two of these I will add Speedlites when I want three or more lights.

Q) Why is it important to you to shoot fantasy portraits of children?

A) I love to create images that realize a child's dreams and fantasies. When they see themselves in the final edited images their reactions are priceless—there is nothing more pleasing than seeing a child's face light up when they see themselves in a fantasy world you have created.

Q) How do you go about setting up a session and preparing the client?

A) I talk through the things that interest the child, such as their likes and hobbies, so I can create a suitable setup for each individual child. I talk about clothing and props that they might like to include and welcome parents to bring along any special items that mean something to the child or the family. I ask the parents to bring a selection of clothes, although I also have a variety of clothing and props in my studio.

Q) What tips do you have for controlling children during the shoot?

A) I try and make it fun and to engage the child. If a child is having fun, they are more likely to co-operate and that enjoyment can also be seen in the images. Drink and snack breaks are important too, so that the child doesn't get bored or hungry. When they lose interest, I find it best to have a break, play for a little while, and then come back to it. There is no point forcing a child to be in front of the camera, as the resulting photos will not look natural.

Q) How do you light your subjects in the studio and combine the location elements?

A) I tend to light from the same side in my photos, with my key light on the left of camera, so when I shoot elements for backgrounds I am mindful of the direction of the light. The quality of the light needs to match as well, so I like to shoot outdoors when the light is softer and lower in the sky to match the lighting setup in the studio. Perspective is also important; I like to be at eye level with the child, so I need to be at a similar height from the ground when capturing any other elements.

Q) How important is postproduction and do you do your own?

A) Postproduction is a vital part of my images—especially the composites—as I couldn't create fantasy worlds without it. I edit in Photoshop and make my final adjustments in Lightroom.

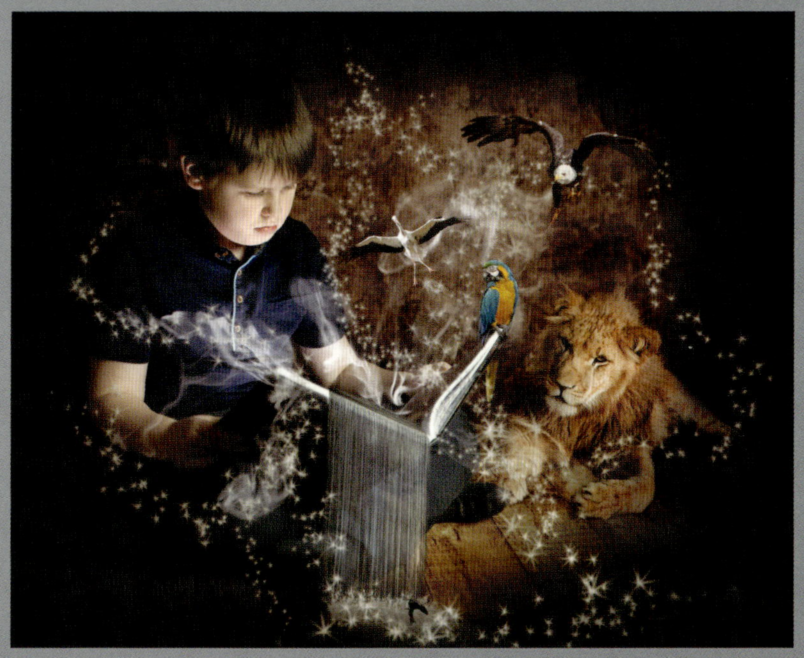

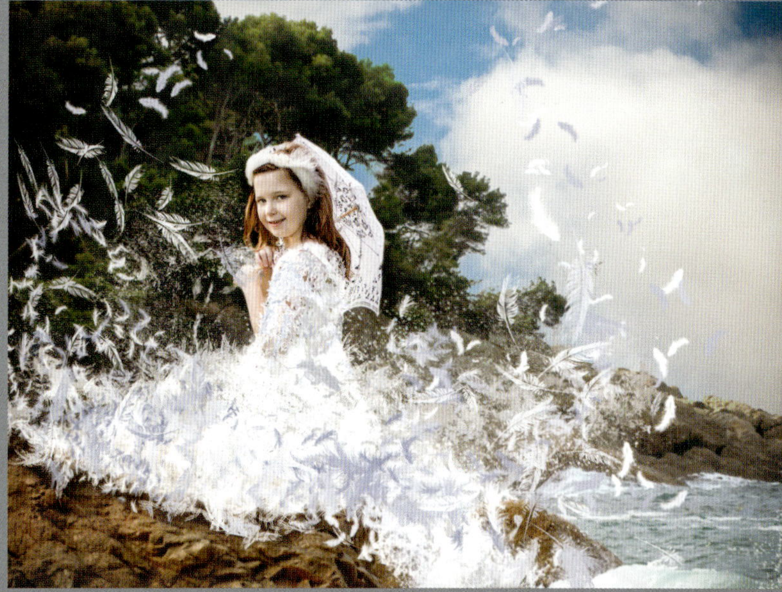

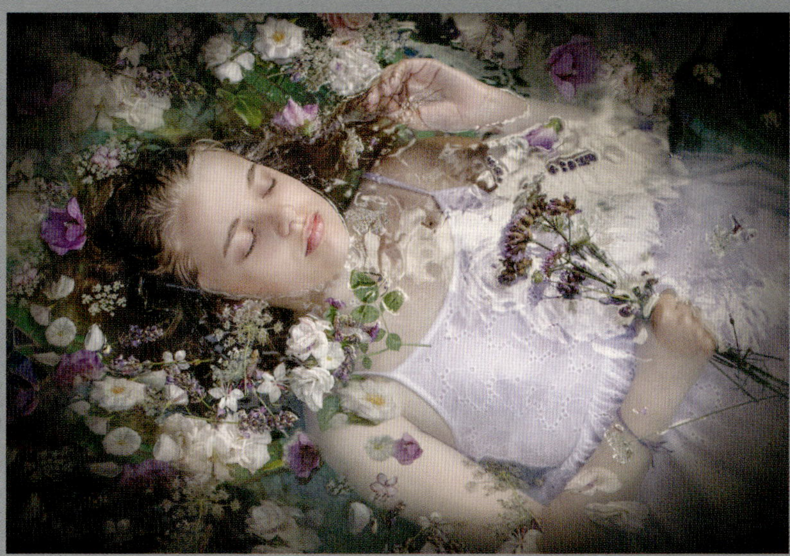

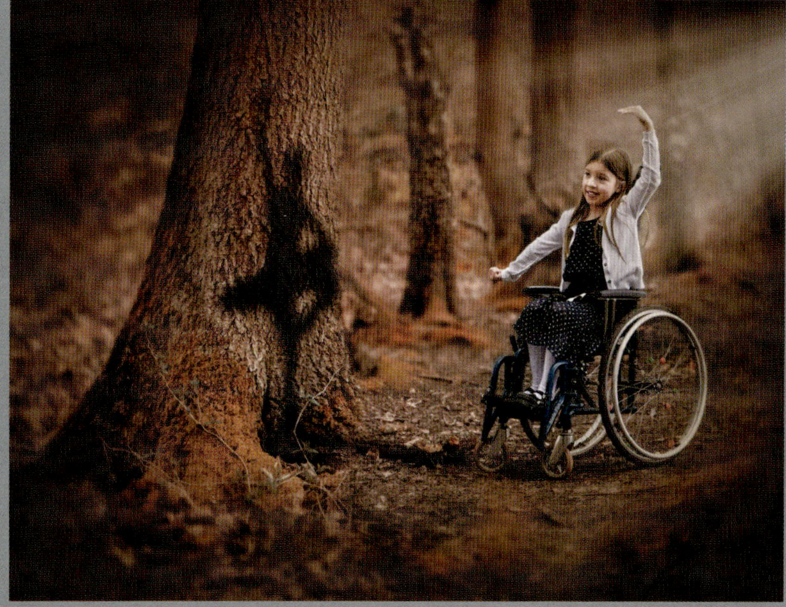

Opposite top center:
Focal length: 105mm
Aperture: f/2.8
Shutter speed: 1/400 sec.
ISO: 100

Opposite top right:
Focal length: 30mm
Aperture: f/5.6
Shutter speed: 1/200 sec.
ISO: 100

Top left:
Focal length: 30mm
Aperture: f/2.8
Shutter speed: 1/160 sec.
ISO: 500

Top right:
Focal length: 50mm
Aperture: f/1.8
Shutter speed: 1/500 sec.
ISO: 100

Bottom left:
Focal length: 30mm
Aperture: f/5
Shutter speed: 1/250 sec.
ISO: 100

Bottom right:
Focal length: 90mm
Aperture: f/2.8
Shutter speed: 1/200 sec.
ISO: 100

Final images are all created by photo composition. The technical details are for the original portrait of the child.

Chapter 8
Babies & Newborns

No child portraiture book would be complete without covering the art of baby and newborn photography. There are many photographers who specialize pretty much exclusively in this genre, and an entire industry has grown up around it: there are specialist newborn photographic societies and annual trade shows devoted to this subject. This perhaps isn't that surprising, because every parent will agree that the first few months of life are a special time, and portraits from that time are highly prized. There is something very unique and very special about very young infants, meaning that baby and newborn images are among the most beautiful and creative child portraits in any portfolio.

Right: The first few months of any child's life are clearly something that all of us will want to capture forever. Baby and newborn images can be very different from other child portraits, so you will need to develop a whole new skill-set.
Focal length: 70mm
Aperture: f/4
Shutter speed: 1/160 sec.
ISO: 640

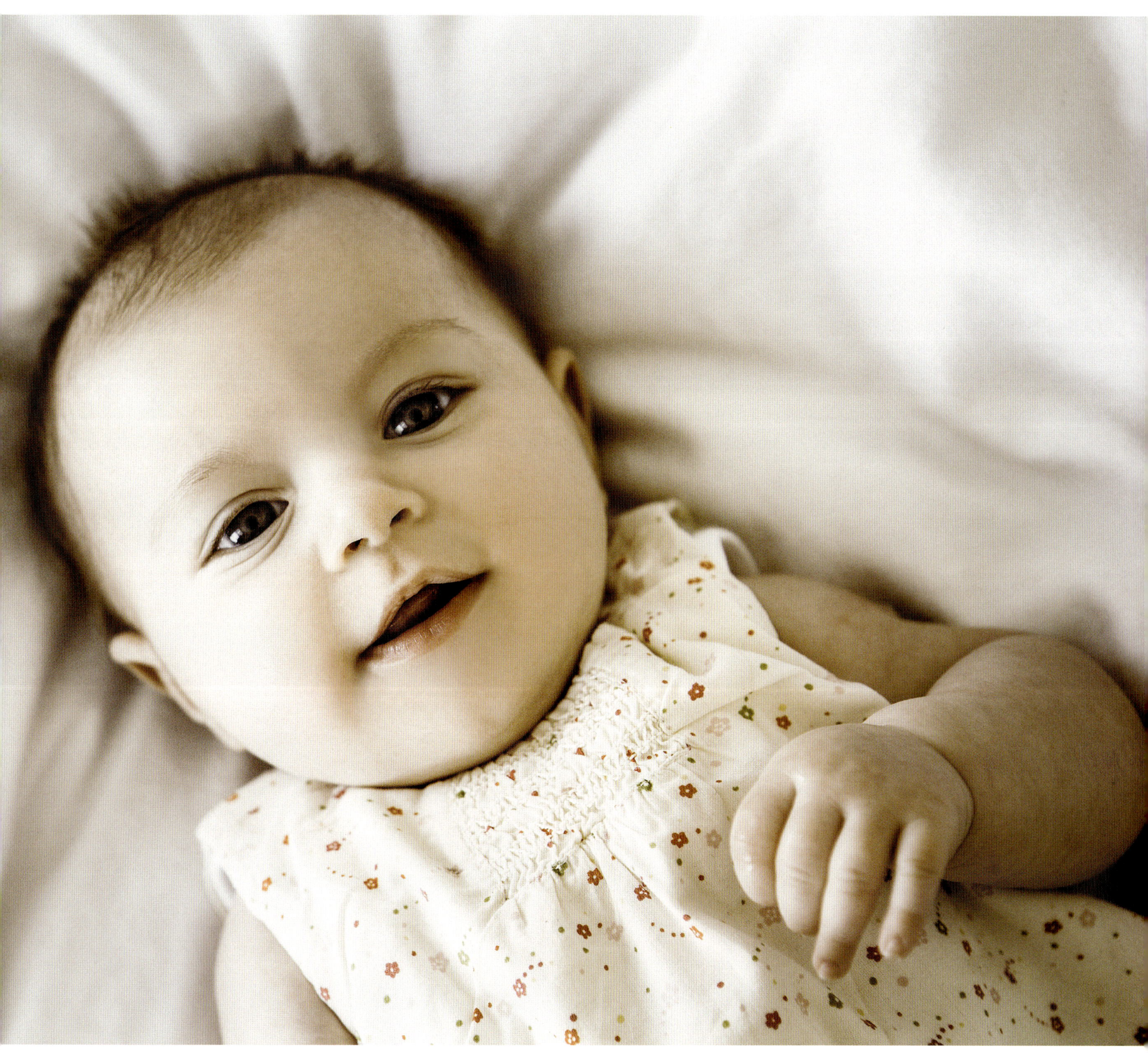

Health & Safety

There is nothing in the world that is more loved, more precious, and more vulnerable than a newborn baby. So along with the technical ability and creativity needed to photograph these tiny humans, there is also a huge emphasis on safety.

Photography studios can be dangerous places to children of all ages, but it is even truer when photographing newborns and babies. Anyone considering this line of specialization should have good liability insurance in place at an early stage, and it is worth highlighting that you intend to photograph newborns. Hopefully you will never need to use it, but make sure you are covered.

Whether you are shooting at your client's home or in your own studio space, you must ensure that all of your props and backgrounds are always in top condition. They should be cleaned, washed, and even sterilized after every shoot.

During a shoot, it is essential that the parent is present at all times and you must *never* leave a baby unattended. You should be particularly aware of babies that can roll over or wriggle unexpectedly, and ensure that they are never in a position where their breathing could be compromised in any way. The temperature of the studio is also important, and should be maintained so it is neither too cold, nor too hot.

Most health and safety is common sense, but it is important that you are aware of any issues that may arise unexpectedly. Basic first aid skills can potentially be very useful, so consider taking an appropriate course if you intend to photograph babies regularly.

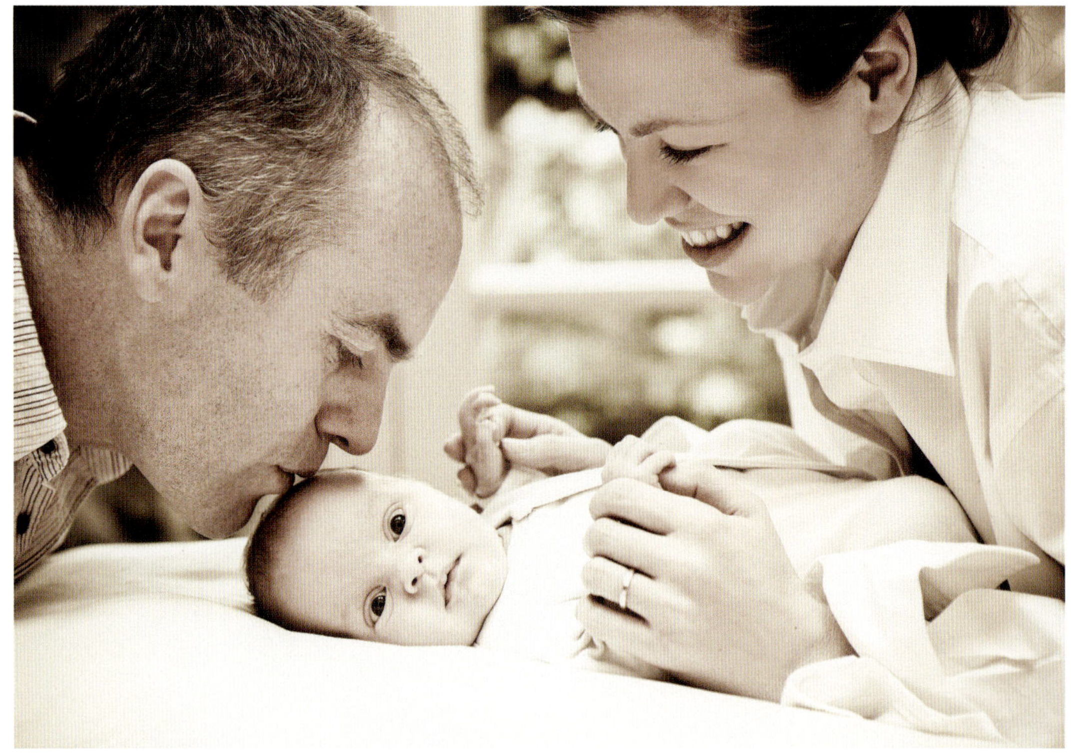

Above: When photographing any child it is important to have the parents present, but with babies and newborns it is essential, so why not think about involving them in the shoot?

Focal length: 70mm

Aperture: f/3.5

Shutter speed: 1/160 sec.

ISO: 500

Working To A System

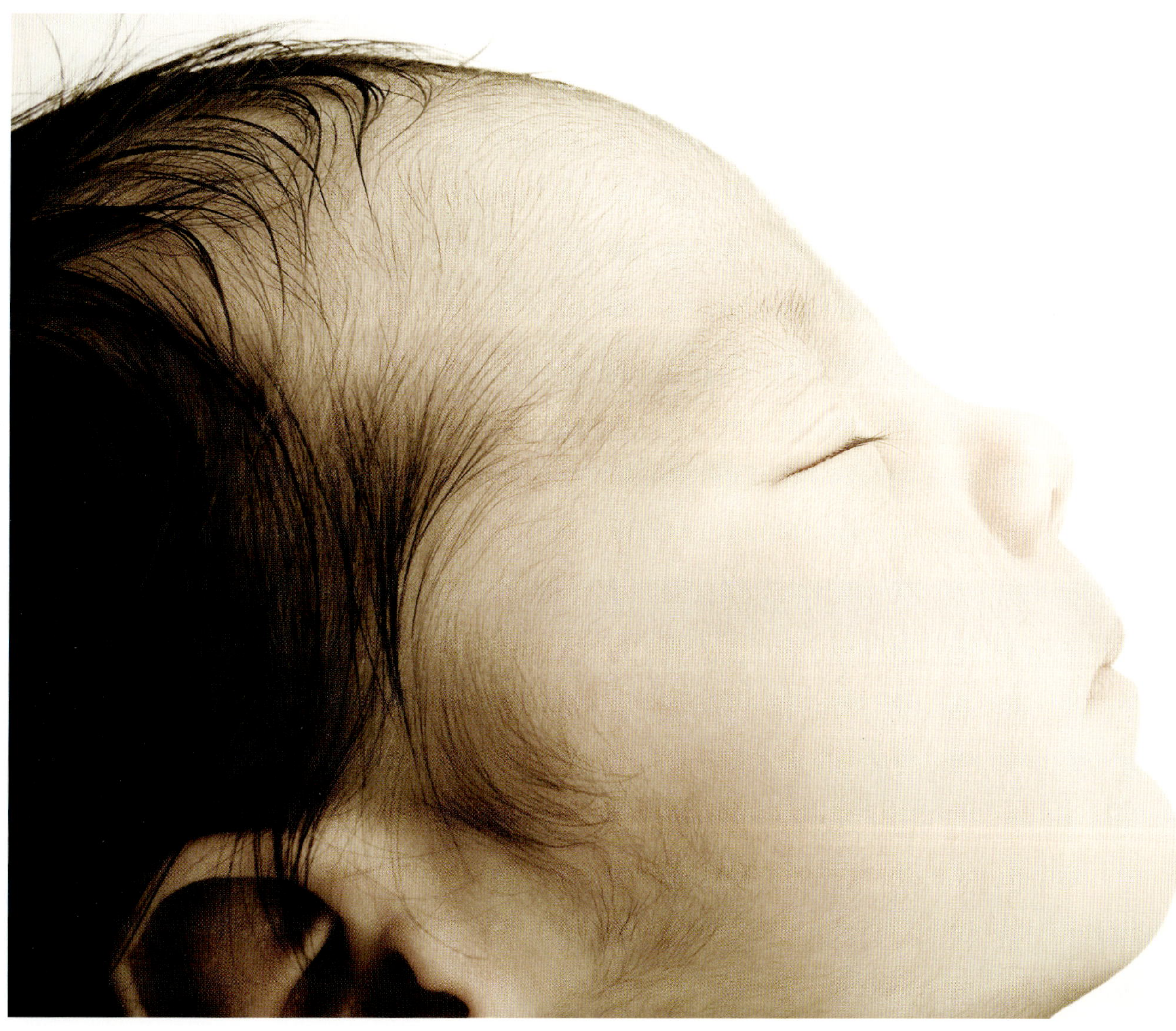

When you photograph babies there is a lot more to get to grips with than there is when photographing older children. It is extremely important that you are completely fluent with your camera, lighting, and other equipment, as it means you can then spend your time concentrating on all the other aspects of a successful shoot.

It is common to photograph babies—especially newborns—while they are sleeping, so it is important to plan the session in advance. However, true "new born" images of a sleeping baby can only be attempted with children up to six weeks old. After that age, babies become considerably more active and awake; wriggling and crying are common, and posing becomes a lot more difficult.

Above: Babies up to six weeks old spend a lot of time sleeping, providing opportunities for very calm shots.

Focal length: 50mm

Aperture: f/20

Shutter speed: 1/160 sec.

ISO: 500

Backgrounds & Props

The creative restrictions encountered when photographing a sleeping child are fairly obvious, so to create variety in your images you need to have visual concepts in mind and props or background options that tell your stories for you.

If you want to specialize in newborns then you will need to build up a good selection of backgrounds and props. My advice is not to overdo it, but the subtle use of baskets, boxes, and containers can add a bit of character and an interesting storyline to your images. Headbands, baby grows, booties, and hats can add a nice touch, so build up a collection and keep them in color order so you and the parents can decide on the best items to include.

A selection of different beanbags and cushions will help you prop up and support the baby. There are now specialist baby prop suppliers, so it pays to familiarize yourself with what is available. Place the supports down first and then drape fabric over them to hide the cushions. Clip the fabric to a background pole behind and allow it to follow the natural flow of the beanbag. As you position the baby you can slide additional cushions under the fabric to add support where necessary: you need to make sure you support the baby safely at all times and never hinder its breathing.

Baby images are all about texture, so think about this when you are purchasing props and backgrounds. Over time you will develop an eye for useful props, but think about soft fabrics, woolly hats, traditional items such as baby baskets, and natural materials such as wooden flooring and old fruit crates. Remember to check wooden items for splinters, though, as this can be a problem when using older props.

As you become more experienced with newborns you will be able to construct some really innovative images, combining clever set building with skilful postproduction to achieve some stunning results.

It is good to bring humor into the shots, but discuss this with the parents and make sure they are happy: babies dressed as elves and other characters can produce some gorgeous results, but they are not to everyone's taste. Develop your own style so that clients come to you for that type of image and use a color scheme (see page 142) to help involve the parents in the final decisions.

Below: Using props in the studio enables you to tell fantastic stories with sleeping newborns.

Focal length: 85mm

Aperture: f/7.1

Shutter speed: 1/200 sec.

ISO: 100

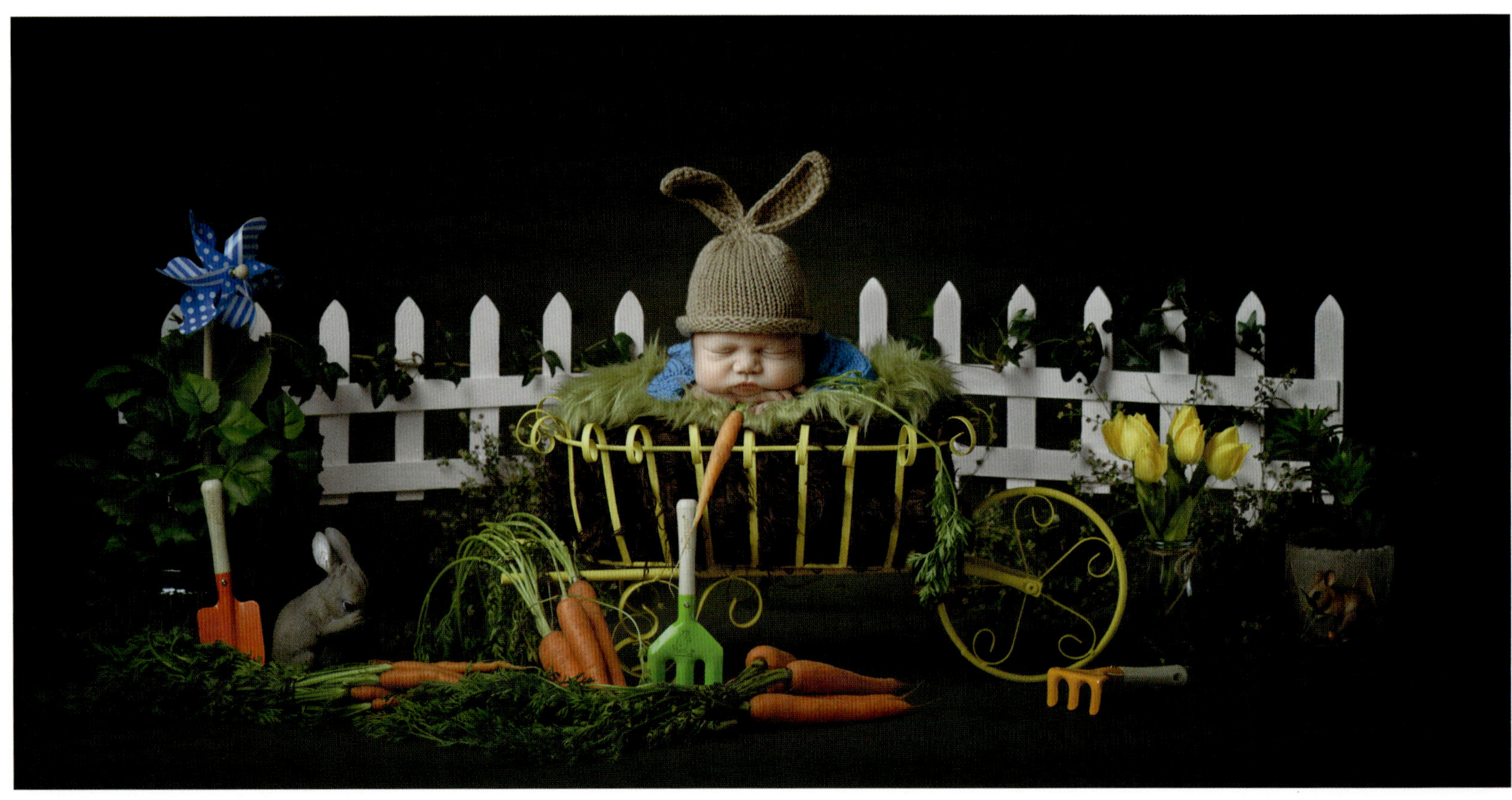

Tips

- Not all baby shoots need to take place in the studio. There are plenty of options for interesting lifestyle shoots. All the same rules apply but learn to use the natural environment to get interesting images of the baby.

- This special time is something that will never be repeated, so think carefully about the variety and range of shots you can offer. Including the parents will usually pay dividends when it comes to selling them prints for family and friends.

- Always remember that today's babies are tomorrow's children: don't forget to let the parents know that you love to photograph children as well!

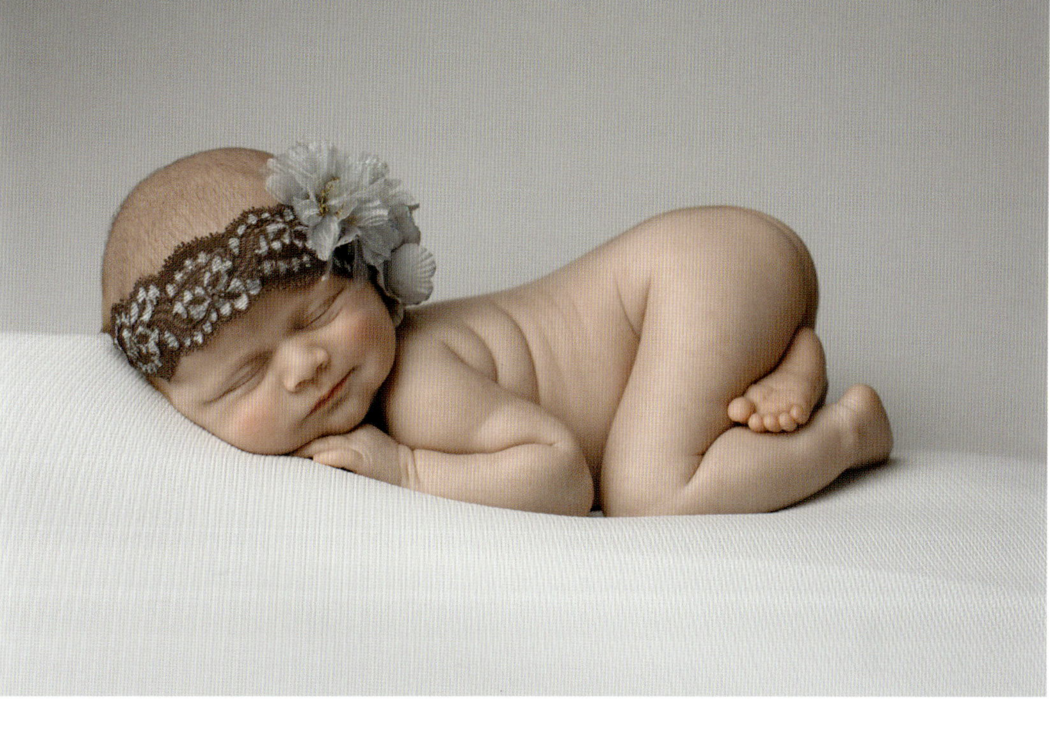

Right top: Buy a collection of beanbags and then drape breathable fabrics over them for a perfect newborn support.

Focal length: 50mm

Aperture: f/4

Shutter speed: 1/200 sec.

ISO: 100

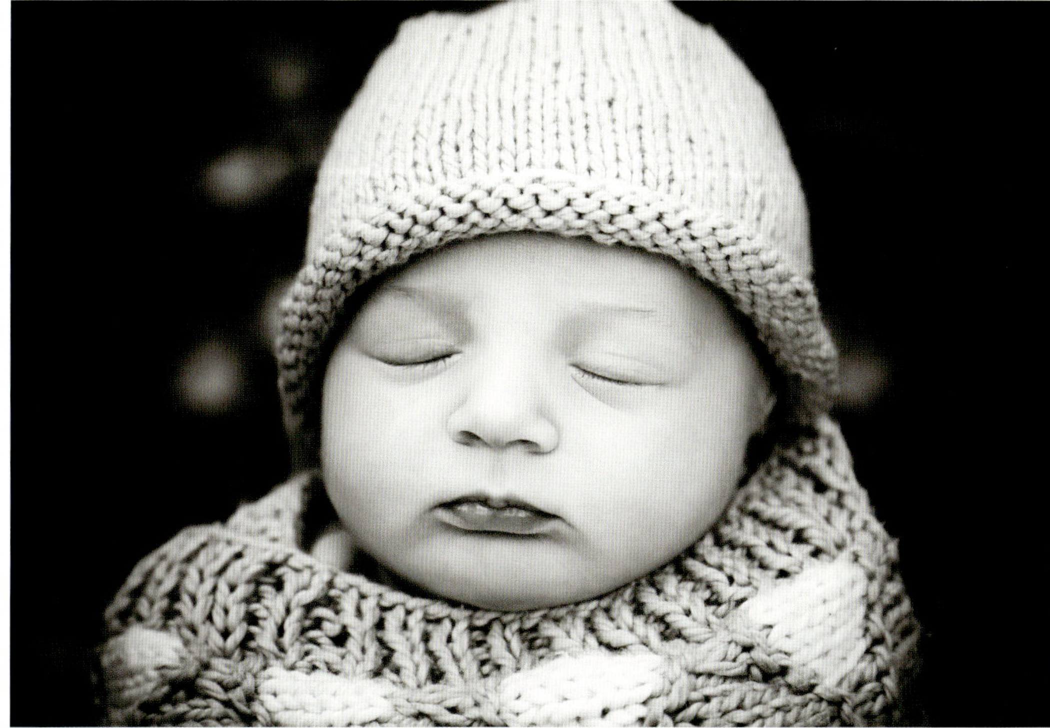

Right: Natural fabrics and woolly hats are great props for young babies.

Focal length: 93mm

Aperture: f/4.5

Shutter speed: 1/250 sec.

ISO: 800

Babies As Still Lifes

Babies and newborns are very different to other children in one major way: they are essentially incapable of controlled self-expression. Most of the tips and techniques that you use to bring out the best in a child portrait shoot are simply irrelevant when it comes to a newborn baby, so you need to approach the shoot in a completely different way.

You should approach your newborn portraits in the same way as you would a still-life shoot. Your lighting will need to be simple and subtle; I recommend one-light setups with white bounce reflectors to soften the shadows. Large, indirect lights will bathe the baby in beautiful soft light, allowing the natural beauty of the child to shine through. The light(s) will probably be quite close, so you won't need too much power.

The lack of movement with young babies also allows you to use continuous light sources if you prefer. With a huge range of LED light panels now available this can be a very easy way to gain experience with studio lighting techniques as you can see exactly what you are going to get. Don't be afraid to set your camera to ISO 800 and shoot at shutter speeds as low as 1/30 sec., although you need to ensure that you can hold the camera steady or use a tripod for extra support.

You can gently pose and re-pose your sleeping baby for different effects. Practice different positions so you can provide a variety of different images. A macro lens or extension tubes fitted to your lens will allow you to move in very close to do detail shots of tiny hands, feet, and eye lashes. These images can be just as effective as the longer shots that all parents will traditionally ask for and add another layer of possibilities to your final set.

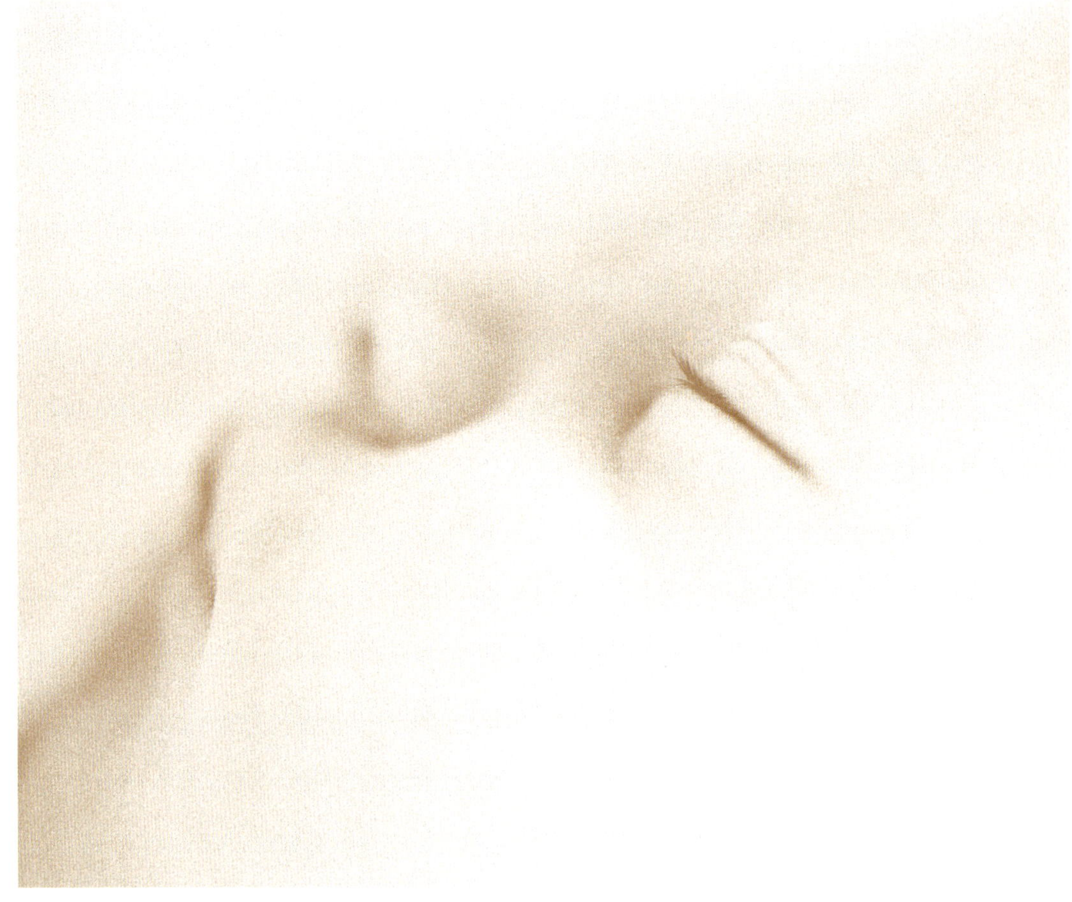

Above: With newborns and pre-toddlers it is nice to shoot close-ups of hands, feet, and eyelashes.

Focal length: 100mm

Aperture: f/2.8

Shutter speed: 1/60 sec.

ISO: 8000

Right: Think carefully about the details of your setups in advance and be prepared to shoot amazing images.

Focal length: 105mm

Aperture: f/5

Shutter speed: 1/200 sec.

ISO: 100

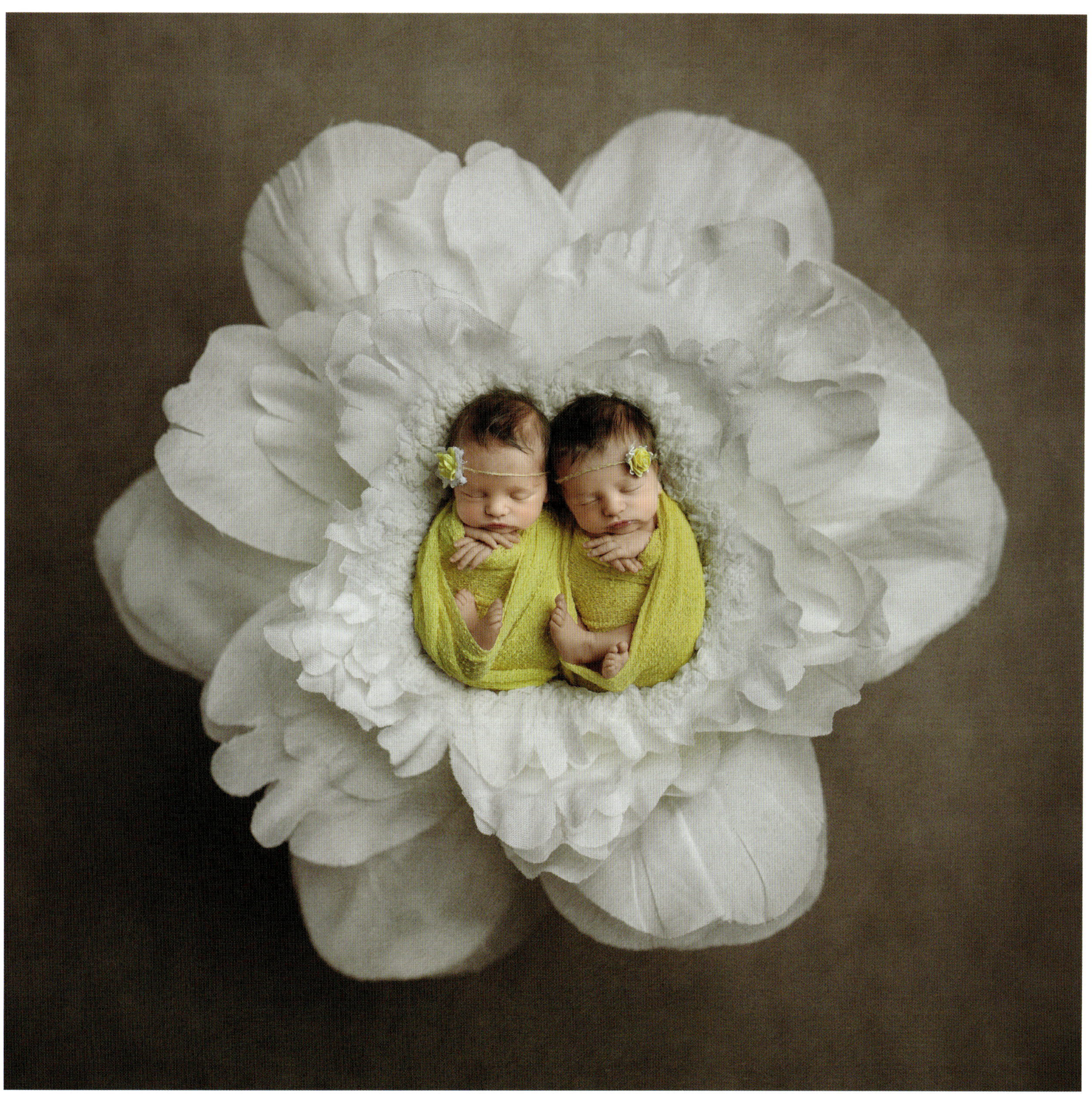

Preparing The Parents

Arranging a color scheme or "color theme" before the shoot begins will give the parent some ideas about what to bring with them, as well as giving them an idea of what they can expect at the end. A good approach is to send a set of your portfolio images to the parents before the shoot date that show a selection of color themes. Ask them to choose a color scheme that they feel is right for them, and you can then ensure that you have the correct backgrounds and props ready before the shoot begins.

As with all child portrait sessions, you should inform the parents in advance about how the session will work. All children are different, but you need to ensure you are in the rhythm of a particular child's sleep pattern, so as to maximize your shoot time. Mom will usually be able to give you a pretty good idea of sleeping times.

The best time to photograph newborns is within the first three to four weeks. After the first few days they sleep a lot and have usually lost most of the obvious signs of birth. They will be flexible and easy to pose. Older babies begin to be a little more reactive, first with open eyes and later on with a smile and other facial expressions.

In terms of the activity levels of a child, there is a fairly clear division between 0–6 weeks and six weeks to six months, so you need to adopt a different approach for each age group. The props you choose will reflect this, so make sure the parent knows what to expect and is on board with any ideas you have.

If you are shooting in your own studio be ready to look after both mother and child on arrival. Your studio space should be clean and tidy at all times, but with babies this is even more important. Mom may not have slept, so a comfortable chair and cup of tea or coffee is always welcome. Have fresh water, biscuits, and fresh fruit available for feeding mothers and an area of privacy if required; babies also need to be changed, so have a changing area set up and ready.

When it comes to the session, you will need to work out your own system, but a suggested order for every shoot might be: mom and baby arrive, tea/coffee, feed baby, calm baby, sleep, shoot. Informing mom of this in advance of the session will not only help her to know what is expected, but also lets her know that you are in charge and know what you are doing. Work quickly and efficiently, as you only have a small window of time when the newborn is sleeping or the baby is in the calm and happy place that he or she needs to be in to get the very best from the shoot.

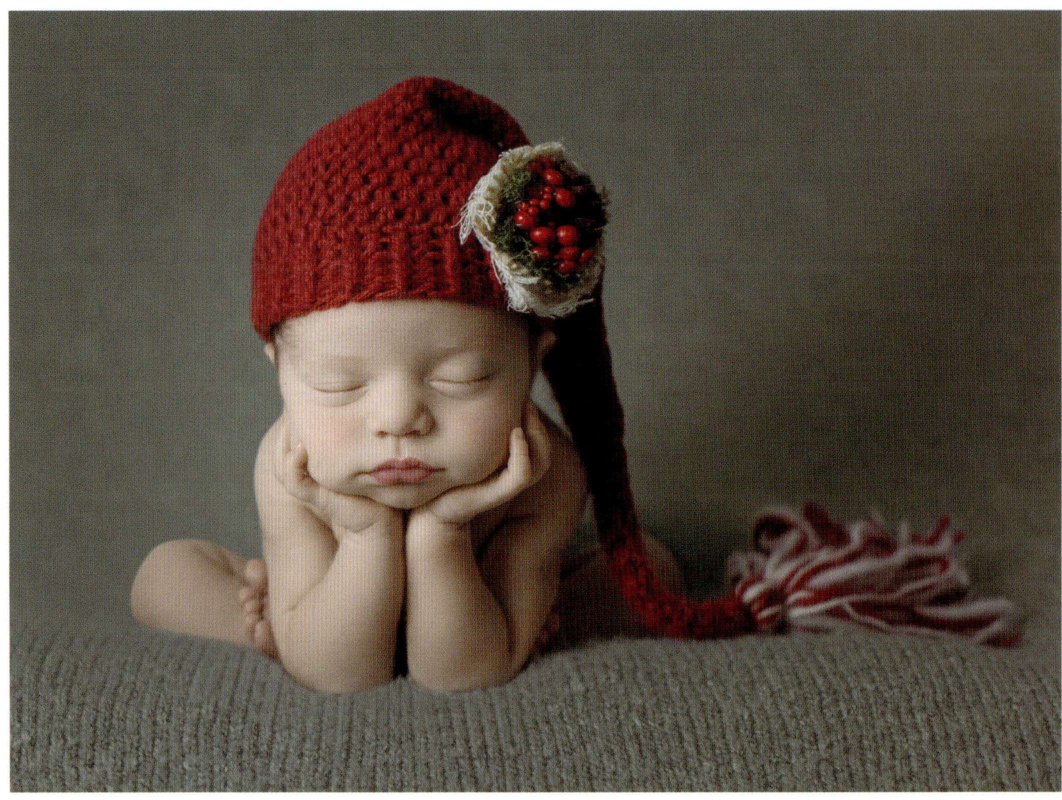

Above: Gray and red is a classic combination for a festive Christmas theme.

Focal length: 50mm

Aperture: f/3.5

Shutter speed: 1/200 sec.

ISO: 100

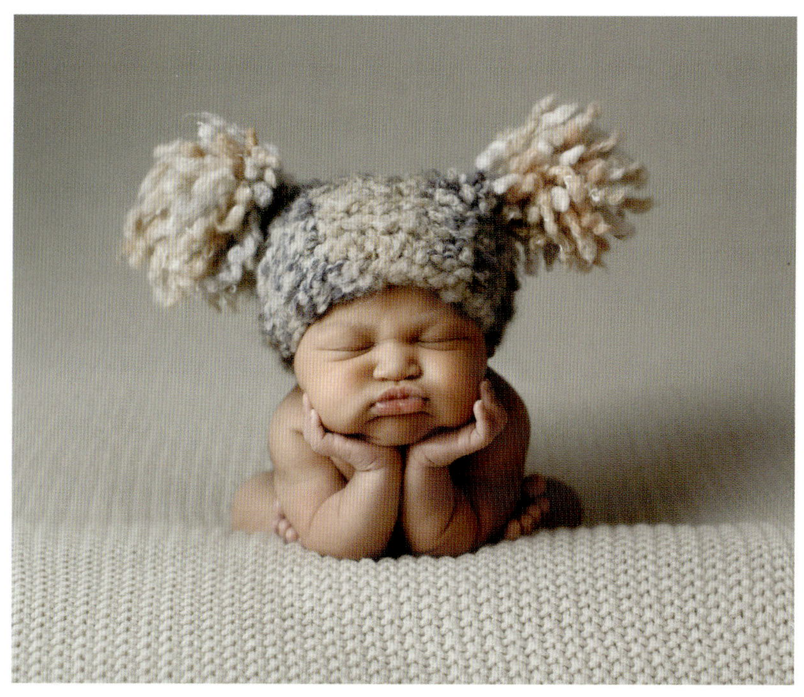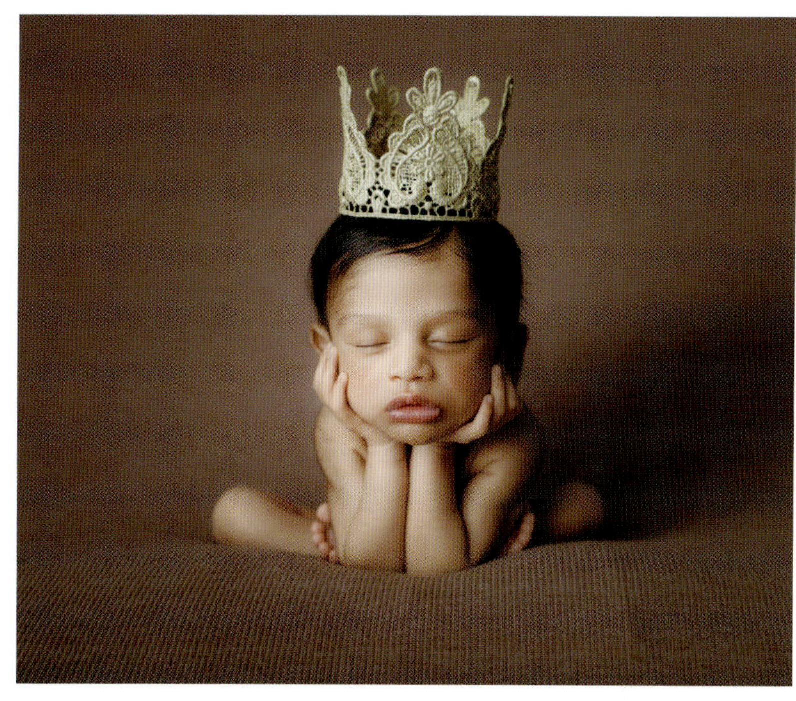

Above left: Beige and blue is a great color theme for a cool look.

Focal length: 50mm

Aperture: f/3.5

Shutter speed: 1/200 sec.

ISO: 100

Above right: Brown and gold will give your images a regal look.

Focal length: 50mm

Aperture: f/4.5

Shutter speed: 1/160 sec.

ISO: 160

Left: Gray and blue is ideal if you're looking for a cute look.

Focal length: 50mm

Aperture: f/3.5

Shutter speed: 1/200 sec.

ISO: 100

Babies Not Newborns

Once children get to around two months they start to have some real personality. They can smile, become more hardy, and sleep less. This opens up many more photographic opportunities, with plenty of options for interesting lifestyle shoots.

Photographing babies is always going to be quite different to photographing children because there is far less physical feedback: they can't run or jump, and don't have the capacity to take actions for themselves. You need to bear this in mind before you begin your shoot and think about the ways you can create interesting images. Here are some ideas to get you started.

Younger babies can be laid on their backs so you have the option of standing over the child and looking down on top of them. Shooting full length with the baby in a central position creates a graphical effect, which is often something that parents have not considered before. I have used this technique both indoors and outdoors and parents love it.

You can zoom in for a closer, waist-up shot, and then closer still for a head and shoulders image, but always ensure that your camera is firmly strapped around your neck—a camera falling on a baby is a very real possibility.

Next, you can lie down to shoot the baby in profile, using a macro lens to blow the background out of focus. Get mom to stand over the baby and make eye contact, as this often promotes a smile. Every now and again click your fingers or make a slight sound so that the baby looks your way.

If there are older brothers and sisters around, think about how you can photograph them with the baby. This can be challenging depending on the age of the older sibling, but if handled correctly will result in some truly memorable shots.

As the child gets a little older they will be able to lie on their tummy and look up. This is a precursor to crawling and makes for great action shots if you position yourself at their eye level. Shoot this with a wideangle lens to get an almost "nature documentary" feel. This works particularly well outdoors on fresh grass or fallen leaves.

At about four to six months babies can sit up and there is a whole host of new possibilities available. Once again, you need to ensure they are always safe, but you can sit babies of this age on the ground or even on a suitable bench or tabletop. Once they can stand you can find trees, walls, benches, or just about anything else for them to hold onto and get some wonderful shots of their first attempts at walking.

Don't forget that there will also be opportunities to get some beautiful images with the parents in the shot. Mom and dad can often get some of the very best reactions from their baby, so direct them and be ready to react to spontaneous expressions. Mothers have a special connection to their babies, so try to shoot them together, capturing the love they feel. Dads are part of the scene, as well, and it's worth remembering that one of the bestselling wall posters of all time was of the male supermodel David Gandy holding a tiny baby in his arms. Remember that this special time will never be repeated, so think carefully about the variety and range of shots you can offer.

Every parent will tell you that toddlers are a real handful. This is a child that can walk, but with very little ability to do so and no concern for their own safety: it's a wonder that any of us survives this challenging time in our lives!

Tips

- Babies sense the world around them by tasting it so just about everything will end up in their mouth. Keep a constant eye on what the little guy is doing at all times, but make sure that mom and dad are clear that their baby is their responsibility at all times.

- Use simple toys as props, but avoid cheap plastic. Wooden toys, vintage toys, and characterful cuddly toys are the best; try to avoid heavily branded items or movie-related merchandise as they usually go out of date and rarely look good in pictures.

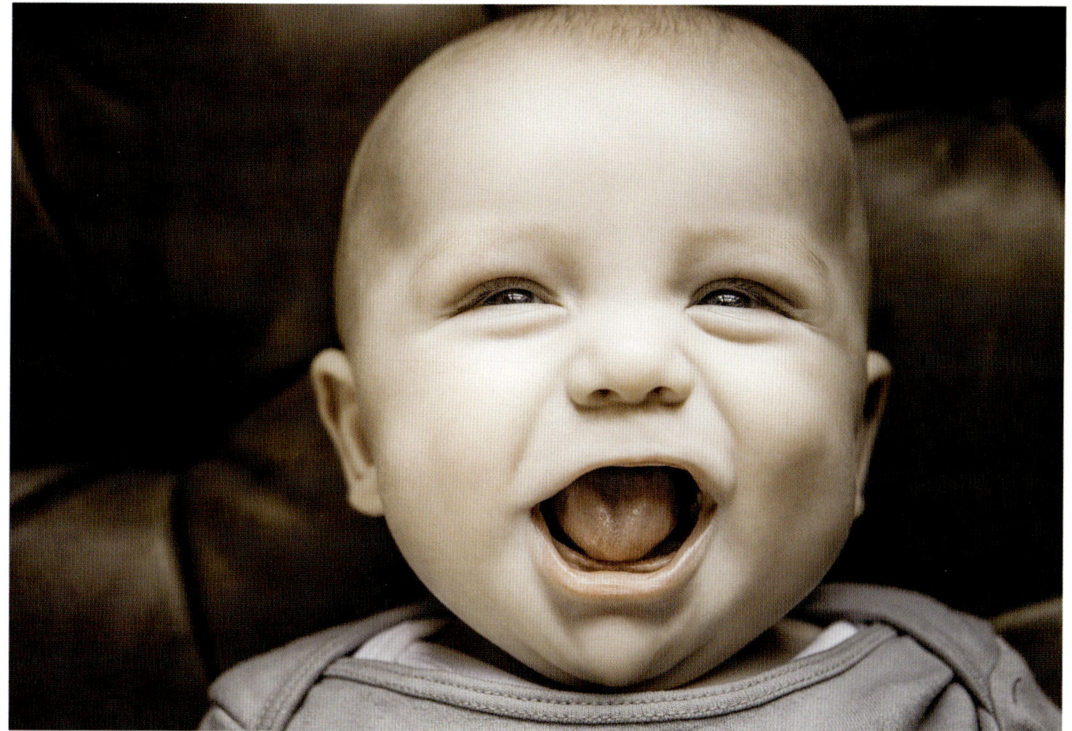

Tip

Get mom to think carefully about outfits before the shoot. Babies are people too, so give them some options. You can create completely different images just by changing outfits. From simple white babygrows to mock sailor suits, there are plenty of possibilities. Don't forget hats for outdoor shoots.

Left: As babies grow they will start to show signs of individual character. Different expressions provide lots of great photo opportunities.

Focal length: 68mm

Aperture: f/5

Shutter speed: 1/200 sec.

ISO: 800

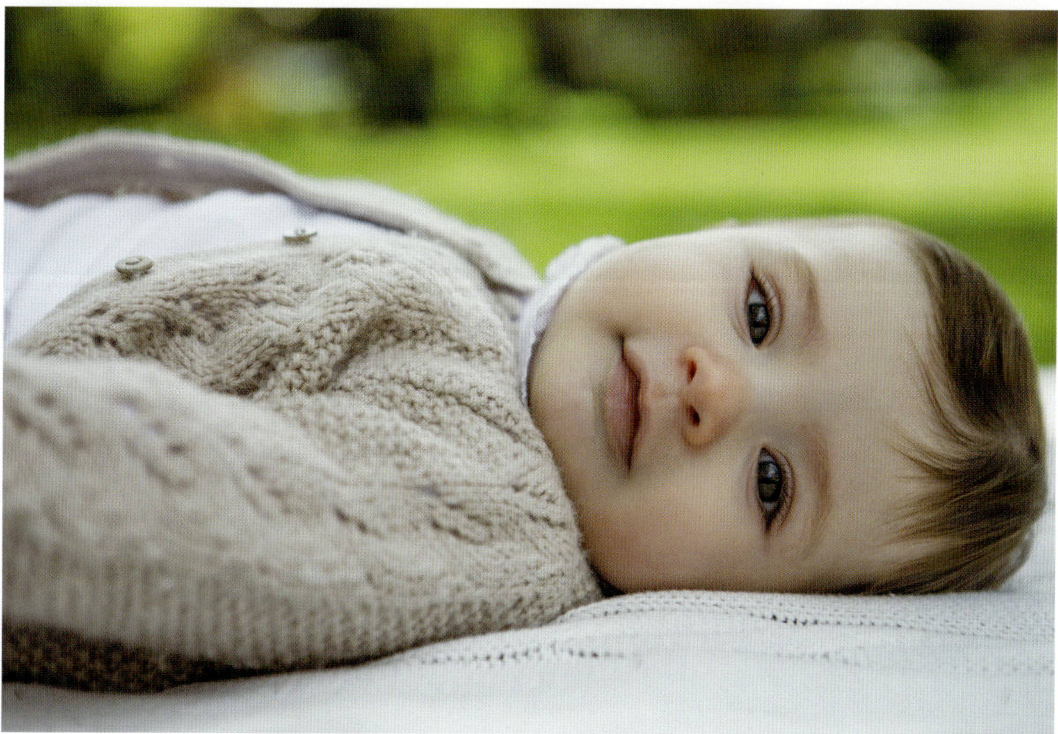

Left: Babies will soon become a lot hardier, so you can now start to shoot beautiful outdoor images, as well as the more familiar indoor locations.

Focal length: 70mm

Aperture: f/3.5

Shutter speed: 1/1000 sec.

ISO: 400

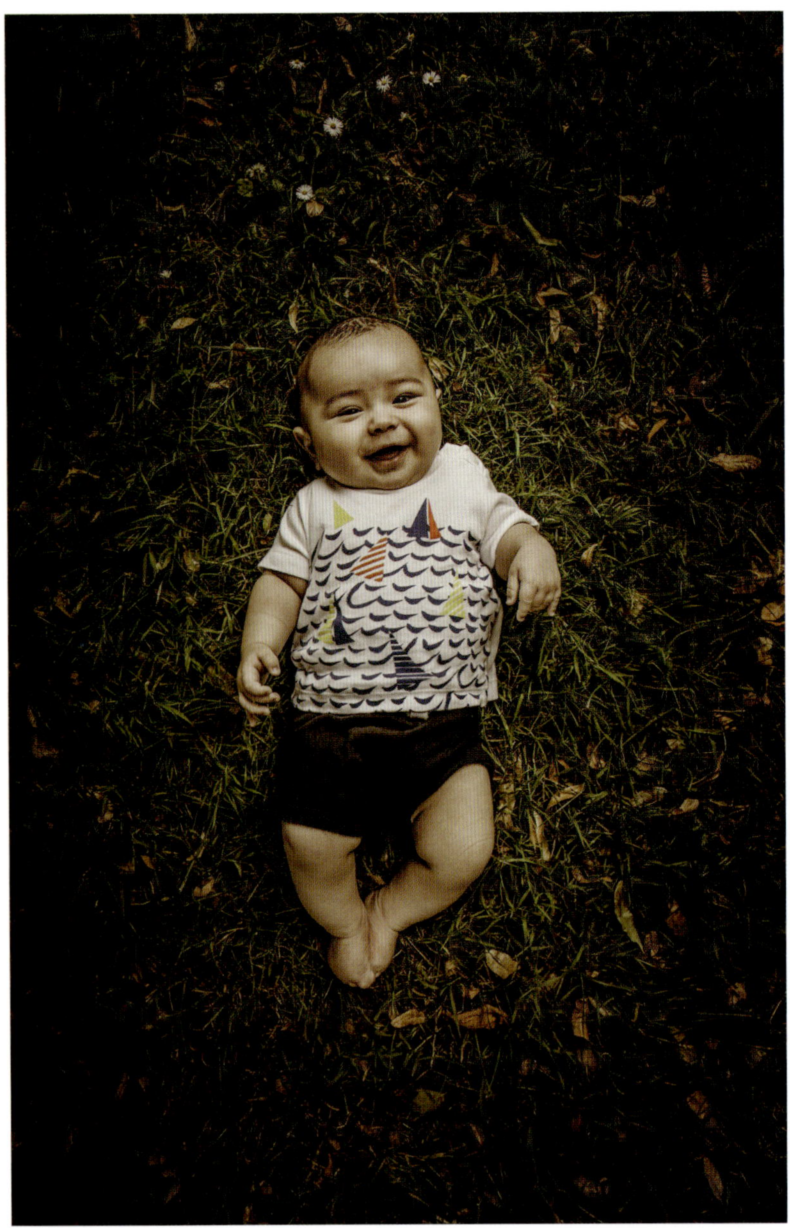

Above: Photographing children and babies isn't easy, but the results can provide a long-lasting memory of a fast changing stage in a young person's life.

Focal length: 32mm

Aperture: f/8

Shutter speed: 1/250 sec.

ISO: 800

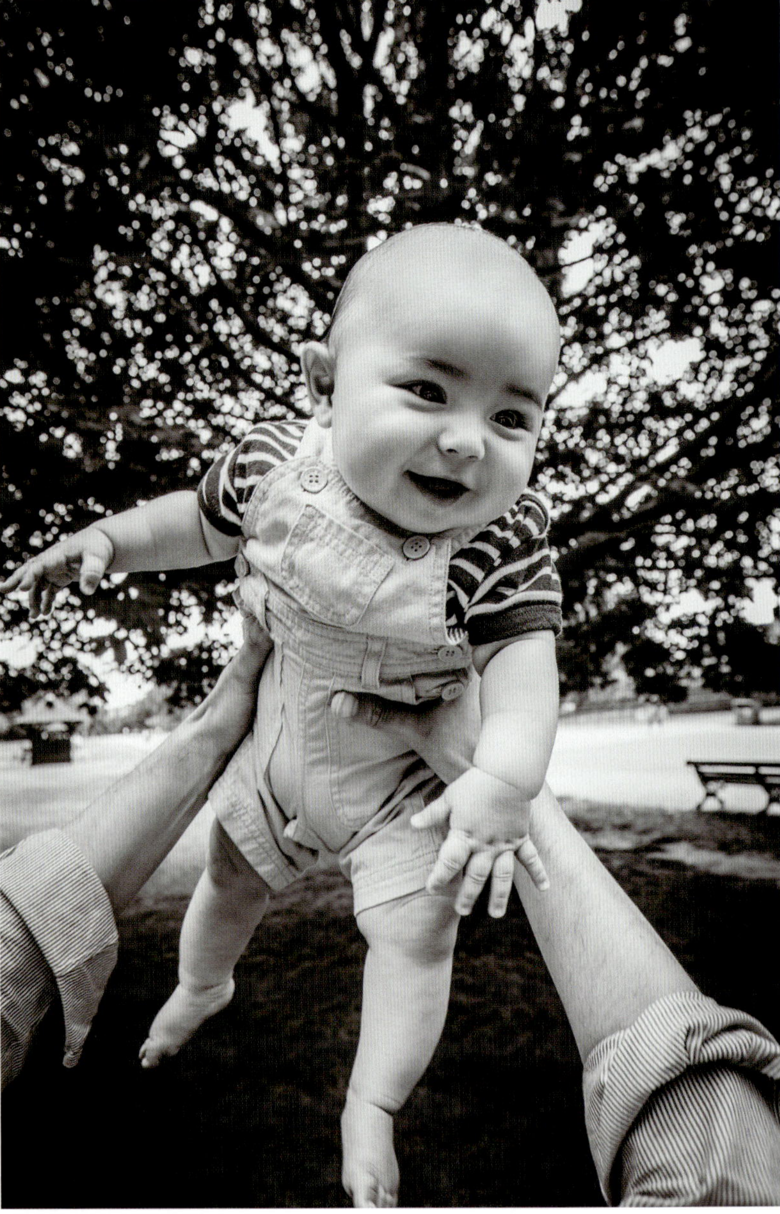

Above: Get mom and dad involved in the shoot for some really interesting images.

Focal length: 24mm

Aperture: f/6.3

Shutter speed: 1/160 sec.

ISO: 800

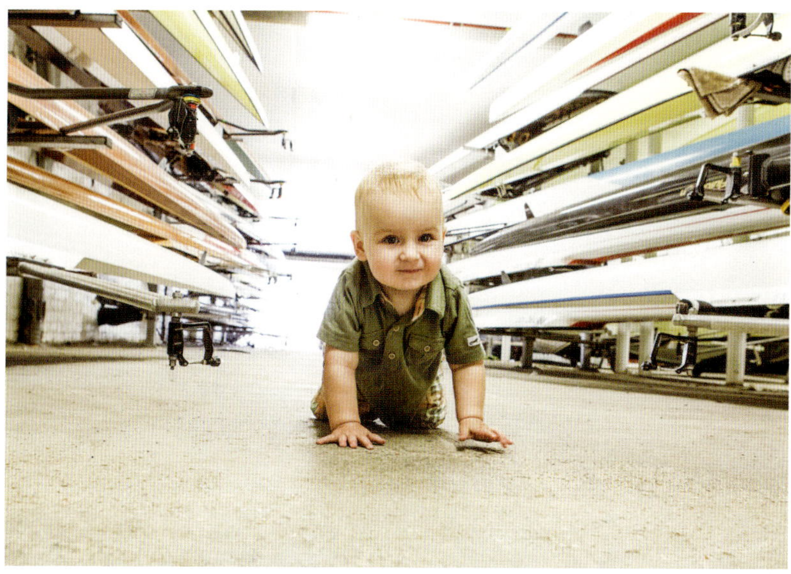

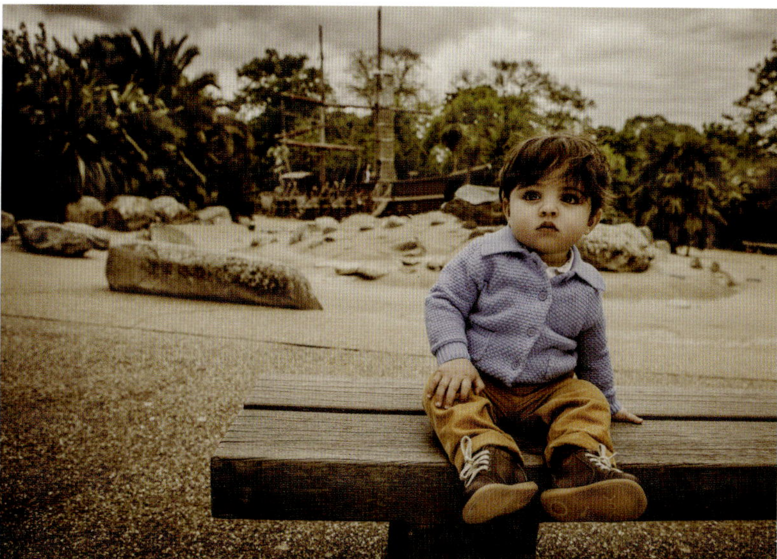

Above: Crawling babies will get into all sorts of trouble, so make sure you are there to record their adventures!

Focal length: 24mm

Aperture: f/5

Shutter speed: 1/100 sec.

ISO: 3200

Above: As a baby gets older you can start to use swings, benches, and tables to sit them on, but keep a safe eye on them at all times.

Focal length: 24mm

Aperture: f/5

Shutter speed: 1/1000 sec.

ISO: 500

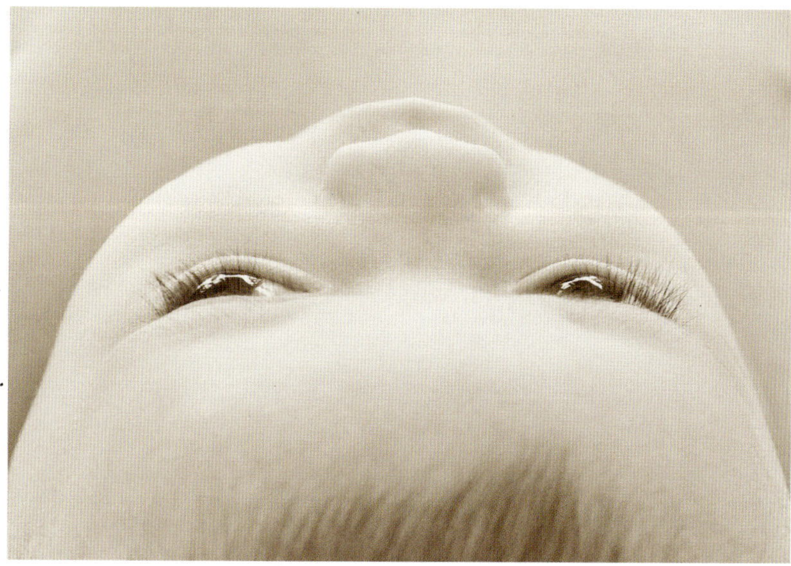

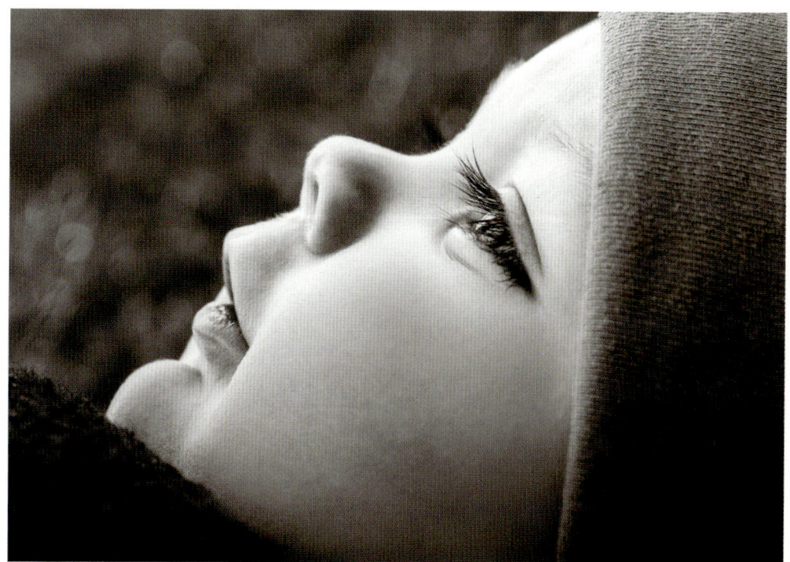

Above: This angle gives a simple and unusual image.

Focal length: 96mm

Aperture: f/7.1

Shutter speed: 1/250 sec.

ISO: 800

Above: Getting down low allows you to concentrate on the baby's profile. Get mom to make eye contact for a guaranteed smile.

Focal length: 105mm

Aperture: f/10

Shutter speed: 1/500 sec.

ISO: 640

Profile: Sarah Wilkes

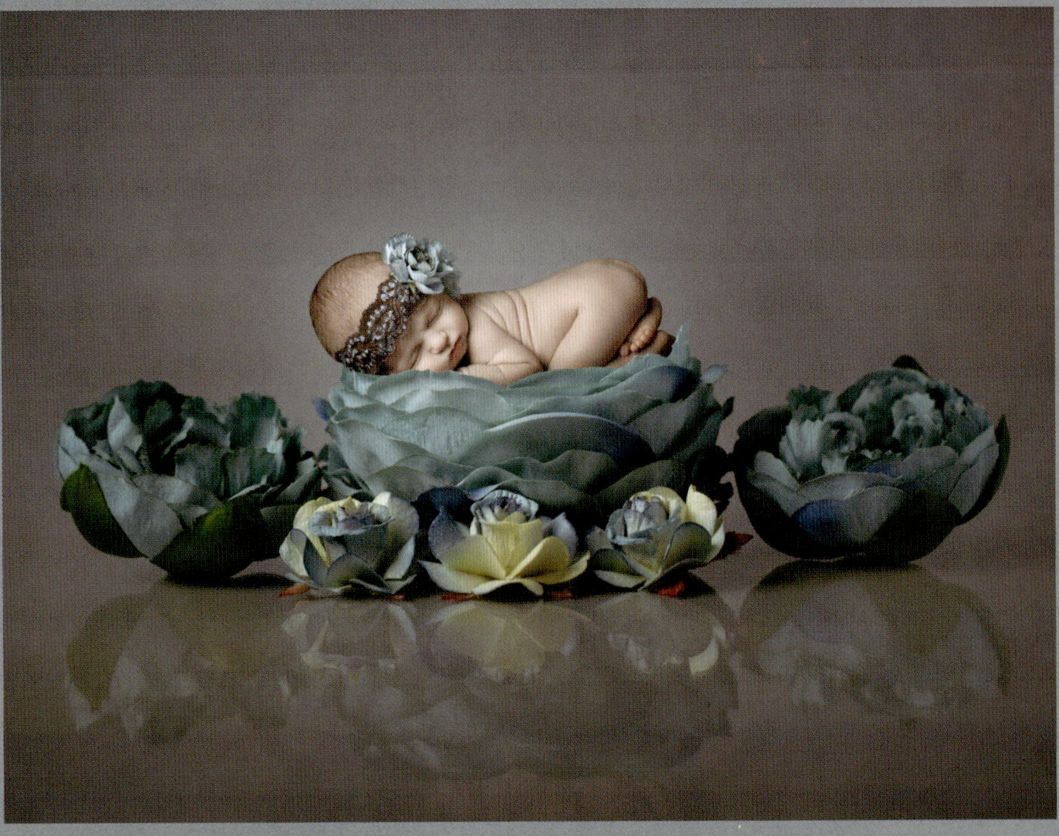

Q) What equipment do you use regularly?
A) I use my Nikon D810 and one of four different lenses depending on what I am shooting. For newborn beanbag work I use my 50mm prime lens, for prop shots and child fine art shoots I use an 85mm lens, a 24–70mm covers aerial floor shots, and a 105mm macro does tiny details.

Q) Why is it important to you to shoot newborns?
A) A baby is only "newborn" for a short period of time, so this is a "one chance" shoot; even after two or three weeks when my clients come back for their viewing, their baby has already changed a lot. I think it is important to capture this time, as you are documenting their baby for generations to come.

Q) How do you go about setting up a session?
A) After looking at my website, many of my clients will come to me with a huge list of things they want, so I often have to set realistic expectations. They are not going to get every single prop and pose, so I'll ask them what is the most important shot they want and try to get that first, before moving on. Above all, I tell them that their baby is the most important thing, and you have to let baby take the lead. I also make sure they are aware that a shoot may last up to four hours and I am very "hands on," so they are not alarmed by the amount of posing and handling that I do.

Q) What tips do you have for controlling babies during the shoot?
A) I want them "milk drunk," so they haven't got the energy to do anything other than sleep. I also play a track on my iPod of womb noise and a heartbeat, as baby has been listening to this for the last nine months, so I think it's a comfort for them to hear something familiar.

Q) How do you go about lighting your subjects?
A) I use Elinchrom lighting and a wide range of modifiers. I started out using daylight, but I like to be in control of my lighting. With newborns I generally "feather" the light from a single strobe and use a reflector to lift the shadows.

Q) How important is postproduction and do you do your own?
A) Postproduction is very important, as newborns are never "perfect"—I regularly see yellow backs, purple hands and feet, and red splotches, and they are often covered in scratches and baby

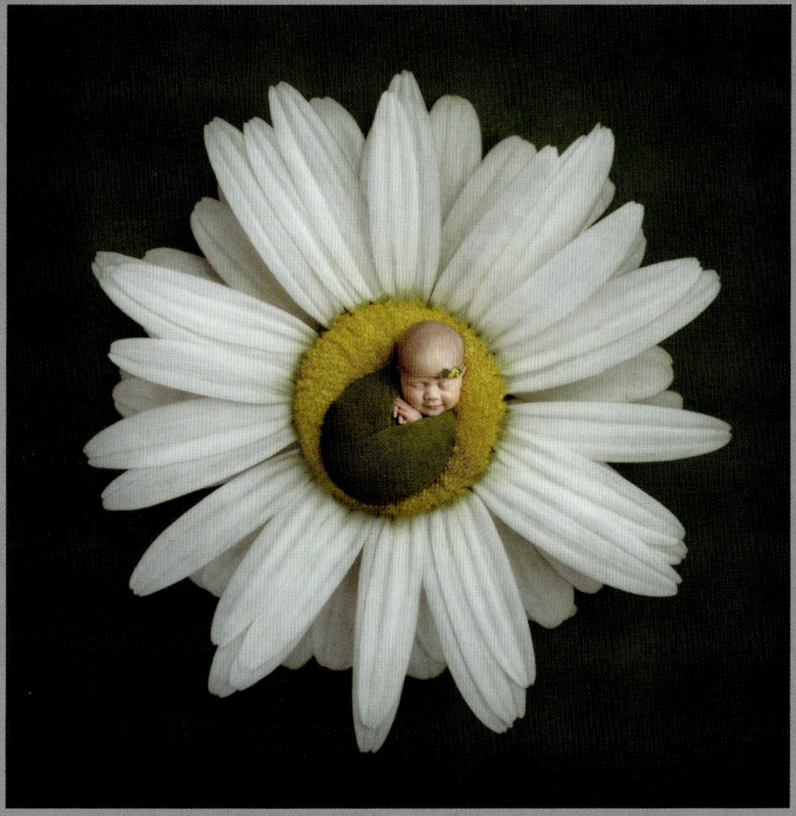

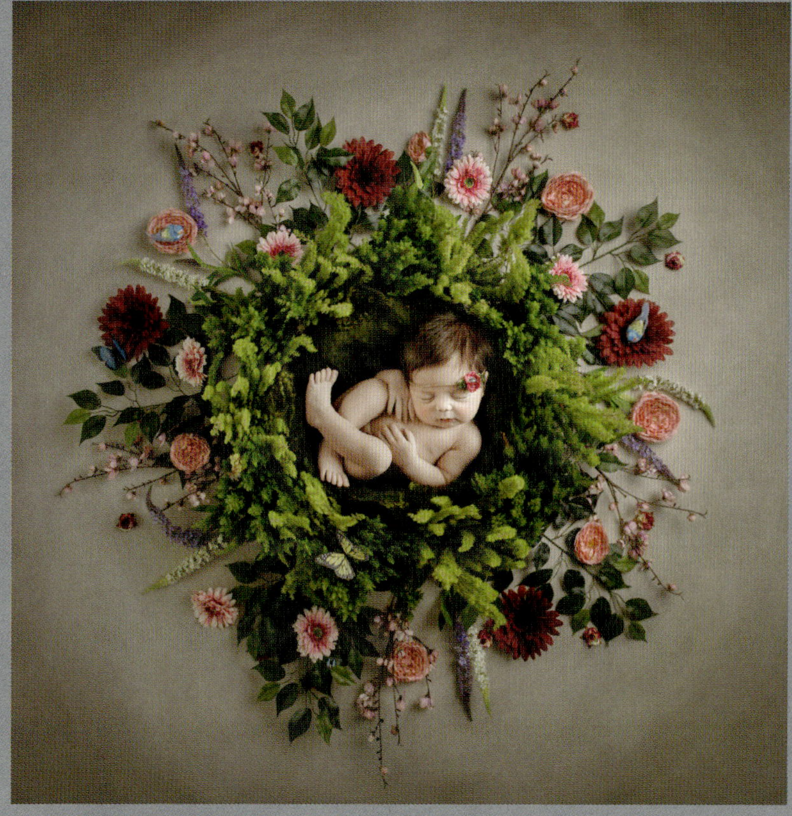

acne. I like to get rid of all that and give them a creamy skin, as my style is all about "newborn art." I also use a lot of composites in my newborn work, as baby safety is paramount. This can involve merging a few images together in Photoshop to get rid of a parent holding baby, or cloning out an adult's fingers and hands, for example.

Q) What is your top tip for newborn child portrait photographers?
A) The best time to bring a baby in for this style of photography is when they are between four and 12 days old, so the process needs to start before the birth. To make your shoots go smoothly you need to learn to read sleep cycles, perfect the basic poses (before moving on to the hero shots), keep the studio warm, and keep calm—newborns can pick up on stress and will not feel as secure.

Final images are all created by photo composition. The technical details are for the original portrait of the child.

Chapter 9
Postproduction

Retouching or "airbrushing" portraits is almost as old as photography itself. Some of the first commercial photographers making early Daguerreotypes would paint onto their images to bring them to life in both black and white and color, with brush strokes often visible in these early photographs. Indeed, retouching became so prolific that in the late 1800s airbrushing "factories" were set up to cope with the demand. Today, of course, retouching has entered the digital realm, with computers and editing software enabling us to edit, fine tune, and perfect our images with the click of a mouse. In this chapter we look at some of the options open to you, as well as techniques for dealing with some fairly specific (and common) portrait problems.

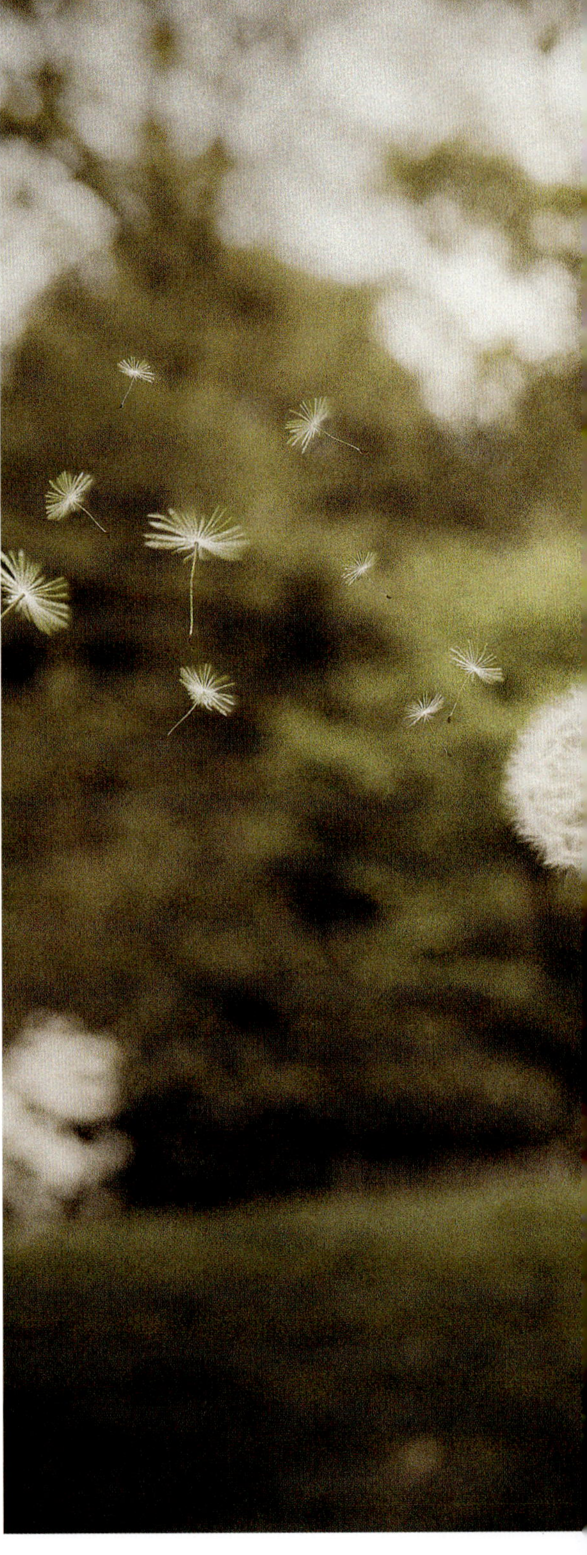

Right: Postproduction is an essential aspect of all child portrait shoots.

Focal length: 63mm

Aperture: f/7.1

Shutter speed: 1/160 sec.

ISO: 1250

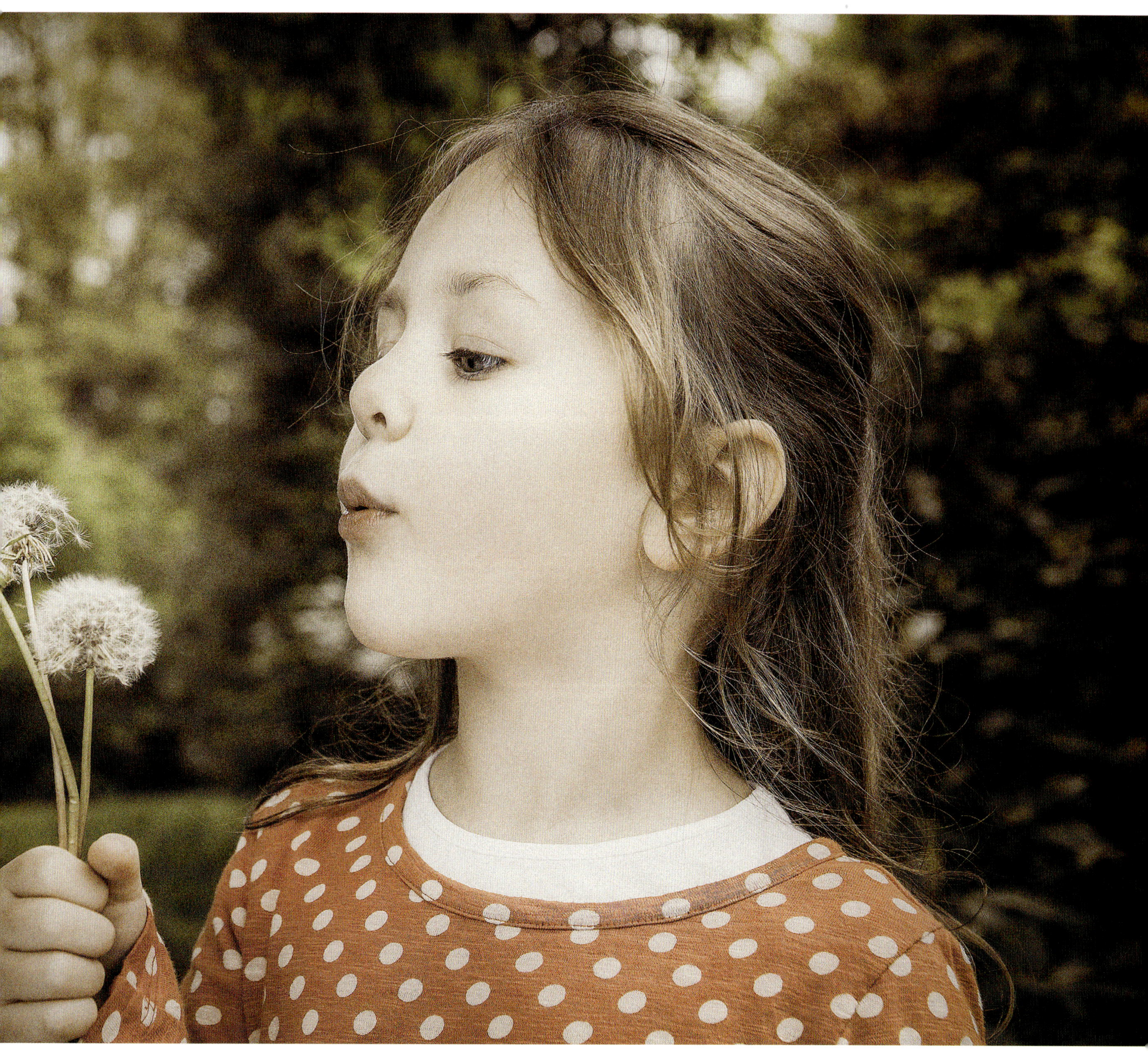

Digital Workflow

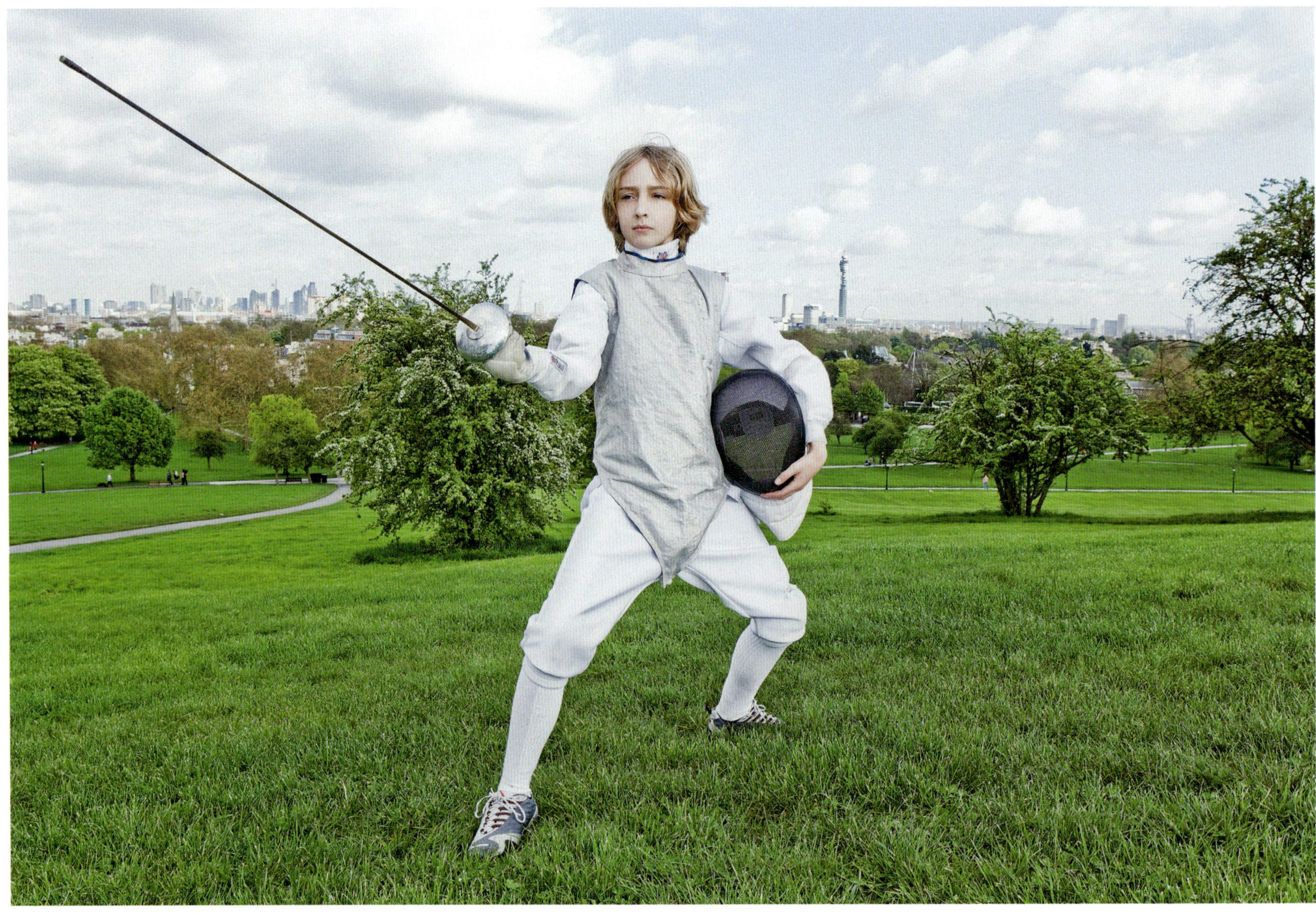

Computers are now a standard part of every photographer's armory and the technology is developing constantly. The "ideal" specification for a postproduction machine is the source of many forum discussions, but essentially, you want a fast computer with a very good graphics card and a lot of RAM so you can handle large image files quickly. Retouching software can suck up a lot of processing power so you need to be prepared to invest in a high-end computer if you want to become a competent retoucher.

As well as the computer, you will also need reliable storage (and plenty of it) in the form of hard drives or SSD (solid state drives); a high-resolution monitor; and you might also find it easier to work with a graphics tablet instead of a mouse. Although using a tablet can take a bit of getting used to, it is a great way to produce professionally

Above: To have an effective digital workflow you need to have the right tools for the job, which means both hardware and the software.

Focal length: 30mm

Aperture: f/10

Shutter speed: 1/200 sec.

ISO: 400

Shooting Raw

finished images. The simple rule here is that the bigger the tablet, the better.

With your hardware in place you can concentrate on the software you need to process your images. There are two aspects to your digital workflow. The first is to develop the individual files and store them; the second is to change and retouch the images to give you the very best results possible. Both of these processes can be handled in several different ways and at different levels, but will inevitably require you to invest in the appropriate software.

Everyone has their own way of working, but I like to make a clear division between the development software and the retouching software: I use Adobe Lightroom for development and storage, and Adobe Photoshop for retouching. Although there is some crossover between the two (Lightroom offers basic retouching, while Photoshop offers basic development options), I prefer to use both without compromise.

Your workflow starts at the shooting stage, which for the highest quality results means shooting Raw. This creates a file that is usually uncompressed and unaltered in any way, so you are in charge of how it is processed. This gives you much more freedom when it comes to creating the "look" of an image, although Raw files tend to look flat and lifeless until they are processed, making this an essential (and time-consuming) step.

The alternative to shooting Raw is to shoot JPEGs, which are often the default file format for lower-end cameras. There is nothing wrong with shooting JPEGs, but the image is processed in-camera, which means the color and contrast are set when you shoot. This is a bit like creating a finished painting, with all the paint in position and dry: if you want to change the painting it's a lot harder to change what's on the canvas. A Raw file, however, is more like a wet painting that you can work and rework more freely.

Raw files are not perfect, though, mainly because all camera manufacturers use their own proprietary Raw format. If you're using a camera that's new to the market—and uses a new Raw format—this can be problematic, as there are often delays between a camera's arrival and the software developers adding its Raw-format "code" to their software's library. If this is the case, you will either have to shoot JPEG until there's an update for your software, or use the software that comes with the camera.

Below: Shooting Raw enables you to bring out every detail in your final image; JPEG is far more restrictive.

Focal length: 24mm

Aperture: f/3.2

Shutter speed: 1/50 sec.

ISO: 640

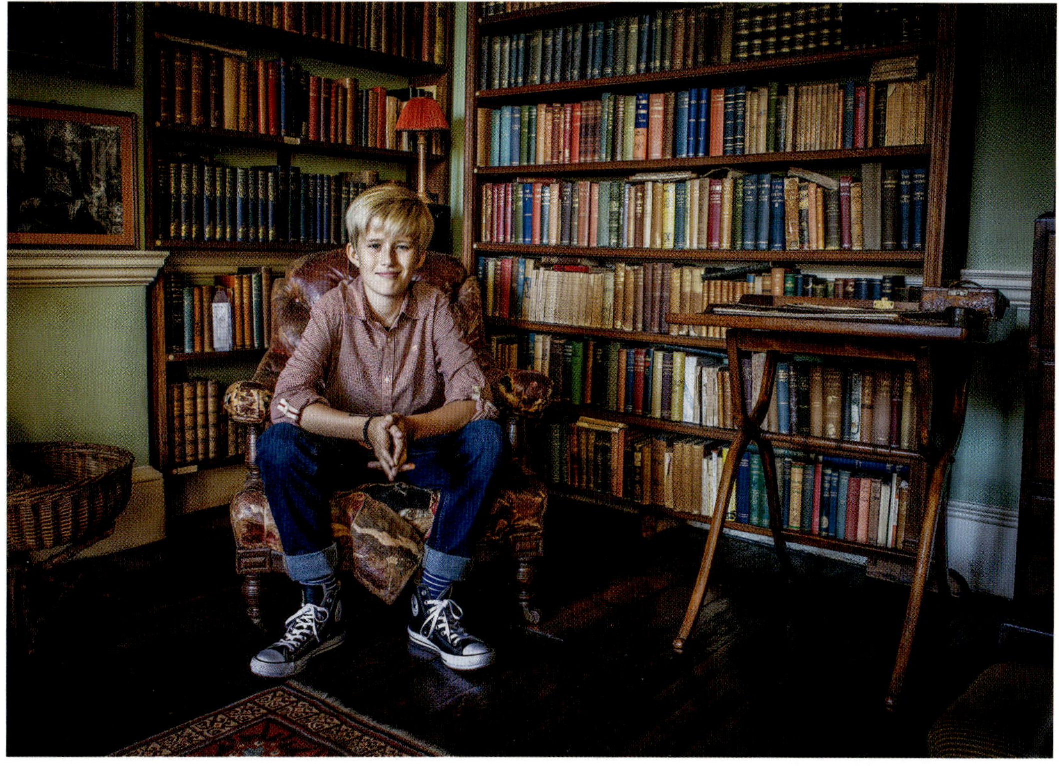

Adobe Lightroom

Lightroom has two functions that can be extremely helpful if you are handling a lot of image data: Library and Develop.

The Library mode can be thought of as your image organization area. It is where you can name and file all of your images so you can find a shot that you took yesterday, last year, or even farther back than that. Using a set of protocols that are infinitely customizable you can automatically rename your images as they are imported to the library, ensure they are filed and backed up, and add searchable keywords. You can then break your images down into smaller categories using star ratings, flags, or colors to sort the multitude of photographs captured during a shoot as you decide which ones are going to make the final cut. Eventually, you will have a shortlist of images that can go forward to be fully developed.

Once you are happy with your selection you can enter Lightroom's Develop module, which is where you will process your Raw files. This is where you decide if they will be black and white or color, whether you want them to have a vintage appearance or a crisp contemporary finish, and generally choose the best "look" for each shot. A good place to start is with the preset profiles listed within the main Develop screen. At the click of a button you can try out several different black-and-white looks and multiple color options, each of which can be fine tuned to suit your own taste. You can also create your own custom profiles to streamline the process even more.

It is worth noting that the changes you make within the Develop module are not actually made to the Raw files themselves. The changes are only implemented when you export your images as a JPEG or TIFF file, which effectively creates a processed copy of your image. This means you can go back and change the Raw image if you change your mind about the processing or want to create multiple versions of the same image.

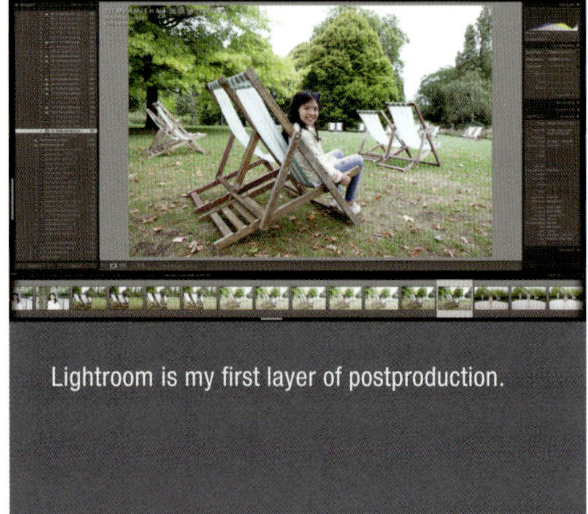

Lightroom is my first layer of postproduction.

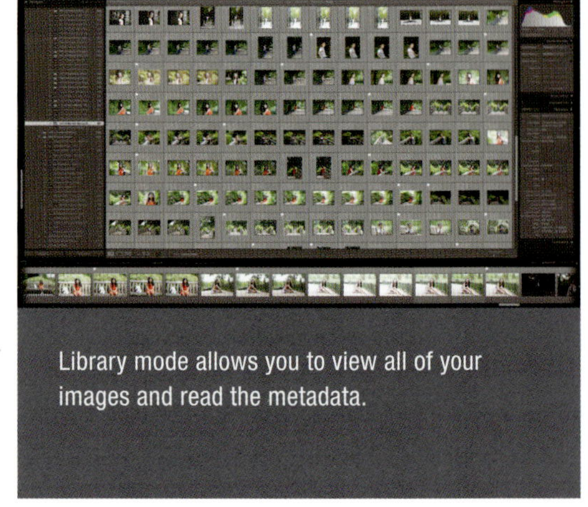

Library mode allows you to view all of your images and read the metadata.

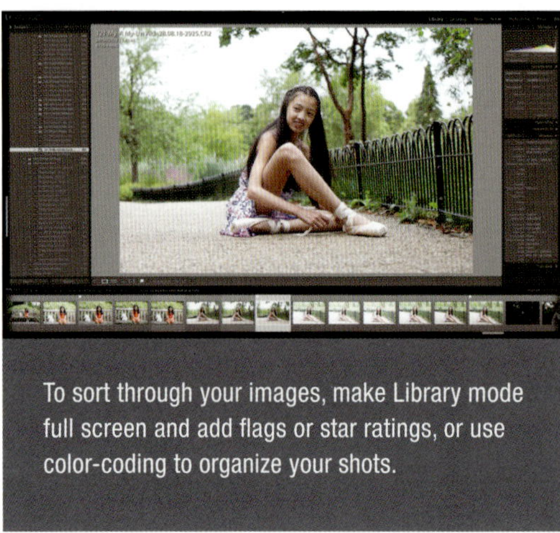

To sort through your images, make Library mode full screen and add flags or star ratings, or use color-coding to organize your shots.

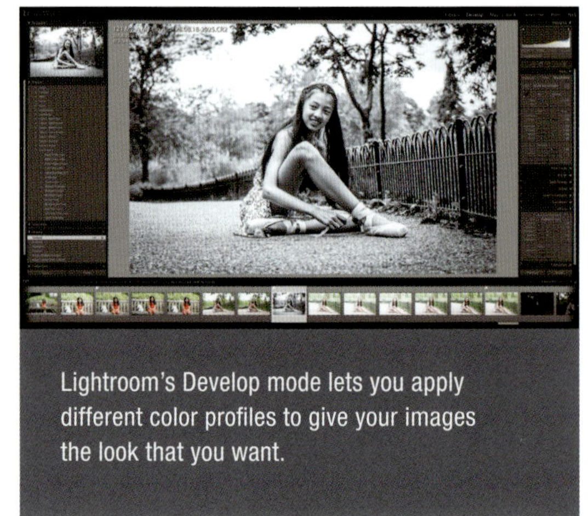

Lightroom's Develop mode lets you apply different color profiles to give your images the look that you want.

Histograms

When you develop your images its pays to keep an eye on the histogram, as this illustrates the spread of highlights and shadows in any given image. The peaks and troughs indicate the levels tonal values that are present in the image with the left side indicating pure black and the right side indicating pure white.

Ideally, you should be looking for a fairly even spread across the graph. If this is not the case, then the basic way to adjust the histogram is to move the Exposure slider or use the Blacks and Whites sliders; you will see the effect of any changes immediately. This should be something you do at the very start of the processing stage as it affects the entire image at a fundamental level.

If you have a significant peak running off the right side of the histogram this indicates that areas of your image have "blown out" to pure white, with no information recorded in them at all. If a peak runs off the left side, you have areas that contain pure black, also with no usable information. In either case you cannot recover detail if it is not in the original exposure, so it also pays to check the histogram on your camera when you shoot.

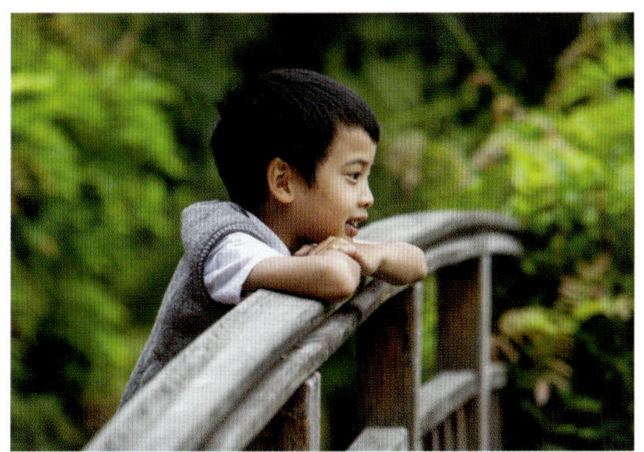

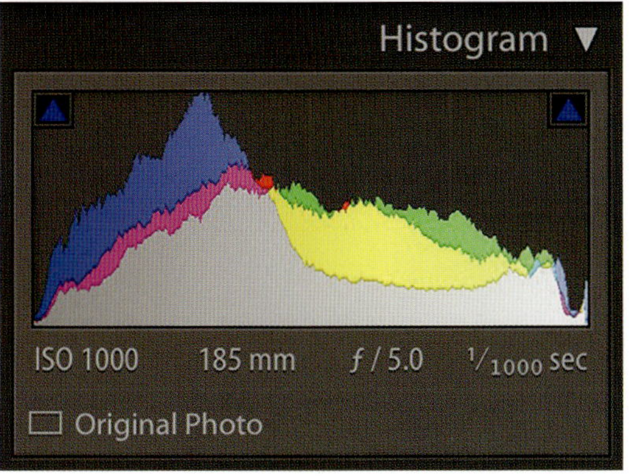

Above: This is a well-exposed image. The histogram shows an even spread of tones with no peak at either end.

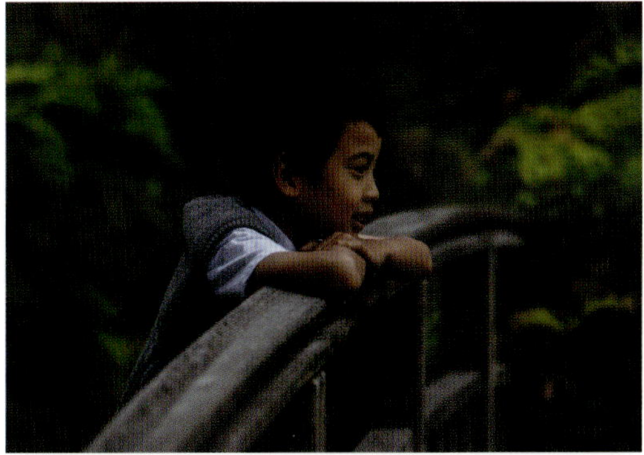

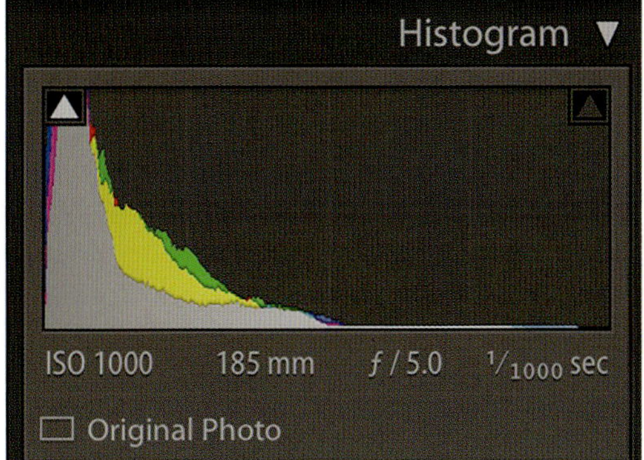

Above: This is the same image with an exposure adjustment of -2 stops. The histogram shows a significant rise toward the left side, indicating that it is too dark and some detail has been lost.

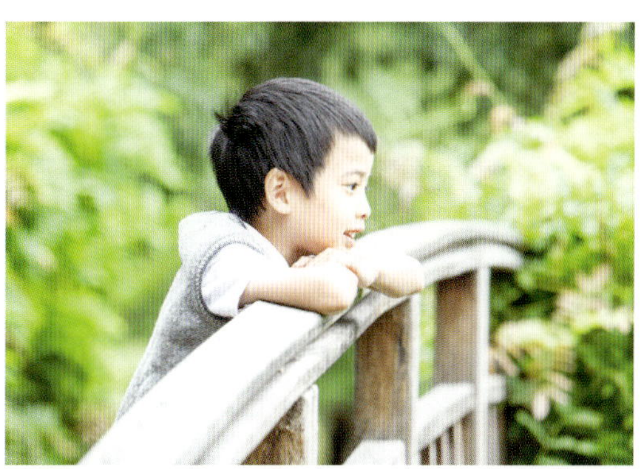

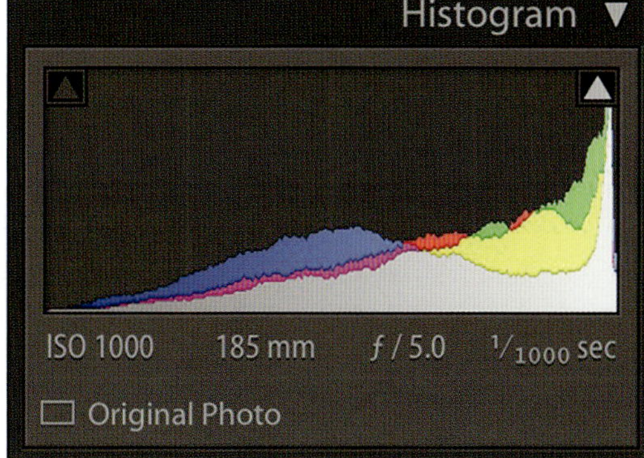

Above: With the exposure increased +2 stops, the histogram shifts to the right. As the histogram runs off the right side this shows that some areas are pure white; detail cannot be recovered in these parts of the image.

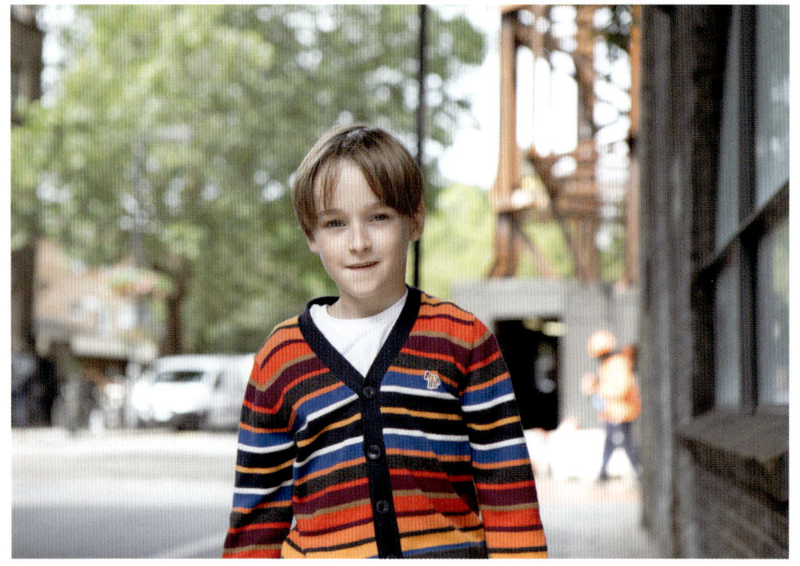

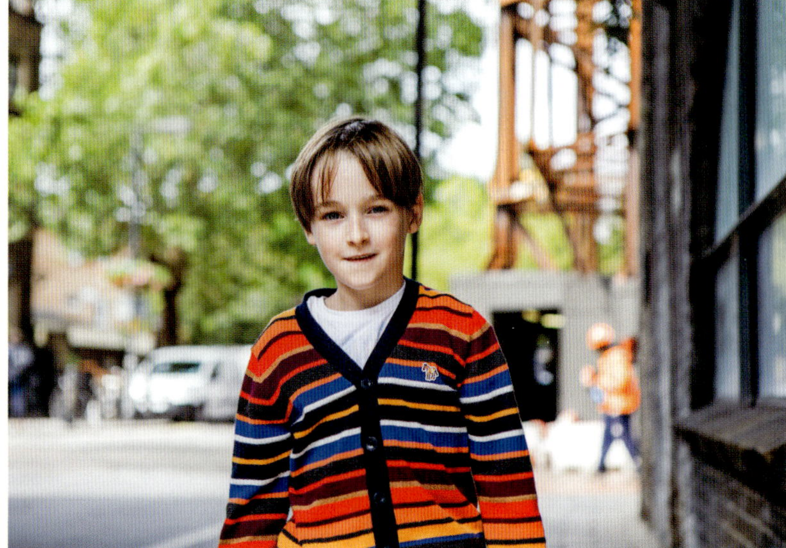

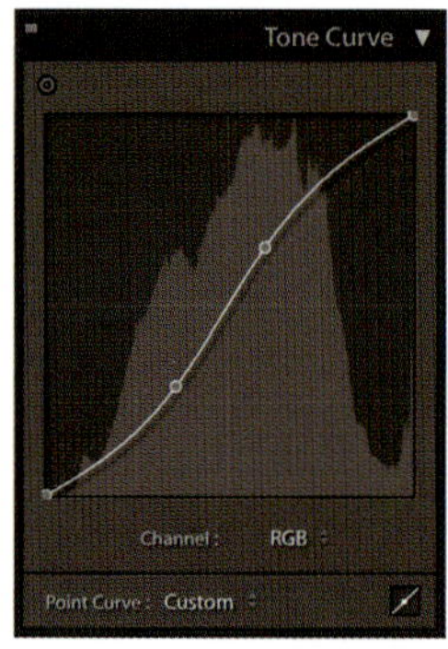

Above & left: In this undeveloped Raw image the tone curve is flat, so is having no effect on the image.

Above & left: Adjusting the curve to create an "S" shape increases the contrast on the image. The same adjustment could also be made by decreasing the Shadows slider and increasing the Highlights sliders.

Shadows & Highlights

The next step in developing an image is often to look at the shadows and highlights in a more specific way. Because Raw files are not processed in the camera they are generally "flat" (low contrast) when they come from the camera. This means you will typically create drama by increasing the contrast between the highlights and shadows.

There are a couple of ways to achieve this: by manipulating the tone curve (usually by adding an "S" shaped curve, as shown above) or by using the Shadows and Highlights sliders found at the right side of the Develop screen. These changes can be seen on screen as you adjust them, so it is up to you to create the image that you want.

Sharpening

All digital images need sharpening to some degree and there are multiple ways of doing this. You will find the sharpening sliders under the Detail tab, but it needs to be applied carefully: it is easy to oversharpen an image and introduce light "halos" along the edges, which will become increasingly obvious as the picture is enlarged.

As you cannot easily get rid of these halos, I would recommend sharpening your images as little as possible in Lightroom, especially as you can always increase the sharpening in Photoshop. Think of sharpening as the salt you sprinkle on your food: if you don't add any, the food will be bland, but too much and it is ruined.

I also like to increase the Clarity (found in the Basic tab) slightly, which increases edge contrast and the impression of sharpness.

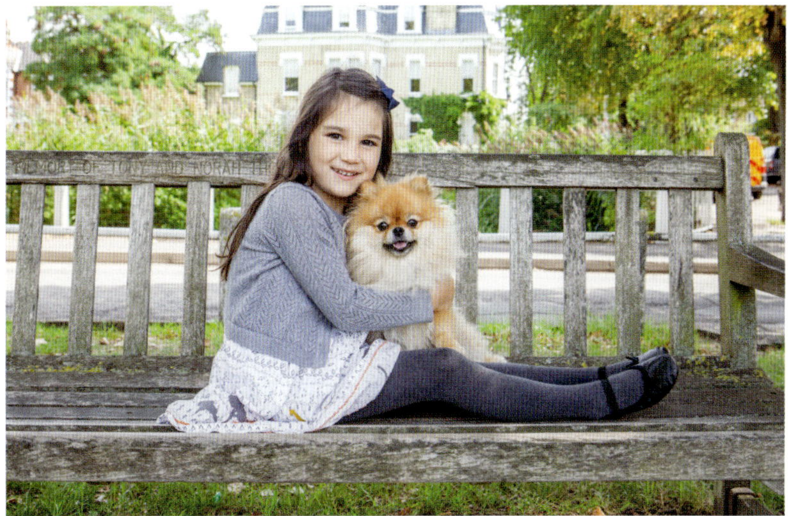

Left: Without any sharpening a Raw image can look slightly "flat."

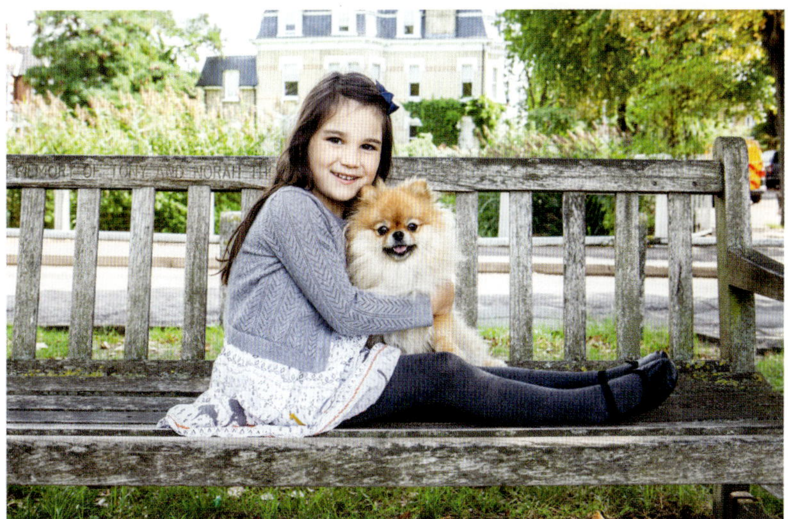

Left: This image has had a small amount of sharpening added in Lightroom.

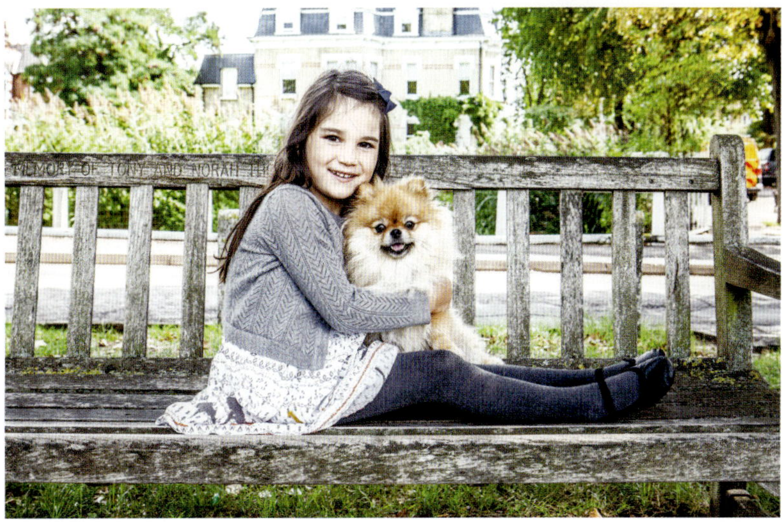

Left: Be careful not to oversharpen an image, as the photograph will start to break up.

Adobe Photoshop

Having developed my images in Lightroom I take them into Photoshop for retouching. The options available within Photoshop are vast. It is impossible to cover everything here, so I will simply outline how I work with my images; this may not be the same way that you end up working with yours.

To start with, I export my selected images from Lightroom as TIFF files. This is because a TIFF is a "lossless," uncompressed file format, so it retains more of the original information than a JPEG. A TIFF can also be saved with its layers intact, enabling you to continue the retouching process at a later stage if you have to.

Spotting & Cloning

The first stage should be to remove anything that should not be in the perfect image. Blobs and dirt spots caused by an unclean sensor are quite common, so look for stain-like marks on the image, especially in the sky or flat, light-colored backgrounds. The Healing tool is a very effective way of getting rid of these, as well as any other problems, such as cigarette ends and garbage in a location shoot, cuts and small blemishes on your subject's skin, or stray hairs.

If the Healing tool struggles, try switching to the Cloning tool instead, which will allow you to copy one area on the image and paste it onto another; if you have some perfect skin next to skin with a scar or mark you can "clone" the good skin over the bad, for example. You can vary the opacity and source of your selected area to control the finished effect, but always be careful that you are not removing so much texture that the image starts to look contrived or "plastic."

A good rule to follow is to always use the largest brush size you can reasonably apply, as this will give you the most general and subtle effect. You can adjust the edge of the brush, as well as its shape and size, but generally you will want to be working with a circular brush with a soft, feathered edge for the most realistic finish. Work carefully to remove all of the obvious marks, scratches, and natural flaws.

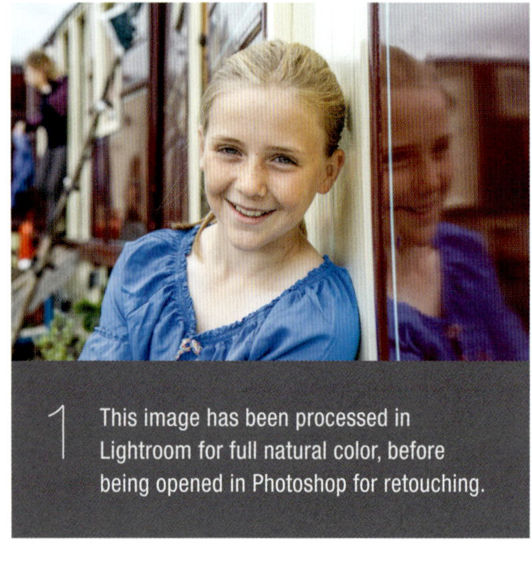

1 This image has been processed in Lightroom for full natural color, before being opened in Photoshop for retouching.

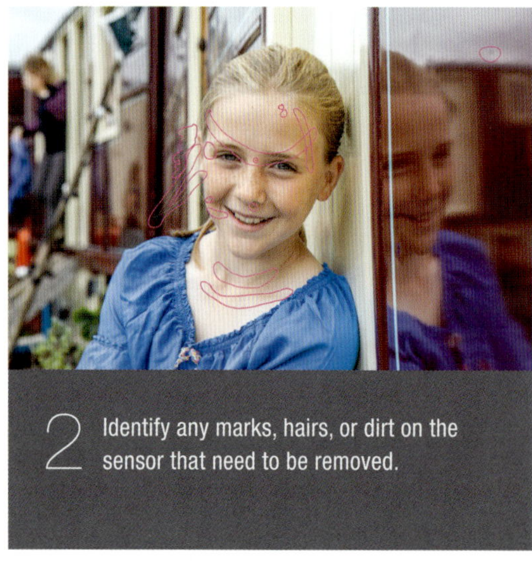

2 Identify any marks, hairs, or dirt on the sensor that need to be removed.

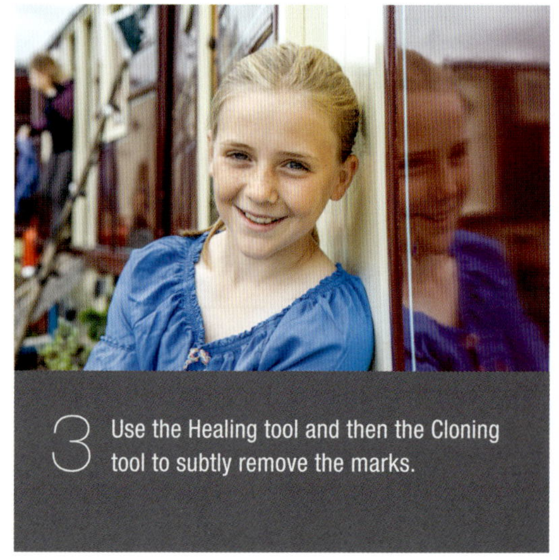

3 Use the Healing tool and then the Cloning tool to subtly remove the marks.

Cropping

If your horizon line is not straight, or your model is not quite in the right place, straighten things up and crop the image to create the perfect composition. The cropping tool can be set to specific dimensions and any resolution, so check before you click "OK" because you don't want to crop your image to a tiny size: keep the resolution as high as reasonably possible because you cannot replace the lost pixels once you have saved your image.

You can create and save your own preset cropping dimensions, which is great if you want a series of images to look similar, as you can make sure they have the same crop.

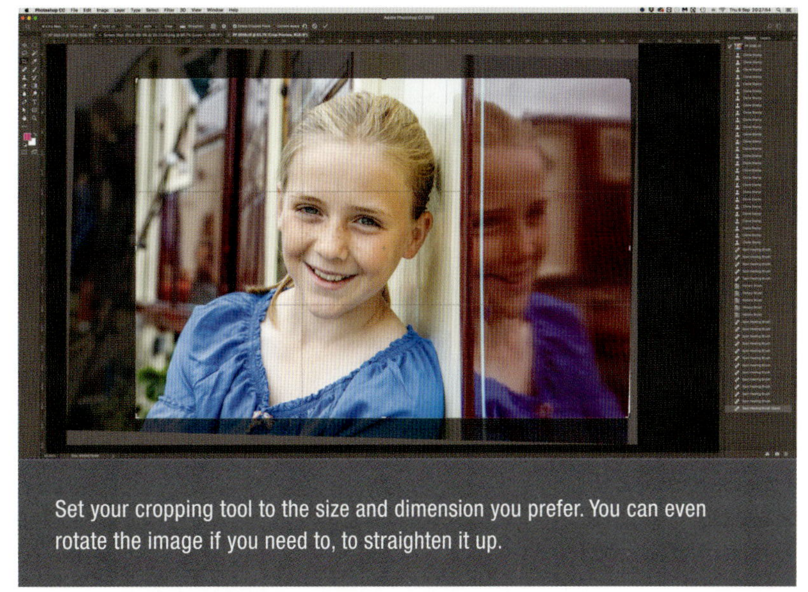

Set your cropping tool to the size and dimension you prefer. You can even rotate the image if you need to, to straighten it up.

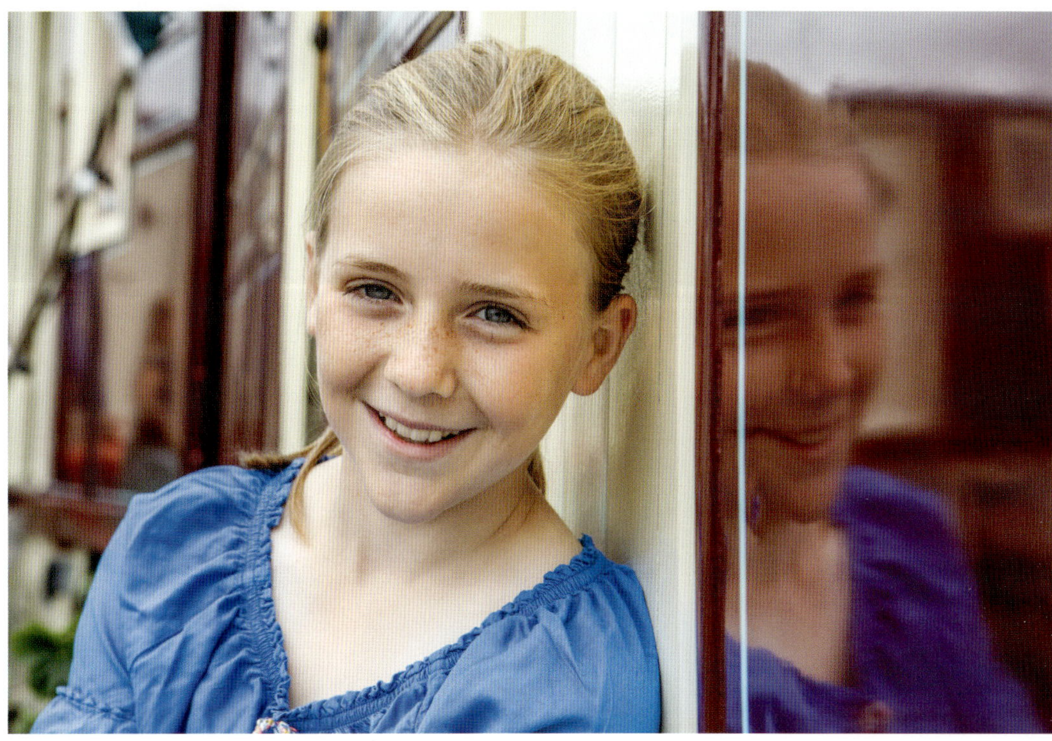

Above: The final image is free of marks and scratches, cropped, and re-composed, with no distracting background issues.

Layers

The concept of Layers can be a little confusing at first, but they are designed so you can adjust and then readjust your image at any stage. In simple terms, think of Layers as being like translucent sheets of film that are laid on top of each other. The image you see on screen is the result of looking through all the sheets, and each individual layer can affect the final view. You can turn layers on or off to see the effect they are having.

Some layers are simply cutout pieces of an image, either taken from the original photograph or from another shot entirely and then laid onto the background image; an extreme example would be to cut out your subject and drop them onto an entirely different background. The trick to achieving a good cutout is to ensure the edge looks natural. There are many ways of doing this, either by automatically feathering the cutout edge, or brushing it in by hand. Try different techniques to find a method that suits you.

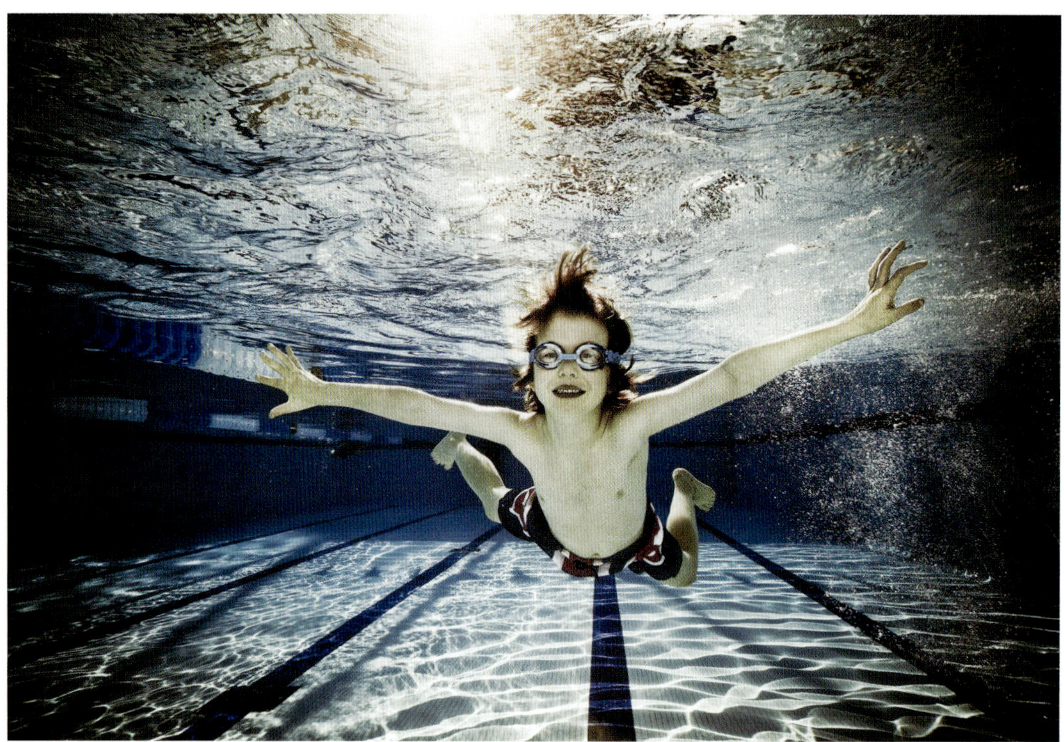

Above: The use of layers can be essential in helping you get the very best result from even the most challenging circumstances.

Focal length: 24mm

Aperture: f/18

Shutter speed: 1/200 sec.

ISO: 320

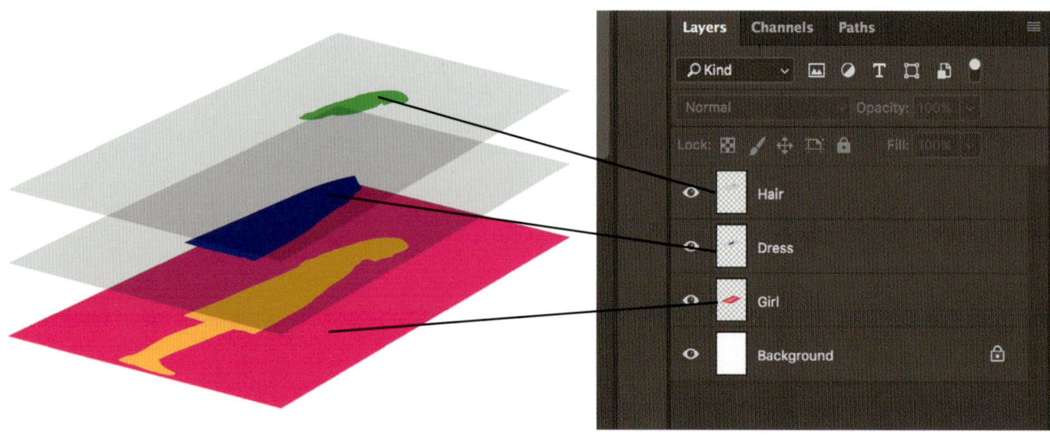

Left: To create a composite image you import a new image element into a different layer. You can adjust everything on that layer independently of the rest of the picture, allowing you to finesse the edges of the cutout, fine tune the color, and so on.

Adjustment Layers

Adjustment layers are a special type of layer that doesn't contain any actual image information. Instead, they contain instructions that adjust all the layers beneath them; they can adjust the exposure, color balance, sharpness, or a multitude of other aspects. They are often used in conjunction with "layer masks," which allow you to isolate specific areas within the image that will be affected by or protected from the adjustment.

As an example, you might want to brighten up a child's eye sockets, which may be a little dark in the original image due to adverse lighting conditions. A Brightness/Contrast adjustment layer could be applied to lift the darkness slightly, but this would affect the entire image. However, you could add a layer mask to the adjustment layer so it only affects the eye sockets, allowing you to set the exact amount of brightness you require in precisely the right area.

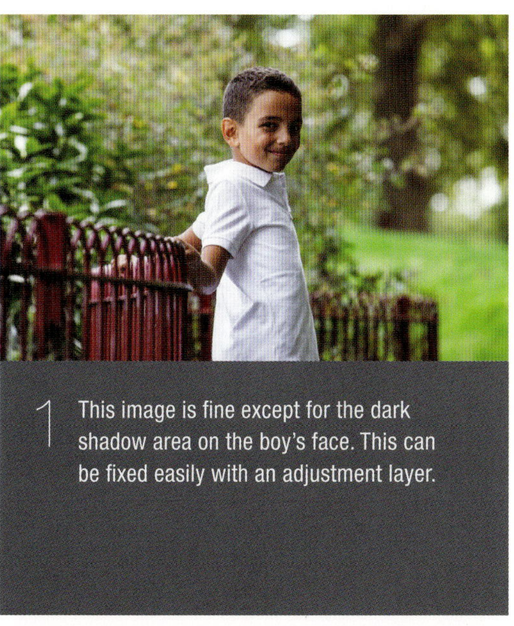

1 This image is fine except for the dark shadow area on the boy's face. This can be fixed easily with an adjustment layer.

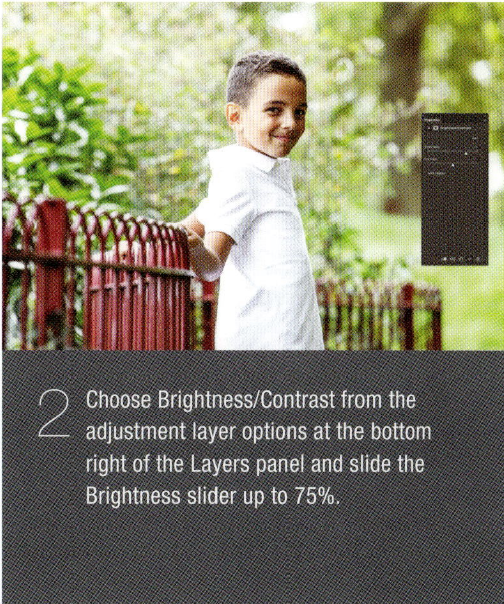

2 Choose Brightness/Contrast from the adjustment layer options at the bottom right of the Layers panel and slide the Brightness slider up to 75%.

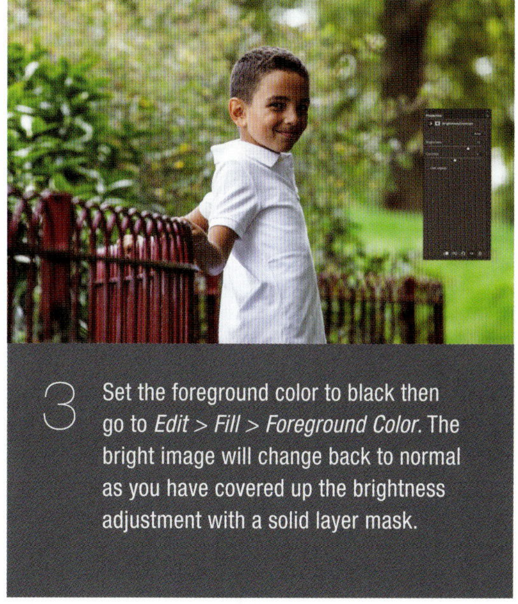

3 Set the foreground color to black then go to *Edit > Fill > Foreground Color*. The bright image will change back to normal as you have covered up the brightness adjustment with a solid layer mask.

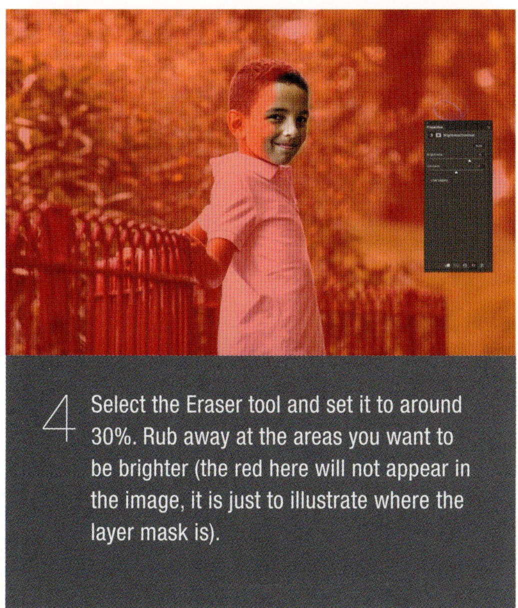

4 Select the Eraser tool and set it to around 30%. Rub away at the areas you want to be brighter (the red here will not appear in the image, it is just to illustrate where the layer mask is).

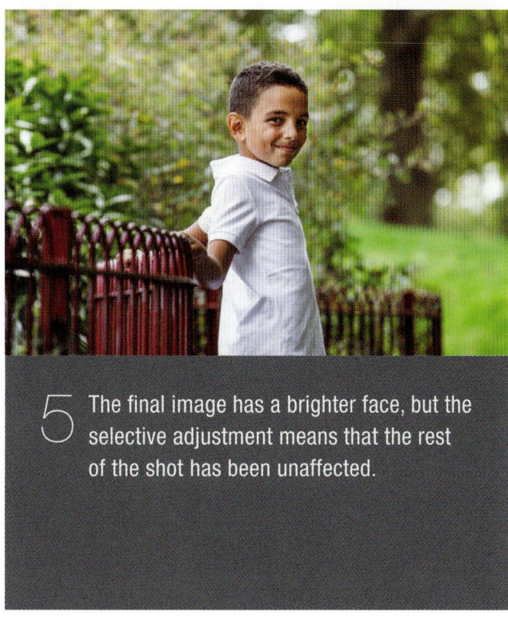

5 The final image has a brighter face, but the selective adjustment means that the rest of the shot has been unaffected.

History

Photoshop's History panel is incredibly useful, as it gives you the freedom to try out virtually any adjustments you like, and then revert back to the original at the click of an icon if things don't work out. History basically records every step you take and lines them up one by one in order down the screen: you can click on any point in the History and the image will revert back to that stage.

You can also use the History panel in conjunction with the History Brush from the tool bar. For example, let's assume that you've made adjustments to your child's hair, which was flying out of the image in an unpleasant way. You then go on to treat some scratches or skin blemishes, but when you've finished you take another look at the image and decide that you now don't like the hair removal. In the History panel you simply check the box to the left of the point you want to go back to. Then, you can use the History Brush to "paint back" the areas from that point. In this way you can selectively undo the changes you have made.

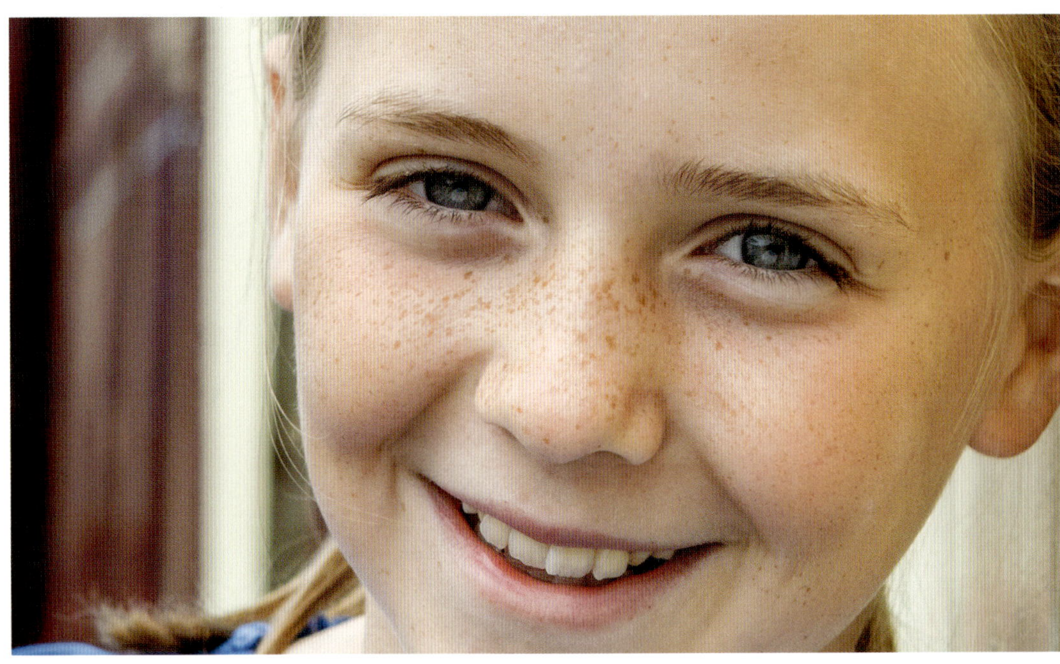

Above: In this image I have removed stray hairs using the Spot Healing tool.

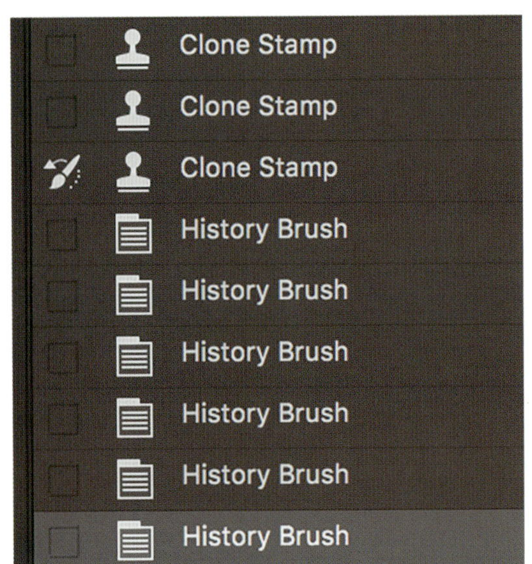

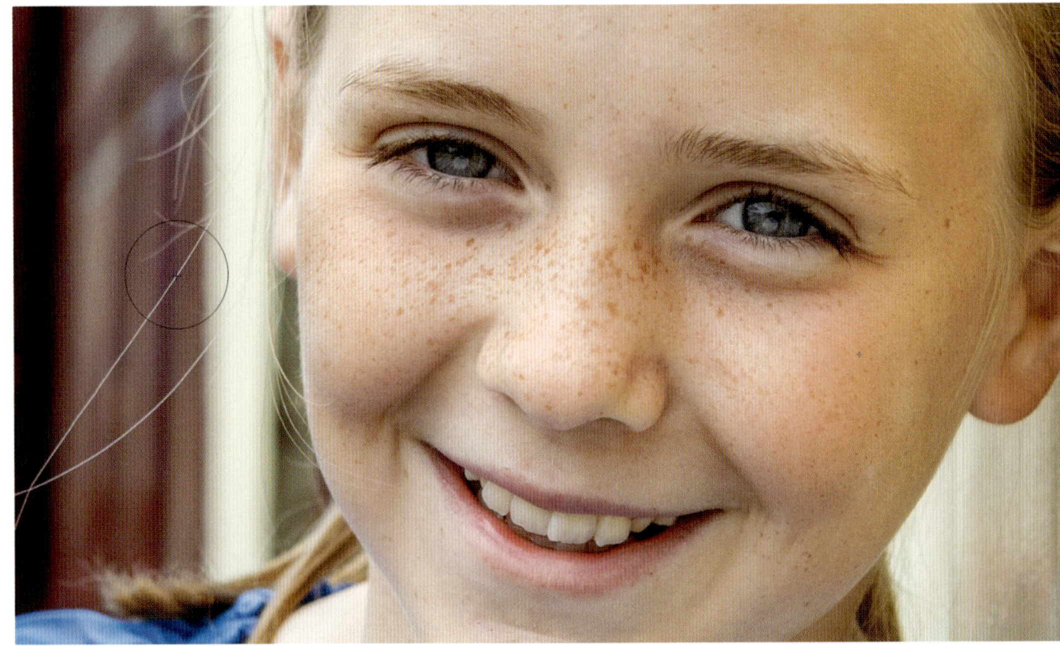

Above & above right: If I want to restore the hairs I can check the box at the left of the point at which they were removed and paint them back in using the History Brush.

Actions

Actions are another very useful facility within Photoshop, as they allow you to perform a sequence of actions on an image that would otherwise be done on an individual basis.

For example, let's say you had a number of images that were all underexposed by 1 stop, had a yellow color cast, and all needed to be reduced in size and saved as JPEGs. You could open each image individually and perform each adjustment, one at a time, but this would require you to manually go through four different processes for each shot.

However, if you recorded the processes as an Action the first time you did them you would simply have to "Play" the action for subsequent images and it would perform each step instantly.

As a practical example, I have an Action called "Grain & Sharp Contrast" that is designed to mimic the look of film, and I use this on most of my images: all I need to do is select the appropriate action from the Actions palette and press Play.

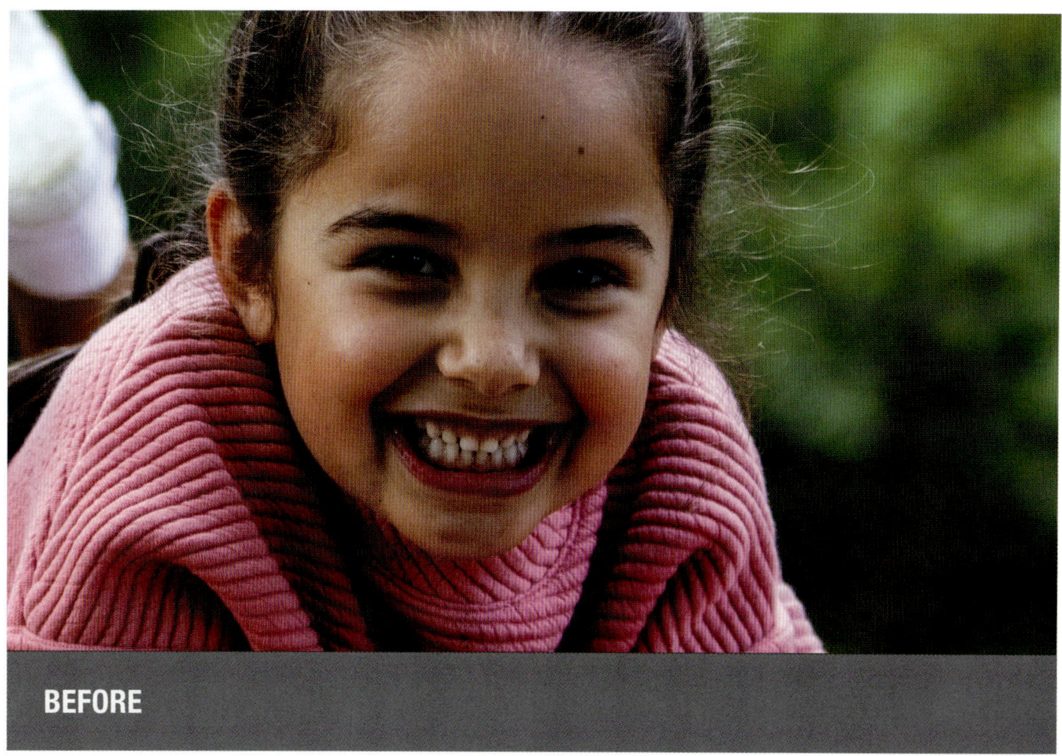

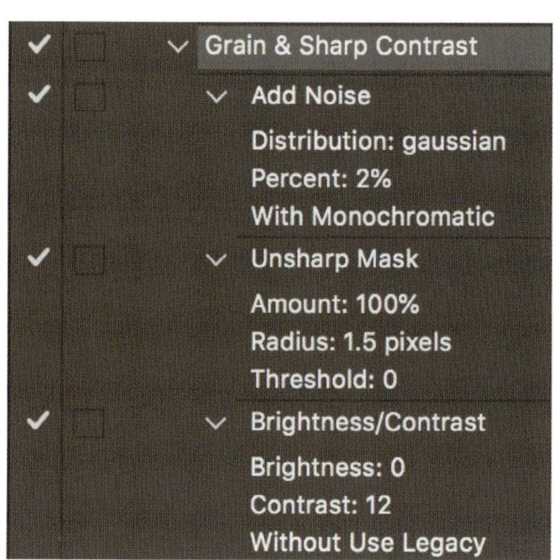

Above: My "Grain & Sharp Contrast" action adds a filmic effect to my images with just a couple of mouse clicks.

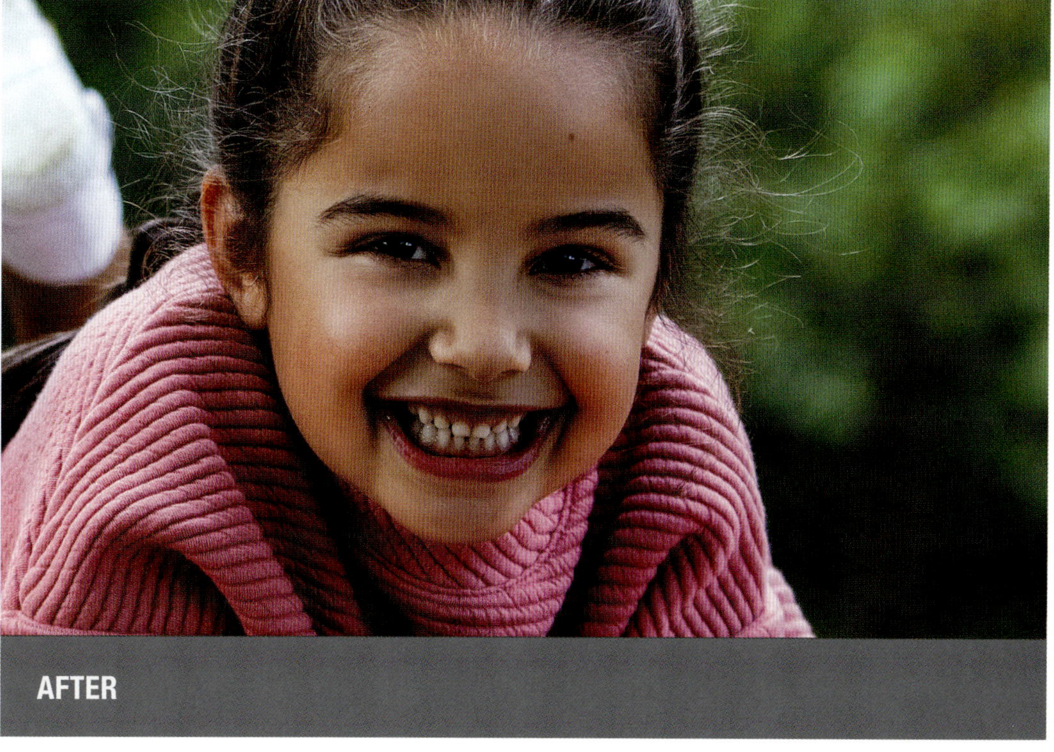

Retouching

Portrait photography has some very specific retouching challenges, which we will look at here. The main thing to remember is that the essence of great retouching is for it to be as minimal as possible and to create a natural-looking image: if your client can see that a shot has been retouched, you have overdone it, so tread softly!

Retouching Skin

Most children have great skin, so don't make the mistake of thinking you have to retouch it if this is not actually needed.

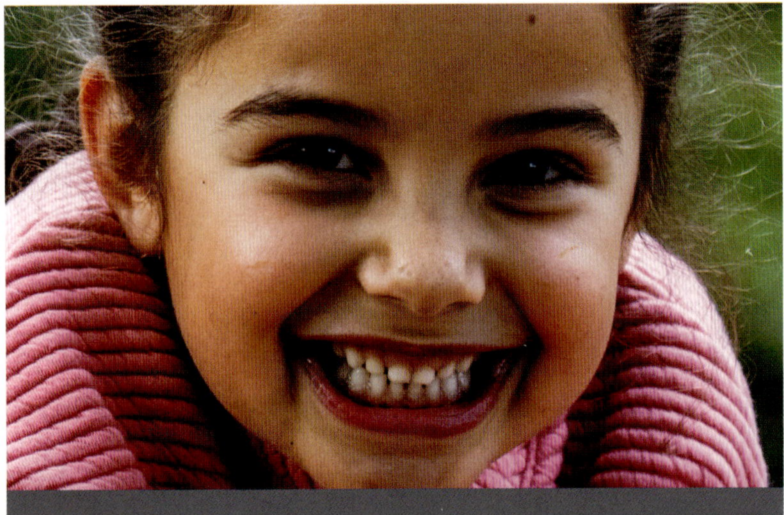

1 In your initial processing stages you should have removed any obvious spots and scratches, so the next thing to look for are any other undesirable elements: look closely at the corners of the eyes and the mouth and nose for any mucus or other "slime," and remove any stray hairs that are distracting or just not in the right place. There is almost always something to be removed, so use the Healing and Cloning tools to do this at a micro level.

When you're done, take a "snapshot" of this state by using the Create New Snapshot icon in the History palette. This will allow you to quickly go back to this point with the History Brush.

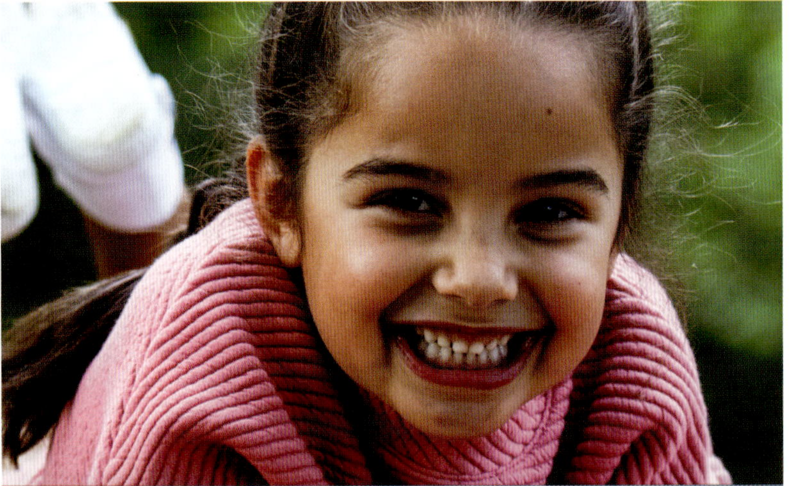

2 Although any undesirable elements have been removed, the skin will still probably have discoloration, annoying shadow areas, and possibly even wrinkles and crease lines that could be improved. Removing these can be more tricky, but work carefully with the Healing and/or Cloning tools.

However, be careful not to remove any freckles or smile dimples that may be part of that child's unique identity, as the parents will want to see these. A simple rule to follow is that if it's a permanent feature, keep it; if it will heal or go away, remove it.

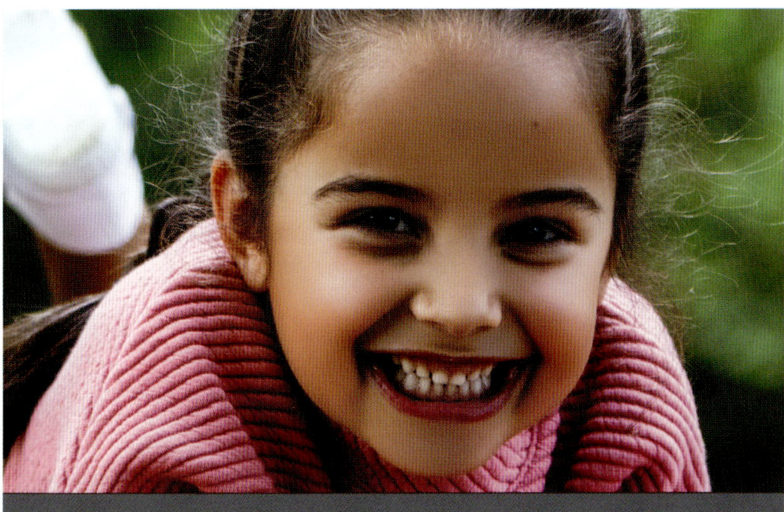

3 When it comes to skin that is flawed or marked (whether it's dirt or deep skin blemishes), you need to clean it up. Some people do this by duplicating the image, applying a blur filter, and then selectively rubbing it back with the Eraser, but I prefer to use the Cloning tool very selectively across virtually all of the skin.

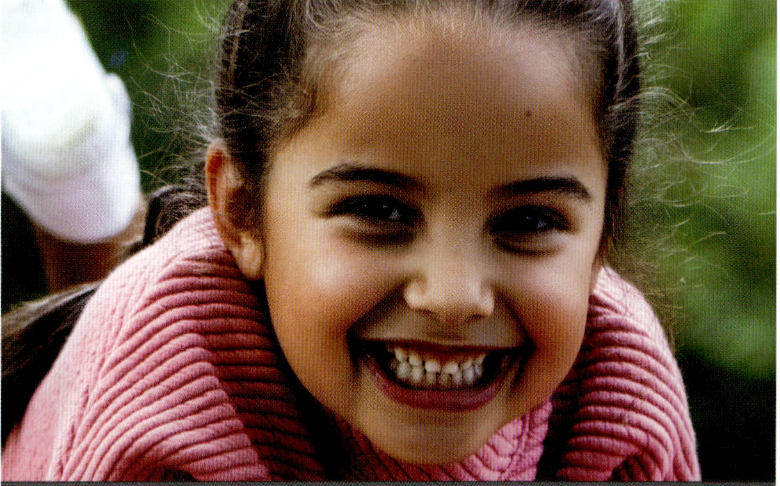

4 Using the Cloning tool to clean the skin results in a rather "plastic" texture that looks very wrong, so the next step is to add a little bit of reality back into the image. Select that History snapshot created at the end of the first step and choose a large, soft History Brush set to an opacity of 10–30%. Carefully brush back some of the original image. Although this will reintroduce some of the flaws you removed in the previous stage this re-establishes a realistic look, although the overall effect is still very clean.

Bags Under The Eyes

To remove bags under eyes you can use either the Cloning tool at a very light opacity setting to fill in darker areas from the lighter areas below, or use the Patch tool. This tool is especially useful if the child has a lot of freckles, and can be found by clicking and holding the Healing brush icon.

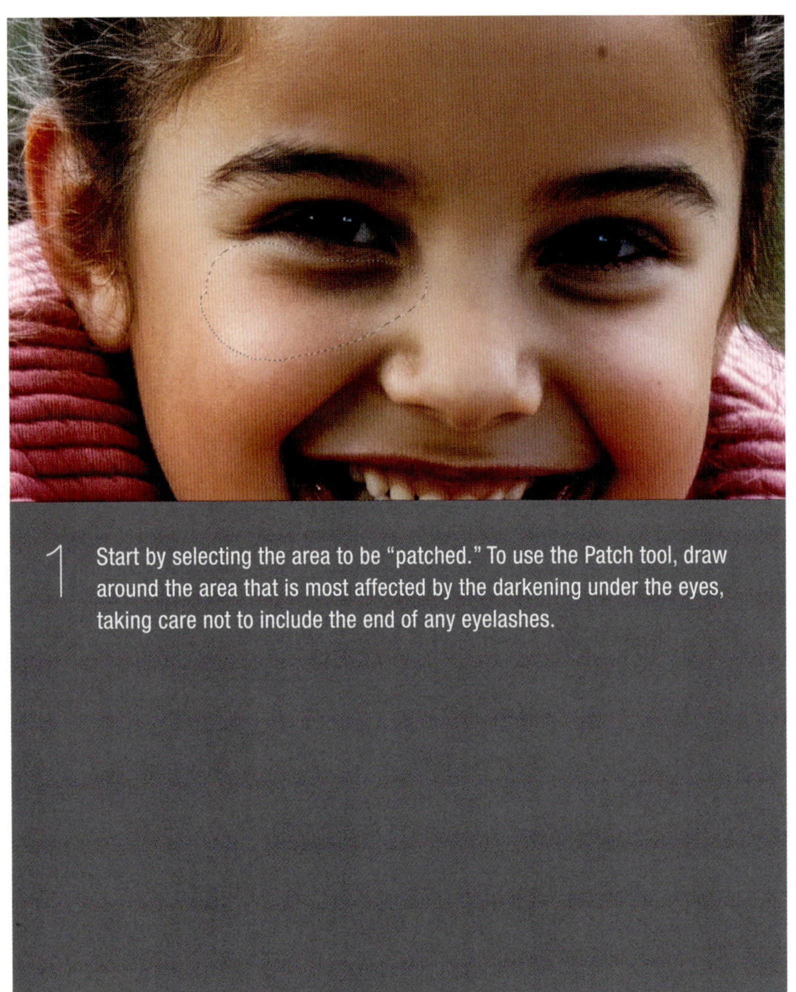

1 Start by selecting the area to be "patched." To use the Patch tool, draw around the area that is most affected by the darkening under the eyes, taking care not to include the end of any eyelashes.

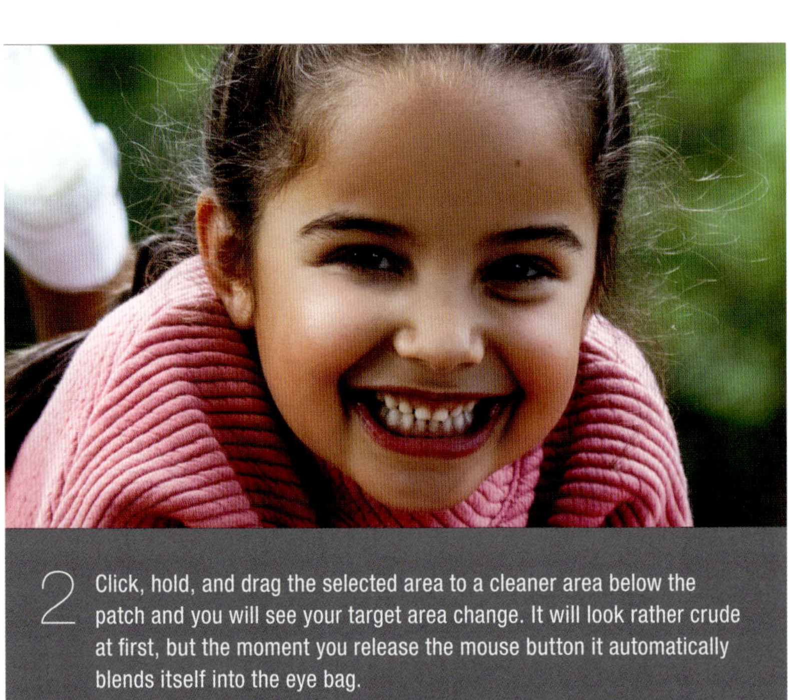

2 Click, hold, and drag the selected area to a cleaner area below the patch and you will see your target area change. It will look rather crude at first, but the moment you release the mouse button it automatically blends itself into the eye bag.

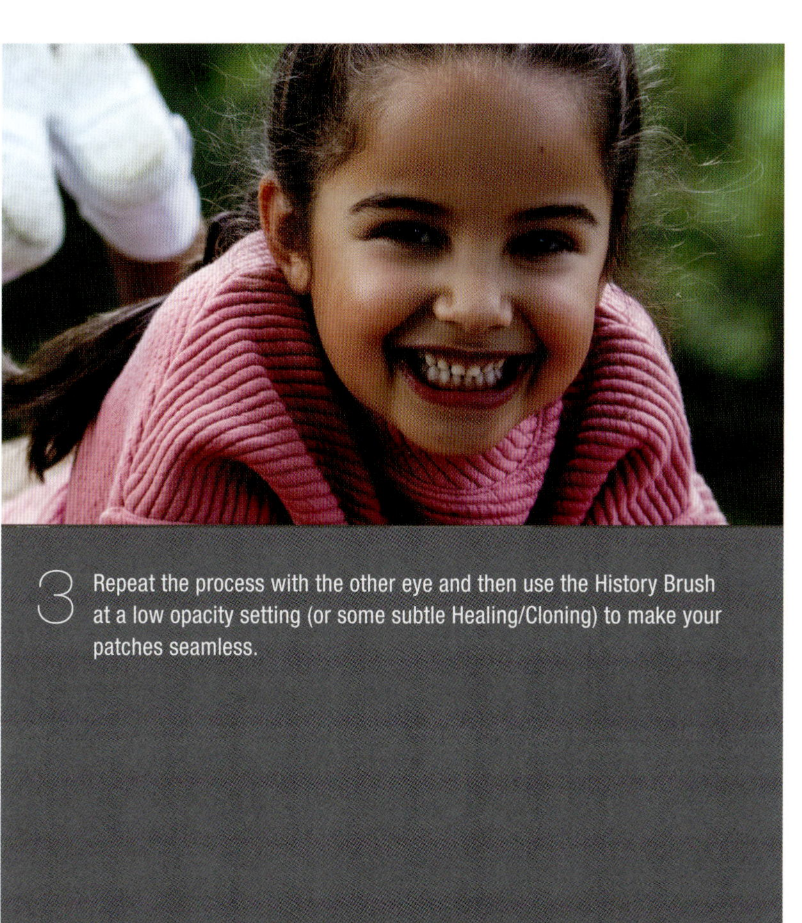

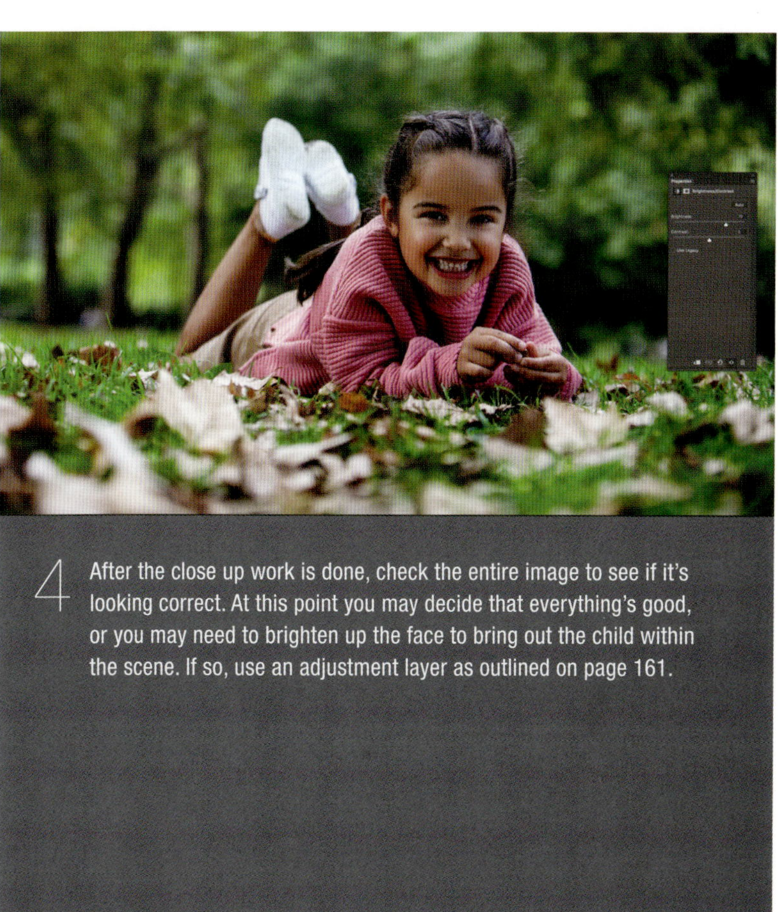

3 Repeat the process with the other eye and then use the History Brush at a low opacity setting (or some subtle Healing/Cloning) to make your patches seamless.

4 After the close up work is done, check the entire image to see if it's looking correct. At this point you may decide that everything's good, or you may need to brighten up the face to bring out the child within the scene. If so, use an adjustment layer as outlined on page 161.

Bloodshot Cheeks

This is a great technique to use if the child has over-reddened cheeks (from being in the cold, running around too much, or because of a postproduction increase in contrast).

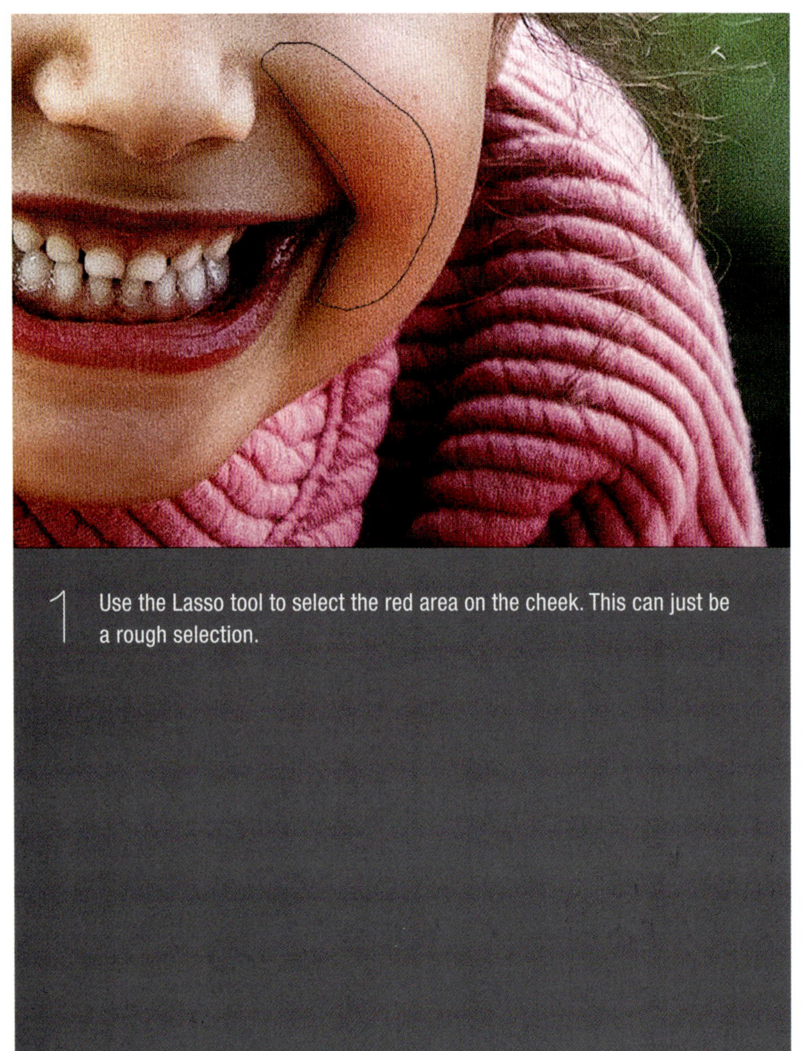

1 Use the Lasso tool to select the red area on the cheek. This can just be a rough selection.

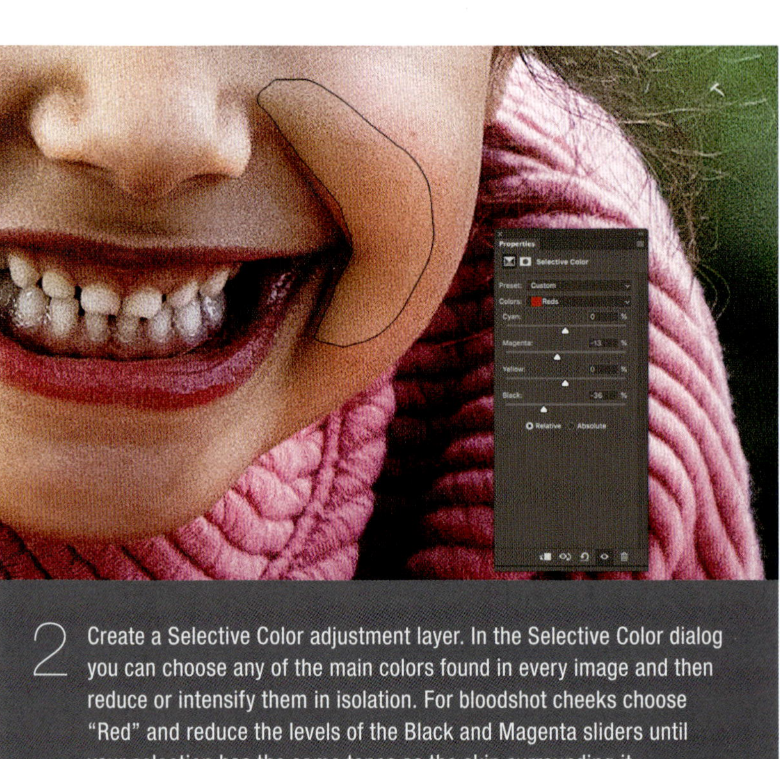

2 Create a Selective Color adjustment layer. In the Selective Color dialog you can choose any of the main colors found in every image and then reduce or intensify them in isolation. For bloodshot cheeks choose "Red" and reduce the levels of the Black and Magenta sliders until your selection has the same tones as the skin surrounding it.

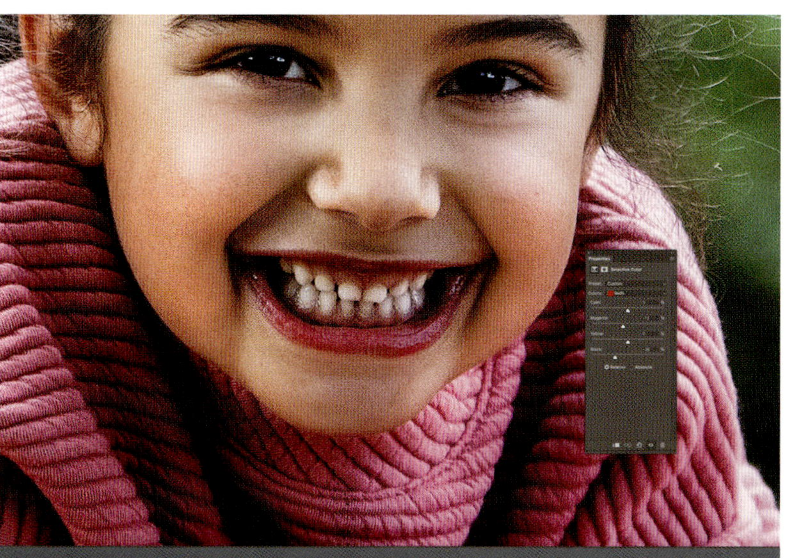

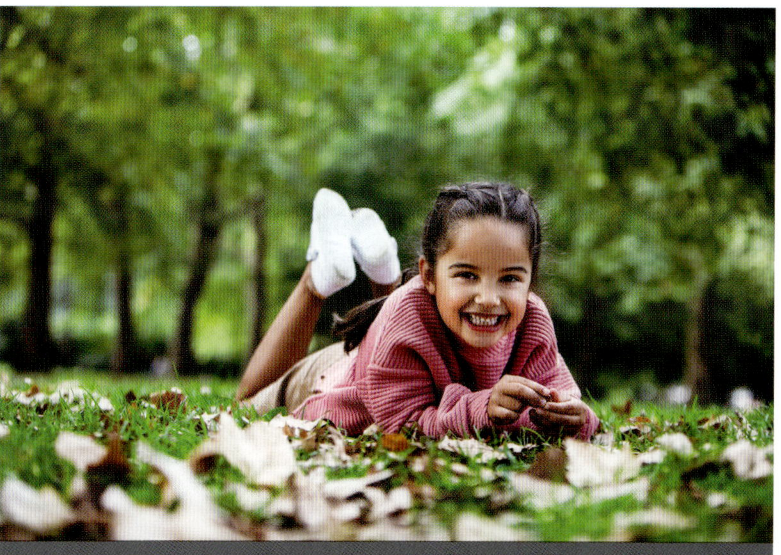

3 Apply a mask and then choose *Edit > Fill > Black.* This will cover the entire image with a mask, returning the image to its original red-cheeked state. Select the Eraser tool, set its opacity to 30%, and erase the mask to remove the redness in the cheeks. It is up to you how far you go with this, but it is usually better to retain a small amount of color, rather than removing it all.

4 You can edit the mask using the regular Paintbrush tool: swap between Black as your "paint" to remove the red cheek color and White to bring back the original color. When you are happy with the final result check the whole image and save it for your client.

Glossary

Aberration An imperfection in a photograph, usually caused by the optics of a lens.

Angle of view The area of a scene that a lens takes in, measured in degrees.

Aperture The variable opening in a camera lens, measured in f/stops, which regulates the amount of light passing through the lens. The aperture setting is also one of the main factors in determining depth of field.

Aperture priority A camera mode that allows the photographer to set the aperture, with the camera automatically choosing the appropriate shutter speed for the correct exposure.

Blue hour The period just before sunset through to just after sunset, when the sky turns a deep blue.

Bracketing The process of taking a sequence of images at varying degrees of exposure, (both under- and overexposed). These images can then be combined in postproduction.

Bulb (B) A manual exposure mode that provides complete control over how long the camera's shutter remains open.

Camera shake A leading cause of blurred images; occurs when the camera is accidentally moved or disturbed while making an exposure.

Center-weighted metering An exposure-metering pattern that determines the exposure from the central part of the image frame.

Chromatic aberration A digital color defect that can appear around the edges of high-contrast image elements. Caused when a lens fails to bring all wavelengths of light to focus at the same point.

Color temperature The color of light, measured in degrees Kelvin (K).

Continuous lighting Any artificial light that is not flash, such as LED, tungsten, and fluorescent.

Contrast The range between bright and dark areas in a scene or image.

Crop factor The size of the camera's sensor measured in reference to a 35mm piece of film or full-frame digital sensor.

Depth of field (DOF) The area in an image in front of and behind the focus point that appears acceptably sharp. The extent of the depth of field is determined by the aperture setting, focal length, and camera-to-subject distance.

Digital workflow The process or processes required after your shoot to develop and present your final image files.

Distortion An optical defect whereby straight lines appear curved in an image.

DSLR (Digital Single Lens Reflex) A camera that uses an internal mirror to reflect the scene from the lens up to the photographer's eye. During the instant that the exposure is made, this mirror flips up out of the way just as the shutter opens, allowing light to reach the image sensor.

Dynamic range The range from light to dark in a scene; also the range that can be recorded by a camera in a single exposure.

Exposure The amount of light allowed to hit the digital sensor, controlled by aperture, shutter speed, and ISO. Also, the act of taking a photograph, as in "making an exposure."

Exposure compensation A manual control that allows you to increase or reduce the camera's recommended exposure.

f/stop The fractional representation of the size of the aperture, based on the focal length of the lens divided by the diameter of the aperture.

Filter A piece of colored or coated glass, or plastic, placed in front of the lens.

Focal length The distance from the optical center of a lens, where the light rays converge to create a sharp image, and the film or sensor.

Full frame A digital camera sensor format the same size as 35mm film frame (36 x 24mm).

Ghosting An effect created when a subject remains still for just long enough to be recorded and then moves quickly to another position, mid-exposure, resulting in a ghost-like appearance.

G.L.O.W. Acronym for the best method for photographing children: Get down low; Light from behind; Open the aperture; Work the subject.

Golden hour The hour after sunrise and before sunset when the light is warm and golden.

Highlights The brightest part of an image.

Histogram A graphical representation of the tones in an image, from pure white to pure black.

ISO The numerical values that represent the sensitivity of the camera's sensor to light.

JPEG A file format where data processing of the image (such as sharpening) is performed internally by the camera, which then compresses the file to save data space.

Lens flare An optical artifact caused by non-image-forming light entering the lens.

Live View A viewing mode that allows images to be viewed and framed using the LCD on the back of the camera, rather than the viewfinder.

Location flash Flash lighting powered by a rechargeable battery; usually used on location.

Megapixel One megapixel equals one million pixels.

Metering The act of measuring the light falling on a scene to determine the exposure required.

Mirrorless Common name given to a camera that doesn't have a reflex mirror (*see* DSLR). The photographer views a live image streamed from the digital sensor to an LCD.

Mirror lock-up The option on some DSLR cameras that enables the mirror to be flipped up and locked in place prior to releasing the shutter. In doing so it minimizes any vibration that may introduce blur into an image.

Multi-zone metering An exposure-metering pattern that divides the frame into zones or segments that are measured individually and then brought together to determine the best overall exposure. Known by various proprietary names, including Evaluative (Canon) and Matrix (Nikon).

Neutral density (ND) filter A filter that limits the amount of light passing through it and into the camera. Commonly used to extend exposure times.

Noise Digital interference that is recorded as a non-image-forming texture.

Overexposure An exposure that is overly bright, often leading to highlight areas being recorded as pure white, with no recoverable image data.

Prime A lens with a fixed focal length.

Raw A file type that records the data captured straight from the image sensor, without applying any processing to this information.

Shutter priority A camera mode that allows the photographer to set the shutter speed, with the camera automatically choosing the appropriate aperture for the correct exposure.

Shutter speed The time that the shutter is open for during an exposure. Adjusted manually or by the camera in automatic modes

Speedlight The brand name used by Nikon for its range of small hotshoe-mounted flash units, but commonly used to refer to any hotshoe-mounted flash, regardless of manufacturer (Canon uses the alternative spelling, "Speedlite").

Spot metering An exposure-metering pattern that determines the exposure based on a small and precise part of the image.

Stop The unit of measurement used to indicate a halving or doubling of light in an exposure.

Studio flash Flash lighting requiring mains power; essentially used indoors.

Underexposure An exposure that is overly dark, often leading to shadow areas being recorded as pure black, with no recoverable image data.

Vignette The darkening of the corners and edges of an image. Although it can be an optical defect in a lens, or caused by a physical obstruction in front of the lens ("mechanical vignetting"), it is also often applied in postproduction as a creative edit.

White balance An in-camera control that allows a particular color temperature of light to be recorded without a color cast.

Zoom A lens with a variable focal length.

Useful Websites

Cameras & Lenses

Canon www.canon.com
Fujifilm www.fujifilm.com
Laowa www.venuslens.net
Leica www.leica-camera.com
Nikon www.nikon.com
Olympus www.olympus-global.com
Panasonic www.panasonic.net
Pentax www.ricoh.com
Sigma www.sigma-photo.com
Sony www.sony.com
Tamron www.tamron.com
Tokina www.tokinalens.com
Zeiss www.zeiss.com

Lighting & Accessories

Broncolor www.broncolor.swiss
Elinchrom www.elinchrom.com
Godox www.godox.com
Lastolite www.manfrotto.com
Lowepro www.lowepro.com
Manfrotto www.manfrotto.com
Phottix www.phottix.com
Profoto www.profoto.com
Rotolight www.rotolight.com

Photography Publications

Ammonite Press www.ammonitepress.com
Black + White Photography magazine www.thegmcgroup.com
Rich Photographer Poor Photographer www.rbradbury.com/RPPP

Printing

Epson www.epson.com
Hahnemühle www.hahnemuehle.de
Harman www.harman-inkjet.com
HP www.hp.com
Ilford www.ilford.com
Kodak www.kodak.com
Marrutt www.marrutt.com

Software

Adobe Lightroom & Photoshop www.adobe.com
Capture One Pro www.phaseone.com
DxO PhotoLab www.dxo.com

Index

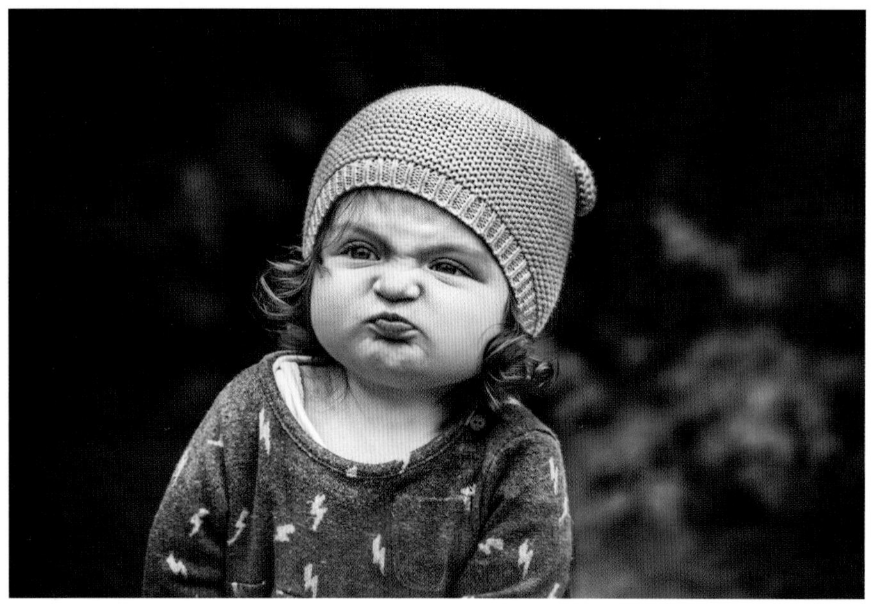

Acknowledgments

Writing a book is the best form of therapy that anyone can have, because most of it is essentially self-analysis. Having said that, it would be impossible to complete a book like this without the help and encouragement of the people that surround and inform you on many levels.

My thanks go to Jason Hook and Robin Shields at Ammonite Press, Chris Gatcum, and my faithful assistant Sarah Abrams for her constant encouragement and picture editing skills.

I also owe a great debt of gratitude to The Flash Centre in London (www.theflashcentre.com) for the loan of Elinchrom flash kit and to Ginger Whisk Studios (www.gingerwhisk.com) in Chiswick for the studio space.

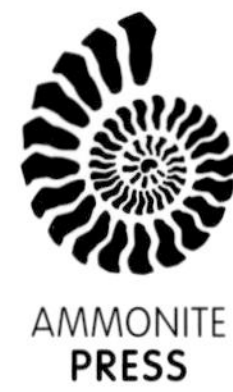

AMMONITE
PRESS

www.ammonitepress.com